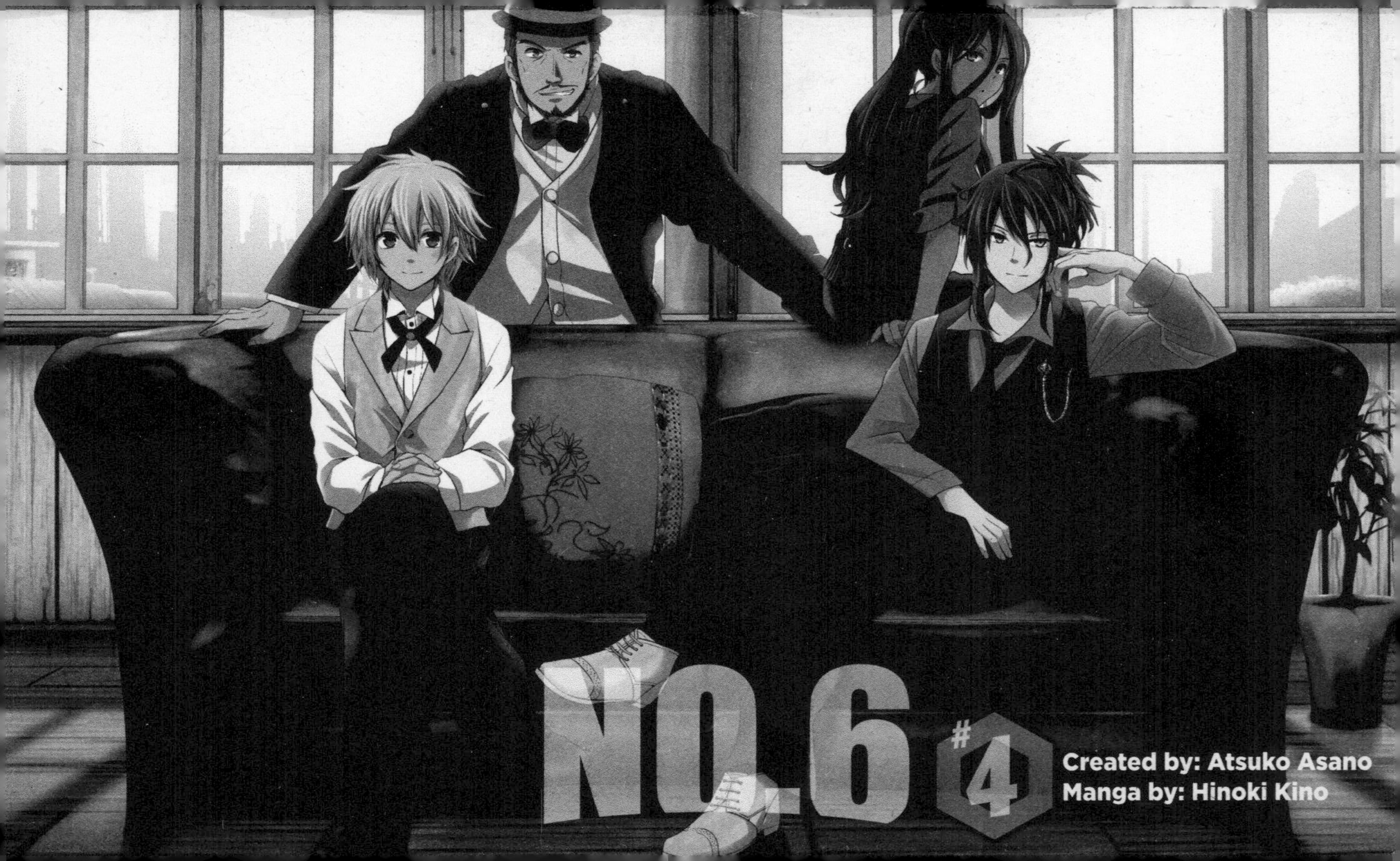
NO.6
#4
Created by: Atsuko Asano
Manga by: Hinoki Kino

NO.6

#4

12 True Lies, False Truths........6

13 Beside the Deceit...............43

14 The Curtain Rises................81

15 The Stage Grows Dark.....122

No. 6 Dubbing Report ... 161

Afterword.......164

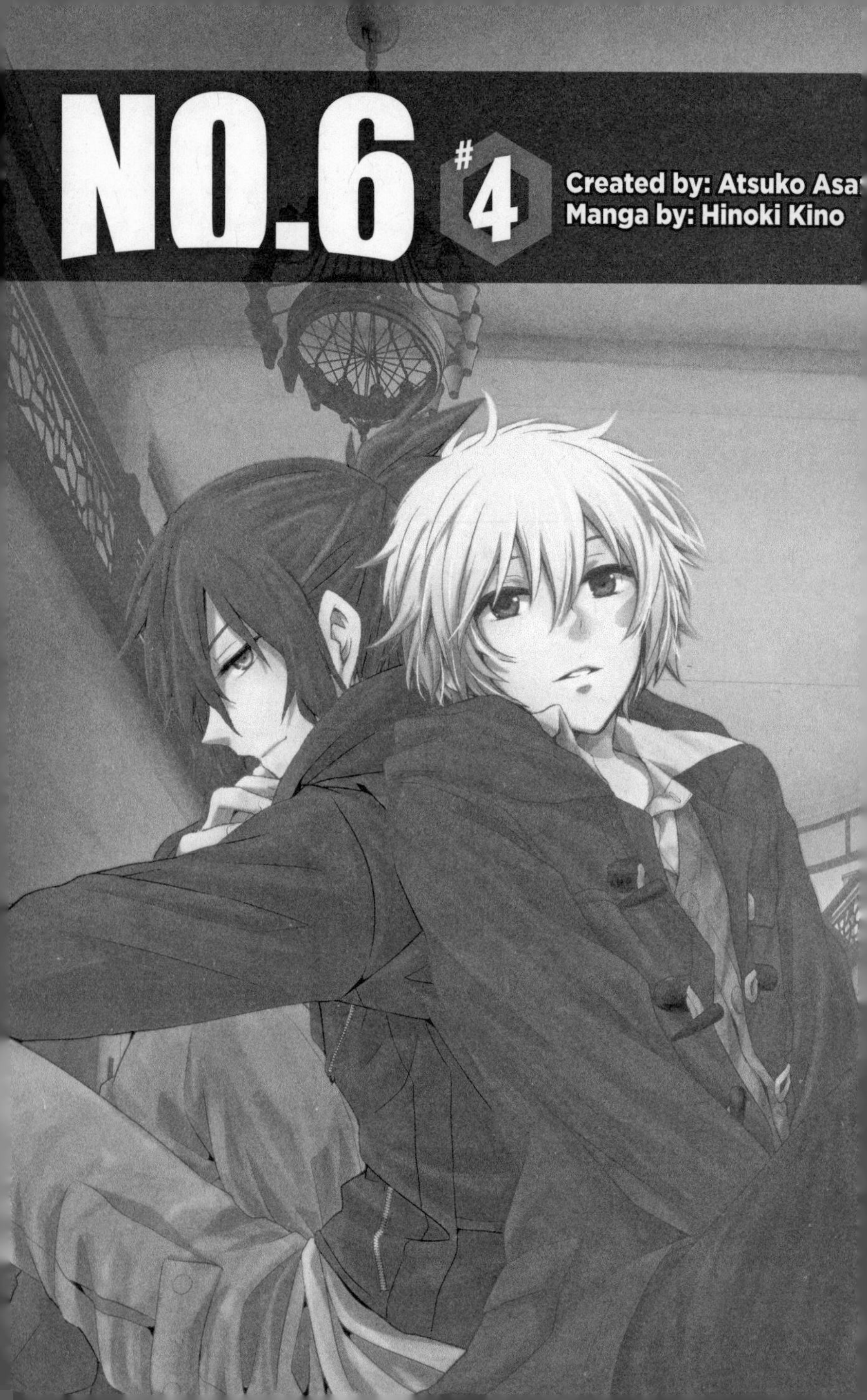
NO.6
#4
Created by: Atsuko Asa
Manga by: Hinoki Kino

NO.6 STORY and CHARACTERS

Shion was raised as a privileged elite in the holy city of No. 6. But after sheltering Rat, a fugitive on the run, Shion was stripped of his elite status and forced to live in Lost Town. Just as he was being arrested by the Security Bureau on suspicion of murder, Rat—the fugitive from four years earlier—came to Shion's rescue, and together they escaped No. 6 for the violence and despair of West Block.

After his body was mysteriously transformed by a parasitic bee, Shion decided to stay with Rat in West Block. After encounters with Dogkeeper and Rikiga, Shion matured into a trustworthy young man.

Meanwhile, Safu returned to No. 6 from her studies abroad, only to be detained by the Security Bureau. Karan sent a message to Rat informing him. He opted not to tell Shion, but by chance, Shion found out that Safu had been taken to the Correctional Facility.

AFU

childhood iend with elings of love r Shion. An ite researcher ho specializes in euroscience.

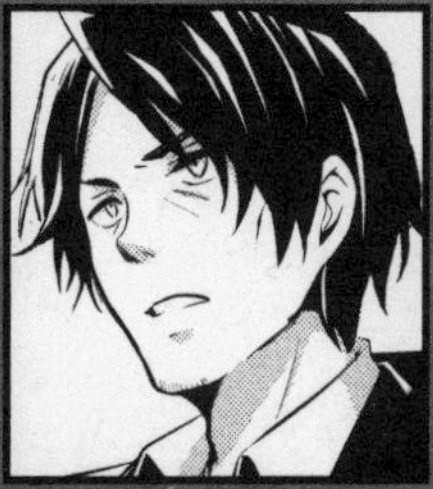

YOMIN

Harbors doubts about No. 6 since losing his wife and child.

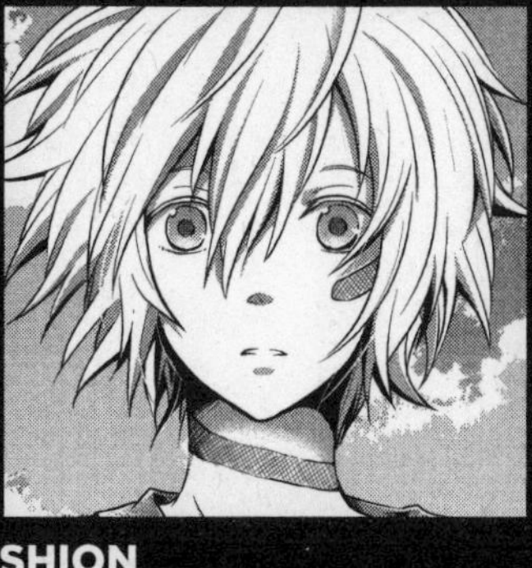

SHION

Fallen from the elite, he escaped to West Block. He was infected by a parasitic bee, but survived.

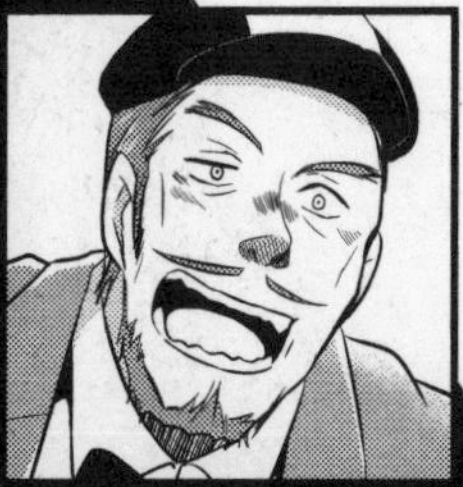

RIKIGA

A former journalist who now publishes a porno magazine in West Block. An old friend of Karan.

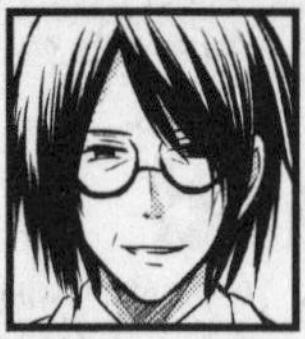

The Man in White

An ambitious research scientist.

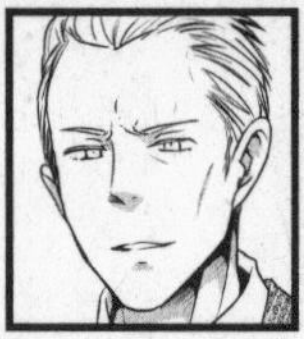

The Mayor

The most powerful man in No. 6.

Inside No. 6

Upper Class

The center of the city, with the Moondrop (City Hall) at its apex.

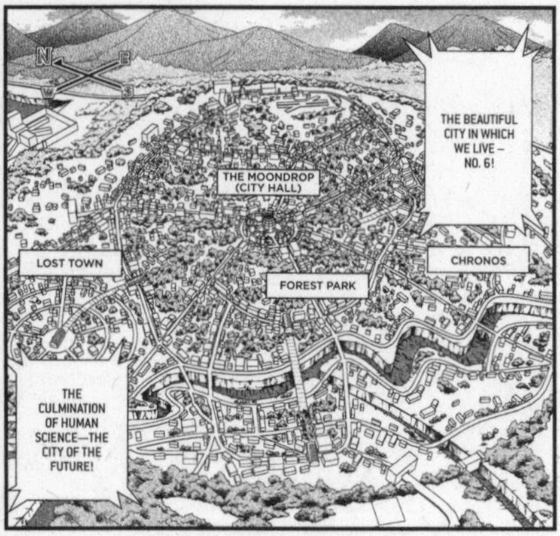

THE BEAUTIFUL CITY IN WHICH WE LIVE – NO. 6!
THE MOONDROP (CITY HALL)
LOST TOWN
CHRONOS
FOREST PARK
THE CULMINATION OF HUMAN SCIENCE—THE CITY OF THE FUTURE!

Chronos

The top-class residential area, open only to special elite citizens.

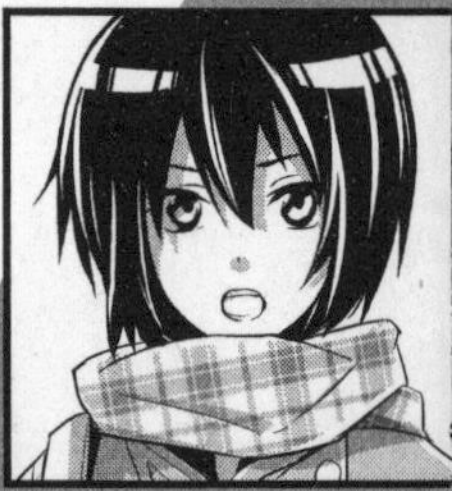

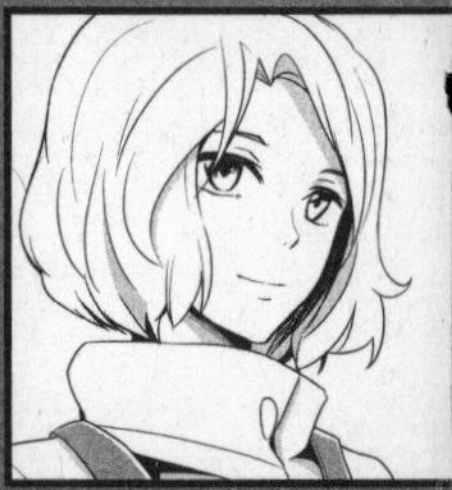

KARAN

Shion's mother. Operates a bakery in Lost Town.

Lost Town

The lower-class residential area for the city's disenfranchised.

The Outskirts

West Block

The dangerous special zone outside the walls of the city. A criminal correctional facility is located there.

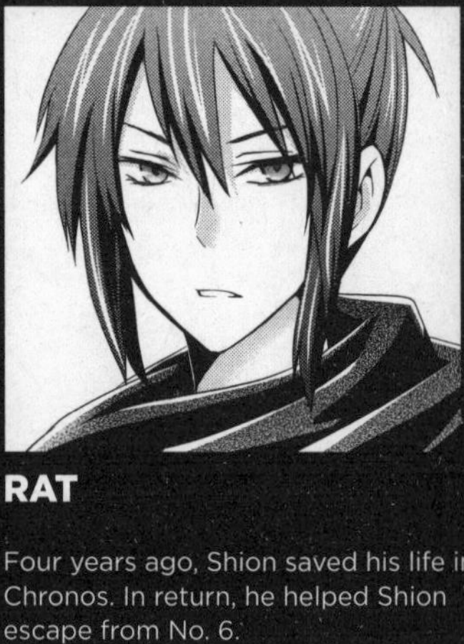

RAT

Four years ago, Shion saved his life in Chronos. In return, he helped Shion escape from No. 6.

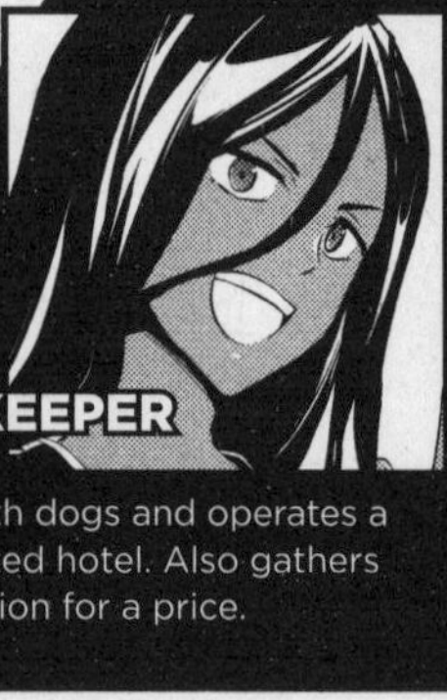

DOGKEEPER

Lives with dogs and operates a dilapidated hotel. Also gathers information for a price.

Chapter 12: True Lies, False Truths

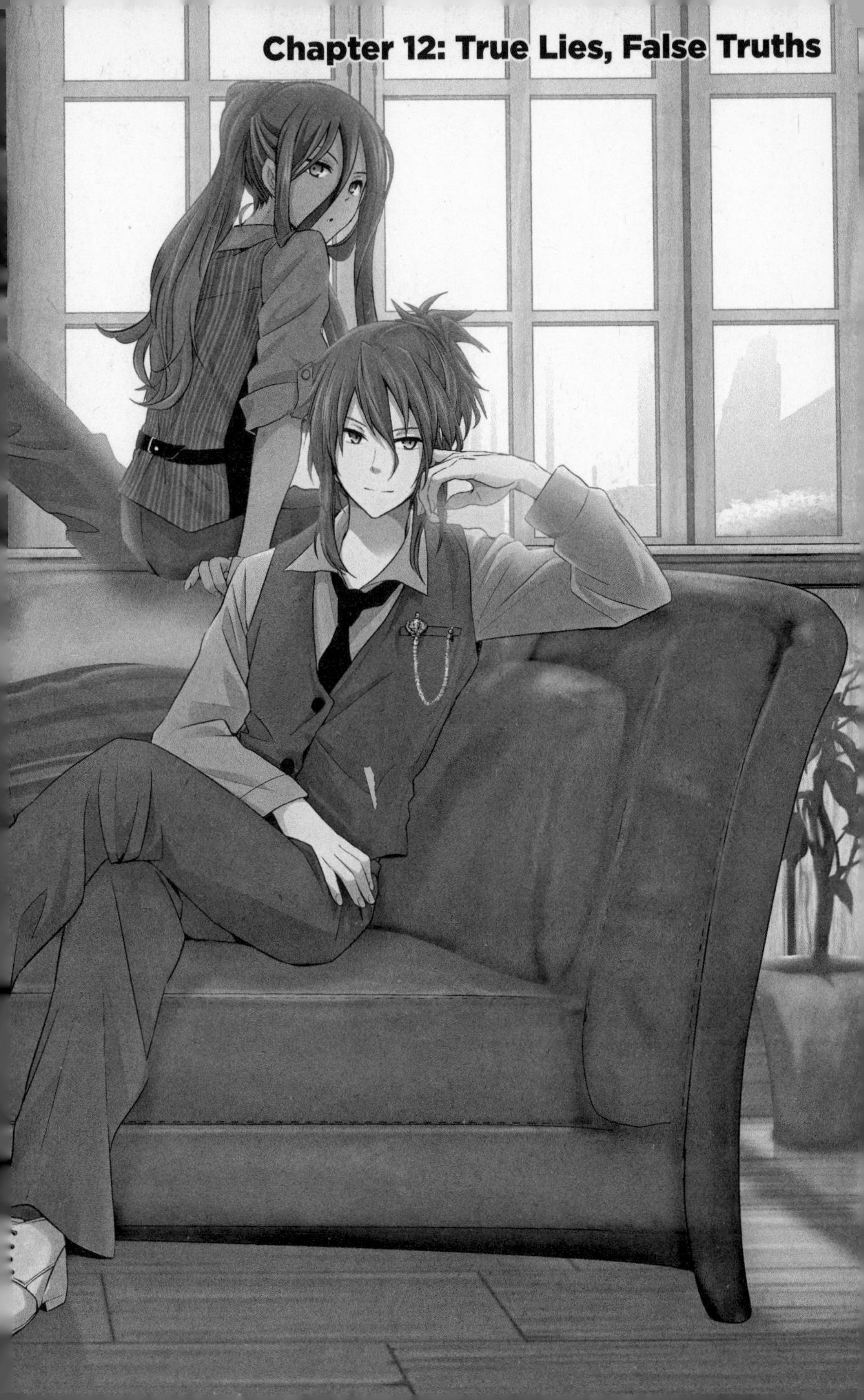

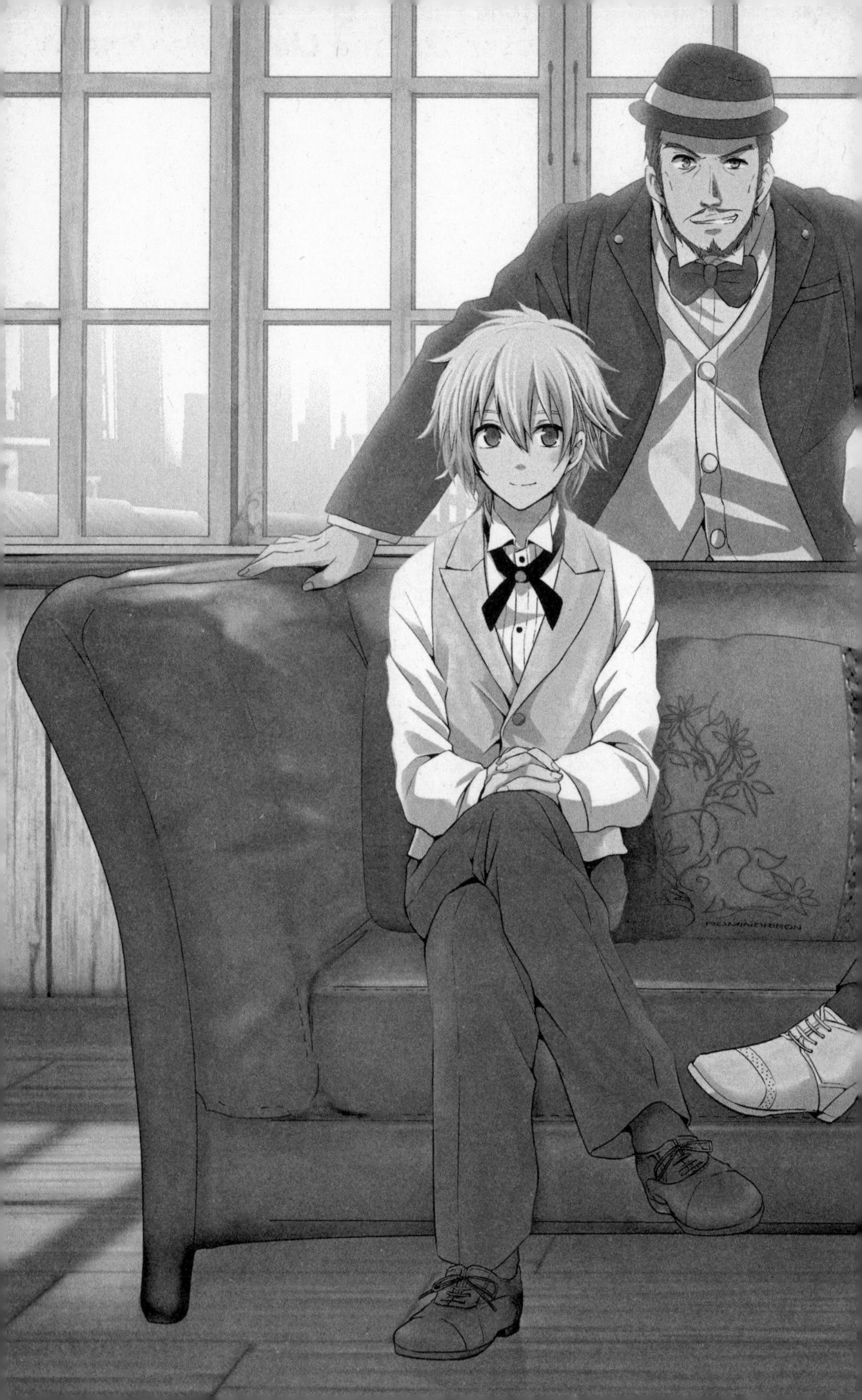

NO.6

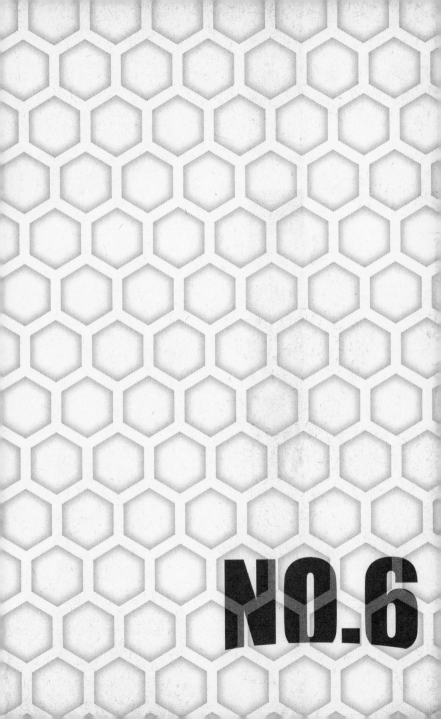

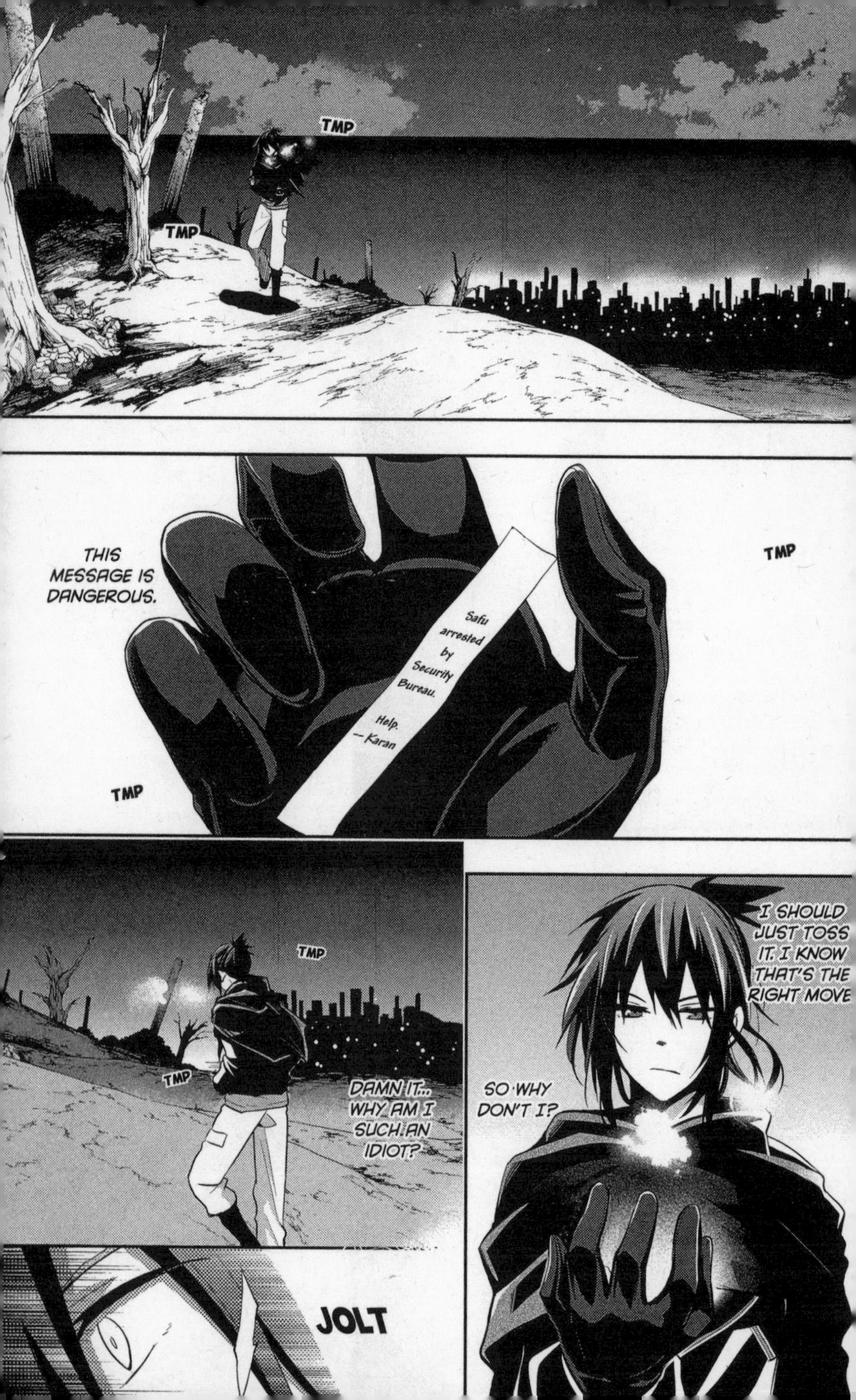
TMP
TMP
TMP
THIS MESSAGE IS DANGEROUS.
Safu arrested by Security Bureau.
Help. --Karan
TMP
I SHOULD JUST TOSS IT. I KNOW THAT'S THE RIGHT MOVE
SO WHY DON'T I?
TMP
TMP
DAMN IT... WHY AM I SUCH AN IDIOT?
JOLT

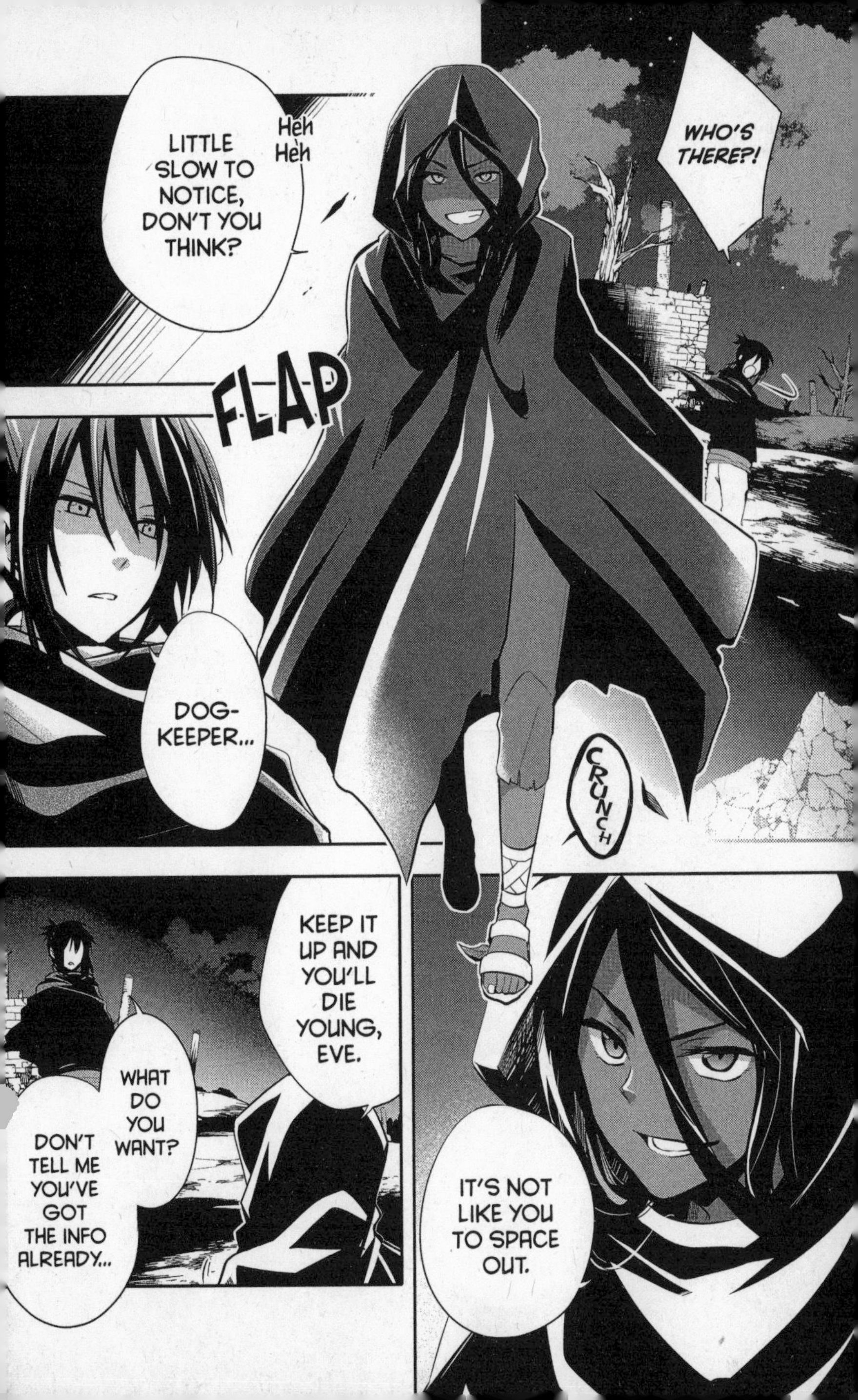
WHO'S THERE?!
Heh Heh
LITTLE SLOW TO NOTICE, DON'T YOU THINK?
FLAP
CRUNCH
DOG-KEEPER...
IT'S NOT LIKE YOU TO SPACE OUT.
KEEP IT UP AND YOU'LL DIE YOUNG, EVE.
WHAT DO YOU WANT?
DON'T TELL ME YOU'VE GOT THE INFO ALREADY...

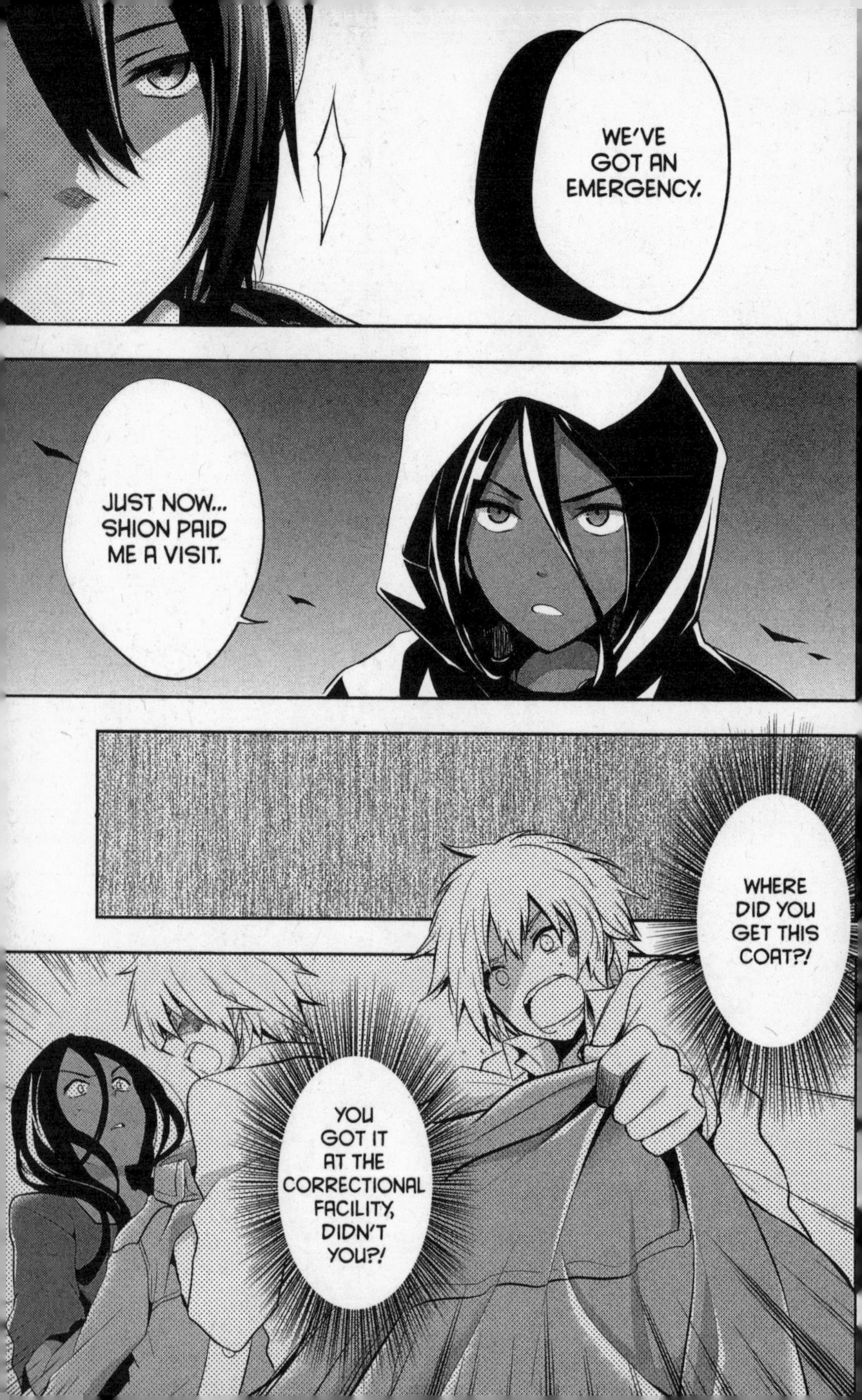
WE'VE GOT AN EMERGENCY.
JUST NOW... SHION PAID ME A VISIT.
WHERE DID YOU GET THIS COAT?!
YOU GOT IT AT THE CORRECTIONAL FACILITY, DIDN'T YOU?!

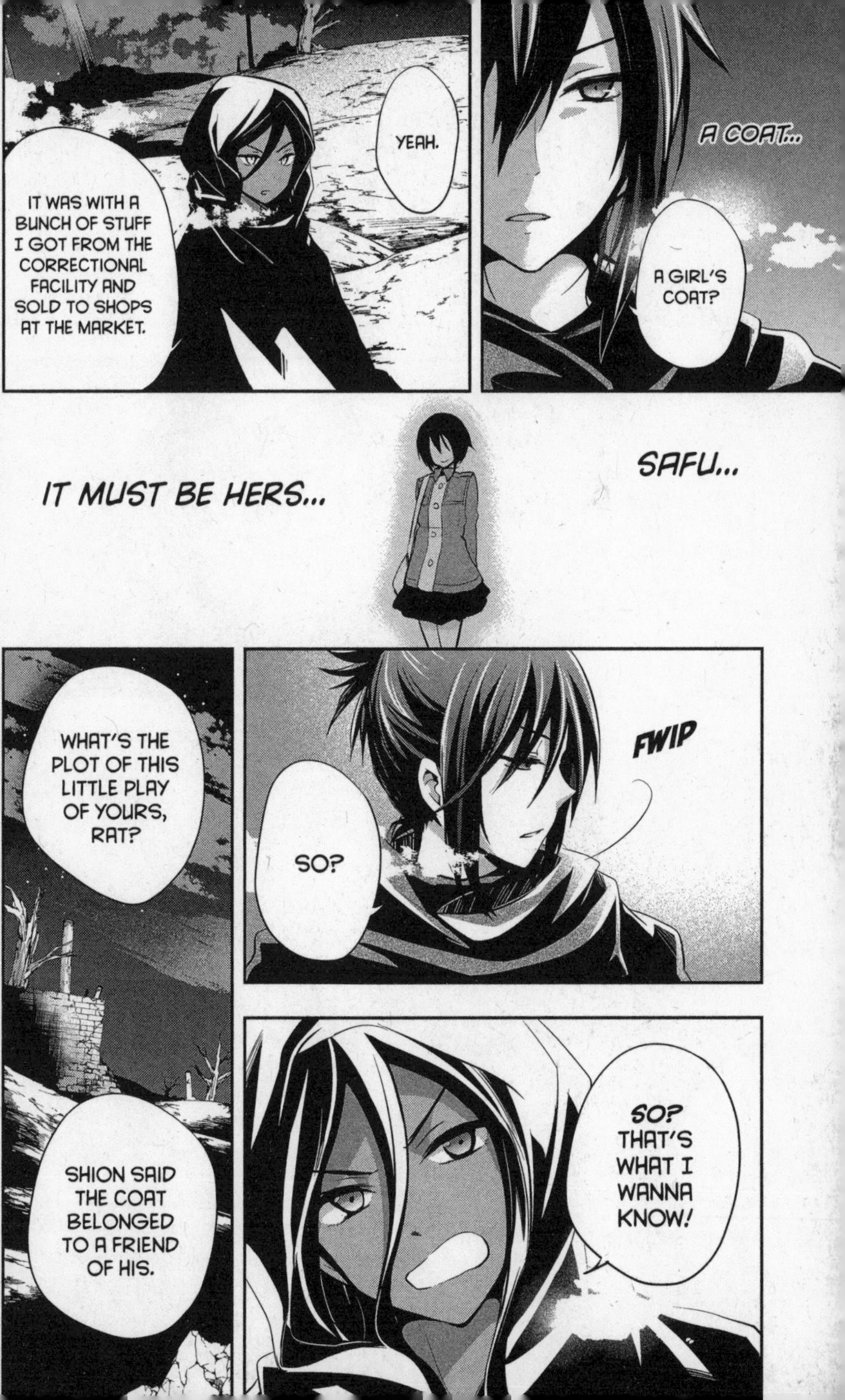
A COAT...
A GIRL'S COAT?
YEAH.
IT WAS WITH A BUNCH OF STUFF I GOT FROM THE CORRECTIONAL FACILITY AND SOLD TO SHOPS AT THE MARKET.
SAFU...
IT MUST BE HERS...
FWIP
SO?
SO? THAT'S WHAT I WANNA KNOW!
WHAT'S THE PLOT OF THIS LITTLE PLAY OF YOURS, RAT?
SHION SAID THE COAT BELONGED TO A FRIEND OF HIS.

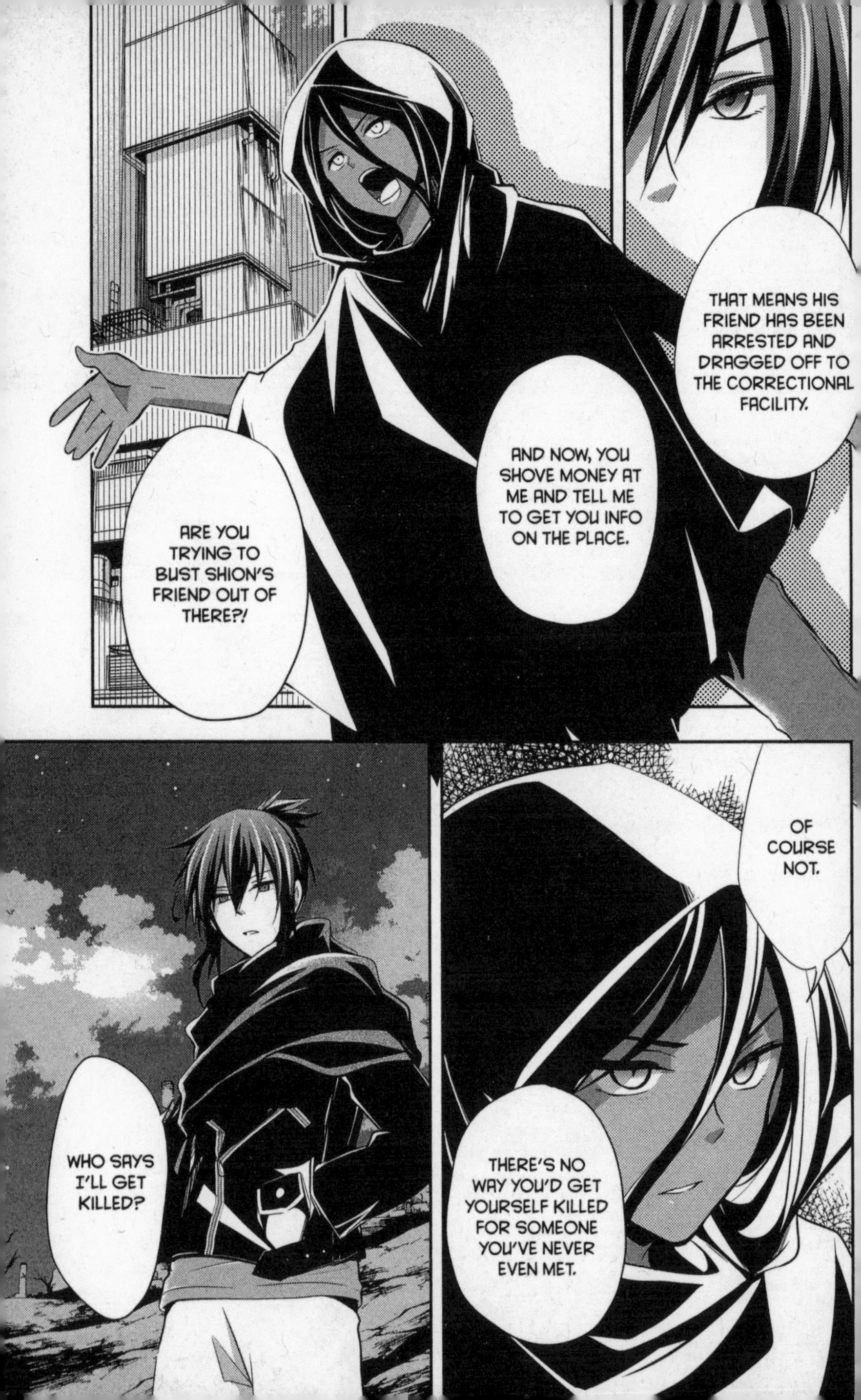
THAT MEANS HIS FRIEND HAS BEEN ARRESTED AND DRAGGED OFF TO THE CORRECTIONAL FACILITY.
AND NOW, YOU SHOVE MONEY AT ME AND TELL ME TO GET YOU INFO ON THE PLACE.
ARE YOU TRYING TO BUST SHION'S FRIEND OUT OF THERE?!
OF COURSE NOT.
THERE'S NO WAY YOU'D GET YOURSELF KILLED FOR SOMEONE YOU'VE NEVER EVEN MET.
WHO SAYS I'LL GET KILLED?

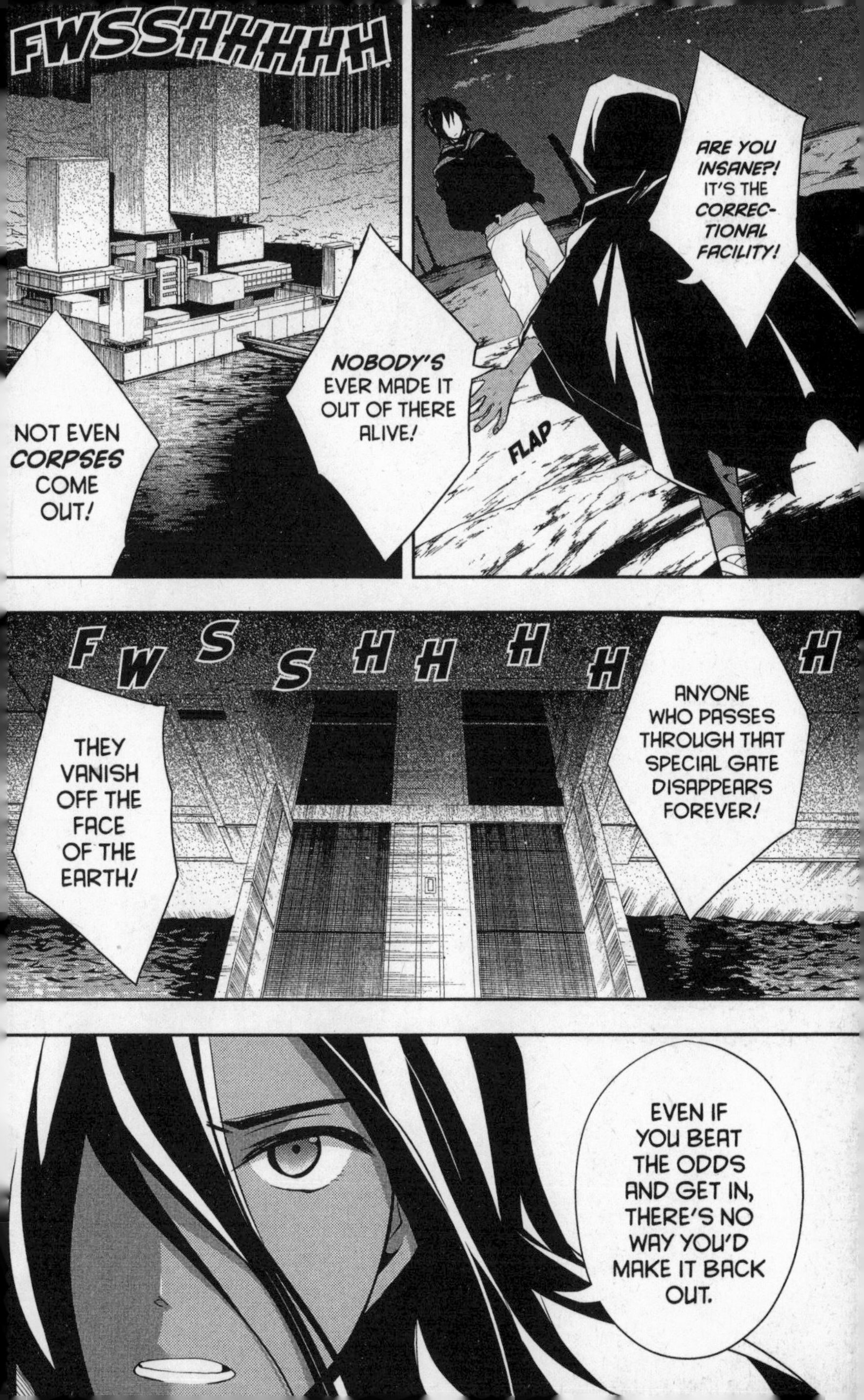
ARE YOU INSANE?! IT'S THE CORRECTIONAL FACILITY!
FLAP
FWSSHHHHHH
NOBODY'S EVER MADE IT OUT OF THERE ALIVE!
NOT EVEN CORPSES COME OUT!
FWSSHHHHH
ANYONE WHO PASSES THROUGH THAT SPECIAL GATE DISAPPEARS FOREVER!
THEY VANISH OFF THE FACE OF THE EARTH!
EVEN IF YOU BEAT THE ODDS AND GET IN, THERE'S NO WAY YOU'D MAKE IT BACK OUT.

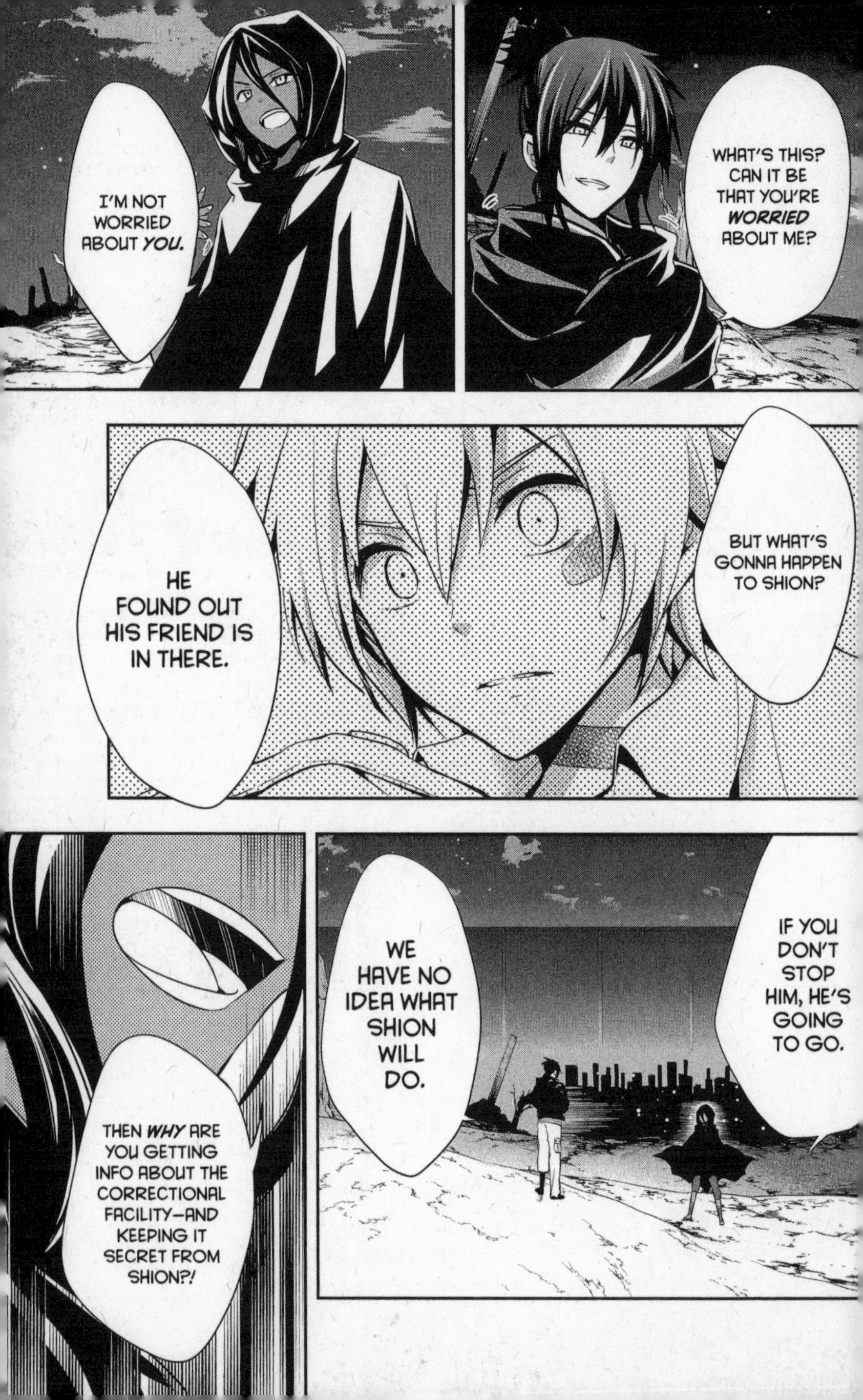
WHAT'S THIS? CAN IT BE THAT YOU'RE *WORRIED* ABOUT ME?
I'M NOT WORRIED ABOUT *YOU.*
BUT WHAT'S GONNA HAPPEN TO SHION?
HE FOUND OUT HIS FRIEND IS IN THERE.
IF YOU DON'T STOP HIM, HE'S GOING TO GO.
WE HAVE NO IDEA WHAT SHION WILL DO.
THEN *WHY* ARE YOU GETTING INFO ABOUT THE CORRECTIONAL FACILITY—AND KEEPING IT SECRET FROM SHION?!

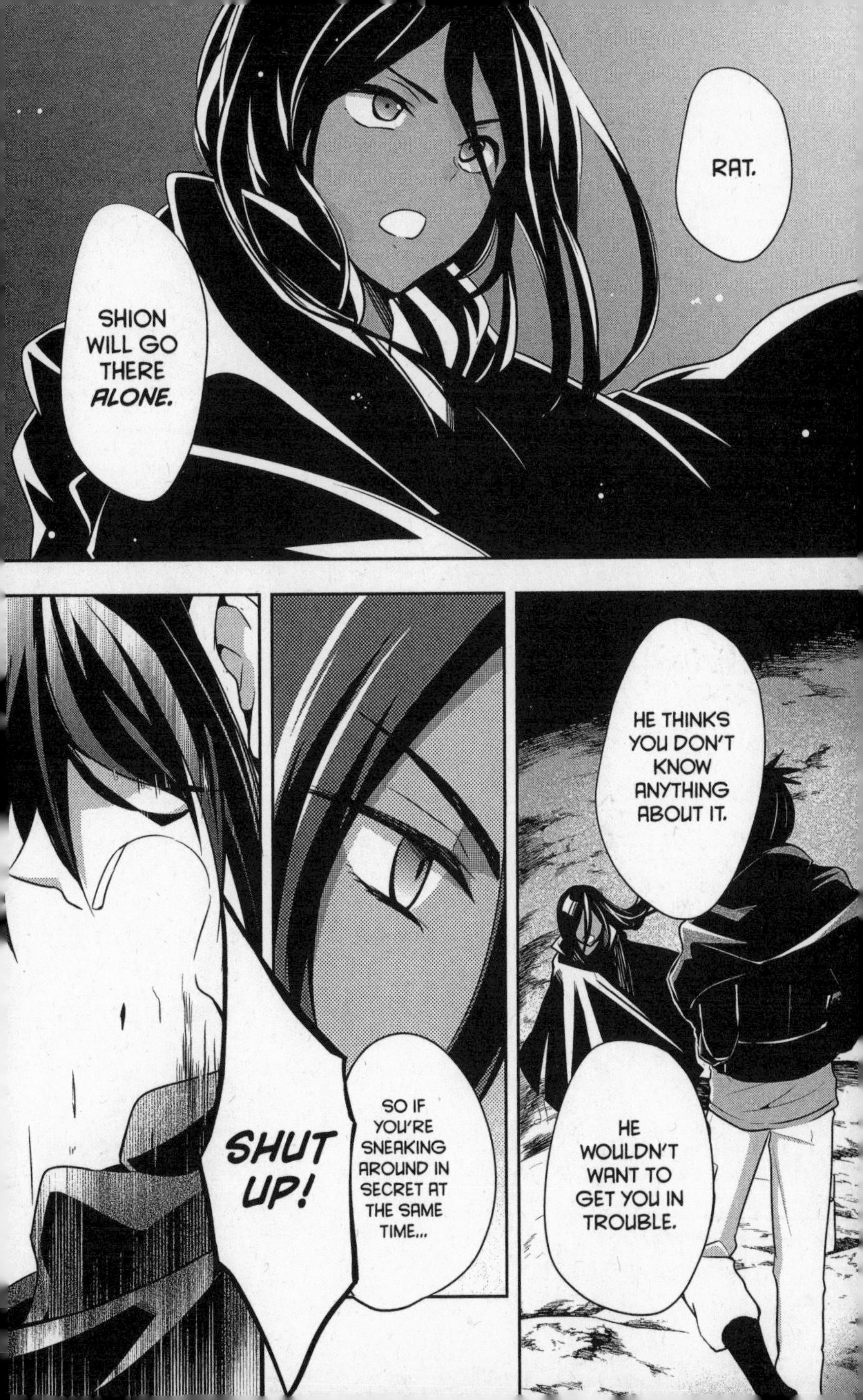
RAT.
SHION WILL GO THERE *ALONE.*
HE THINKS YOU DON'T KNOW ANYTHING ABOUT IT.
HE WOULDN'T WANT TO GET YOU IN TROUBLE.
SO IF YOU'RE SNEAKING AROUND IN SECRET AT THE SAME TIME...
SHUT UP!

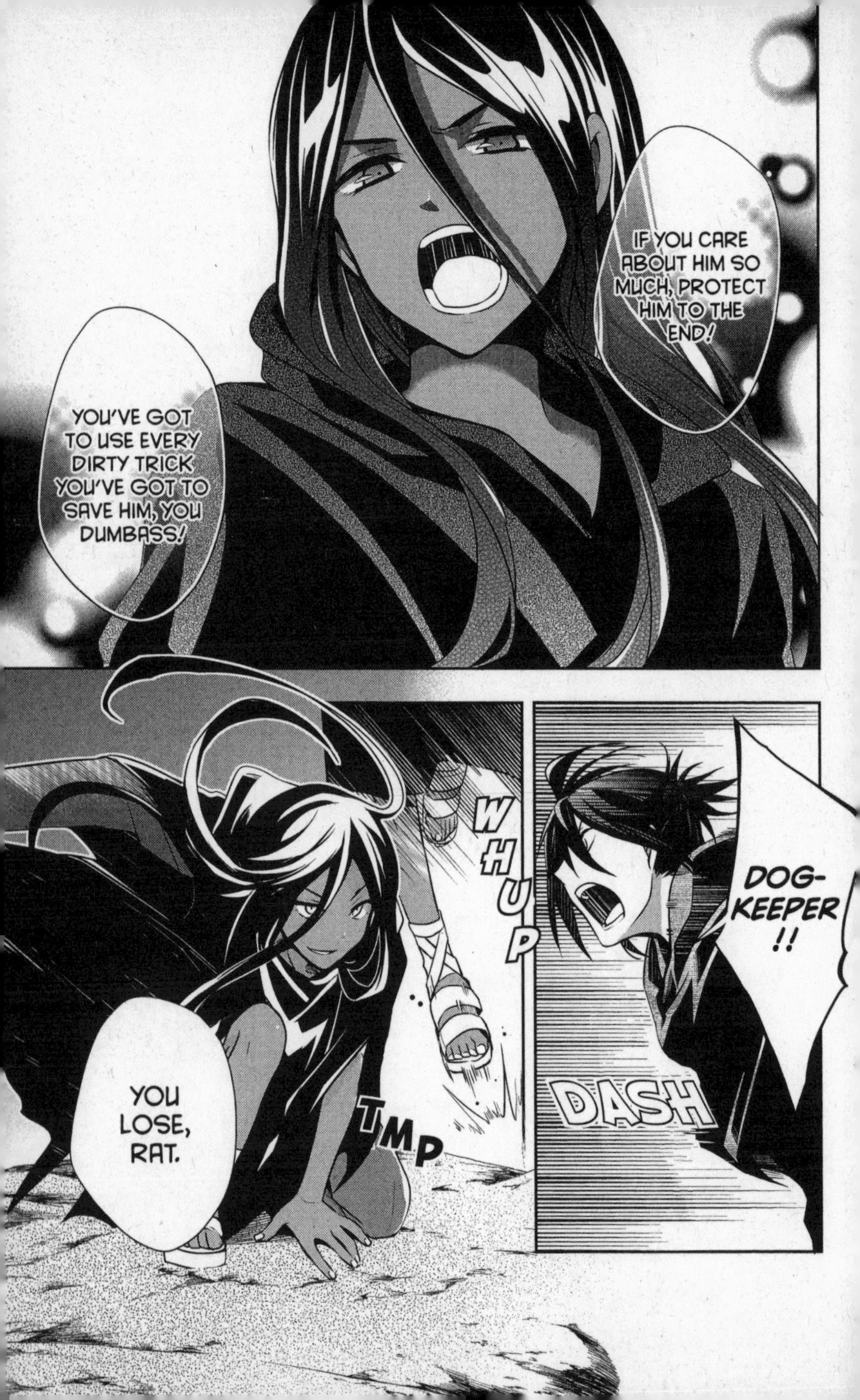
IF YOU CARE ABOUT HIM SO MUCH, PROTECT HIM TO THE END!
YOU'VE GOT TO USE EVERY DIRTY TRICK YOU'VE GOT TO SAVE HIM, YOU DUMBASS!
DOG-KEEPER !!
DASH
WHUP
YOU LOSE, RAT.
TMP

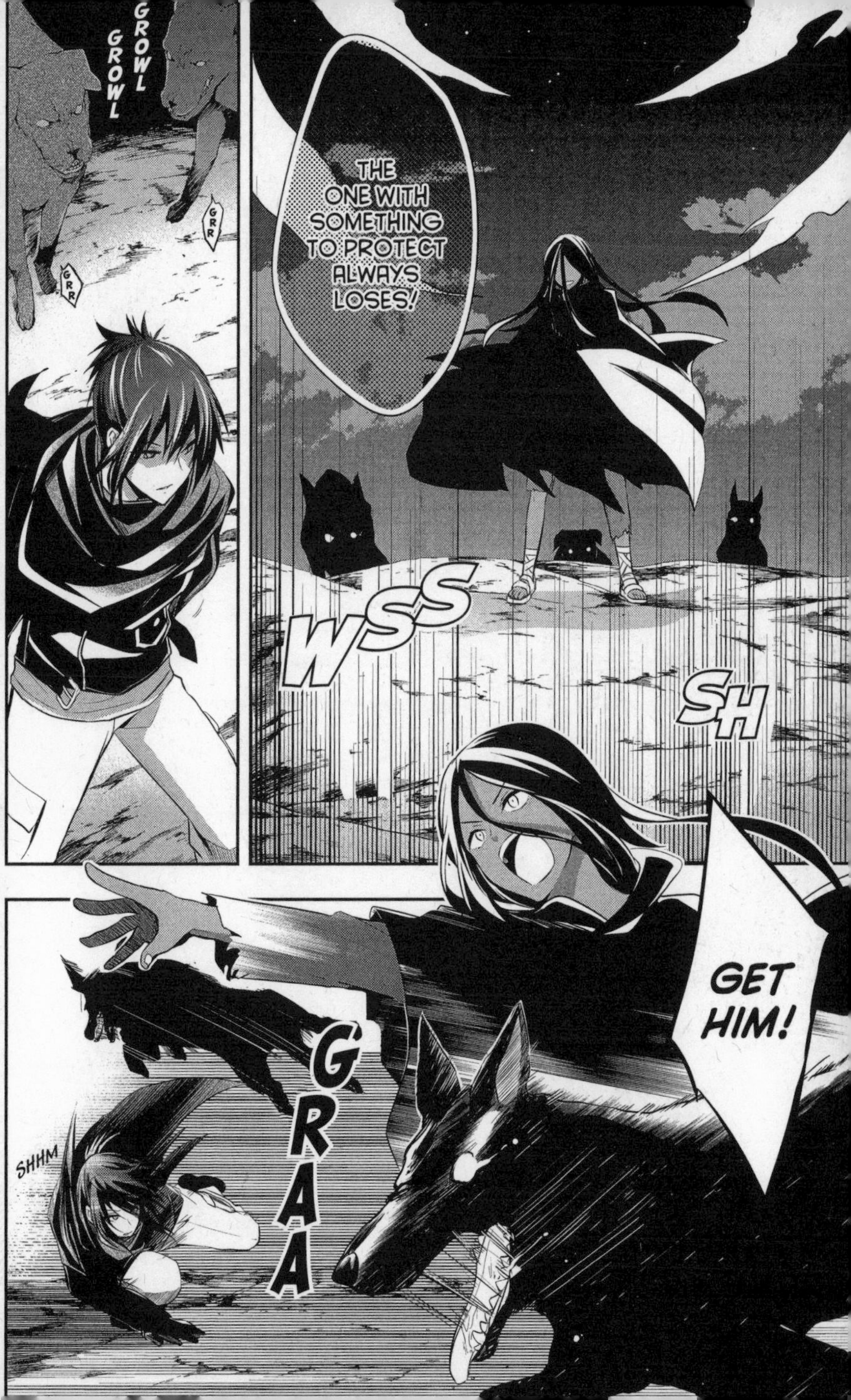
THE ONE WITH SOMETHING TO PROTECT ALWAYS LOSES!
WSS
SH
GROWL
GROWL
GRR
GRR
GET HIM!
GRAA
SHHM

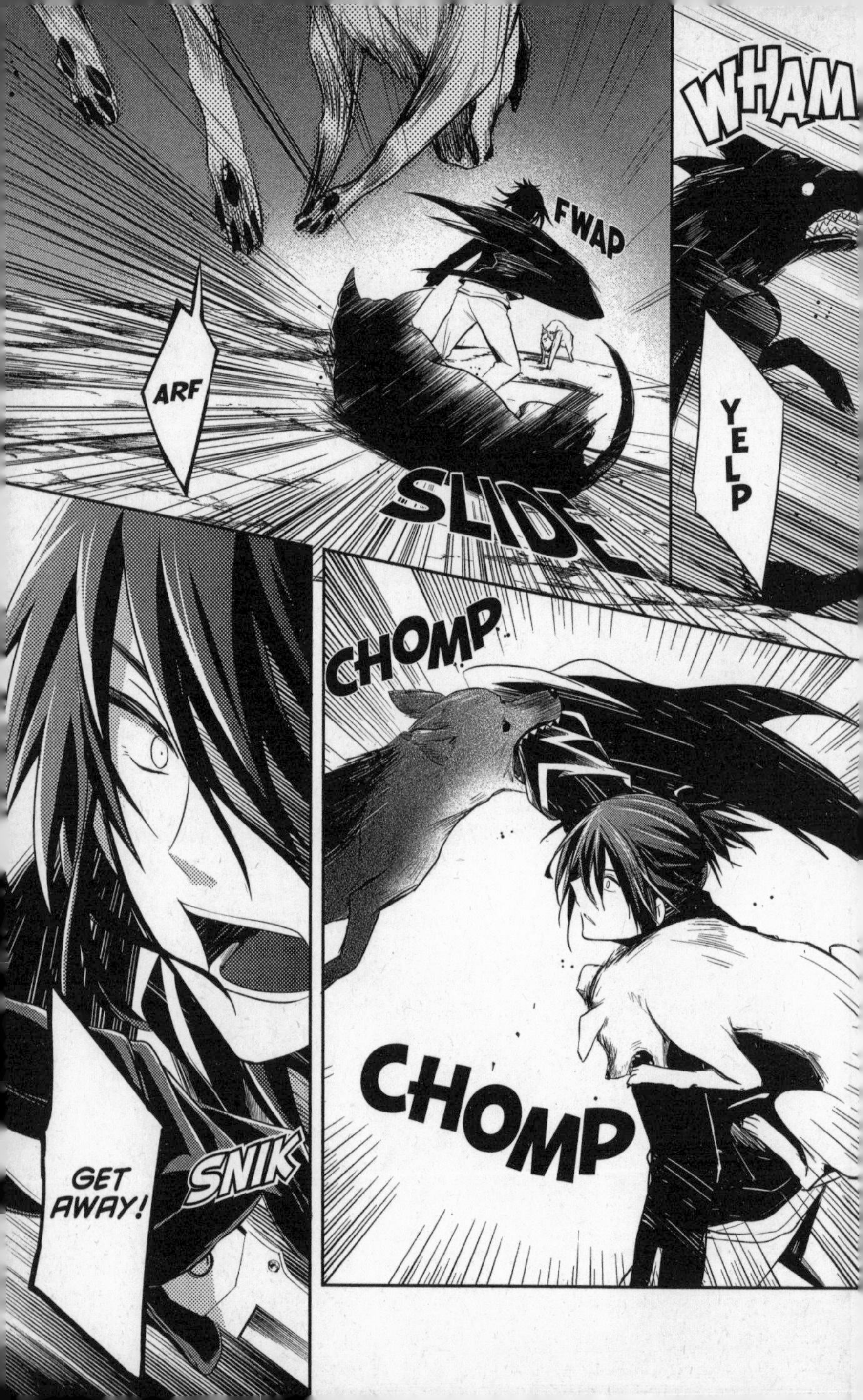
WHAM
YELP
FWAP
ARF
SLIDE
CHOMP
CHOMP
SNIK
GET AWAY!

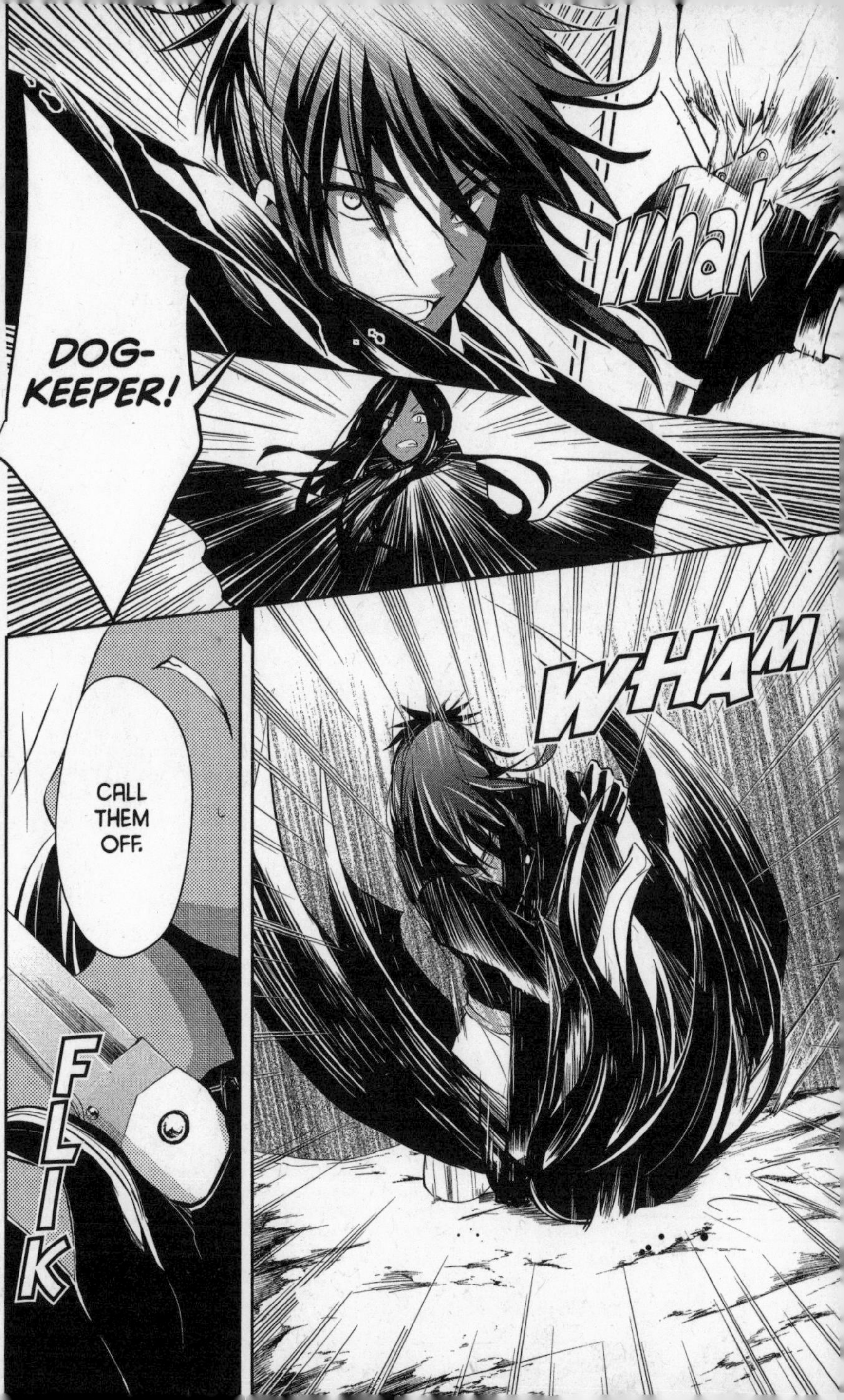
WHAK
DOG-KEEPER!
WHAM
CALL THEM OFF.
FLIK

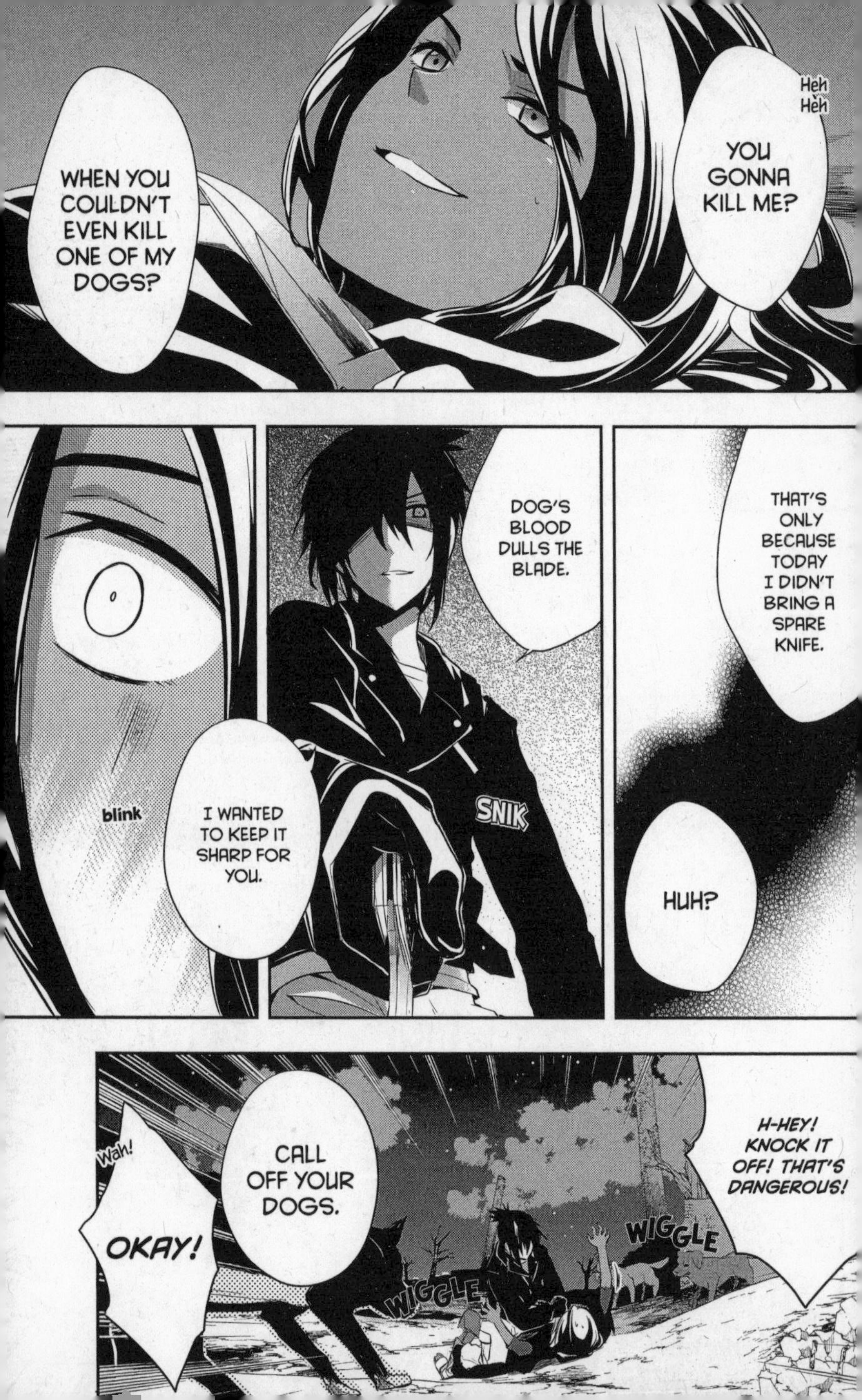
Heh Heh
YOU GONNA KILL ME?
WHEN YOU COULDN'T EVEN KILL ONE OF MY DOGS?
THAT'S ONLY BECAUSE TODAY I DIDN'T BRING A SPARE KNIFE.
HUH?
DOG'S BLOOD DULLS THE BLADE.
SNIK
I WANTED TO KEEP IT SHARP FOR YOU.
blink
H-HEY! KNOCK IT OFF! THAT'S DANGEROUS!
WIGGLE
CALL OFF YOUR DOGS.
WIGGLE
Wah!
OKAY!

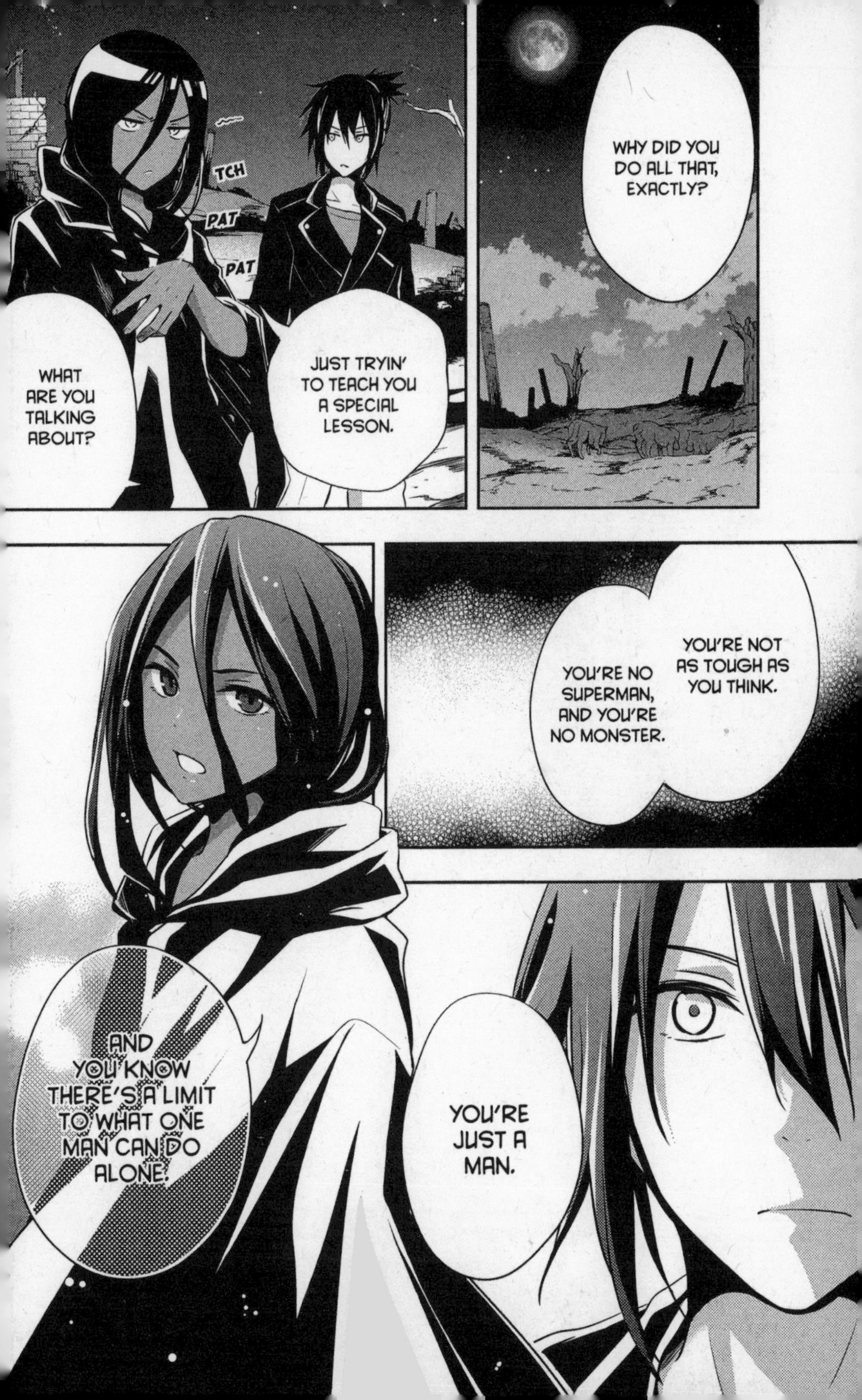
WHY DID YOU DO ALL THAT, EXACTLY?
TCH
PAT
PAT
JUST TRYIN' TO TEACH YOU A SPECIAL LESSON.
WHAT ARE YOU TALKING ABOUT?
YOU'RE NOT AS TOUGH AS YOU THINK.
YOU'RE NO SUPERMAN, AND YOU'RE NO MONSTER.
YOU'RE JUST A MAN.
AND YOU KNOW THERE'S A LIMIT TO WHAT ONE MAN CAN DO ALONE.

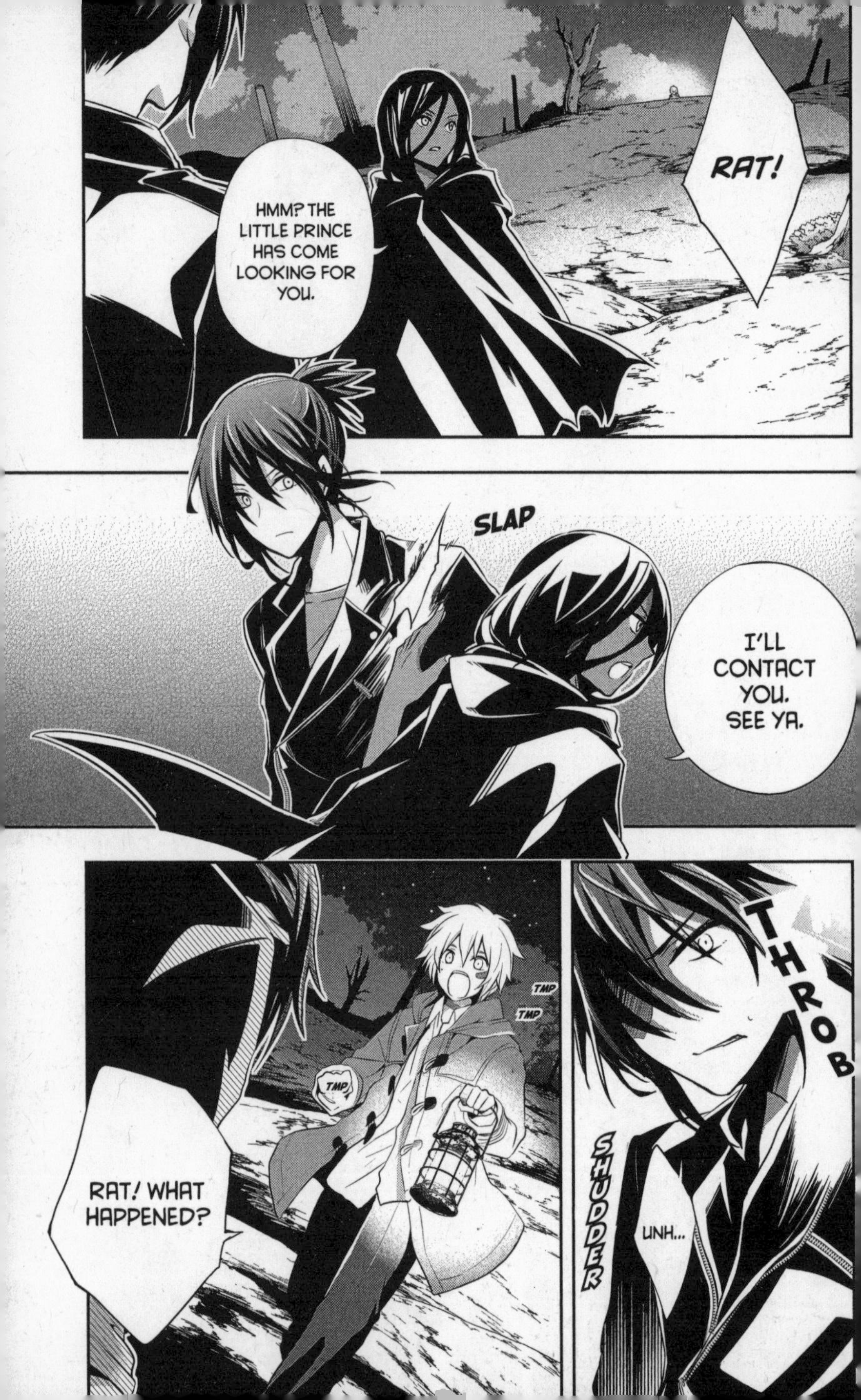
RAT!
HMM? THE LITTLE PRINCE HAS COME LOOKING FOR YOU.
SLAP
I'LL CONTACT YOU. SEE YA.
THROB
SHUDDER
UNH...
TMP
TMP
TMP
RAT! WHAT HAPPENED?

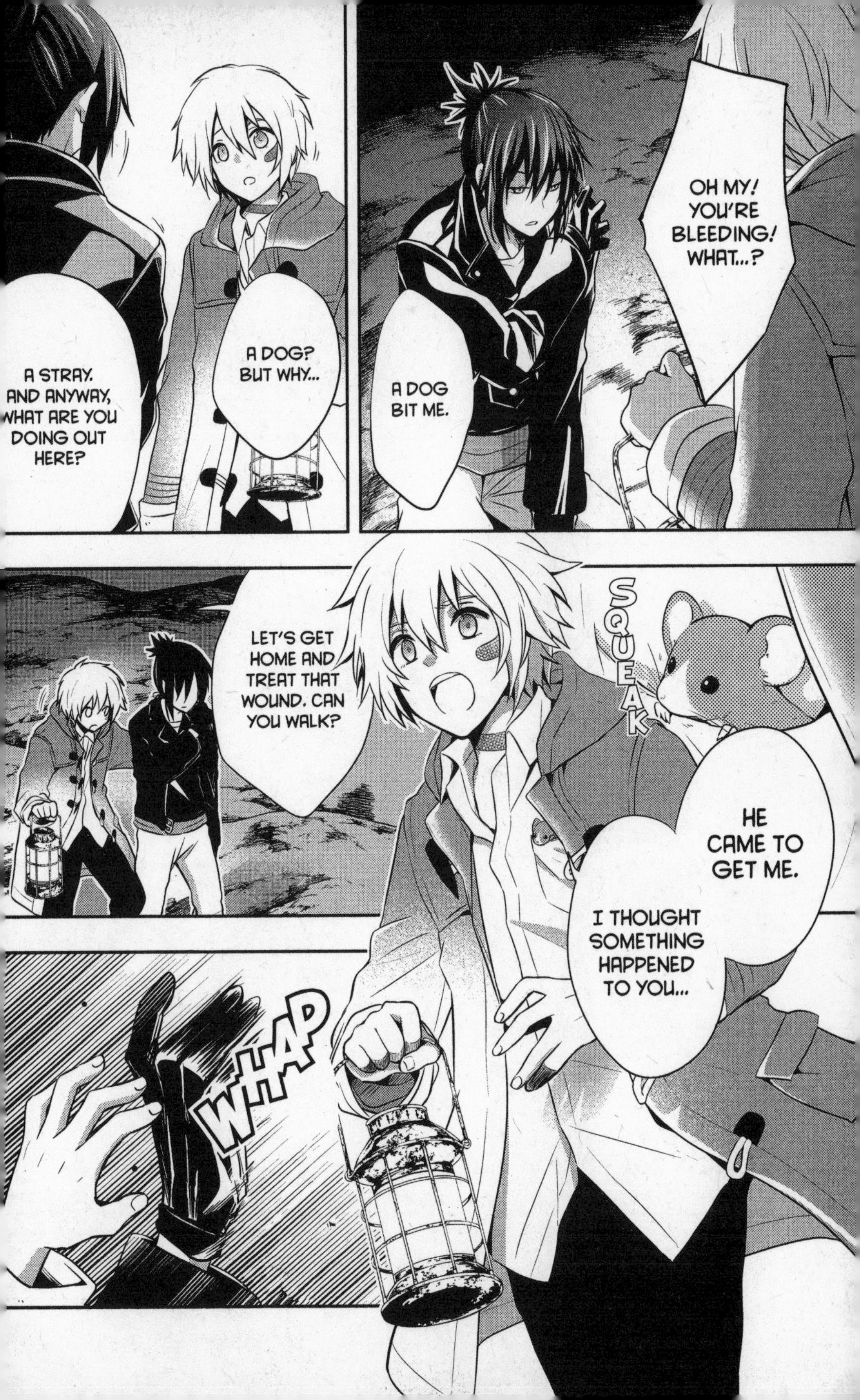
OH MY! YOU'RE BLEEDING! WHAT...?
A DOG BIT ME.
A DOG? BUT WHY...
A STRAY. AND ANYWAY, WHAT ARE YOU DOING OUT HERE?
SQUEAK
HE CAME TO GET ME.
I THOUGHT SOMETHING HAPPENED TO YOU...
LET'S GET HOME AND TREAT THAT WOUND. CAN YOU WALK?
WHAP

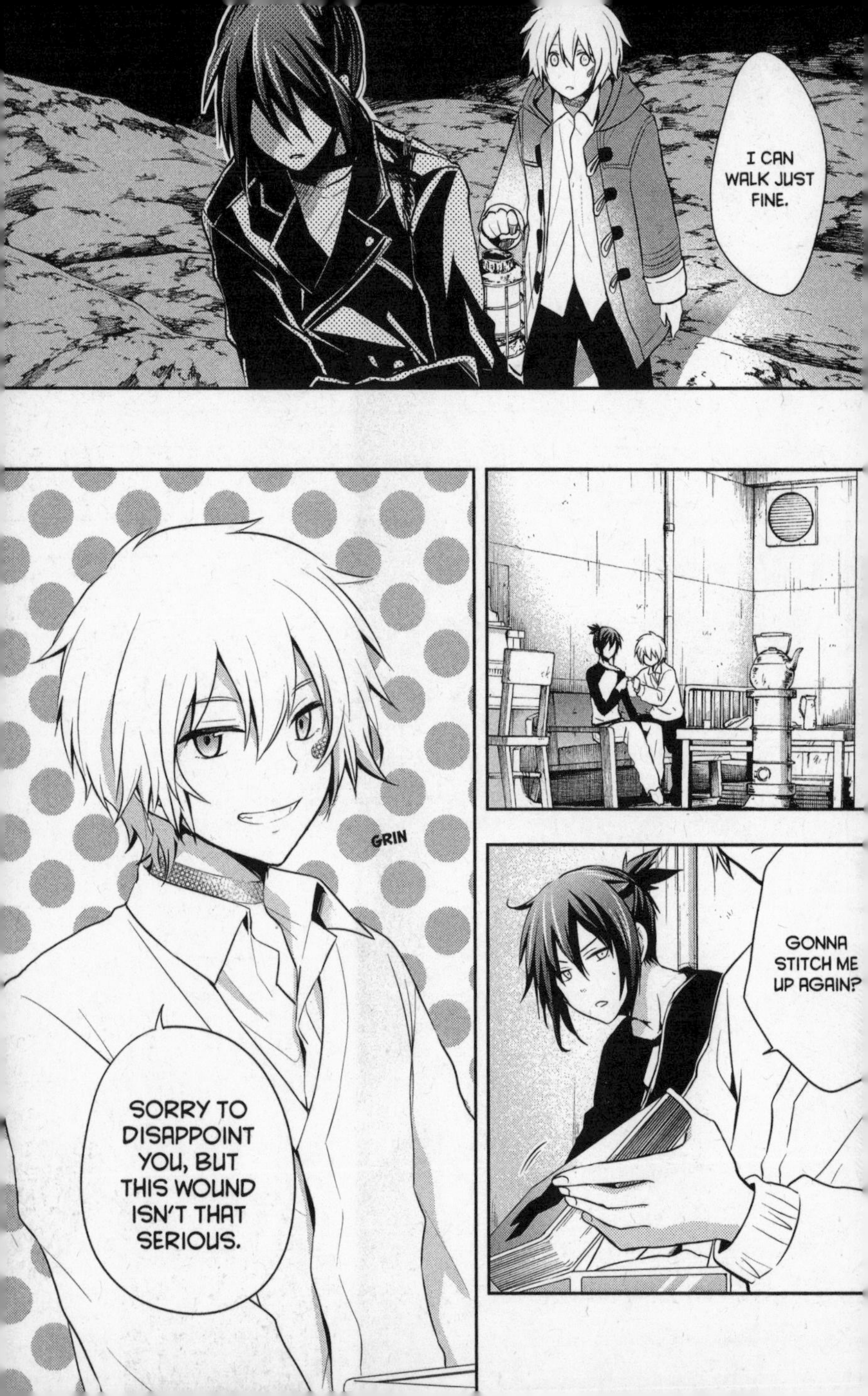
I CAN WALK JUST FINE.
GONNA STITCH ME UP AGAIN?
GRIN
SORRY TO DISAPPOINT YOU, BUT THIS WOUND ISN'T THAT SERIOUS.

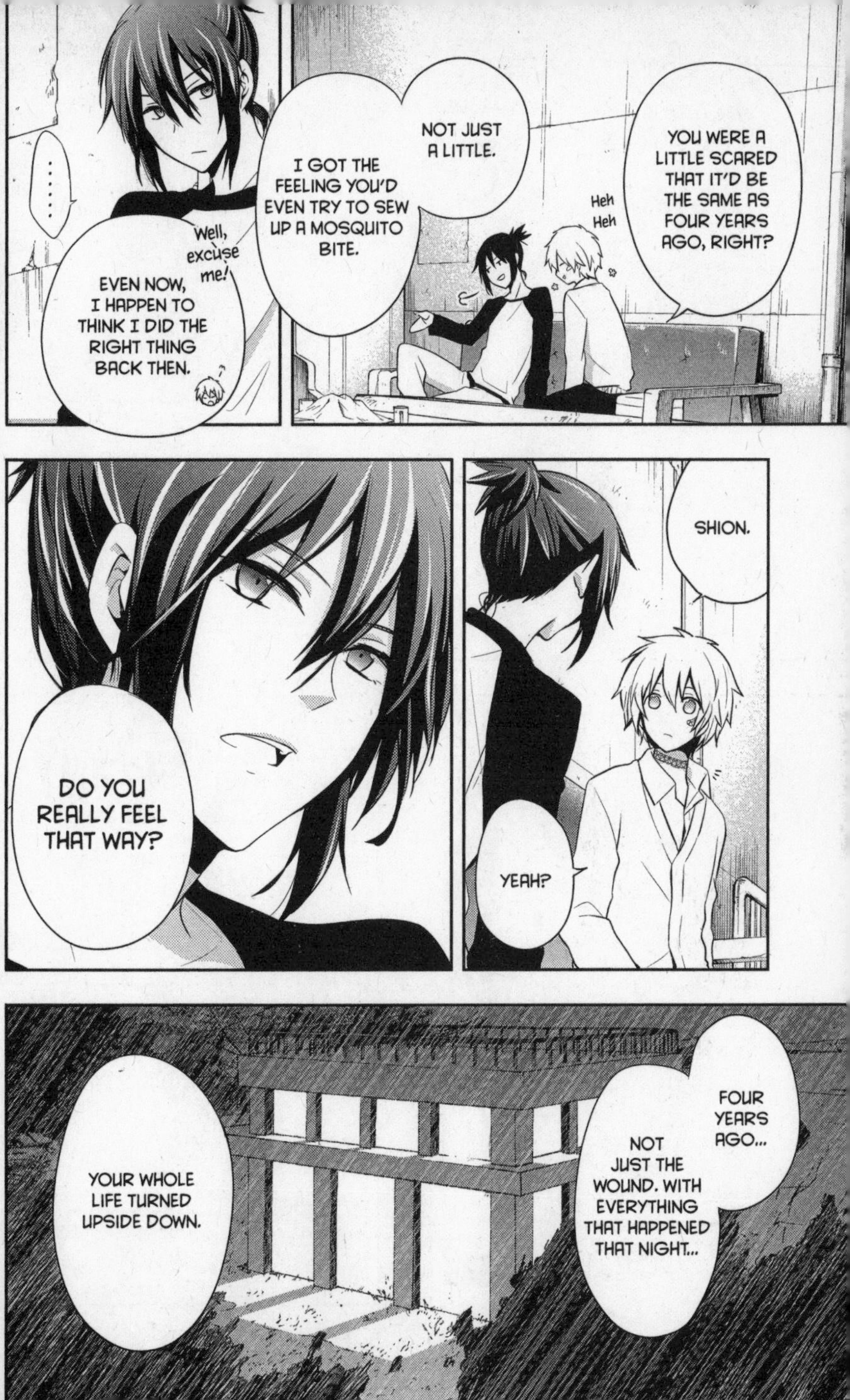
YOU WERE A LITTLE SCARED THAT IT'D BE THE SAME AS FOUR YEARS AGO, RIGHT?
Heh Heh
NOT JUST A LITTLE.
I GOT THE FEELING YOU'D EVEN TRY TO SEW UP A MOSQUITO BITE.
Well, excuse me!
EVEN NOW, I HAPPEN TO THINK I DID THE RIGHT THING BACK THEN.
......
SHION.
YEAH?
DO YOU REALLY FEEL THAT WAY?
FOUR YEARS AGO...
NOT JUST THE WOUND. WITH EVERYTHING THAT HAPPENED THAT NIGHT...
YOUR WHOLE LIFE TURNED UPSIDE DOWN.

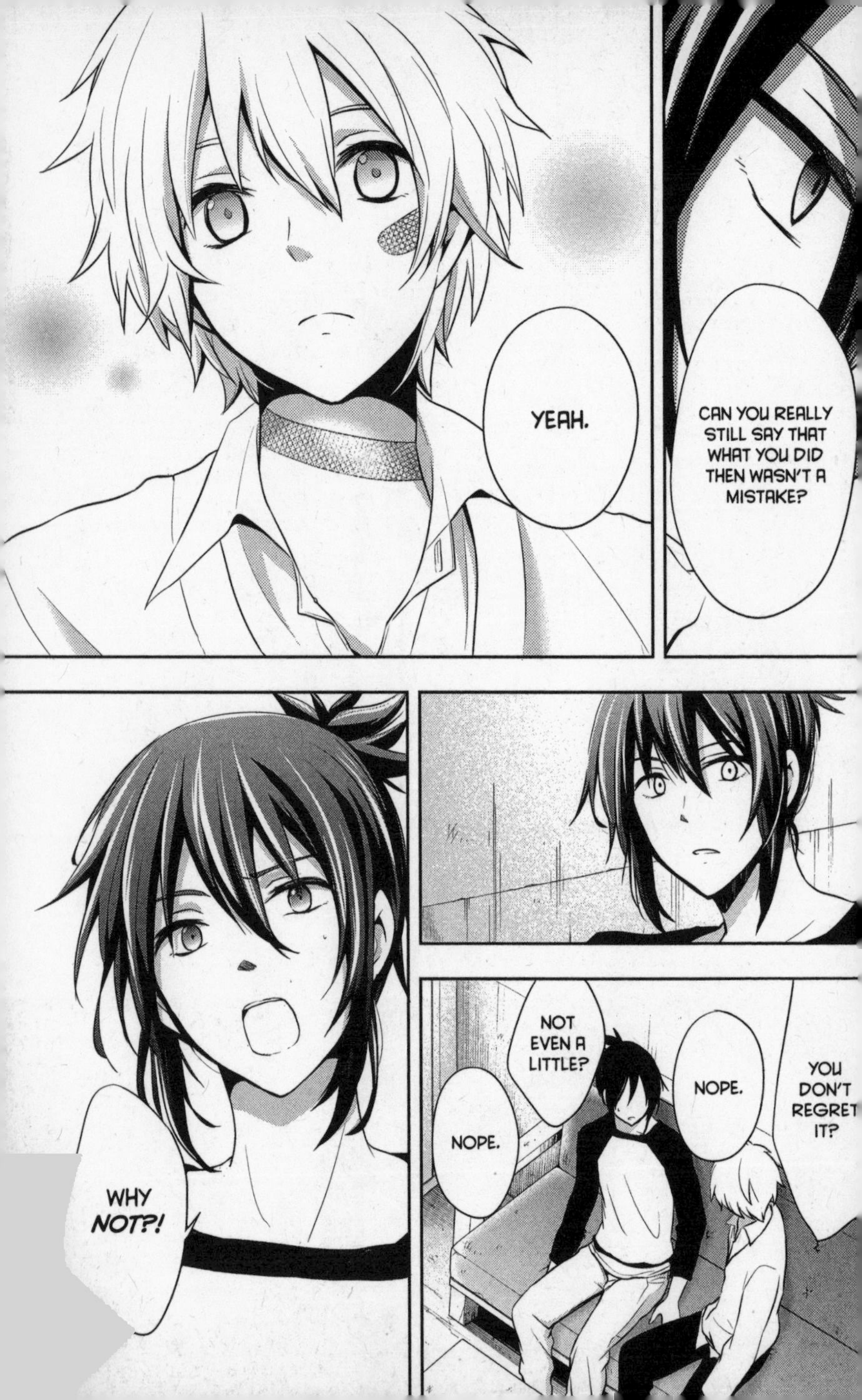
CAN YOU REALLY STILL SAY THAT WHAT YOU DID THEN WASN'T A MISTAKE?
YEAH.
YOU DON'T REGRET IT?
NOPE.
NOT EVEN A LITTLE?
NOPE.
WHY *NOT?!*

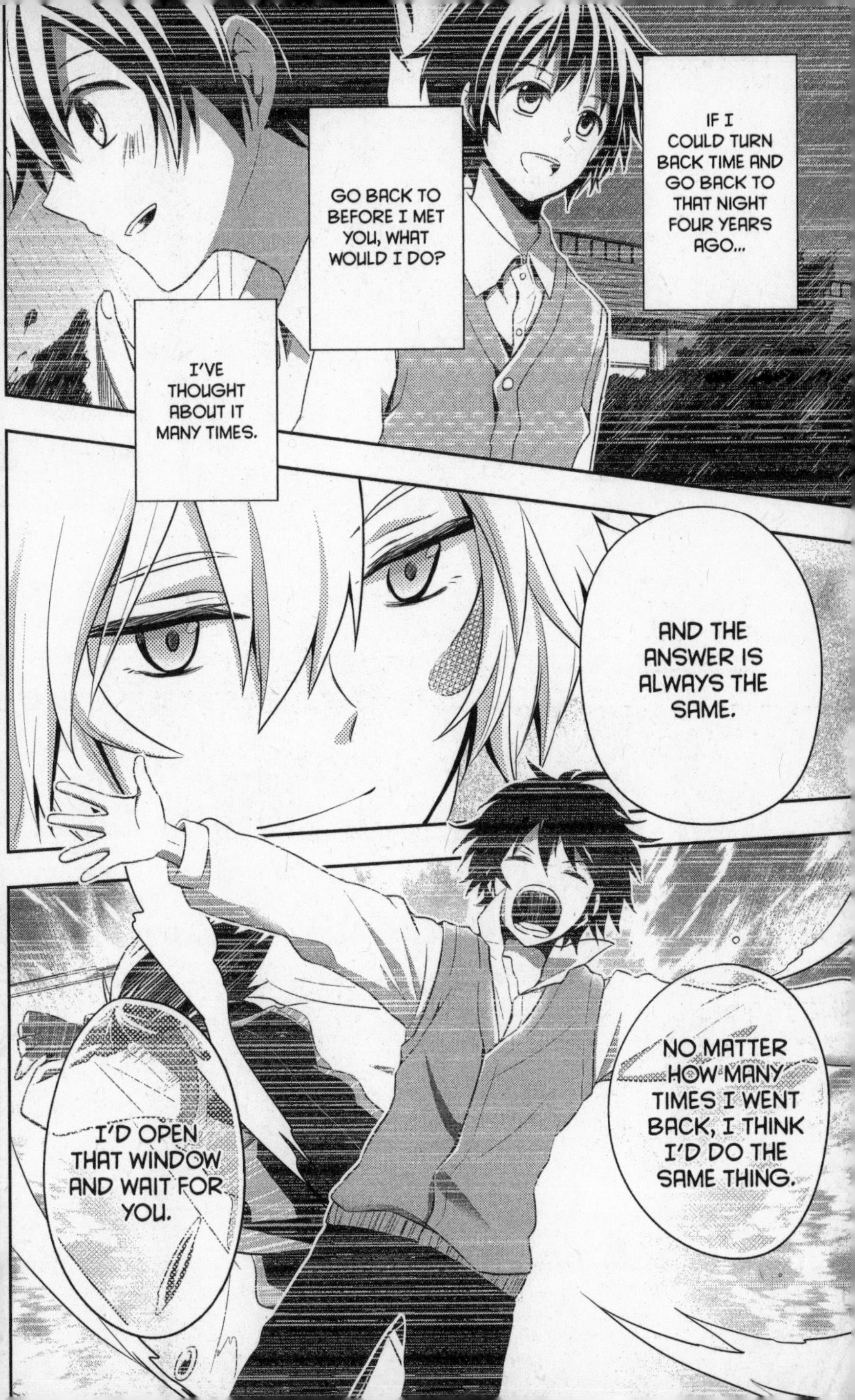
IF I COULD TURN BACK TIME AND GO BACK TO THAT NIGHT FOUR YEARS AGO...
GO BACK TO BEFORE I MET YOU, WHAT WOULD I DO?
I'VE THOUGHT ABOUT IT MANY TIMES.
AND THE ANSWER IS ALWAYS THE SAME.
NO MATTER HOW MANY TIMES I WENT BACK, I THINK I'D DO THE SAME THING.
I'D OPEN THAT WINDOW AND WAIT FOR YOU.

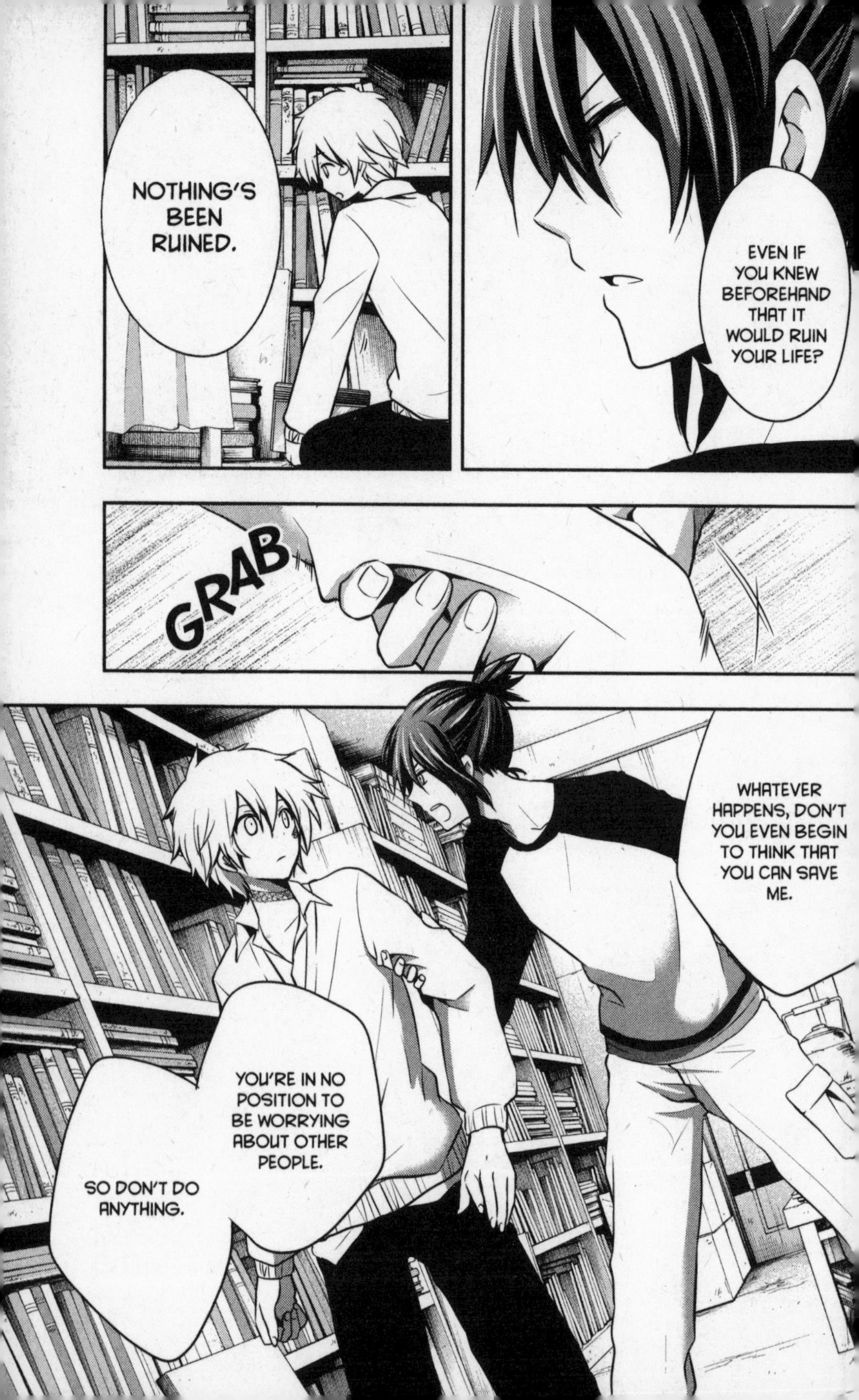
EVEN IF YOU KNEW BEFOREHAND THAT IT WOULD RUIN YOUR LIFE?
NOTHING'S BEEN RUINED.
GRAB
WHATEVER HAPPENS, DON'T YOU EVEN BEGIN TO THINK THAT YOU CAN SAVE ME.
YOU'RE IN NO POSITION TO BE WORRYING ABOUT OTHER PEOPLE.
SO DON'T DO ANYTHING.

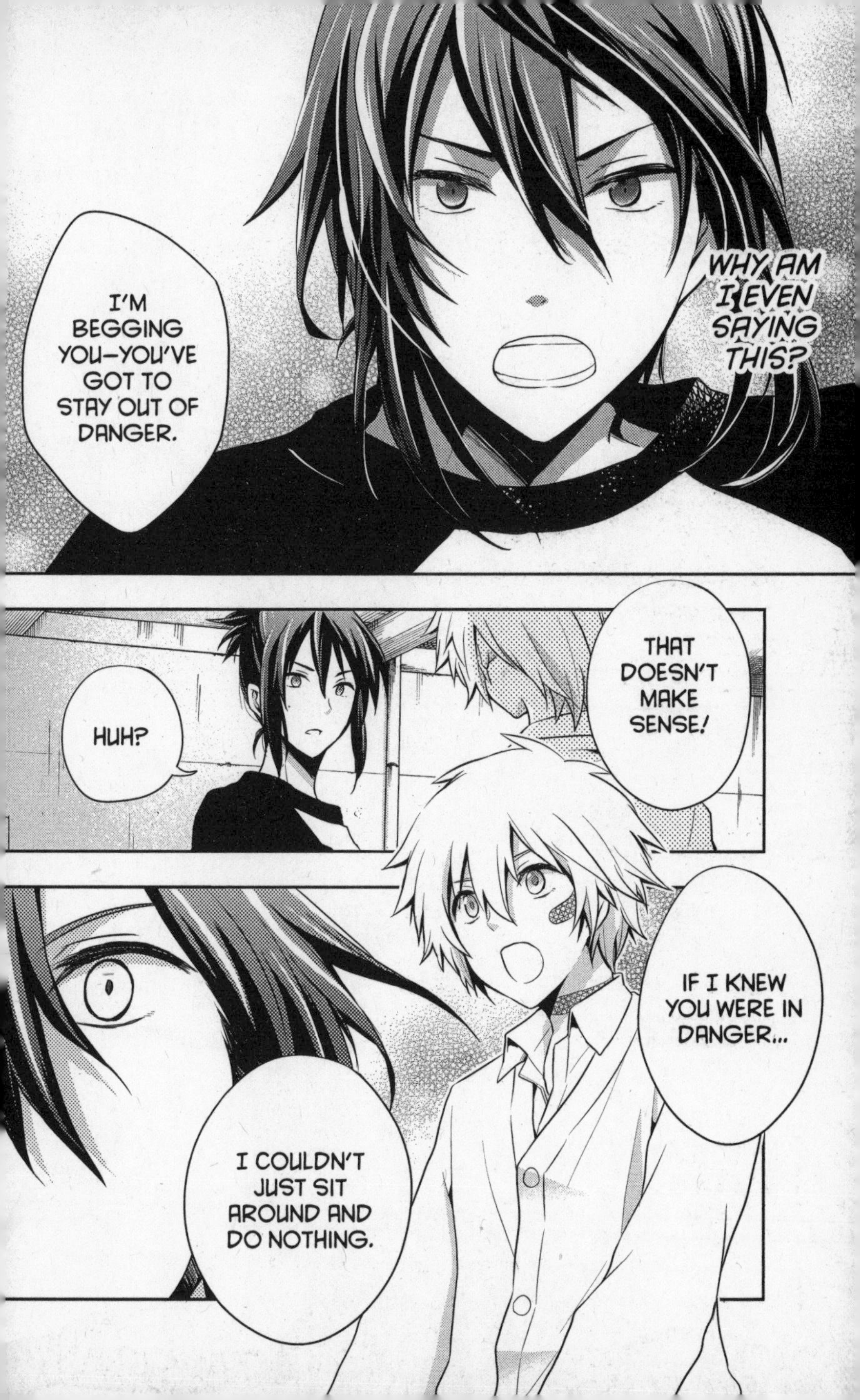
WHY AM I EVEN SAYING THIS?
I'M BEGGING YOU—YOU'VE GOT TO STAY OUT OF DANGER.
THAT DOESN'T MAKE SENSE!
HUH?
IF I KNEW YOU WERE IN DANGER...
I COULDN'T JUST SIT AROUND AND DO NOTHING.

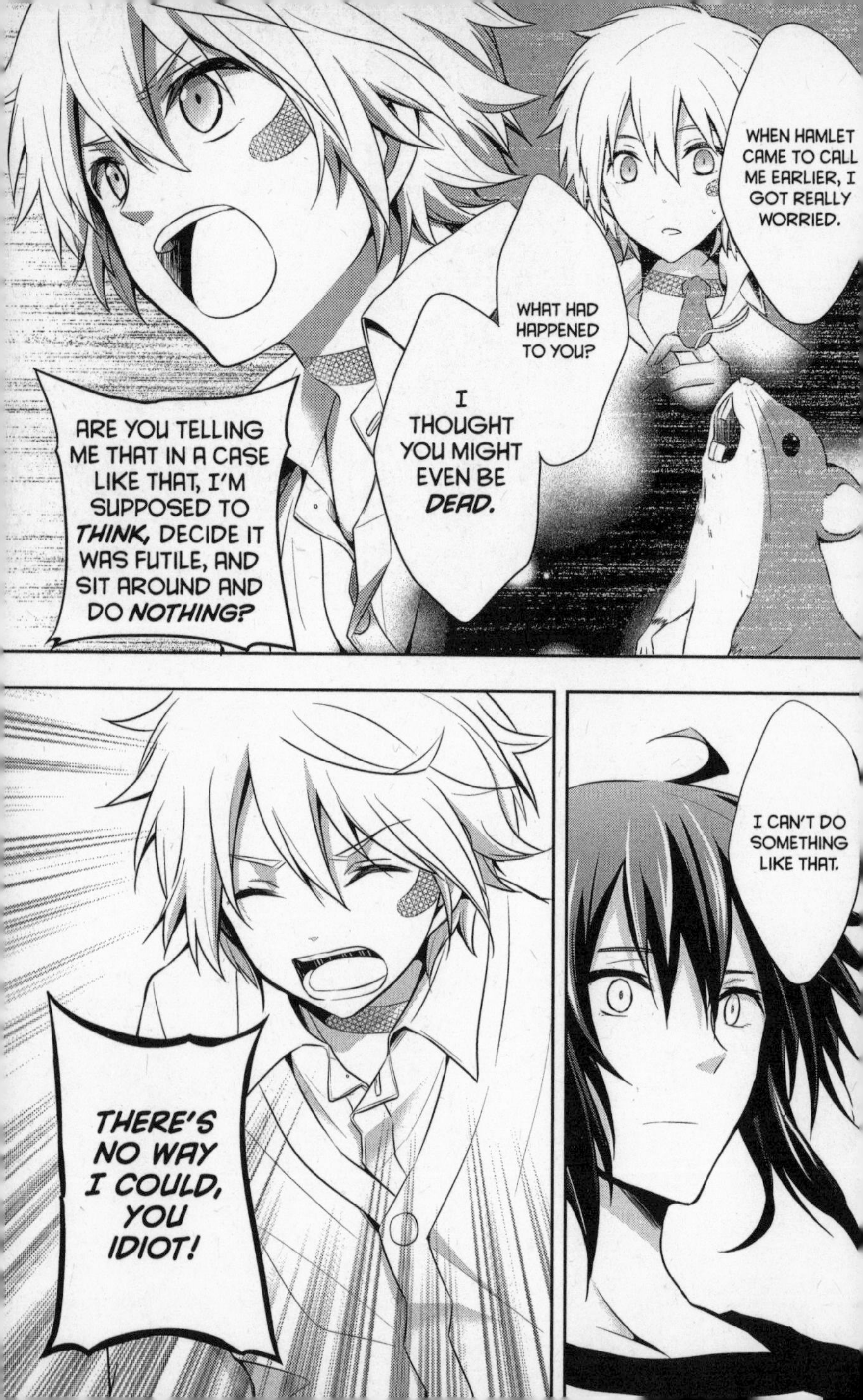
WHEN HAMLET CAME TO CALL ME EARLIER, I GOT REALLY WORRIED.
WHAT HAD HAPPENED TO YOU?
I THOUGHT YOU MIGHT EVEN BE *DEAD.*
ARE YOU TELLING ME THAT IN A CASE LIKE THAT, I'M SUPPOSED TO *THINK,* DECIDE IT WAS FUTILE, AND SIT AROUND AND DO *NOTHING?*
I CAN'T DO SOMETHING LIKE THAT.
THERE'S NO WAY I COULD, YOU IDIOT!

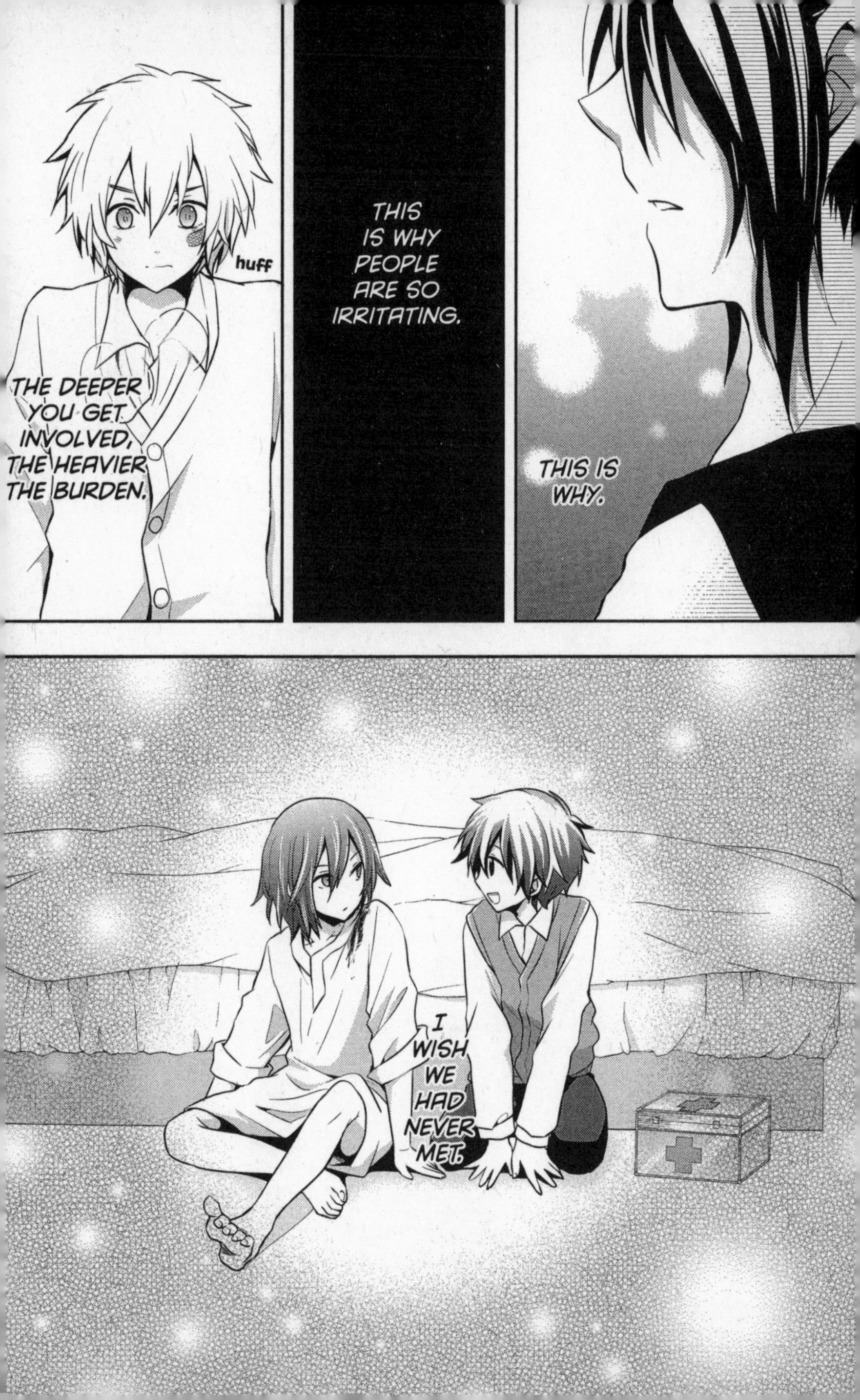
THIS IS WHY.
THIS IS WHY PEOPLE ARE SO IRRITATING.
huff
THE DEEPER YOU GET INVOLVED, THE HEAVIER THE BURDEN.
I WISH WE HAD NEVER MET.

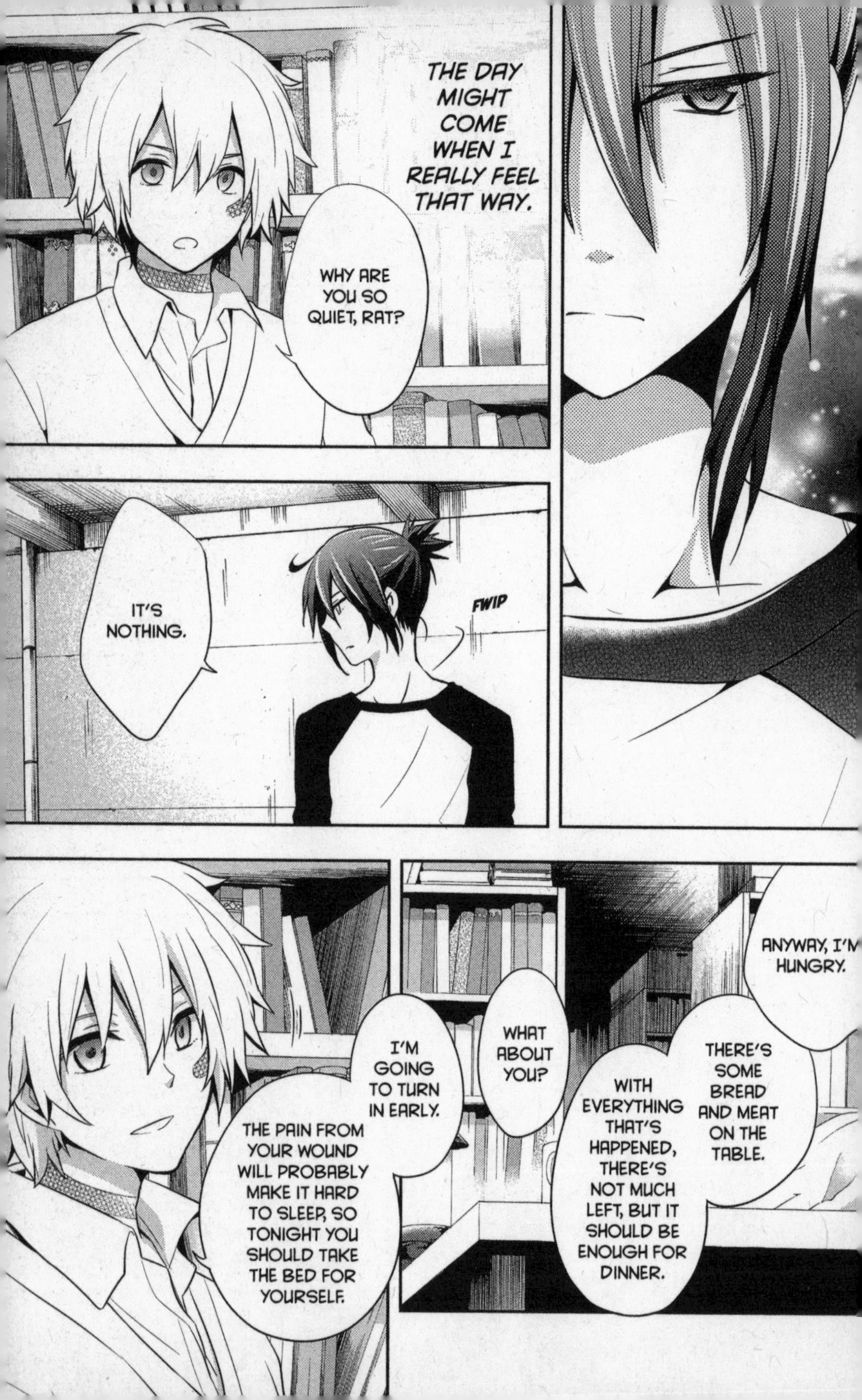
THE DAY MIGHT COME WHEN I REALLY FEEL THAT WAY.
WHY ARE YOU SO QUIET, RAT?
FWIP
IT'S NOTHING.
ANYWAY, I'M HUNGRY.
THERE'S SOME BREAD AND MEAT ON THE TABLE.
WITH EVERYTHING THAT'S HAPPENED, THERE'S NOT MUCH LEFT, BUT IT SHOULD BE ENOUGH FOR DINNER.
WHAT ABOUT YOU?
I'M GOING TO TURN IN EARLY.
THE PAIN FROM YOUR WOUND WILL PROBABLY MAKE IT HARD TO SLEEP, SO TONIGHT YOU SHOULD TAKE THE BED FOR YOURSELF.

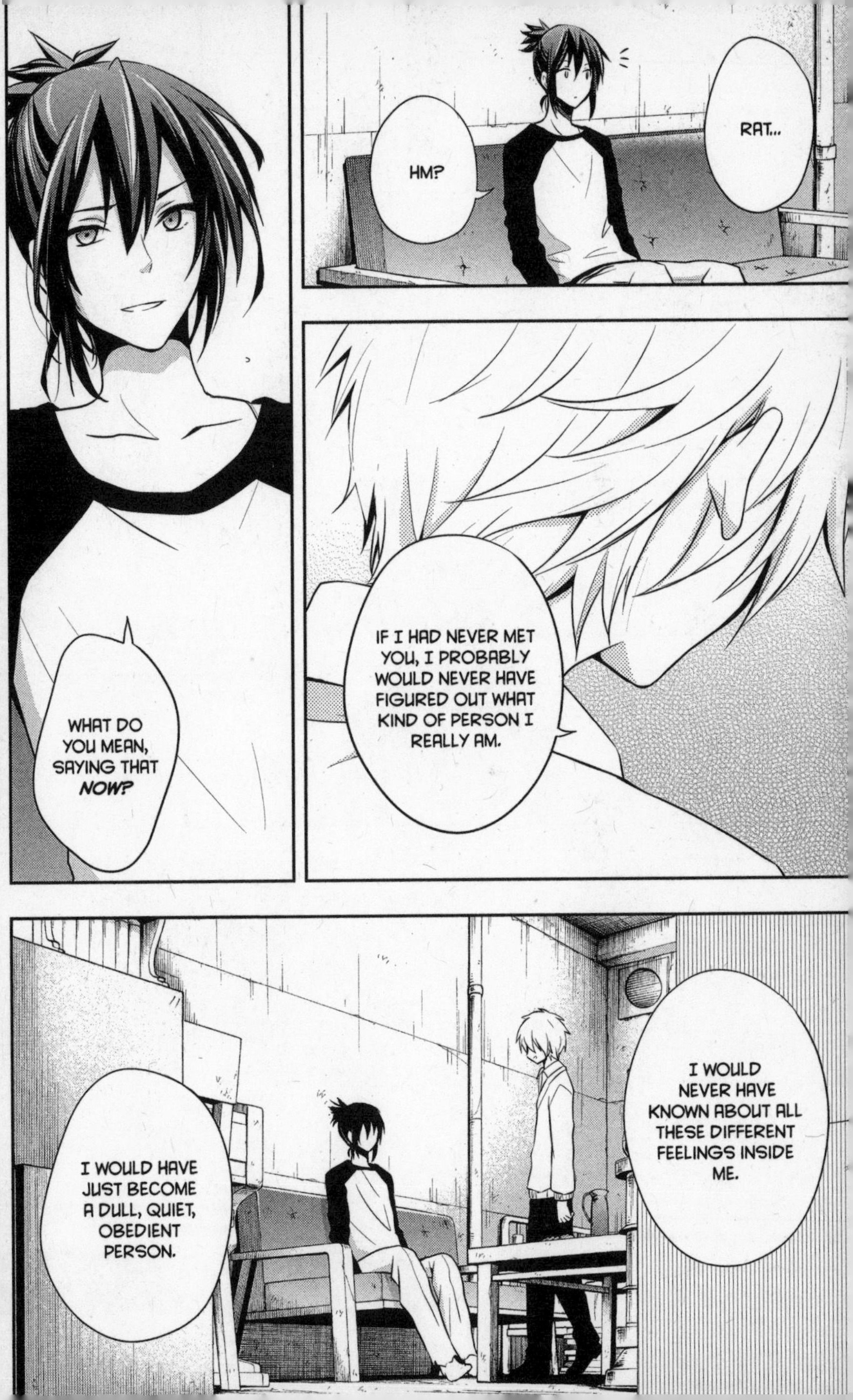
RAT...
HM?
IF I HAD NEVER MET YOU, I PROBABLY WOULD NEVER HAVE FIGURED OUT WHAT KIND OF PERSON I REALLY AM.
WHAT DO YOU MEAN, SAYING THAT *NOW?*
I WOULD NEVER HAVE KNOWN ABOUT ALL THESE DIFFERENT FEELINGS INSIDE ME.
I WOULD HAVE JUST BECOME A DULL, QUIET, OBEDIENT PERSON.

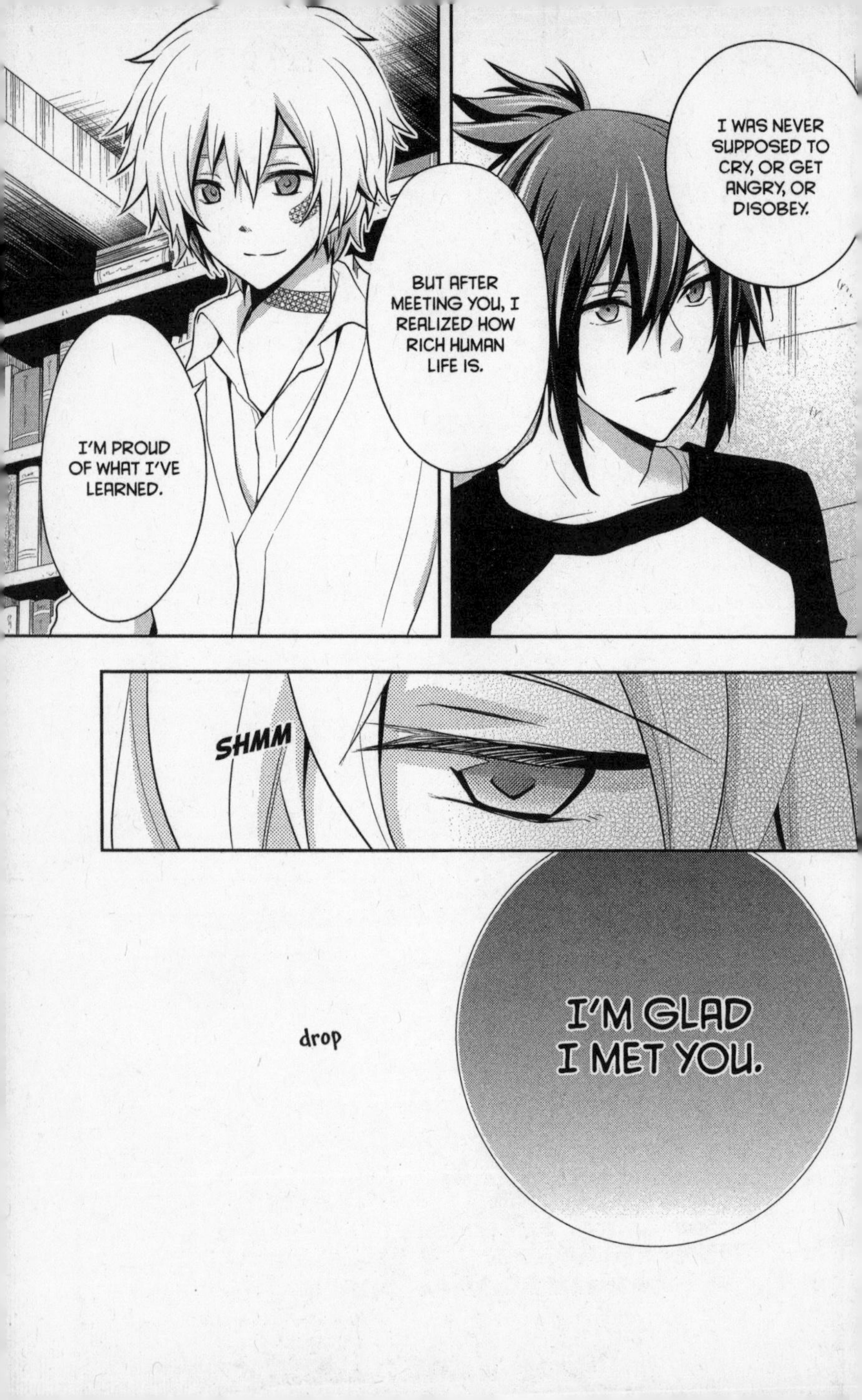
I WAS NEVER SUPPOSED TO CRY, OR GET ANGRY, OR DISOBEY.
BUT AFTER MEETING YOU, I REALIZED HOW RICH HUMAN LIFE IS.
I'M PROUD OF WHAT I'VE LEARNED.
SHMM
I'M GLAD I MET YOU.
drop

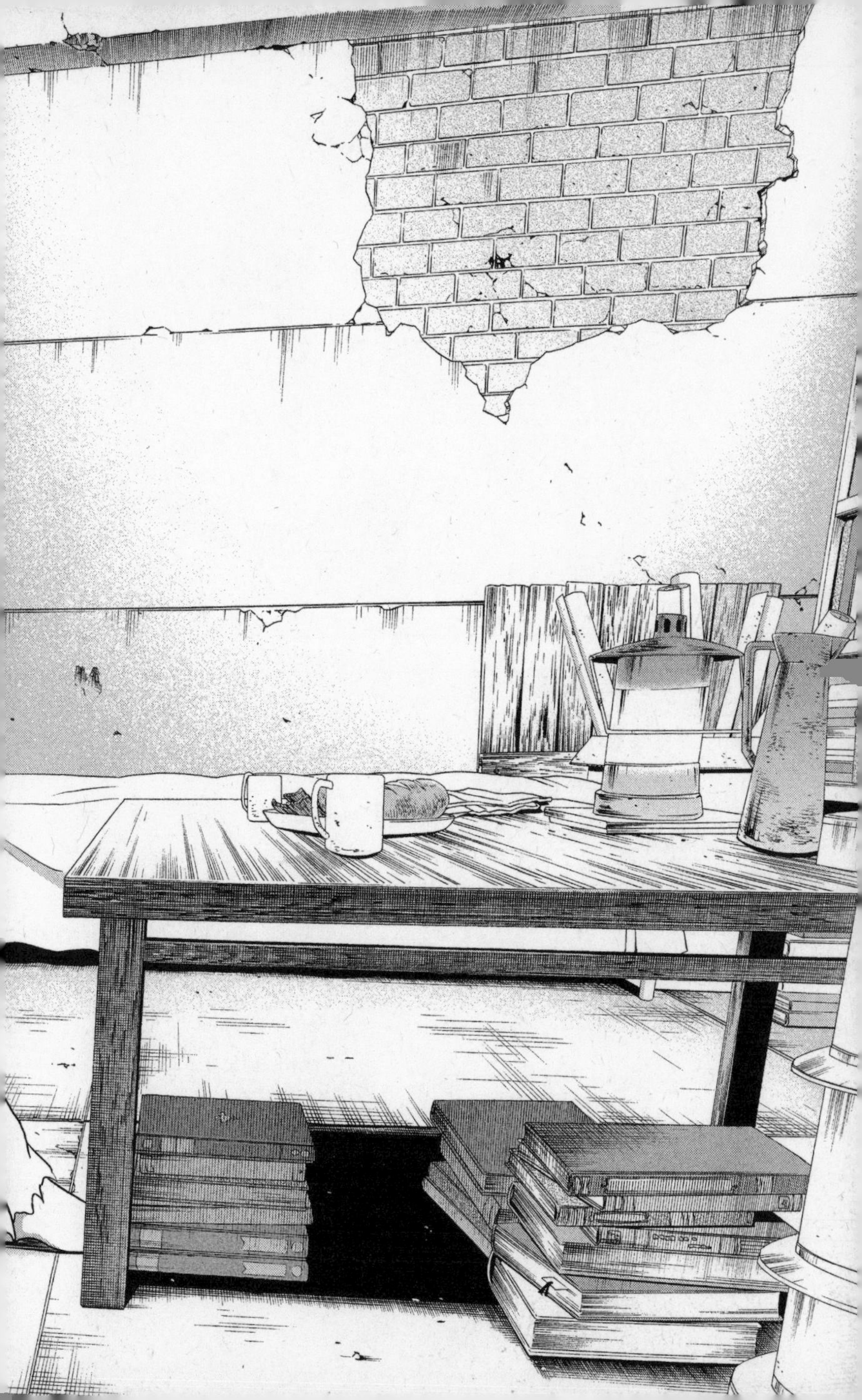

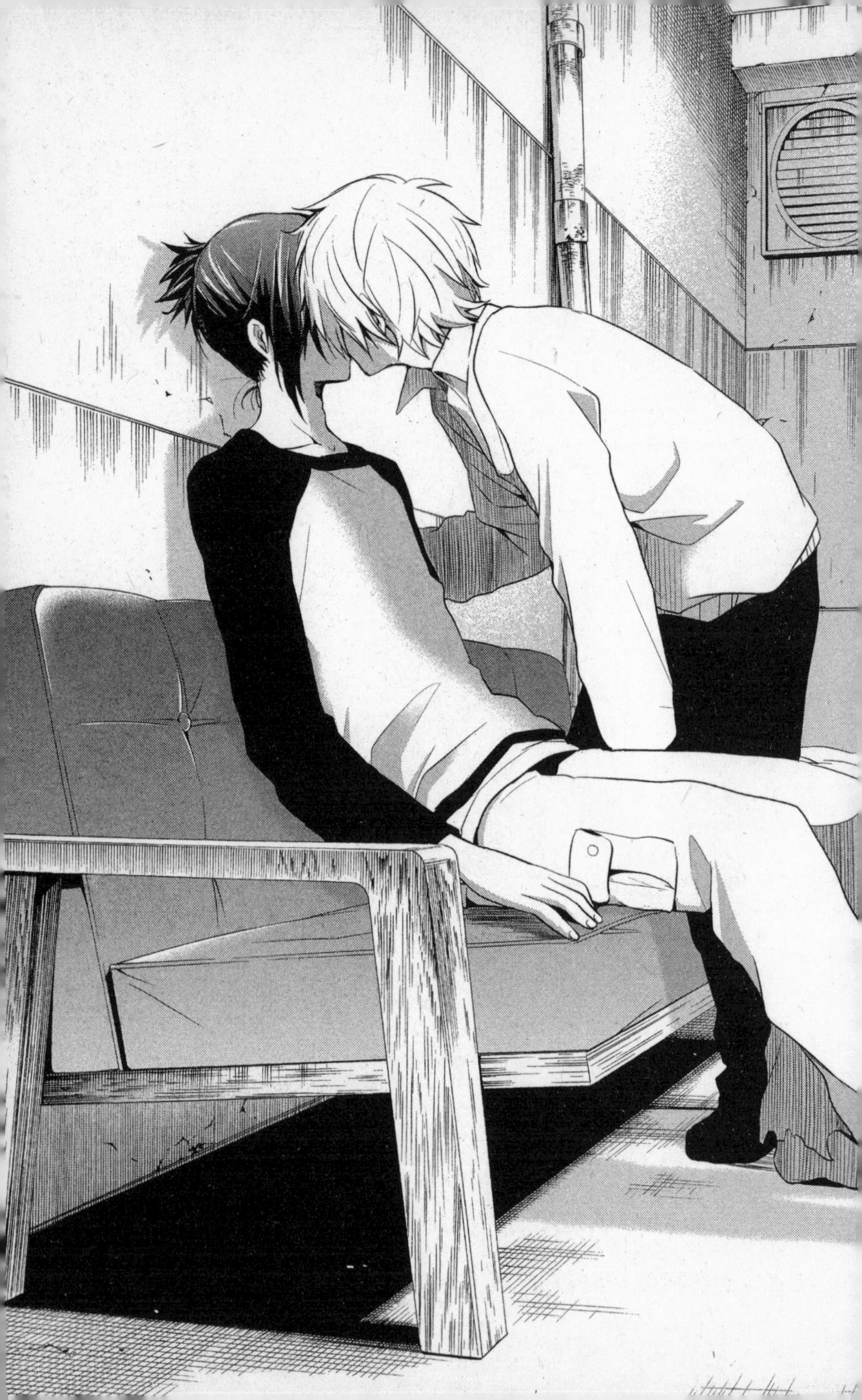

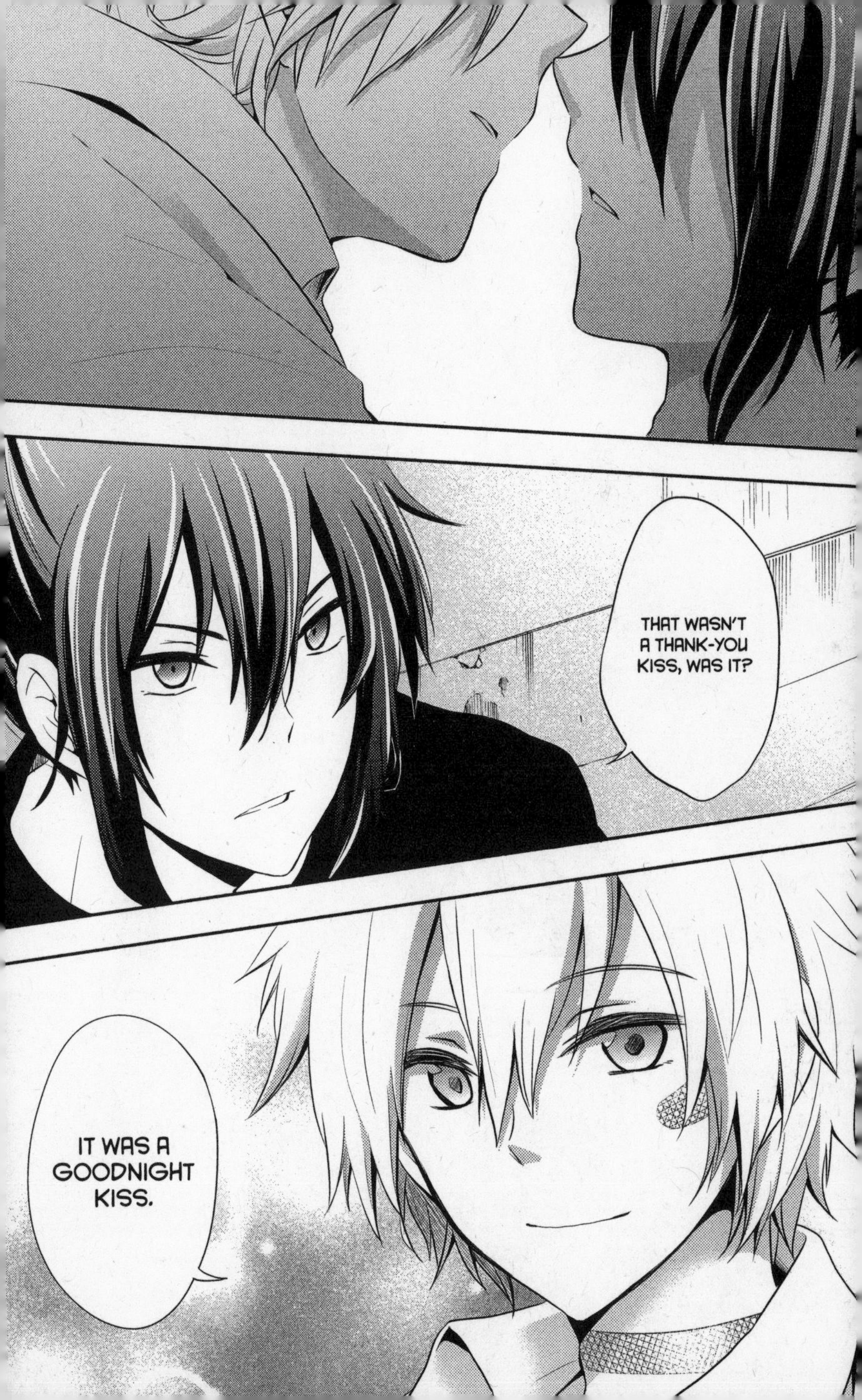
THAT WASN'T A THANK-YOU KISS, WAS IT?
IT WAS A GOODNIGHT KISS.

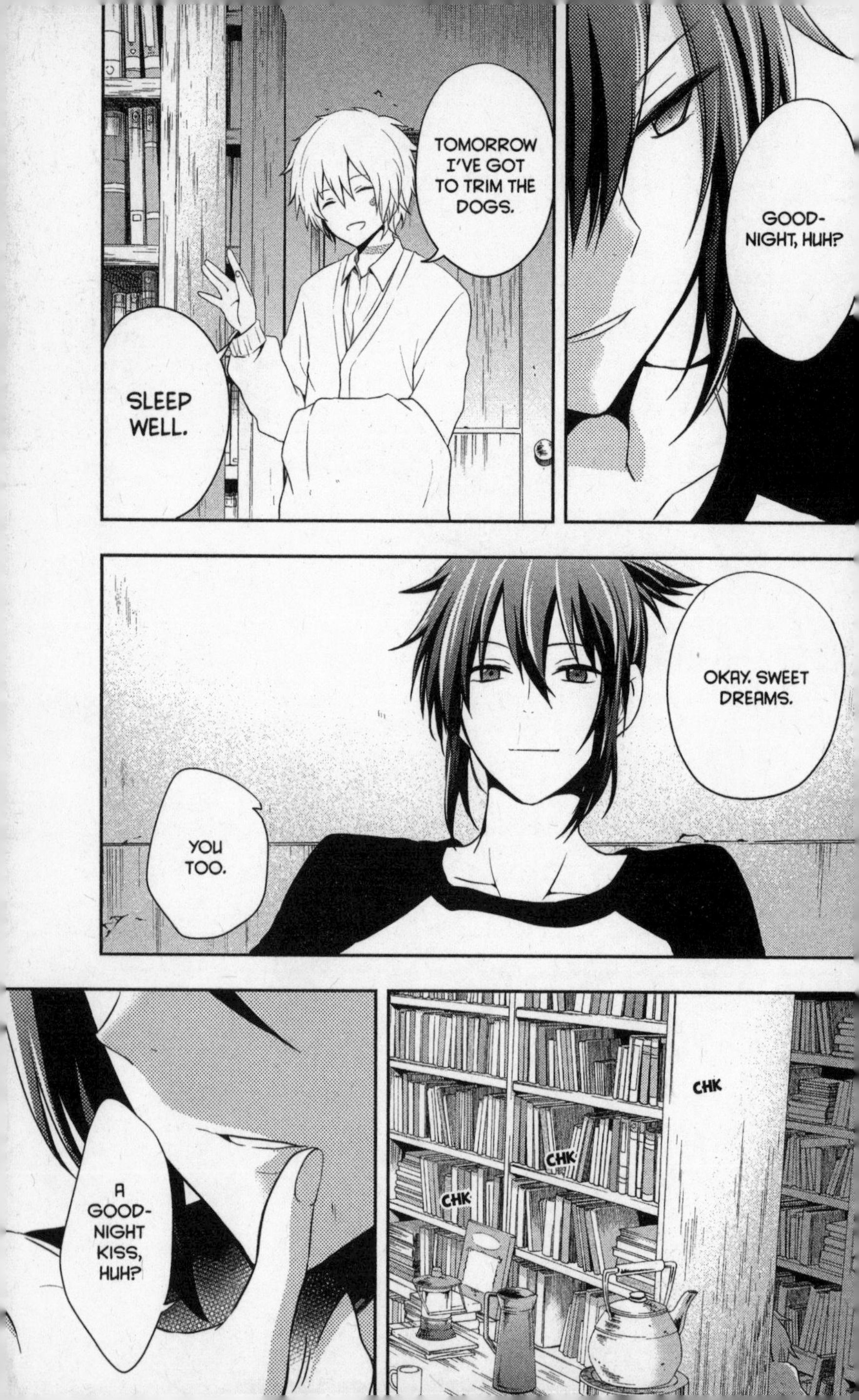
GOOD-NIGHT, HUH?
TOMORROW I'VE GOT TO TRIM THE DOGS.
SLEEP WELL.
OKAY. SWEET DREAMS.
YOU TOO.
CHK
CHK
CHK
A GOOD-NIGHT KISS, HUH?

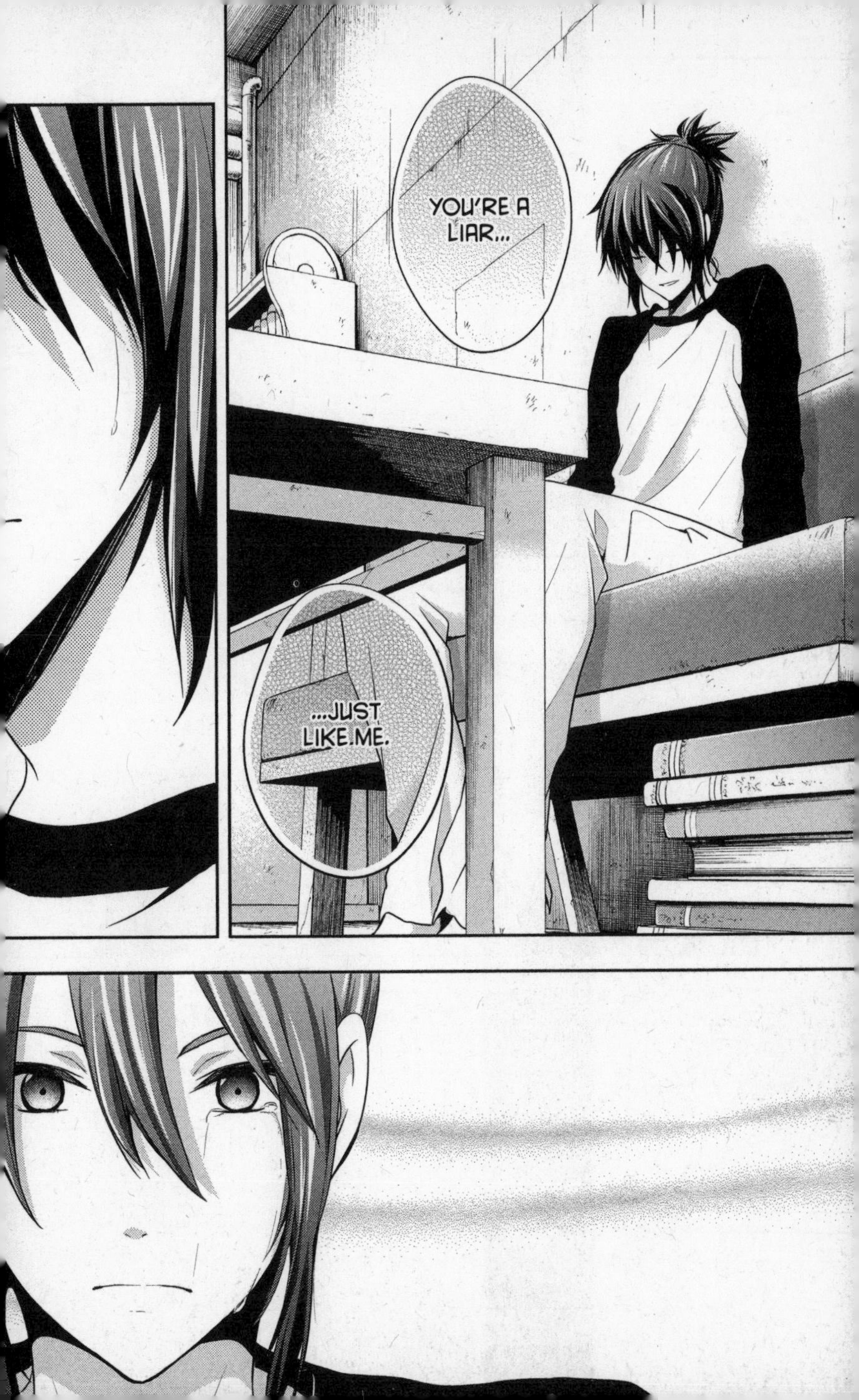
YOU'RE A LIAR...
...JUST LIKE ME.

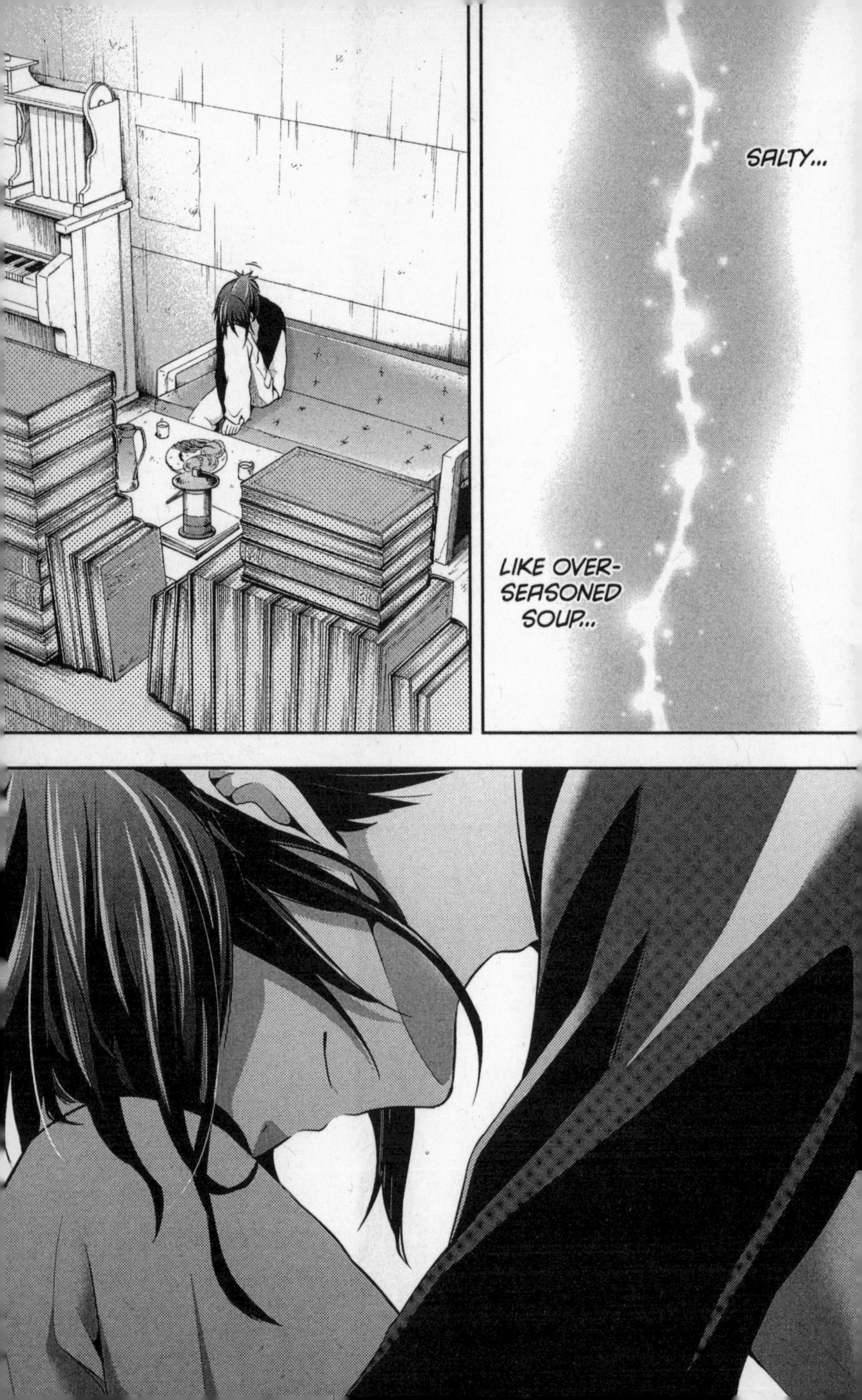
SALTY...
LIKE OVER-SEASONED SOUP...

NO.6

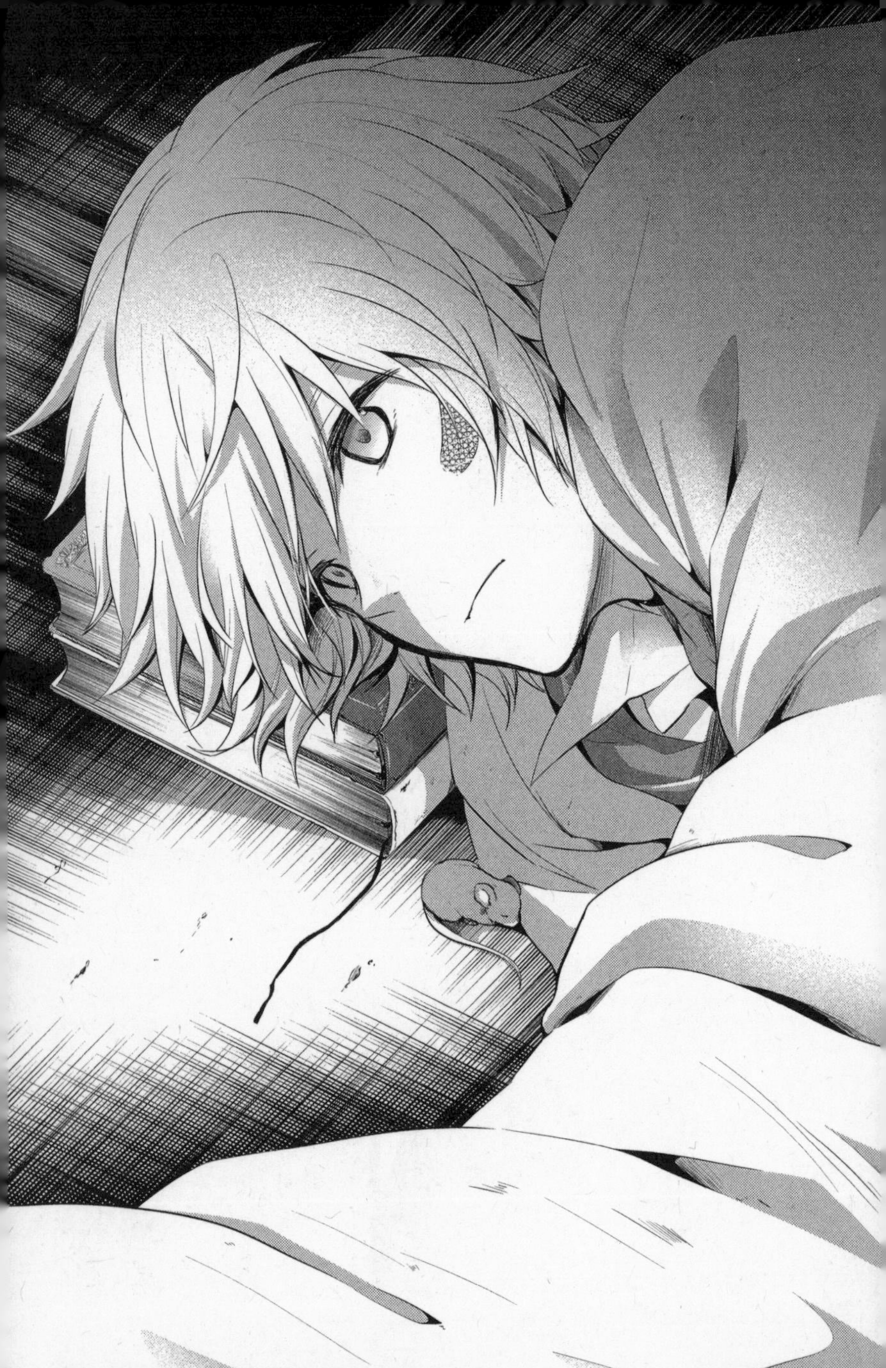

Chapter 13: Beside the Deceit

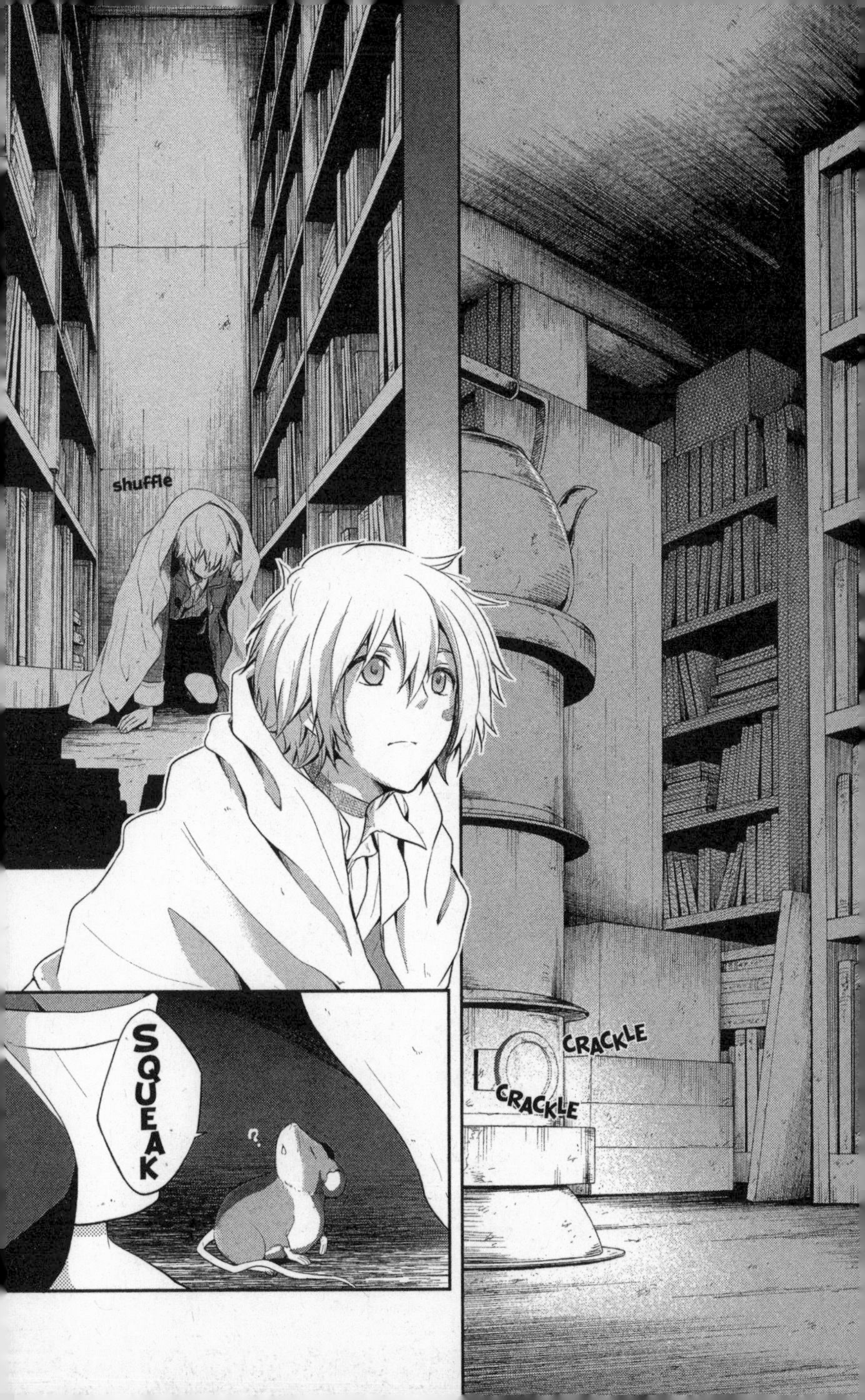
CRACKLE
CRACKLE
shuffle
SQUEAK

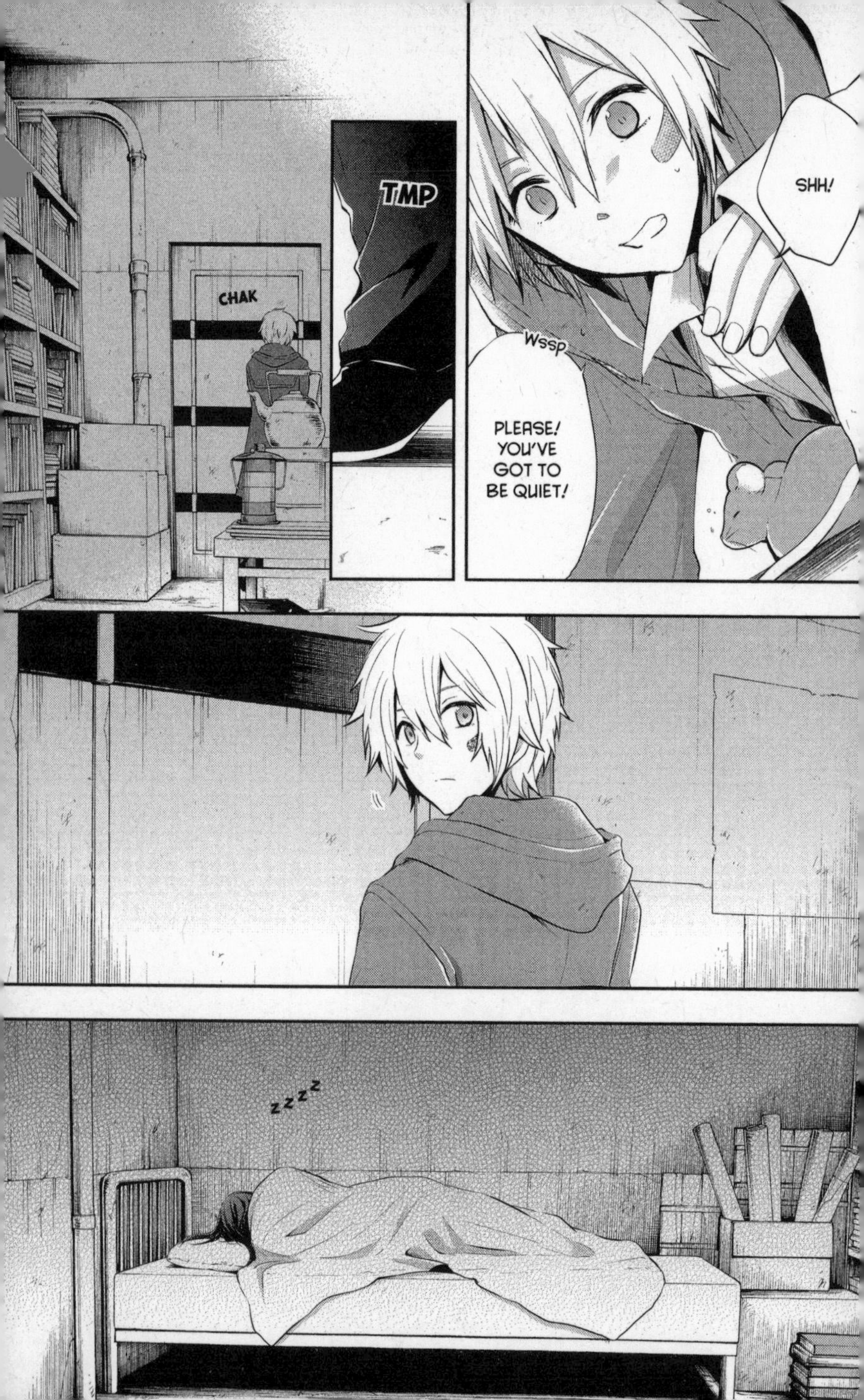
SHH!
Wssp
PLEASE! YOU'VE GOT TO BE QUIET!
TMP
CHAK
ZZZZ

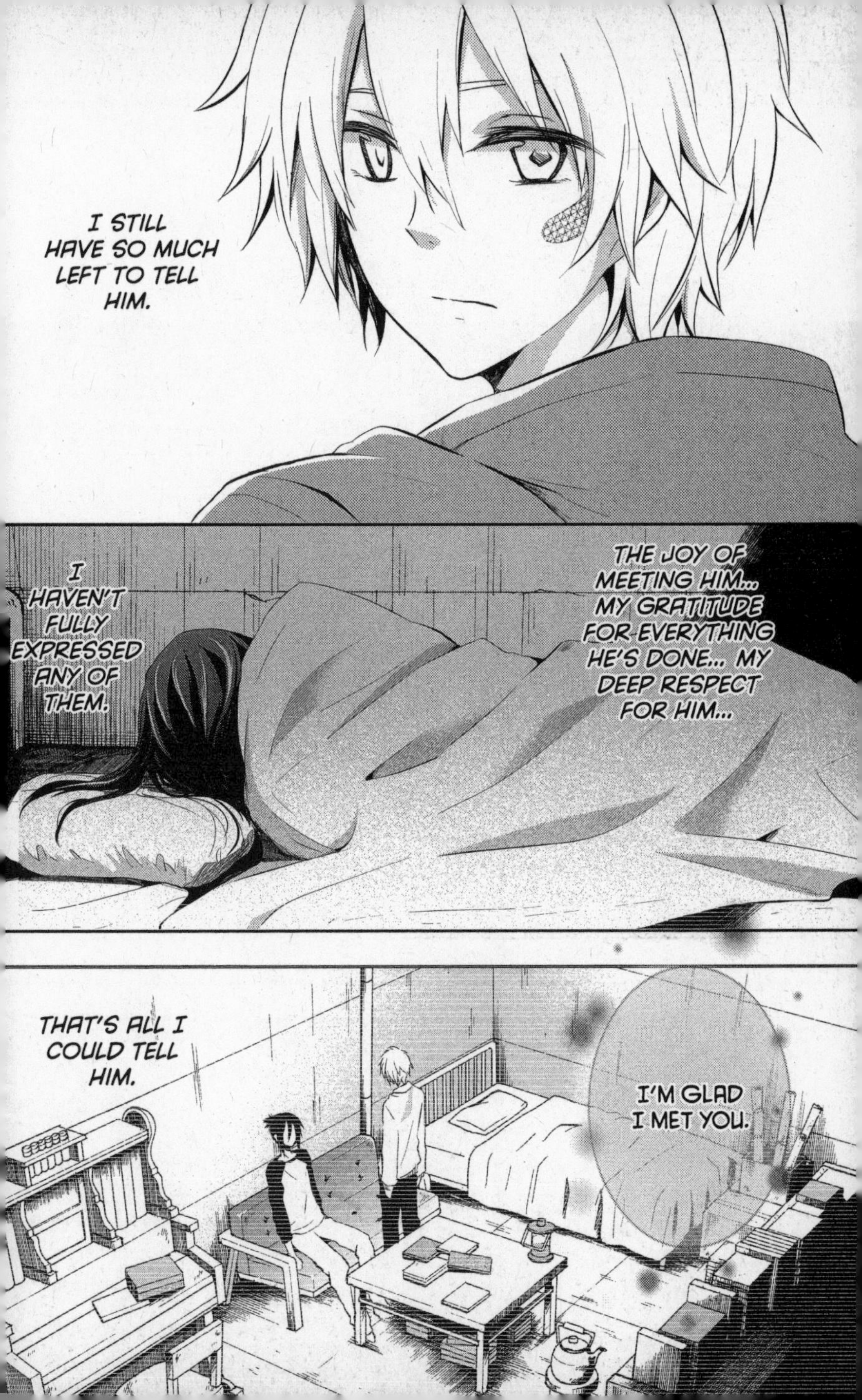
I STILL HAVE SO MUCH LEFT TO TELL HIM.
THE JOY OF MEETING HIM... MY GRATITUDE FOR EVERYTHING HE'S DONE... MY DEEP RESPECT FOR HIM...
I HAVEN'T FULLY EXPRESSED ANY OF THEM.
I'M GLAD I MET YOU.
THAT'S ALL I COULD TELL HIM.

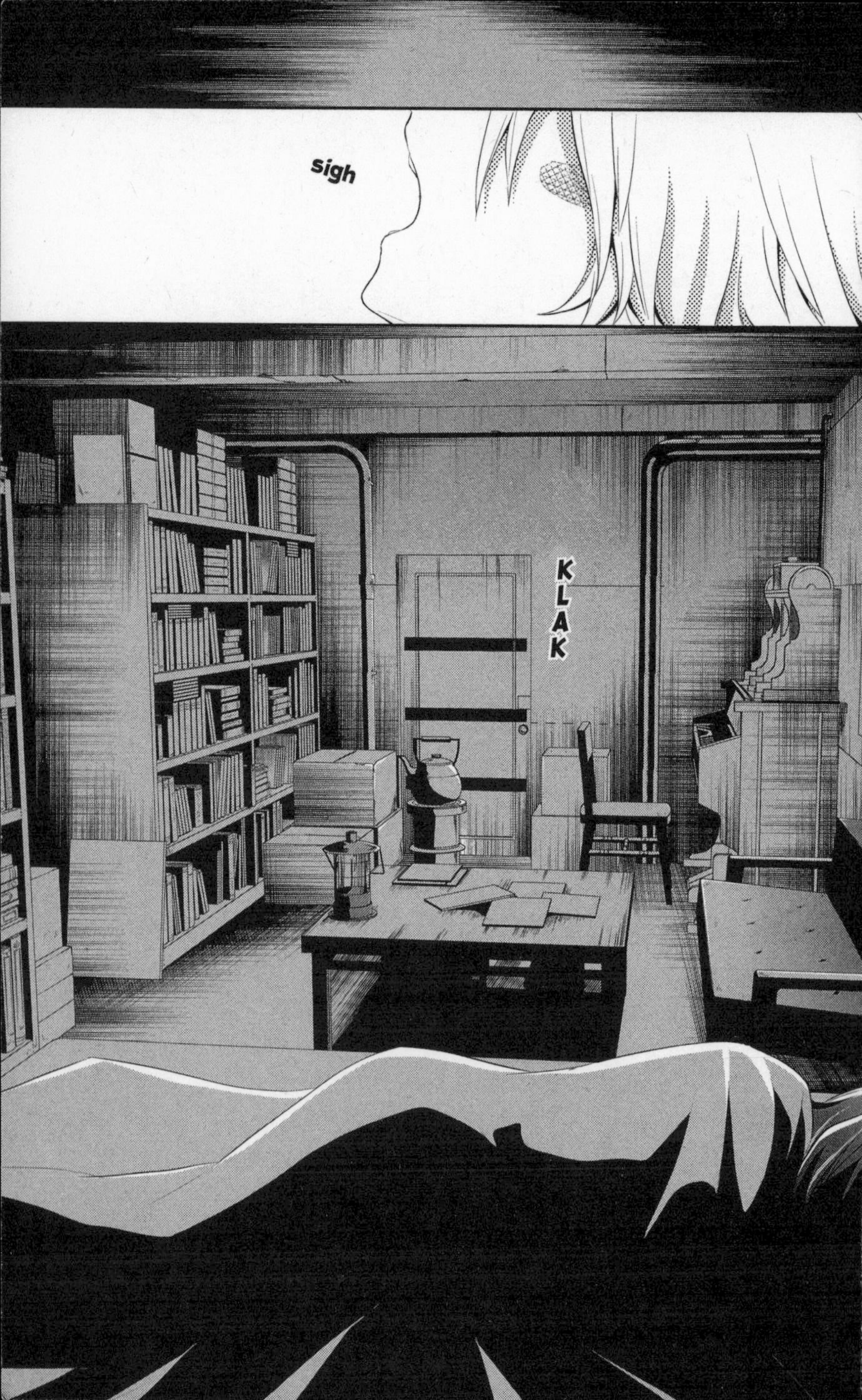
sigh
KLAK

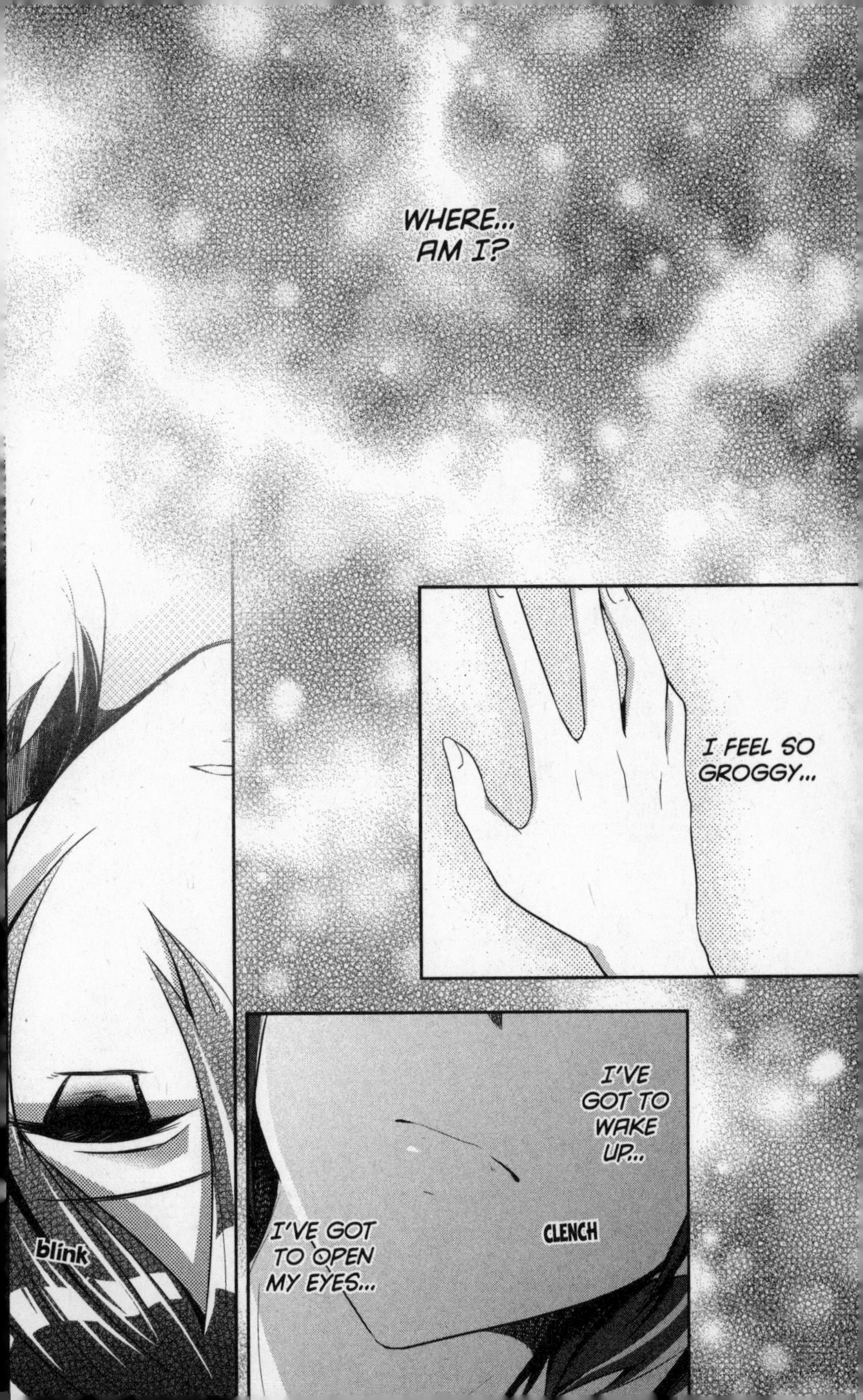
WHERE... AM I?
I FEEL SO GROGGY...
I'VE GOT TO WAKE UP...
CLENCH
I'VE GOT TO OPEN MY EYES...
blink

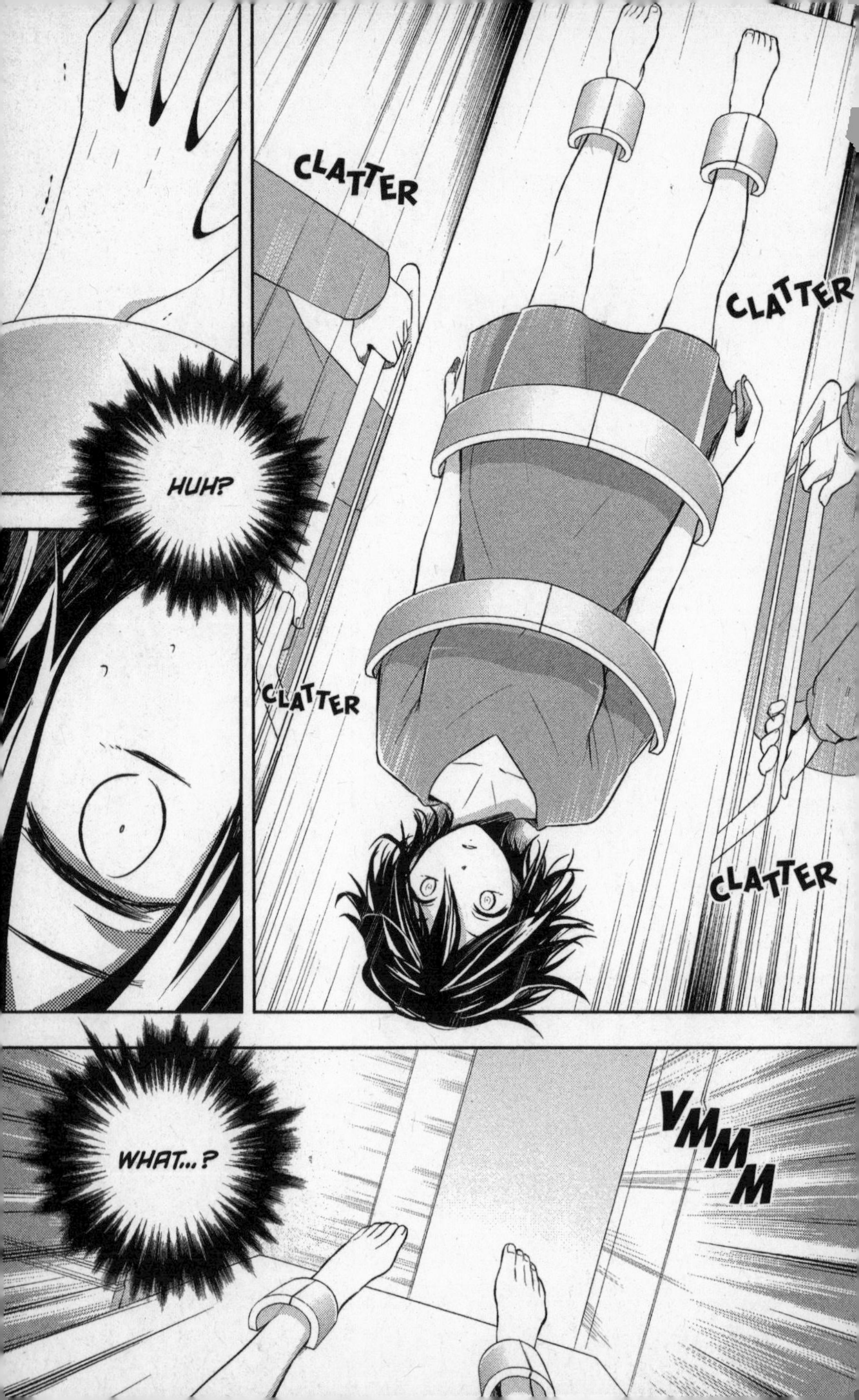
CLATTER
CLATTER
CLATTER
CLATTER
HUH?
VMMM
WHAT...?

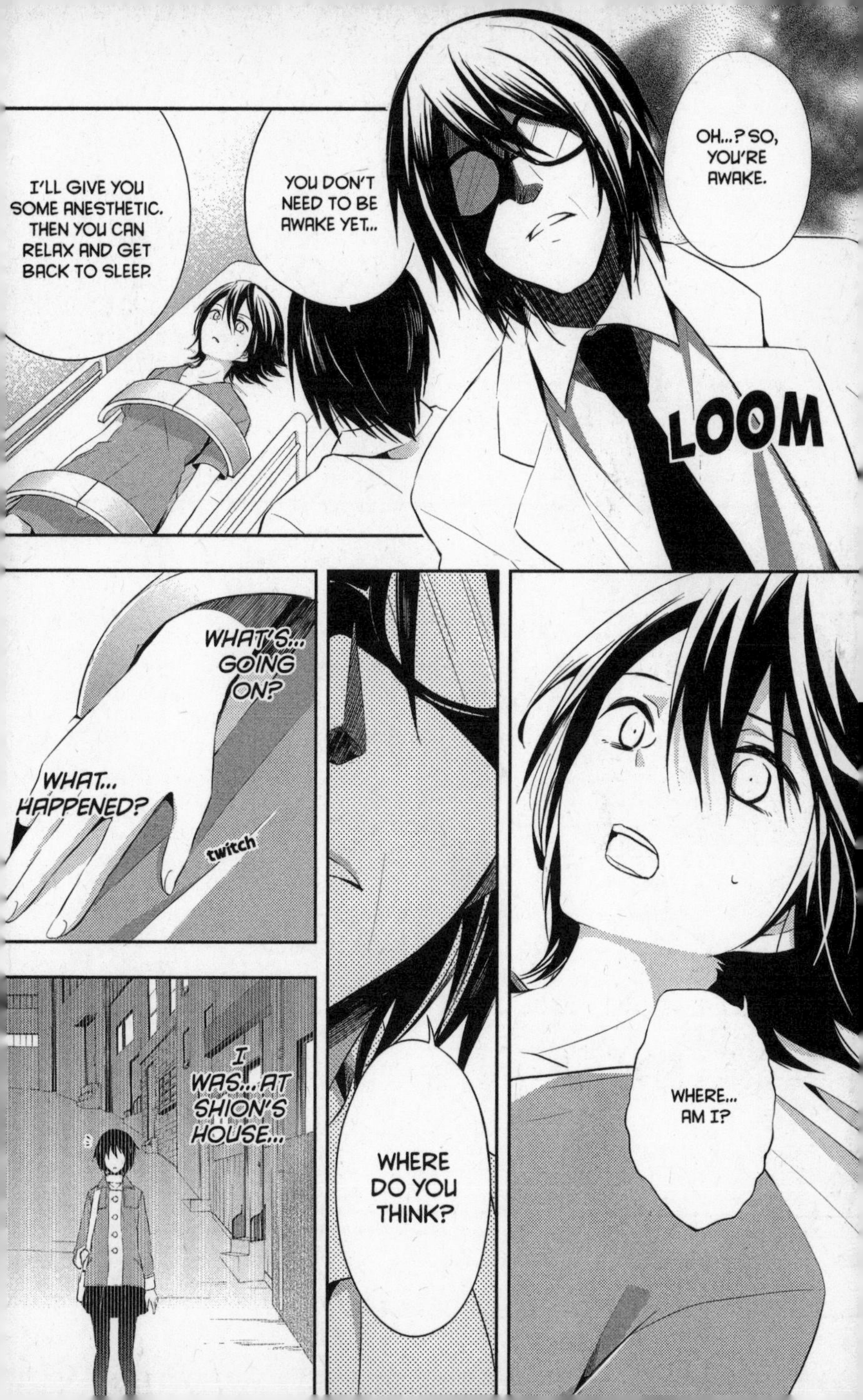
OH...? SO, YOU'RE AWAKE.
LOOM
YOU DON'T NEED TO BE AWAKE YET...
I'LL GIVE YOU SOME ANESTHETIC. THEN YOU CAN RELAX AND GET BACK TO SLEEP.
WHERE... AM I?
WHERE DO YOU THINK?
WHAT'S... GOING ON?
WHAT... HAPPENED?
twitch
I WAS... AT SHION'S HOUSE...

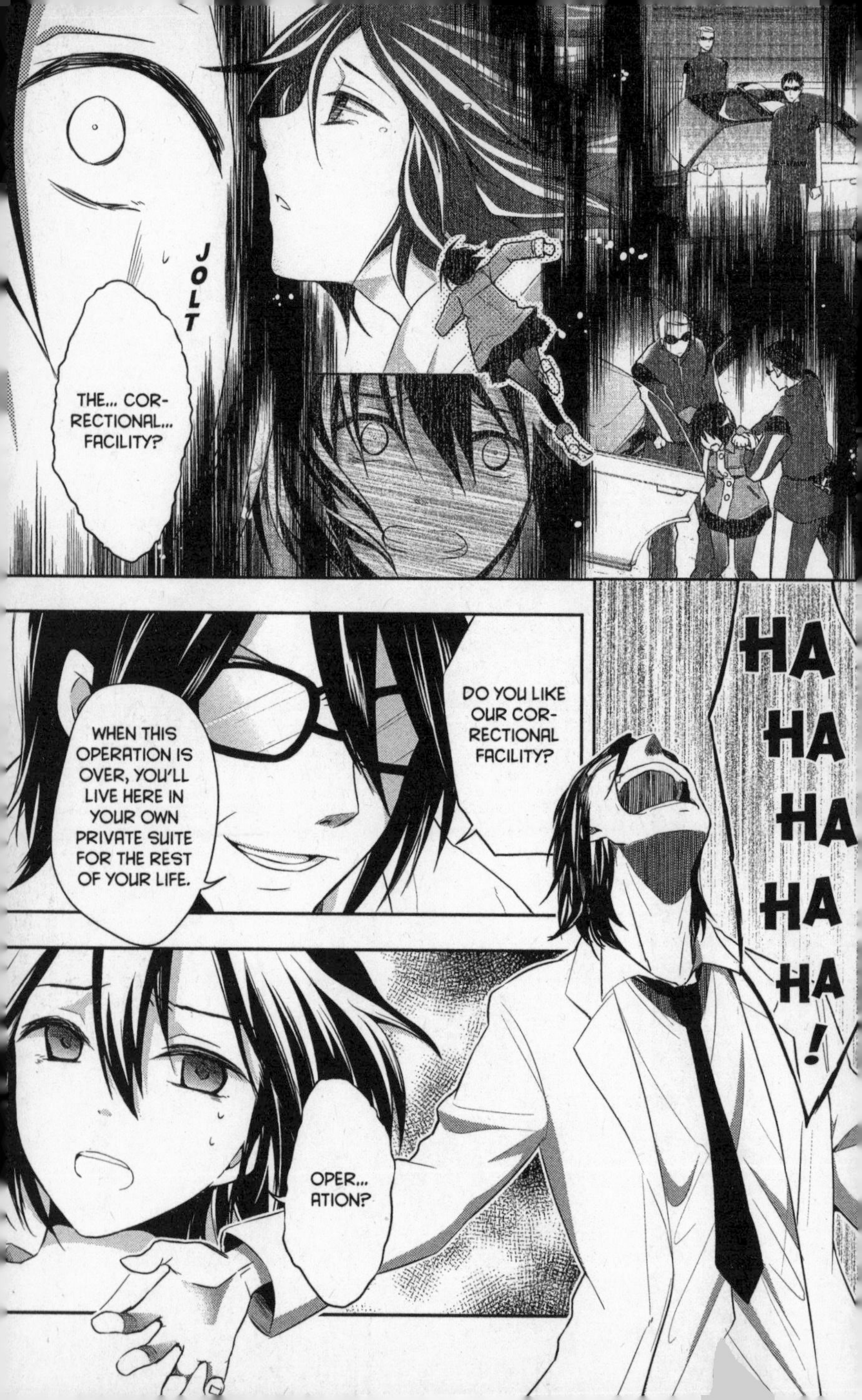
JOLT
THE... COR-RECTIONAL... FACILITY?
HA HA HA HA HA HA!
DO YOU LIKE OUR COR-RECTIONAL FACILITY?
WHEN THIS OPERATION IS OVER, YOU'LL LIVE HERE IN YOUR OWN PRIVATE SUITE FOR THE REST OF YOUR LIFE.
OPER... ATION?

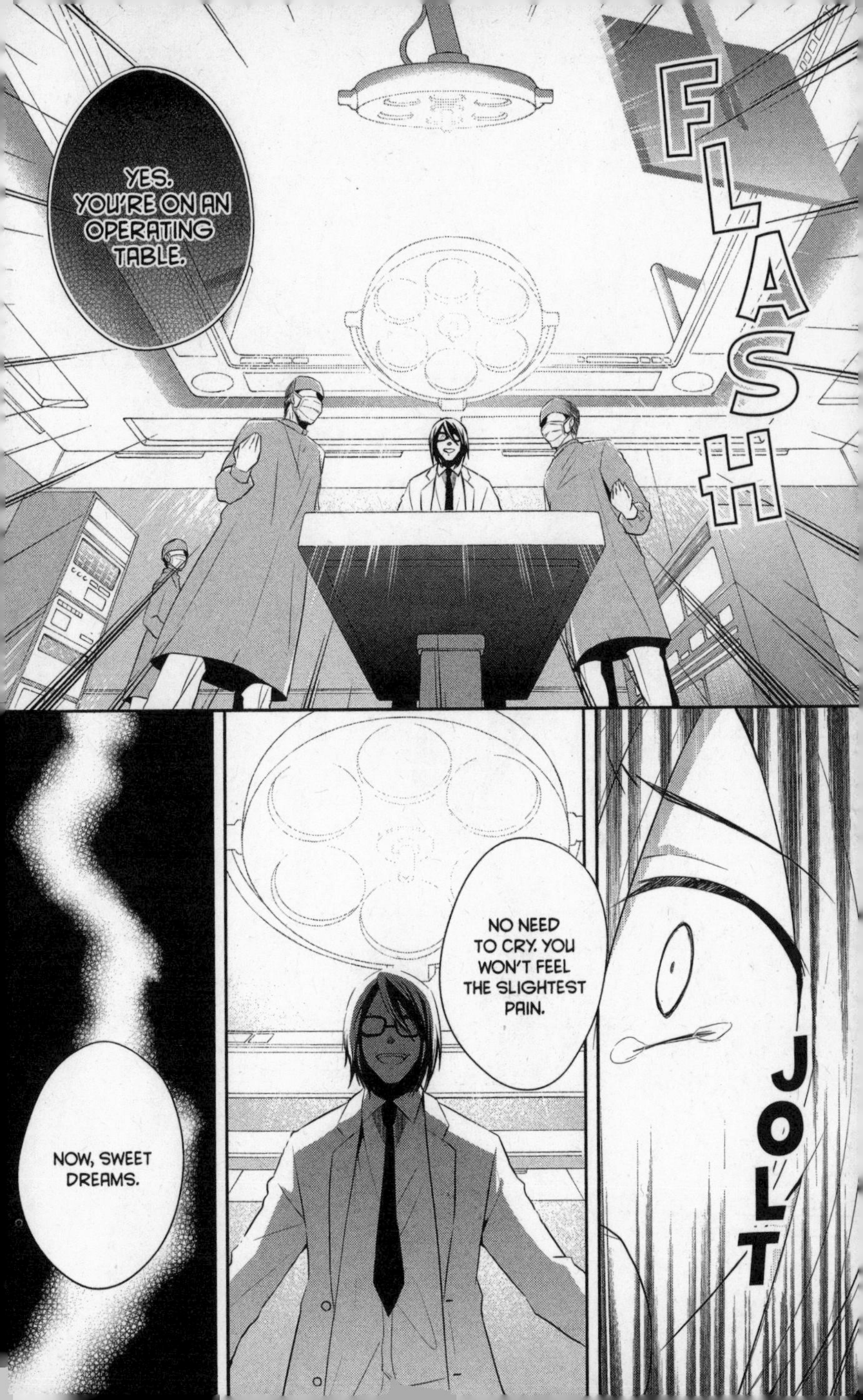
FLASHH
YES. YOU'RE ON AN OPERATING TABLE.
JOLT
NO NEED TO CRY. YOU WON'T FEEL THE SLIGHTEST PAIN.
NOW, SWEET DREAMS.

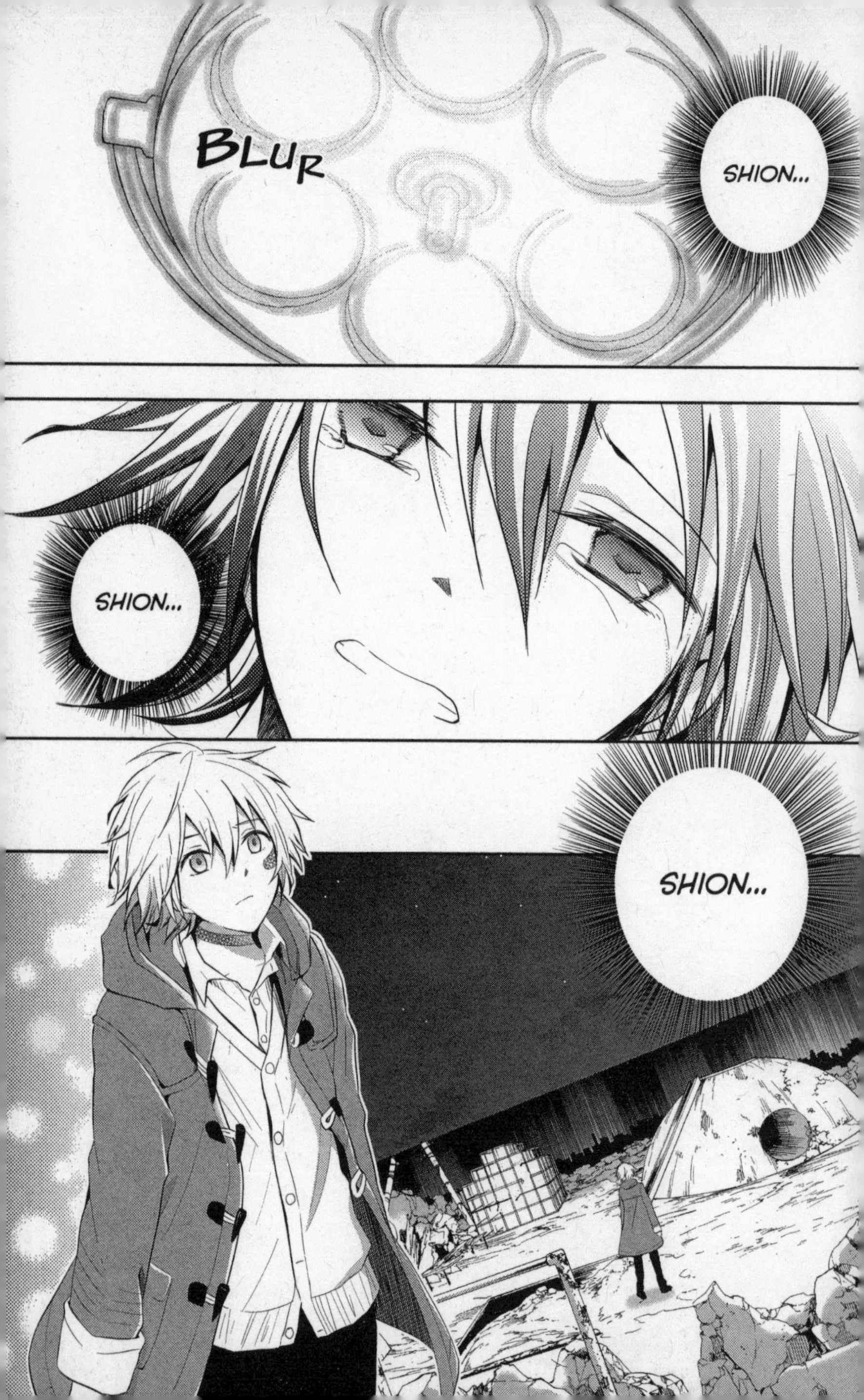
SHION...
BLUR
SHION...
SHION...

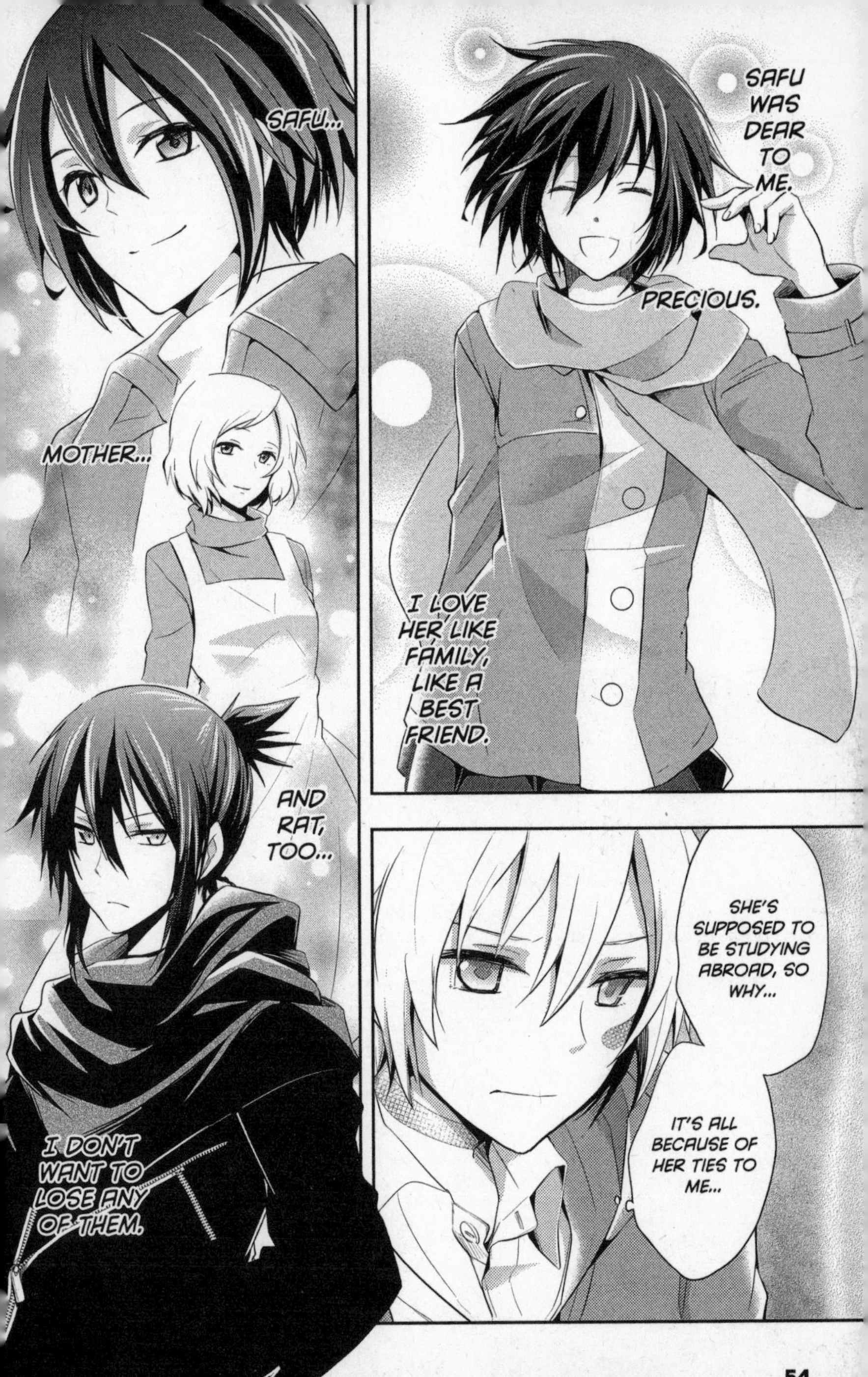
SAFU WAS DEAR TO ME.
PRECIOUS.
I LOVE HER LIKE FAMILY, LIKE A BEST FRIEND.
SHE'S SUPPOSED TO BE STUDYING ABROAD, SO WHY...
IT'S ALL BECAUSE OF HER TIES TO ME...
SAFU...
MOTHER...
AND RAT, TOO...
I DON'T WANT TO LOSE ANY OF THEM.

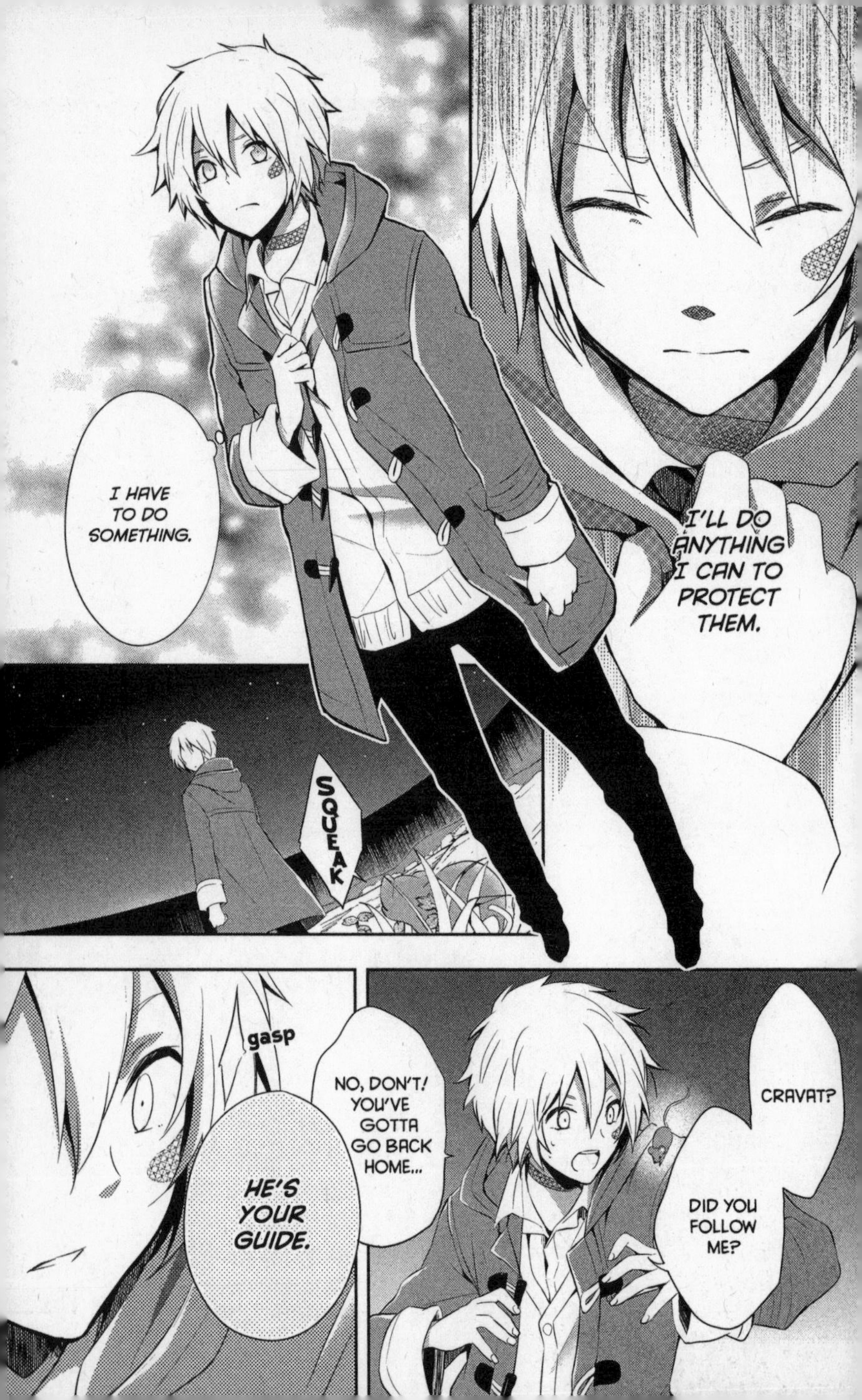
I'LL DO ANYTHING I CAN TO PROTECT THEM.
I HAVE TO DO SOMETHING.
SQUEAK
CRAVAT?
DID YOU FOLLOW ME?
NO, DON'T! YOU'VE GOTTA GO BACK HOME...
gasp
HE'S YOUR GUIDE.

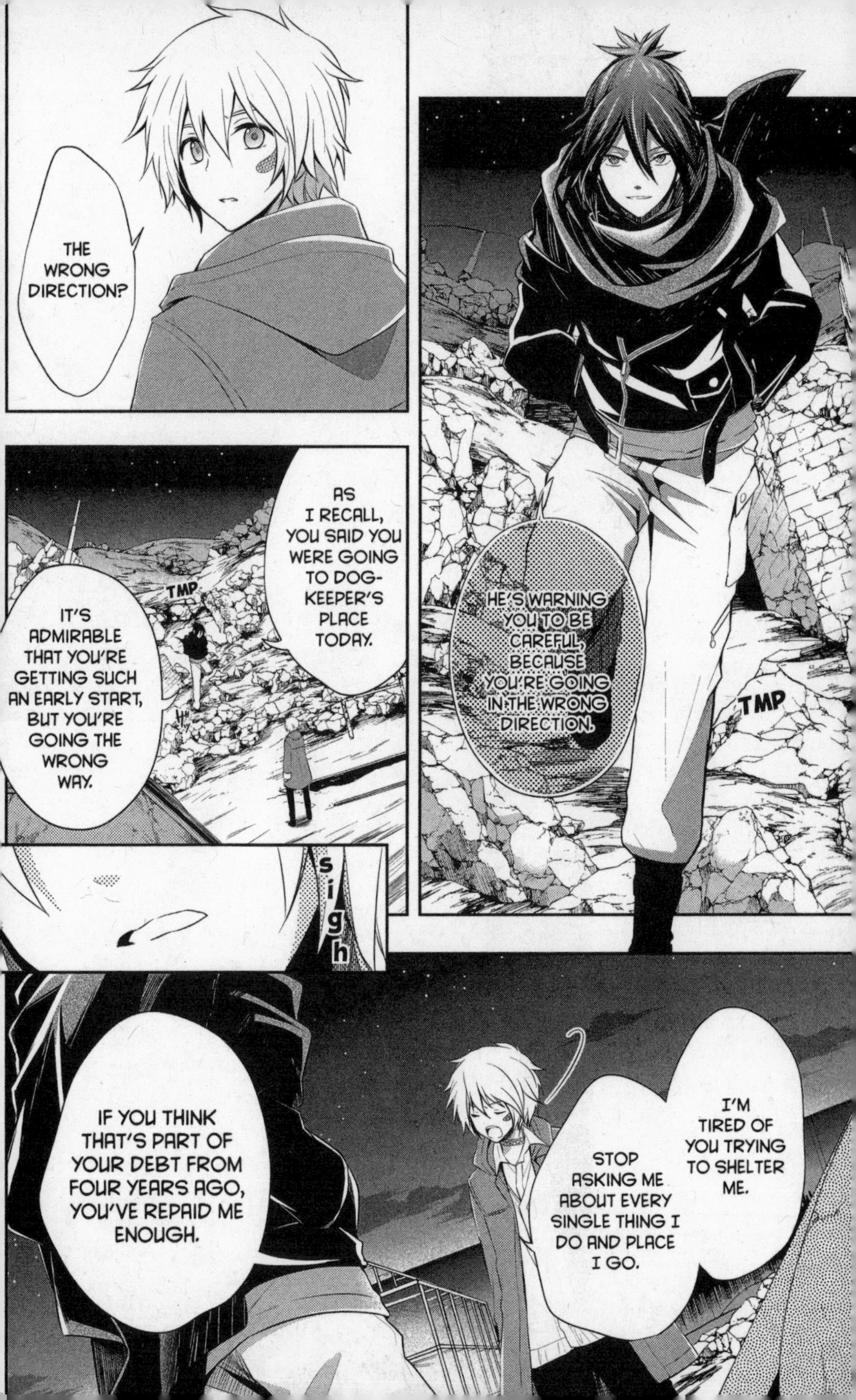
TMP
HE'S WARNING YOU TO BE CAREFUL, BECAUSE YOU'RE GOING IN THE WRONG DIRECTION.
THE WRONG DIRECTION?
AS I RECALL, YOU SAID YOU WERE GOING TO DOG-KEEPER'S PLACE TODAY.
TMP
IT'S ADMIRABLE THAT YOU'RE GETTING SUCH AN EARLY START, BUT YOU'RE GOING THE WRONG WAY.
sigh
I'M TIRED OF YOU TRYING TO SHELTER ME.
STOP ASKING ME ABOUT EVERY SINGLE THING I DO AND PLACE I GO.
IF YOU THINK THAT'S PART OF YOUR DEBT FROM FOUR YEARS AGO, YOU'VE REPAID ME ENOUGH.

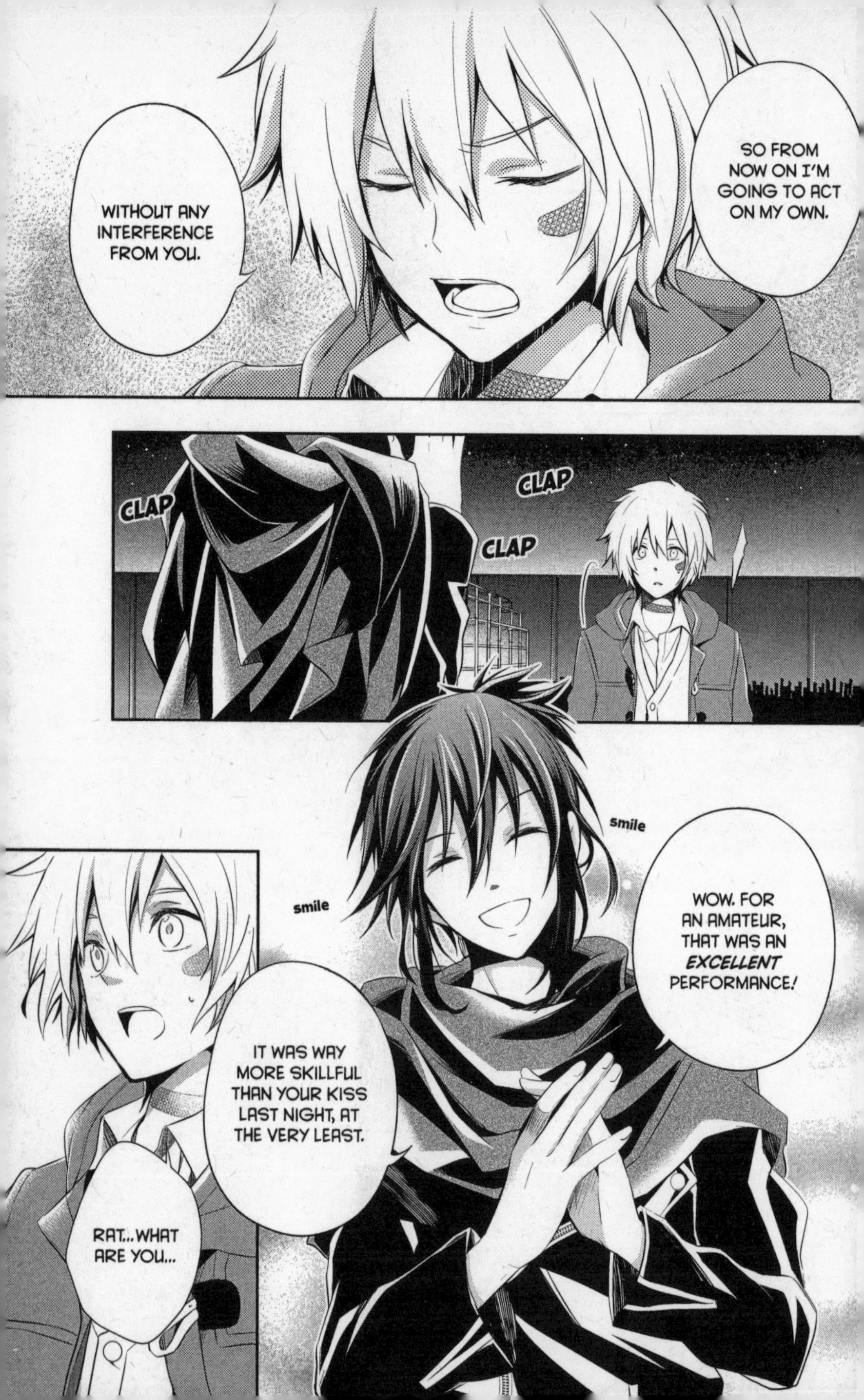
SO FROM NOW ON I'M GOING TO ACT ON MY OWN.
WITHOUT ANY INTERFERENCE FROM YOU.
CLAP
CLAP
CLAP
smile
WOW. FOR AN AMATEUR, THAT WAS AN *EXCELLENT* PERFORMANCE!
smile
IT WAS WAY MORE SKILLFUL THAN YOUR KISS LAST NIGHT, AT THE VERY LEAST.
RAT...WHAT ARE YOU...

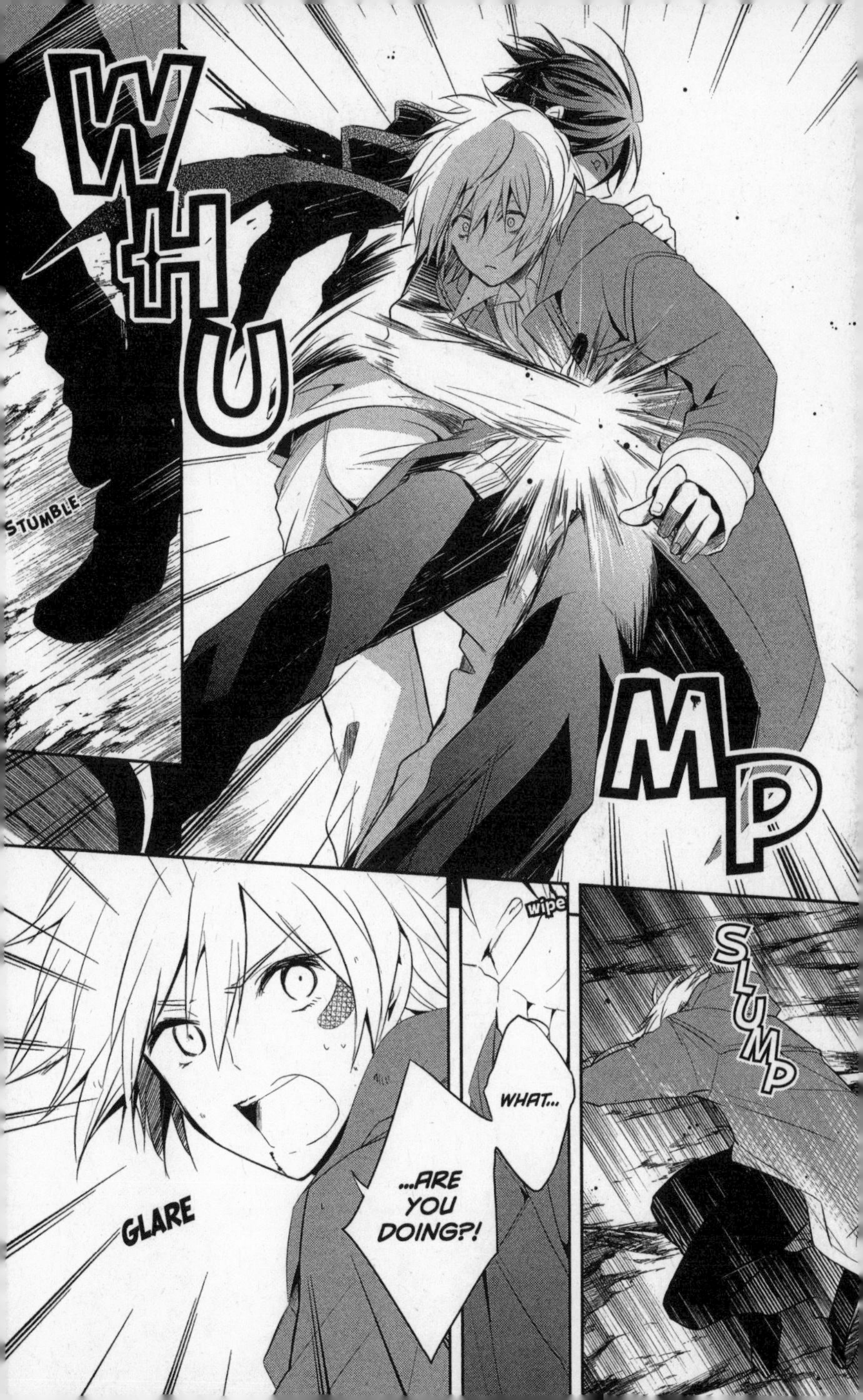
WHUMP
STUMBLE
SLUMP
wipe
WHAT...
...ARE YOU DOING?!
GLARE

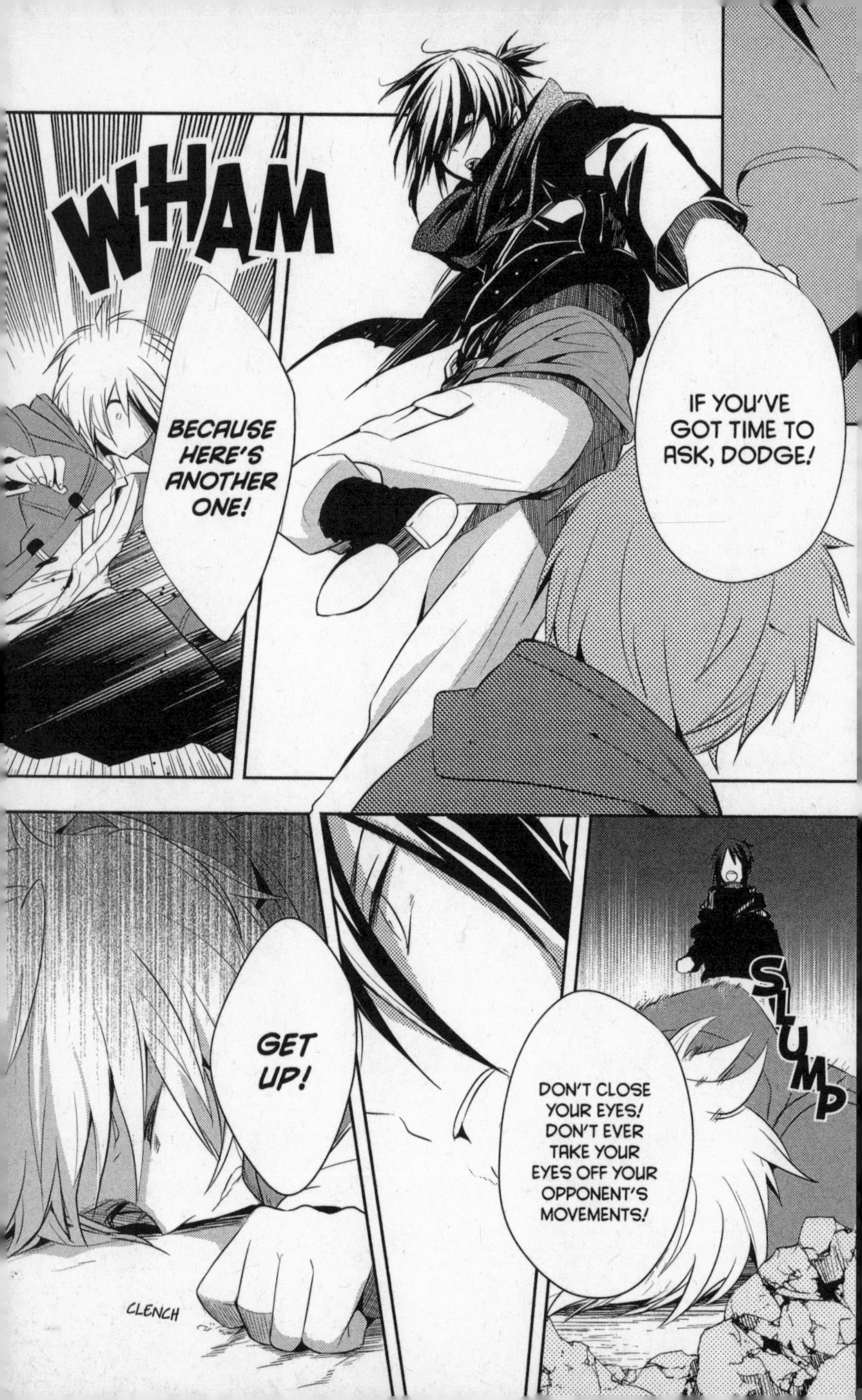
IF YOU'VE GOT TIME TO ASK, DODGE!
WHAM
BECAUSE HERE'S ANOTHER ONE!
SLUMP
DON'T CLOSE YOUR EYES! DON'T EVER TAKE YOUR EYES OFF YOUR OPPONENT'S MOVEMENTS!
GET UP!
CLENCH

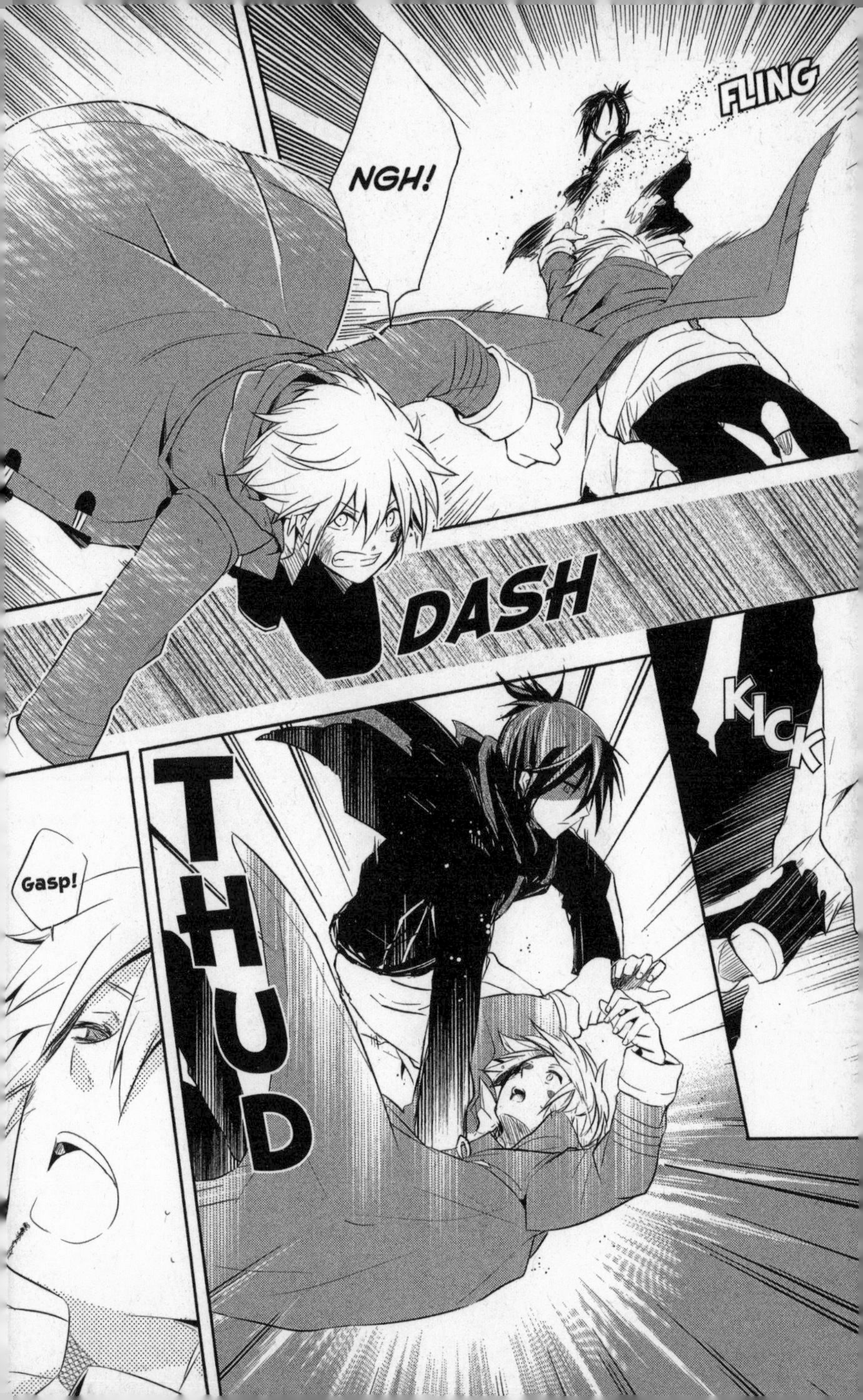
FLING
NGH!
DASH
KICK
THUD
Gasp!

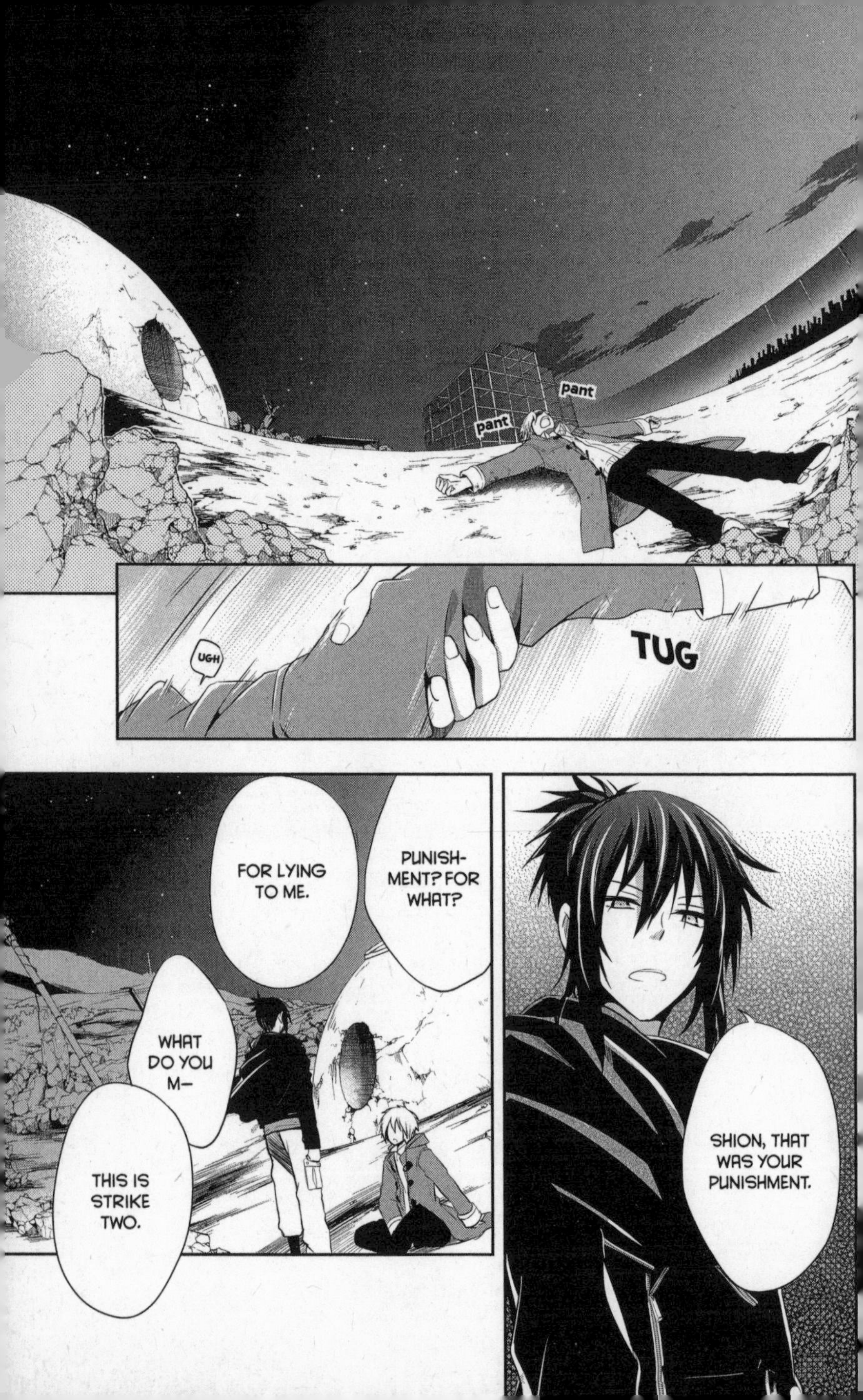
pant
pant
TUG
UGH
SHION, THAT WAS YOUR PUNISHMENT.
PUNISH-MENT? FOR WHAT?
FOR LYING TO ME.
WHAT DO YOU M—
THIS IS STRIKE TWO.

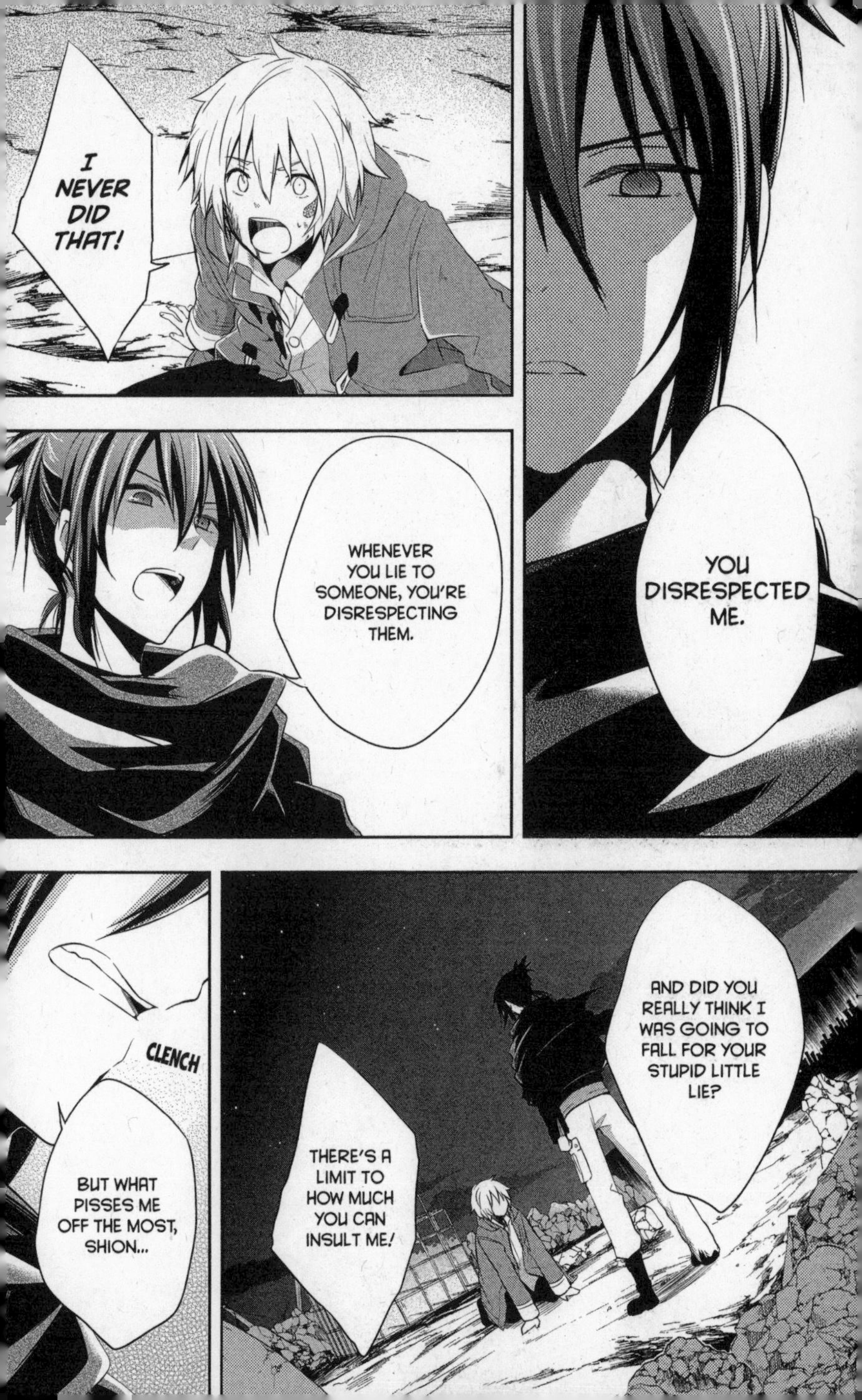
YOU DISRESPECTED ME.
I NEVER DID THAT!
WHENEVER YOU LIE TO SOMEONE, YOU'RE DISRESPECTING THEM.
AND DID YOU REALLY THINK I WAS GOING TO FALL FOR YOUR STUPID LITTLE LIE?
THERE'S A LIMIT TO HOW MUCH YOU CAN INSULT ME!
CLENCH
BUT WHAT PISSES ME OFF THE MOST, SHION...

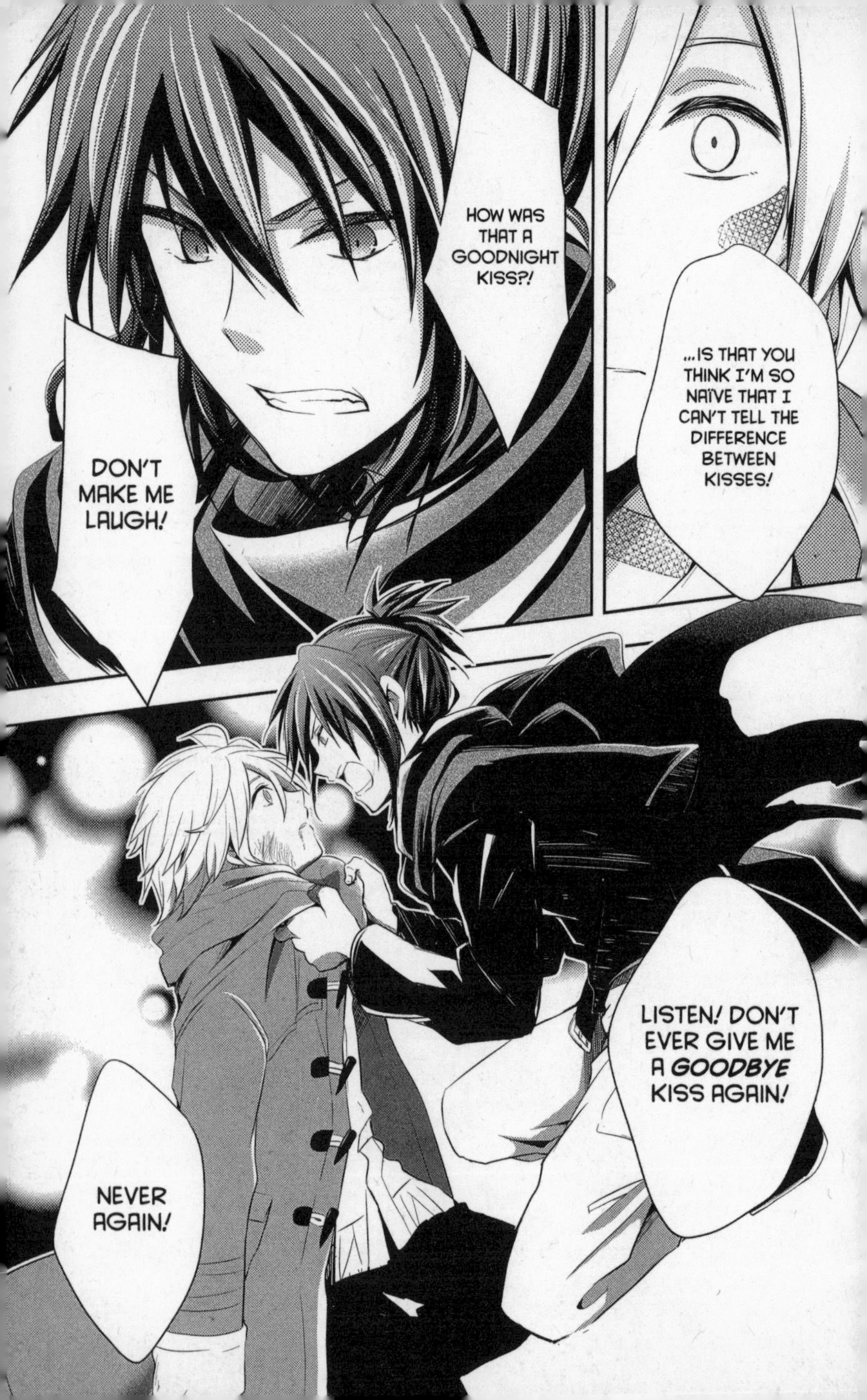
...IS THAT YOU THINK I'M SO NAÏVE THAT I CAN'T TELL THE DIFFERENCE BETWEEN KISSES!
HOW WAS THAT A GOODNIGHT KISS?!
DON'T MAKE ME LAUGH!
LISTEN! DON'T EVER GIVE ME A ***GOODBYE*** KISS AGAIN!
NEVER AGAIN!

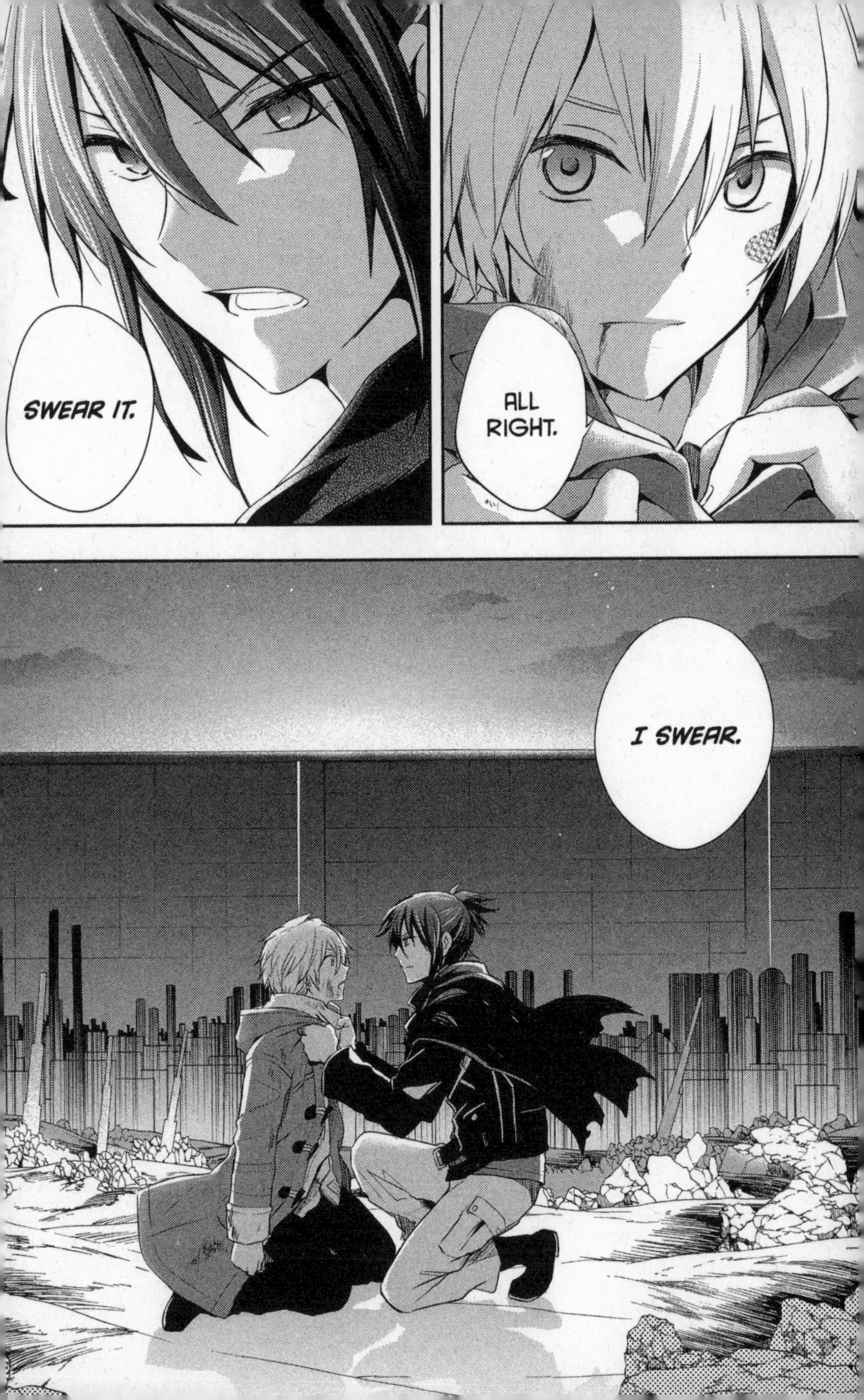
ALL RIGHT.
SWEAR IT.
I SWEAR.

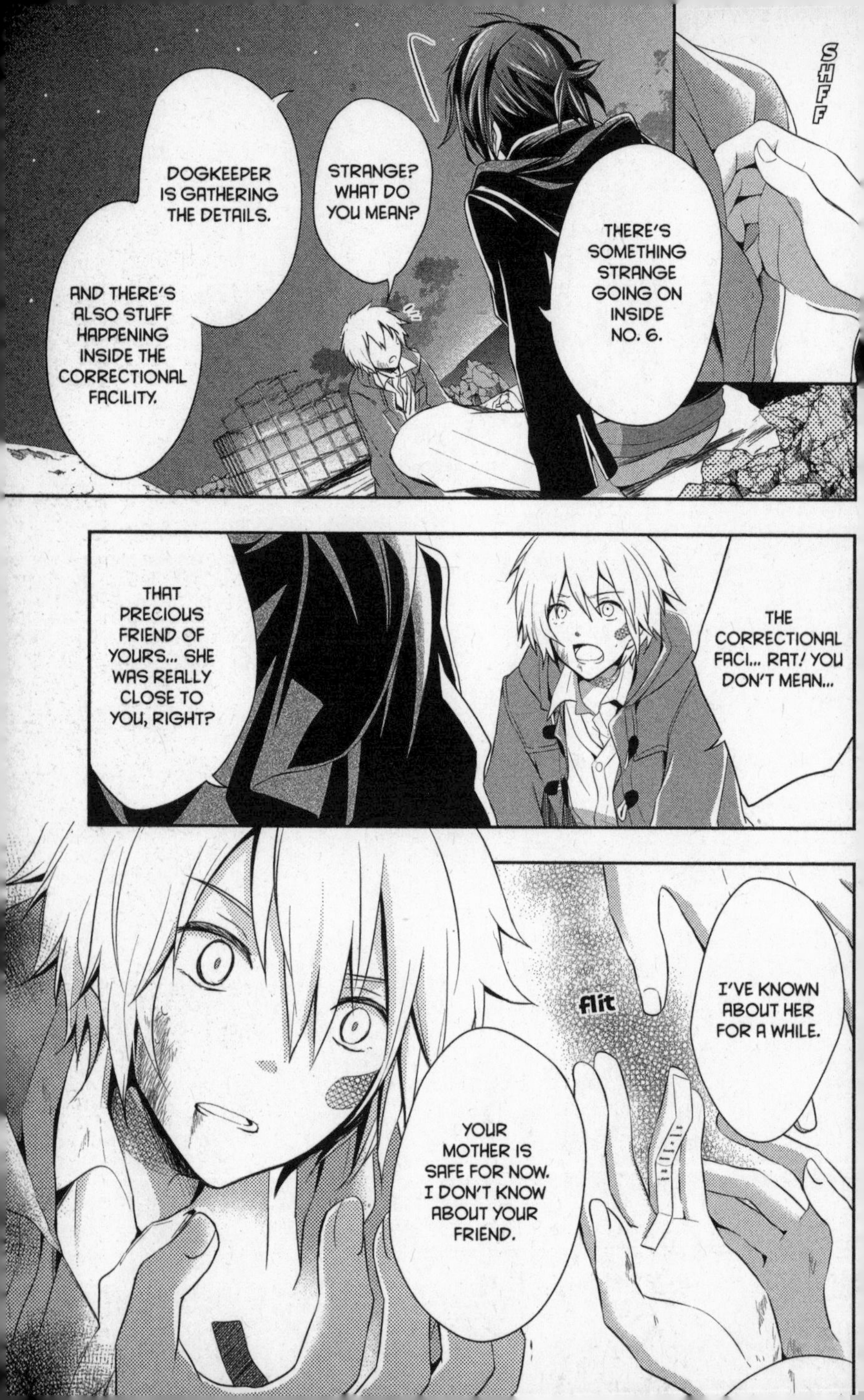
SHFF
THERE'S SOMETHING STRANGE GOING ON INSIDE NO. 6.
STRANGE? WHAT DO YOU MEAN?
DOGKEEPER IS GATHERING THE DETAILS.
AND THERE'S ALSO STUFF HAPPENING INSIDE THE CORRECTIONAL FACILITY.
THE CORRECTIONAL FACI... RAT! YOU DON'T MEAN...
THAT PRECIOUS FRIEND OF YOURS... SHE WAS REALLY CLOSE TO YOU, RIGHT?
I'VE KNOWN ABOUT HER FOR A WHILE.
flit
YOUR MOTHER IS SAFE FOR NOW. I DON'T KNOW ABOUT YOUR FRIEND.

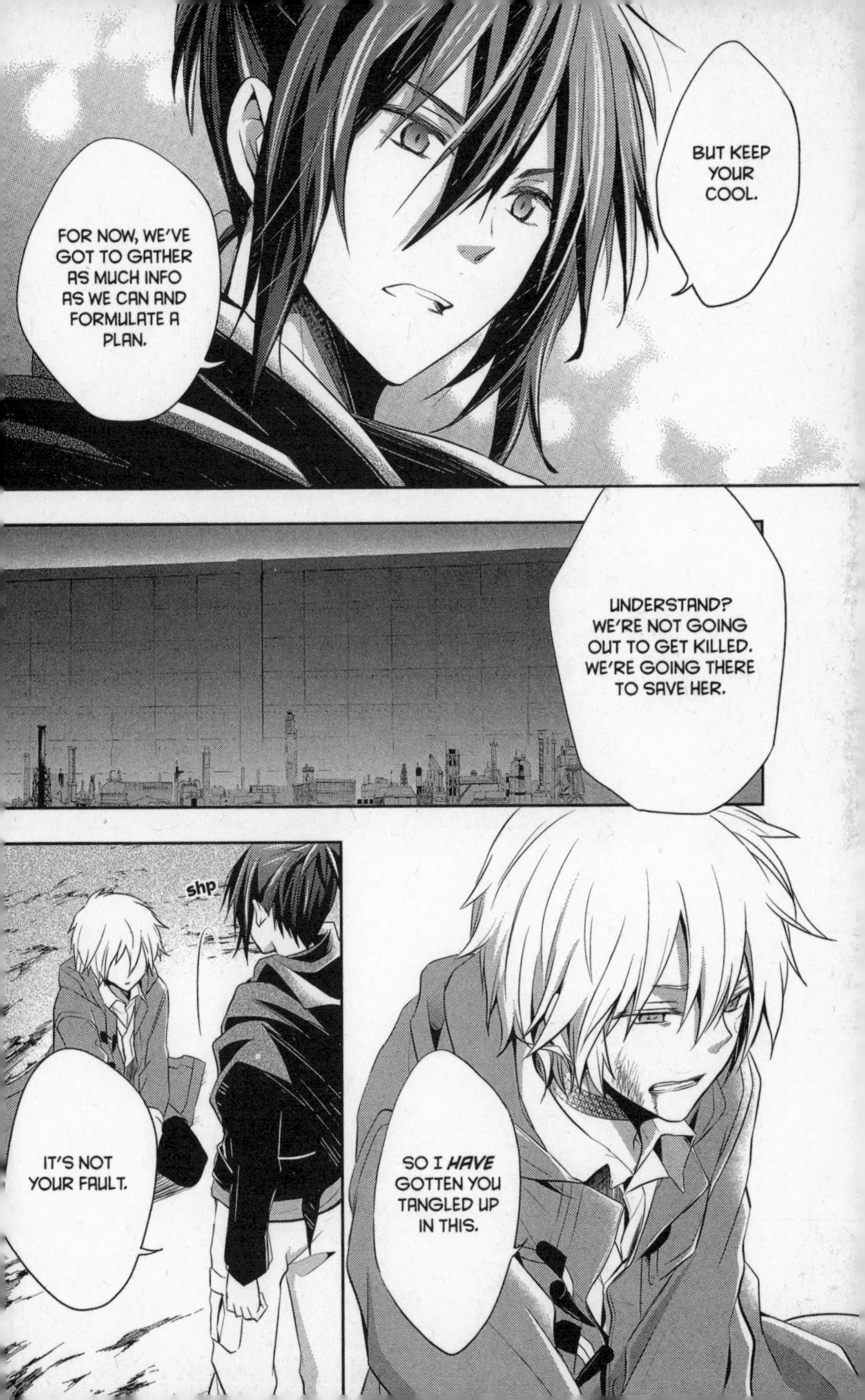
BUT KEEP YOUR COOL.
FOR NOW, WE'VE GOT TO GATHER AS MUCH INFO AS WE CAN AND FORMULATE A PLAN.
UNDERSTAND? WE'RE NOT GOING OUT TO GET KILLED. WE'RE GOING THERE TO SAVE HER.
SO I *HAVE* GOTTEN YOU TANGLED UP IN THIS.
shp
IT'S NOT YOUR FAULT.

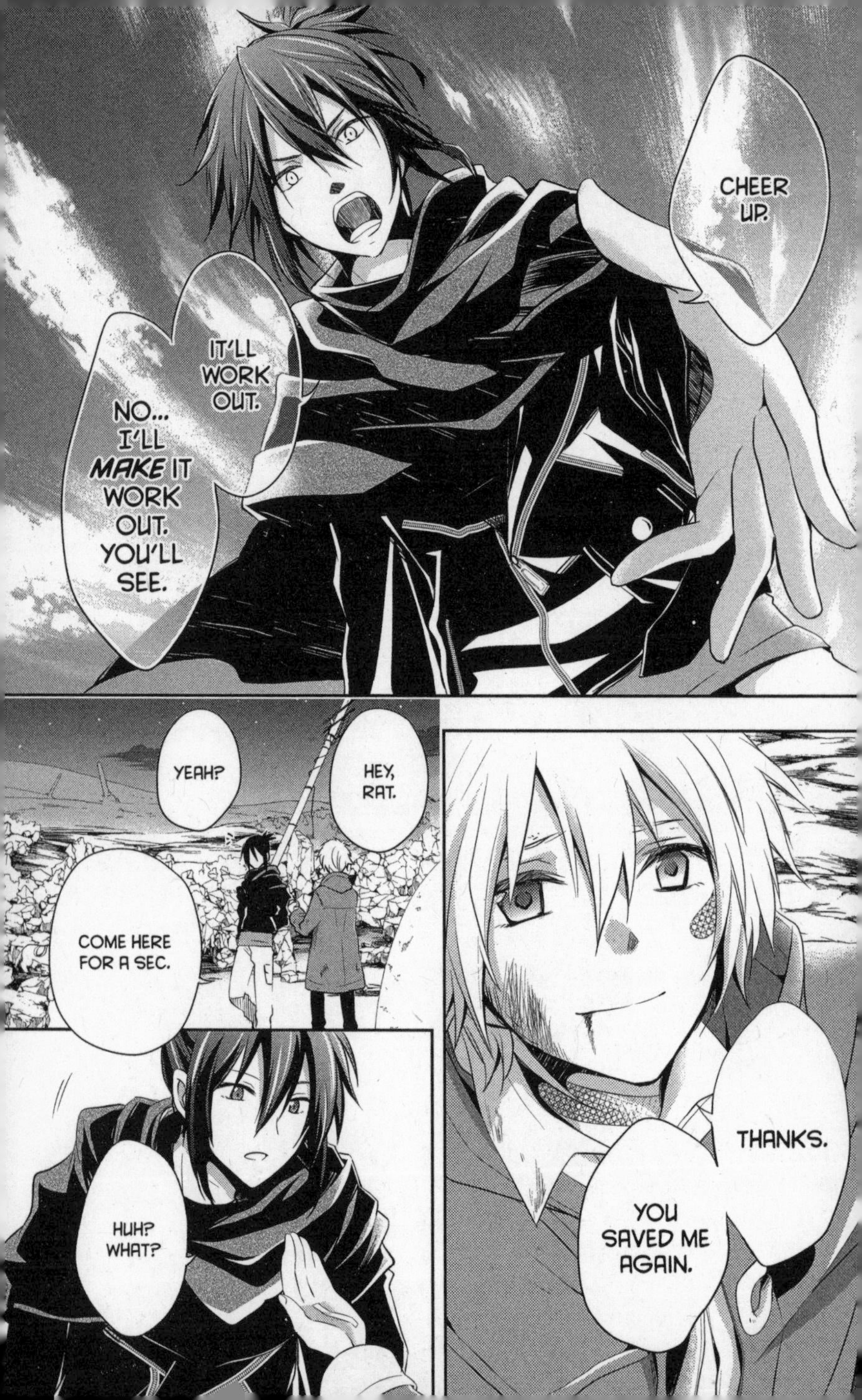
CHEER UP.
IT'LL WORK OUT.
NO... I'LL *MAKE* IT WORK OUT. YOU'LL SEE.
THANKS.
YOU SAVED ME AGAIN.
HEY, RAT.
YEAH?
COME HERE FOR A SEC.
HUH? WHAT?

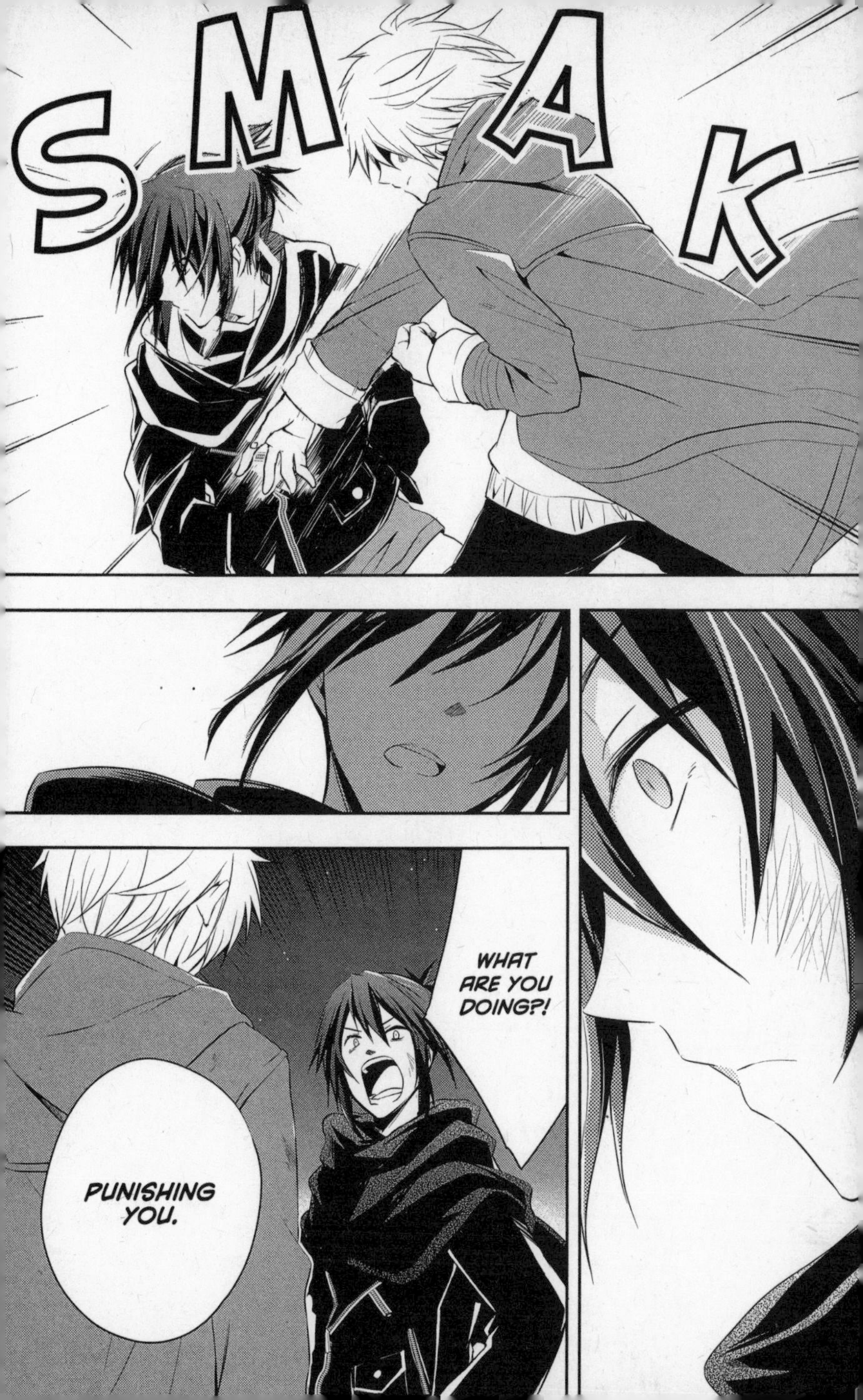
SMAK
WHAT ARE YOU DOING?!
PUNISHING YOU.

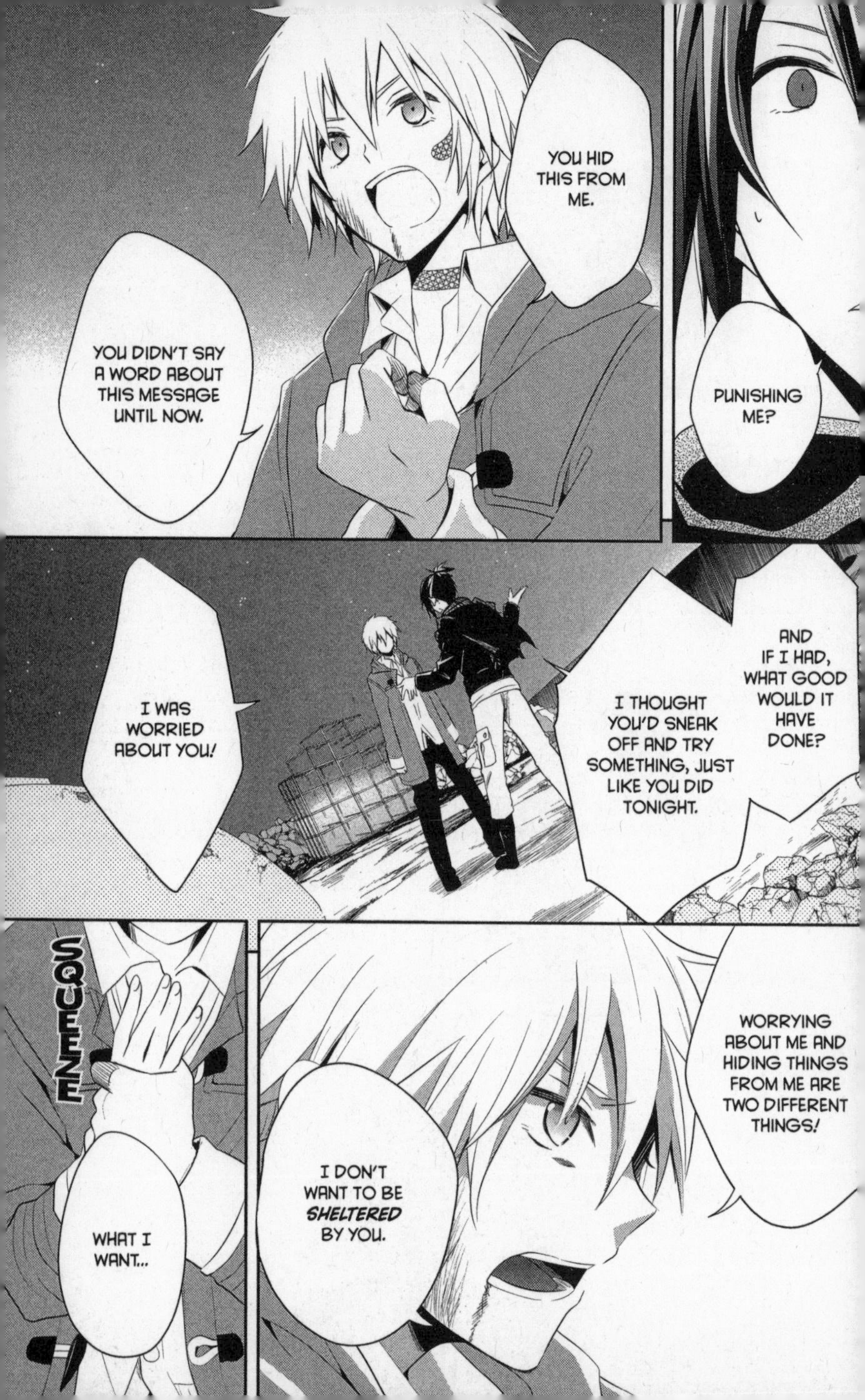
PUNISHING ME?
YOU HID THIS FROM ME.
YOU DIDN'T SAY A WORD ABOUT THIS MESSAGE UNTIL NOW.
AND IF I HAD, WHAT GOOD WOULD IT HAVE DONE?
I THOUGHT YOU'D SNEAK OFF AND TRY SOMETHING, JUST LIKE YOU DID TONIGHT.
I WAS WORRIED ABOUT YOU!
WORRYING ABOUT ME AND HIDING THINGS FROM ME ARE TWO DIFFERENT THINGS!
I DON'T WANT TO BE *SHELTERED* BY YOU.
SQUEEZE
WHAT I WANT...

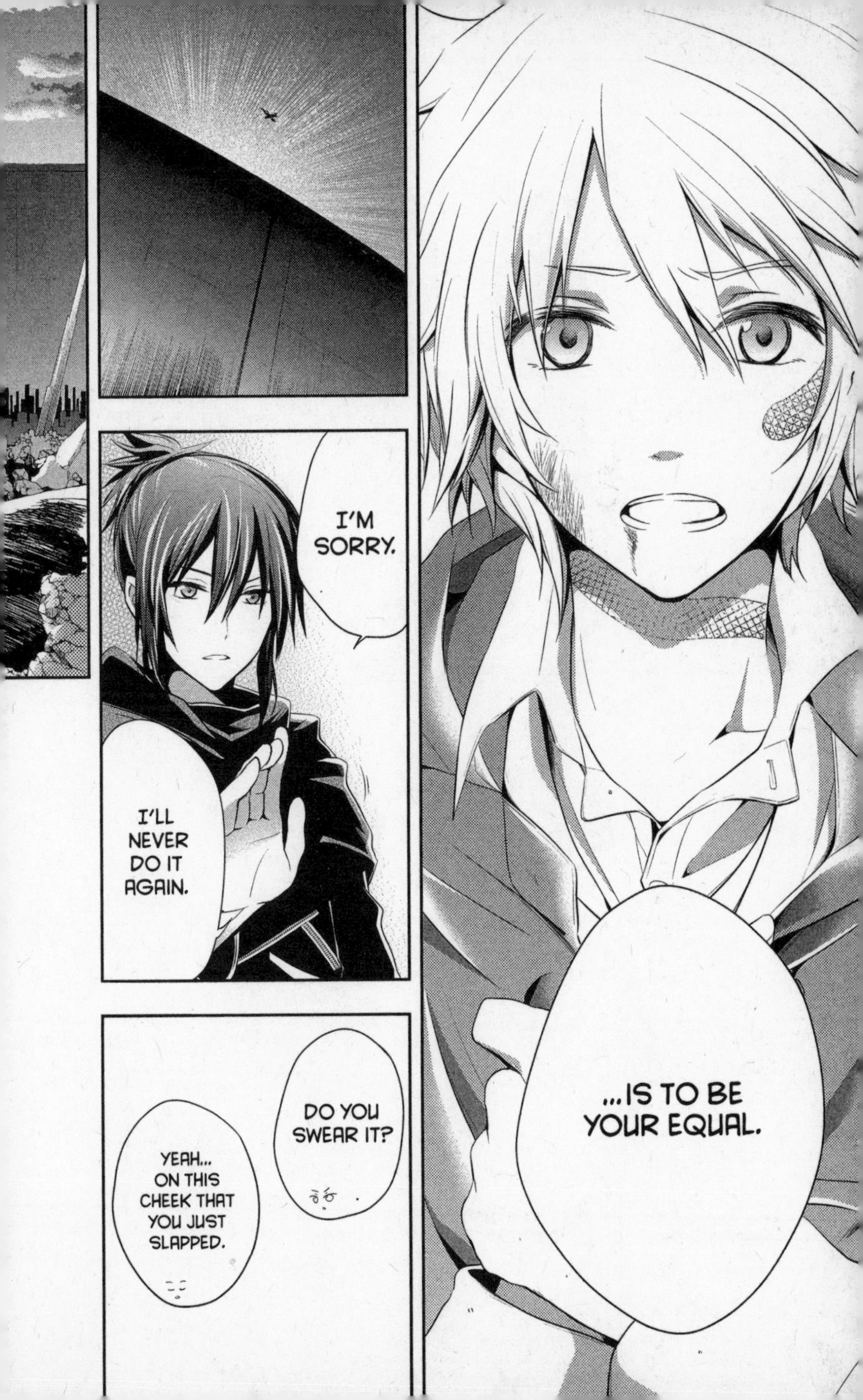
...IS TO BE YOUR EQUAL.
I'M SORRY.
I'LL NEVER DO IT AGAIN.
DO YOU SWEAR IT?
YEAH... ON THIS CHEEK THAT YOU JUST SLAPPED.

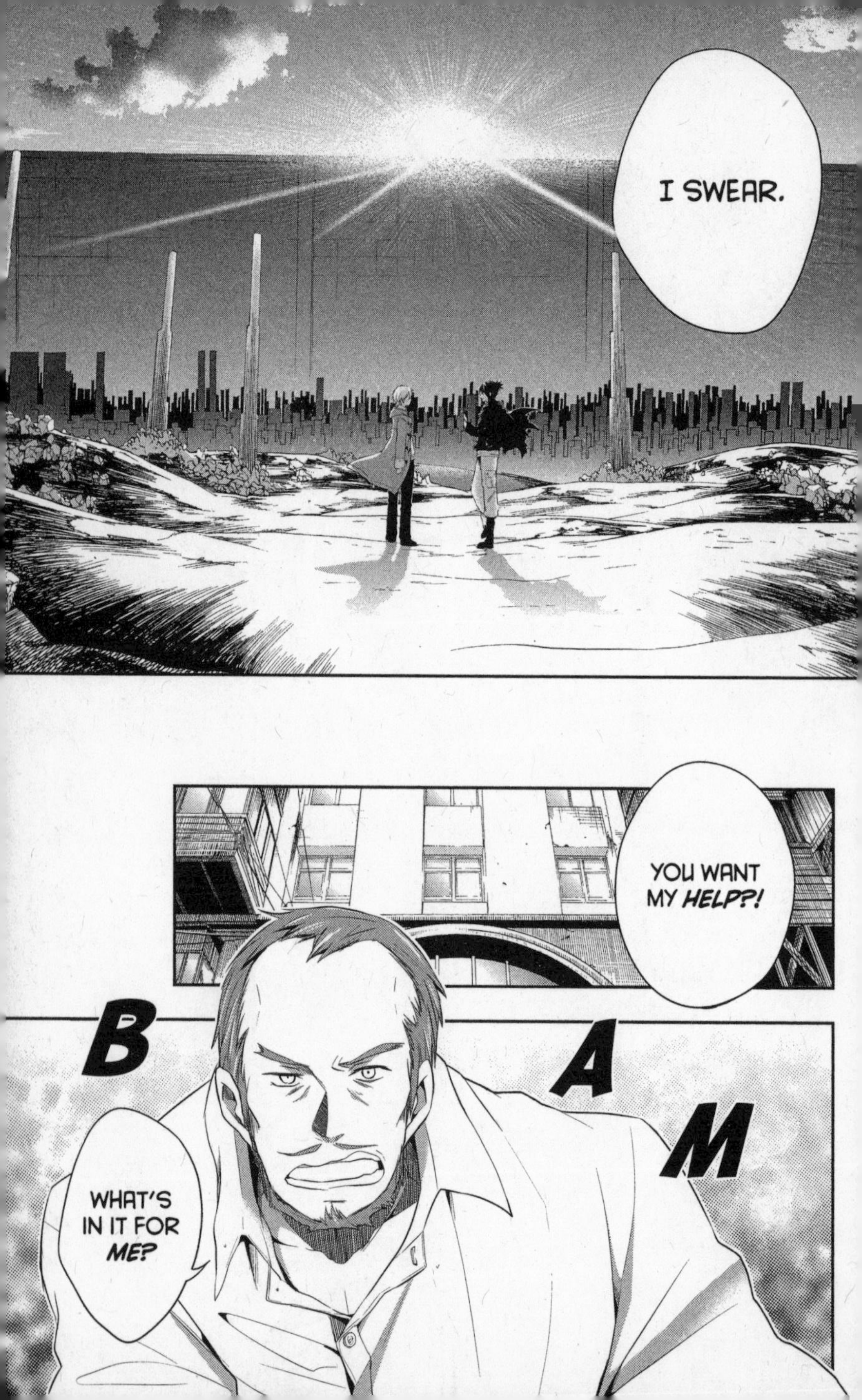
I SWEAR.
YOU WANT MY *HELP?!*
BAM
WHAT'S IN IT FOR *ME?*

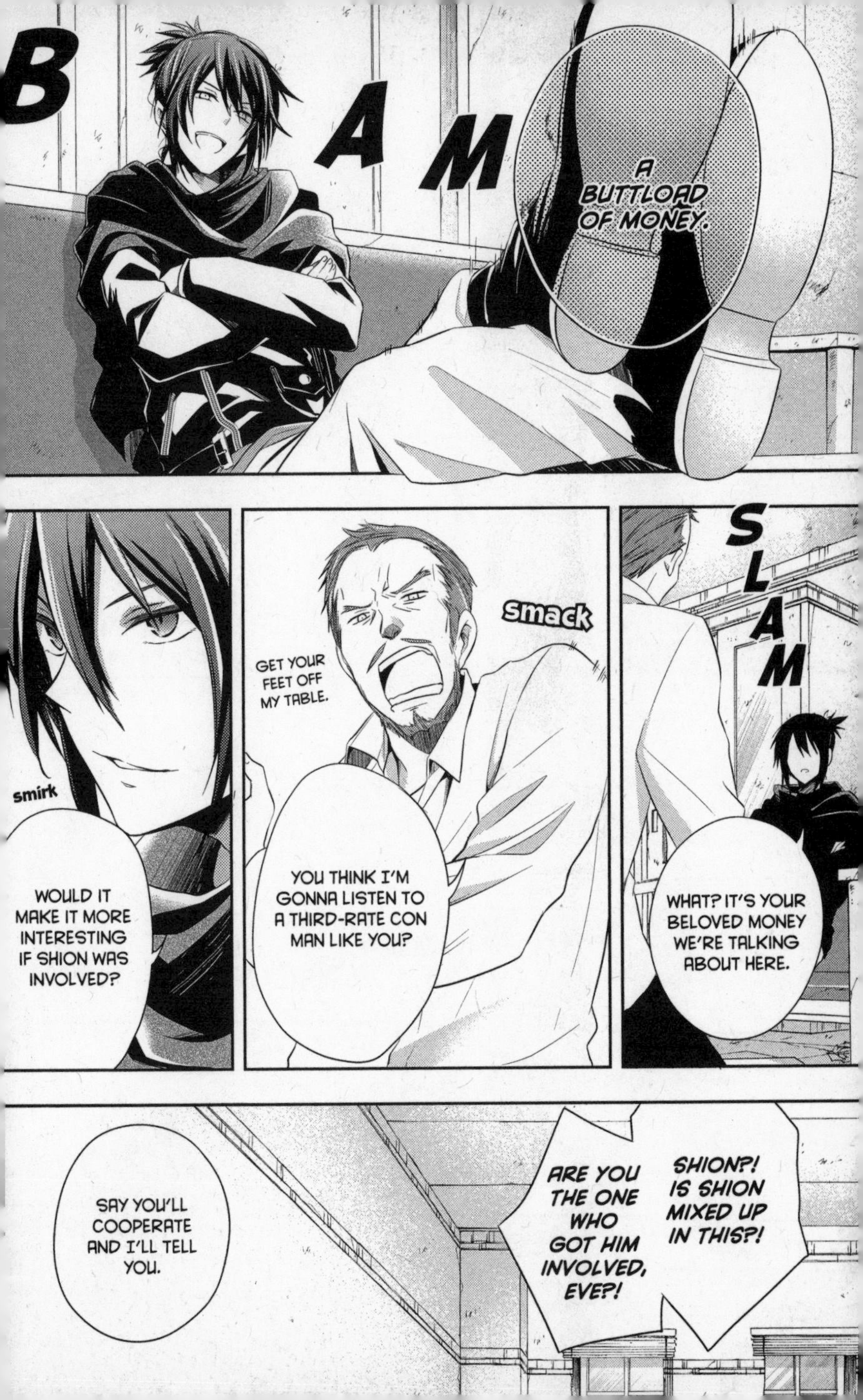
BAM
A BUTTLOAD OF MONEY.
SLAM
WHAT? IT'S YOUR BELOVED MONEY WE'RE TALKING ABOUT HERE.
smack
GET YOUR FEET OFF MY TABLE.
YOU THINK I'M GONNA LISTEN TO A THIRD-RATE CON MAN LIKE YOU?
smirk
WOULD IT MAKE IT MORE INTERESTING IF SHION WAS INVOLVED?
SHION?! IS SHION MIXED UP IN THIS?!
ARE YOU THE ONE WHO GOT HIM INVOLVED, EVE?!
SAY YOU'LL COOPERATE AND I'LL TELL YOU.

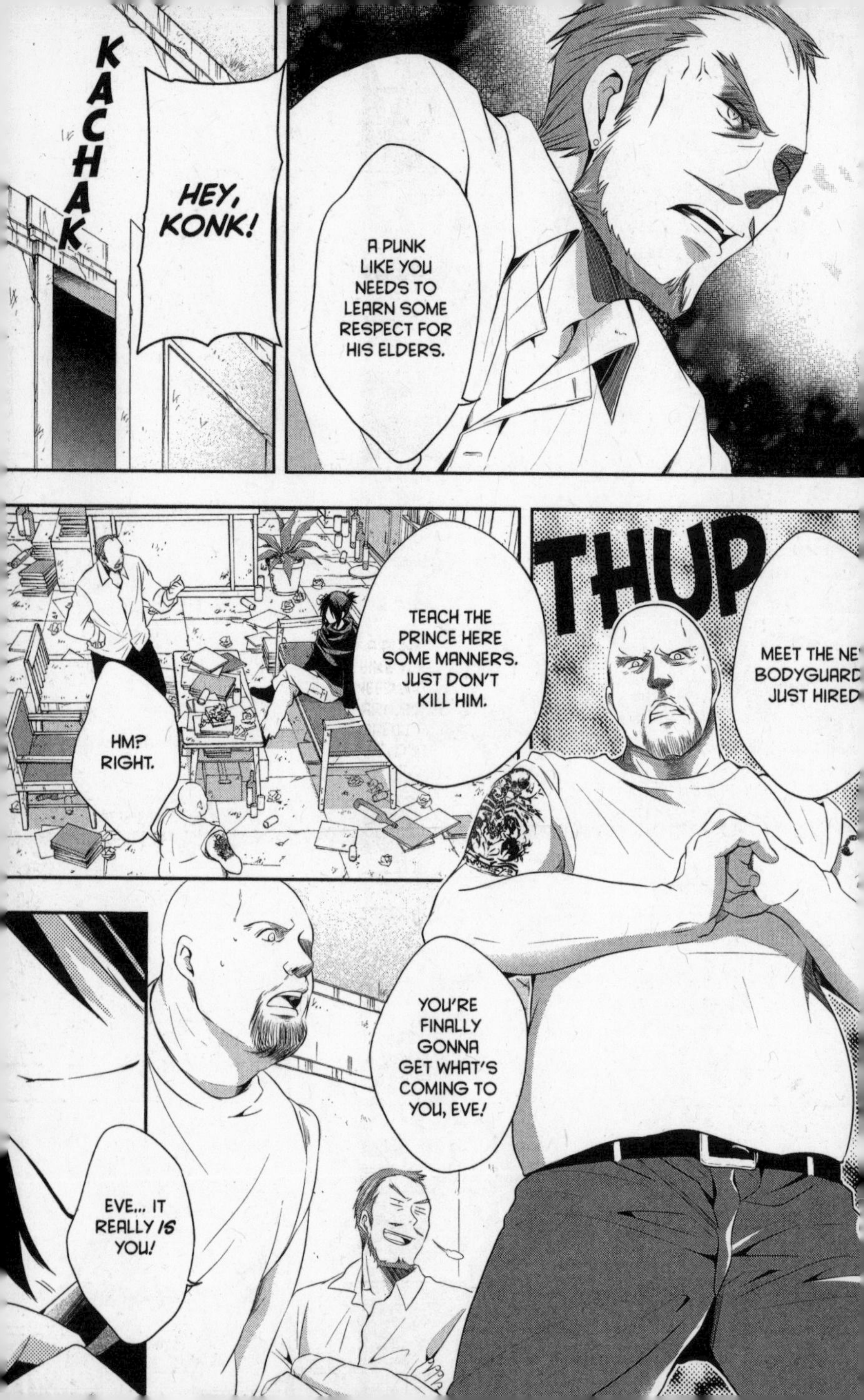

A PUNK LIKE YOU NEEDS TO LEARN SOME RESPECT FOR HIS ELDERS.
KACHAK
HEY, KONK!
THUP
MEET THE NE BODYGUARD JUST HIRED
TEACH THE PRINCE HERE SOME MANNERS. JUST DON'T KILL HIM.
HM? RIGHT.
YOU'RE FINALLY GONNA GET WHAT'S COMING TO YOU, EVE!
EVE... IT REALLY *IS* YOU!

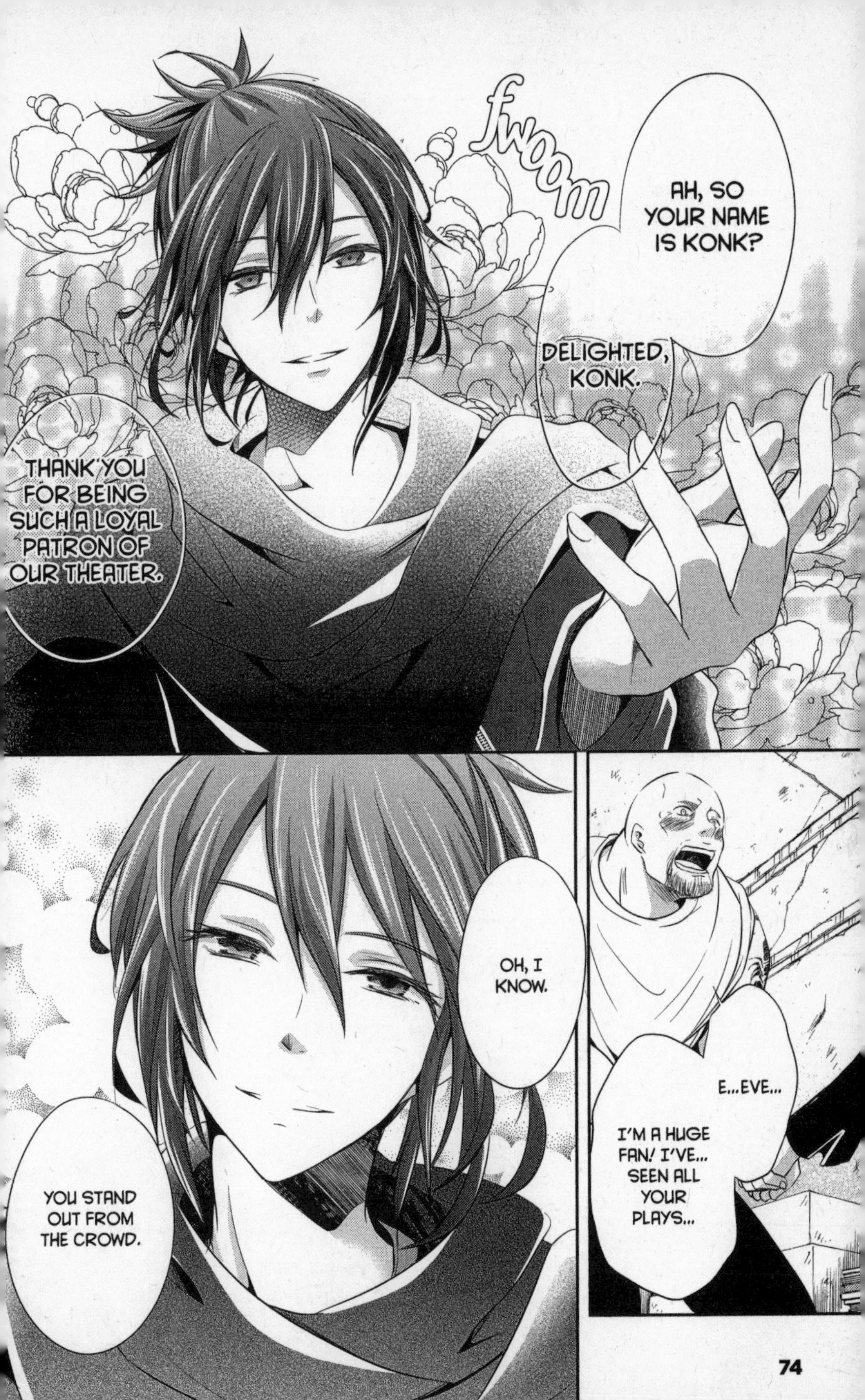
fwoom
AH, SO YOUR NAME IS KONK?
DELIGHTED, KONK.
THANK YOU FOR BEING SUCH A LOYAL PATRON OF OUR THEATER.
E...EVE...
I'M A HUGE FAN! I'VE... SEEN ALL YOUR PLAYS...
OH, I KNOW.
YOU STAND OUT FROM THE CROWD.

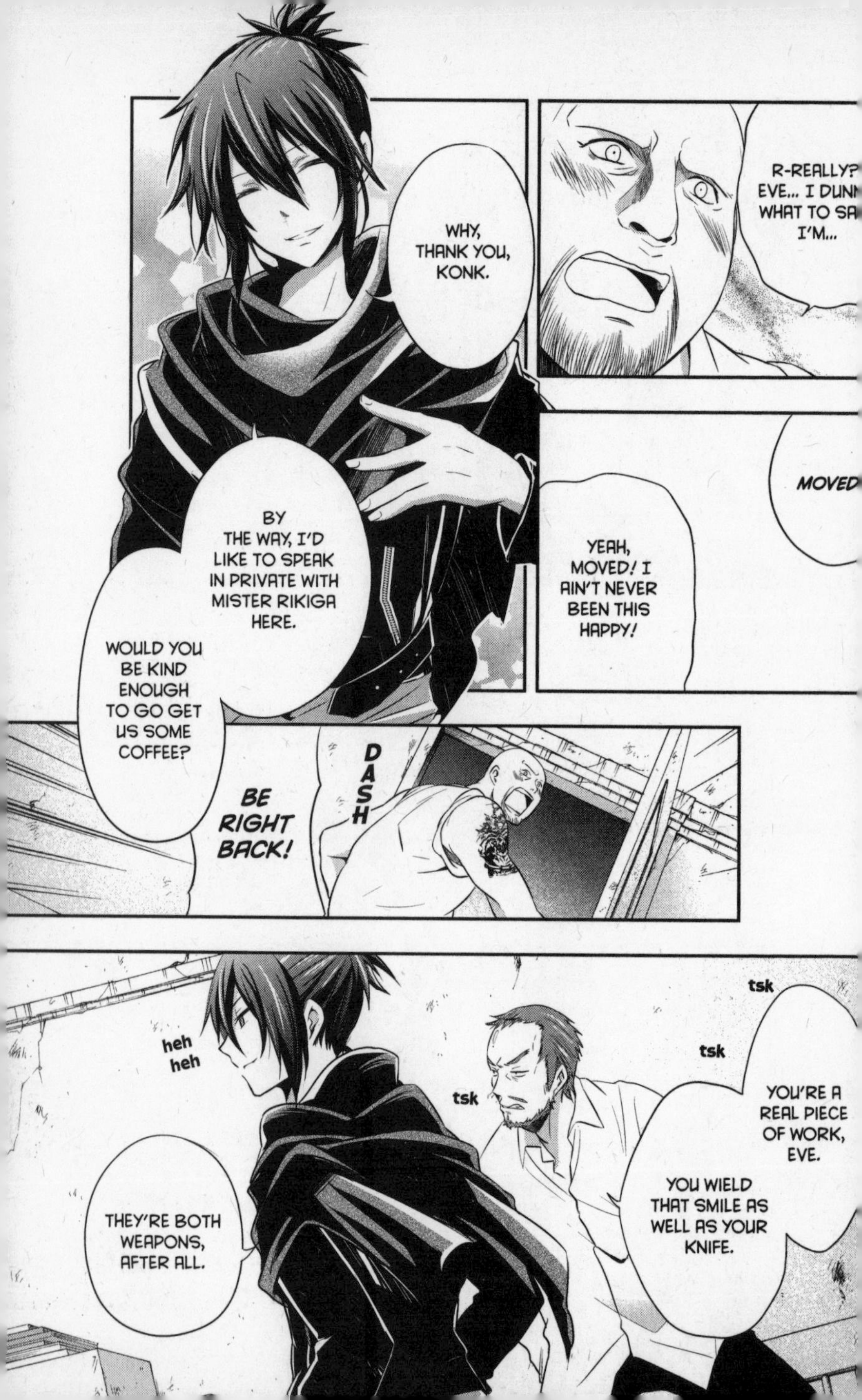
R-REALLY? EVE... I DUNN WHAT TO SA I'M...
MOVED
YEAH, MOVED! I AIN'T NEVER BEEN THIS HAPPY!
WHY, THANK YOU, KONK.
BY THE WAY, I'D LIKE TO SPEAK IN PRIVATE WITH MISTER RIKIGA HERE.
WOULD YOU BE KIND ENOUGH TO GO GET US SOME COFFEE?
DASH
BE RIGHT BACK!
tsk
tsk
YOU'RE A REAL PIECE OF WORK, EVE.
YOU WIELD THAT SMILE AS WELL AS YOUR KNIFE.
tsk
heh heh
THEY'RE BOTH WEAPONS, AFTER ALL.

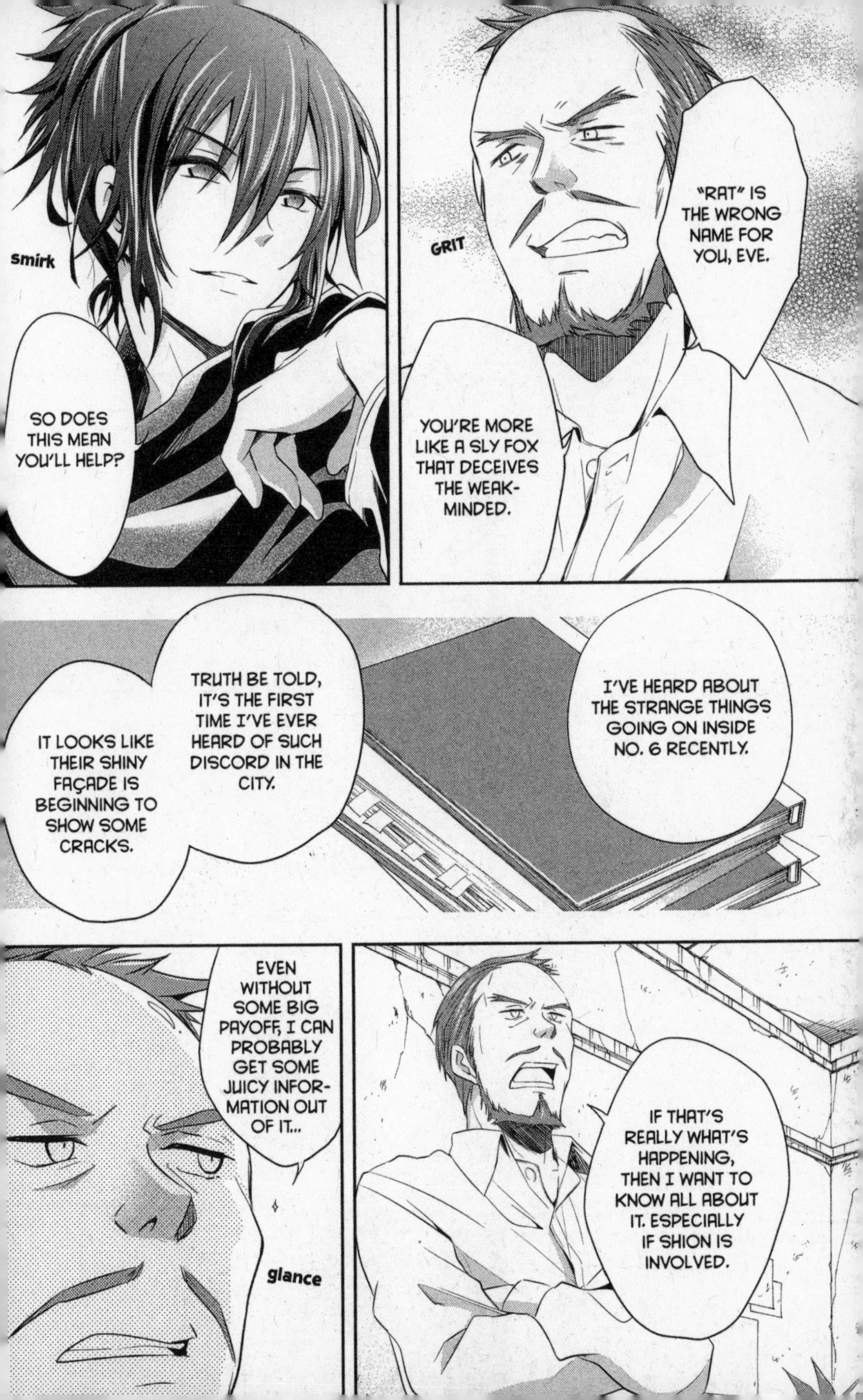
"RAT" IS THE WRONG NAME FOR YOU, EVE.
GRIT
YOU'RE MORE LIKE A SLY FOX THAT DECEIVES THE WEAK-MINDED.
smirk
SO DOES THIS MEAN YOU'LL HELP?
I'VE HEARD ABOUT THE STRANGE THINGS GOING ON INSIDE NO. 6 RECENTLY.
TRUTH BE TOLD, IT'S THE FIRST TIME I'VE EVER HEARD OF SUCH DISCORD IN THE CITY.
IT LOOKS LIKE THEIR SHINY FAÇADE IS BEGINNING TO SHOW SOME CRACKS.
IF THAT'S REALLY WHAT'S HAPPENING, THEN I WANT TO KNOW ALL ABOUT IT. ESPECIALLY IF SHION IS INVOLVED.
EVEN WITHOUT SOME BIG PAYOFF, I CAN PROBABLY GET SOME JUICY INFORMATION OUT OF IT...
glance

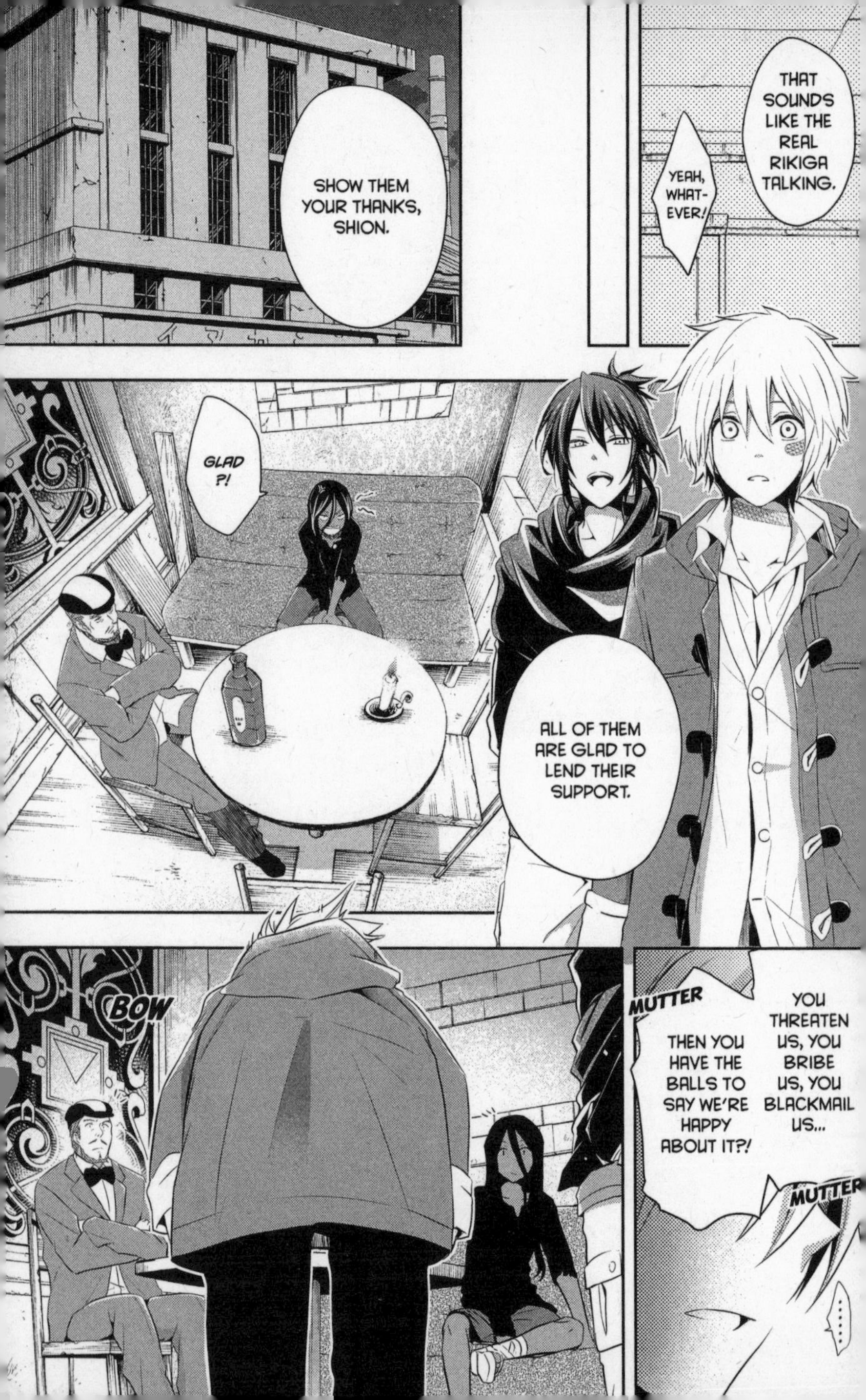
THAT SOUNDS LIKE THE REAL RIKIGA TALKING.
YEAH, WHAT-EVER!
SHOW THEM YOUR THANKS, SHION.
ALL OF THEM ARE GLAD TO LEND THEIR SUPPORT.
GLAD ?!
MUTTER
YOU THREATEN US, YOU BRIBE US, YOU BLACKMAIL US...
THEN YOU HAVE THE BALLS TO SAY WE'RE HAPPY ABOUT IT?!
MUTTER
......
BOW

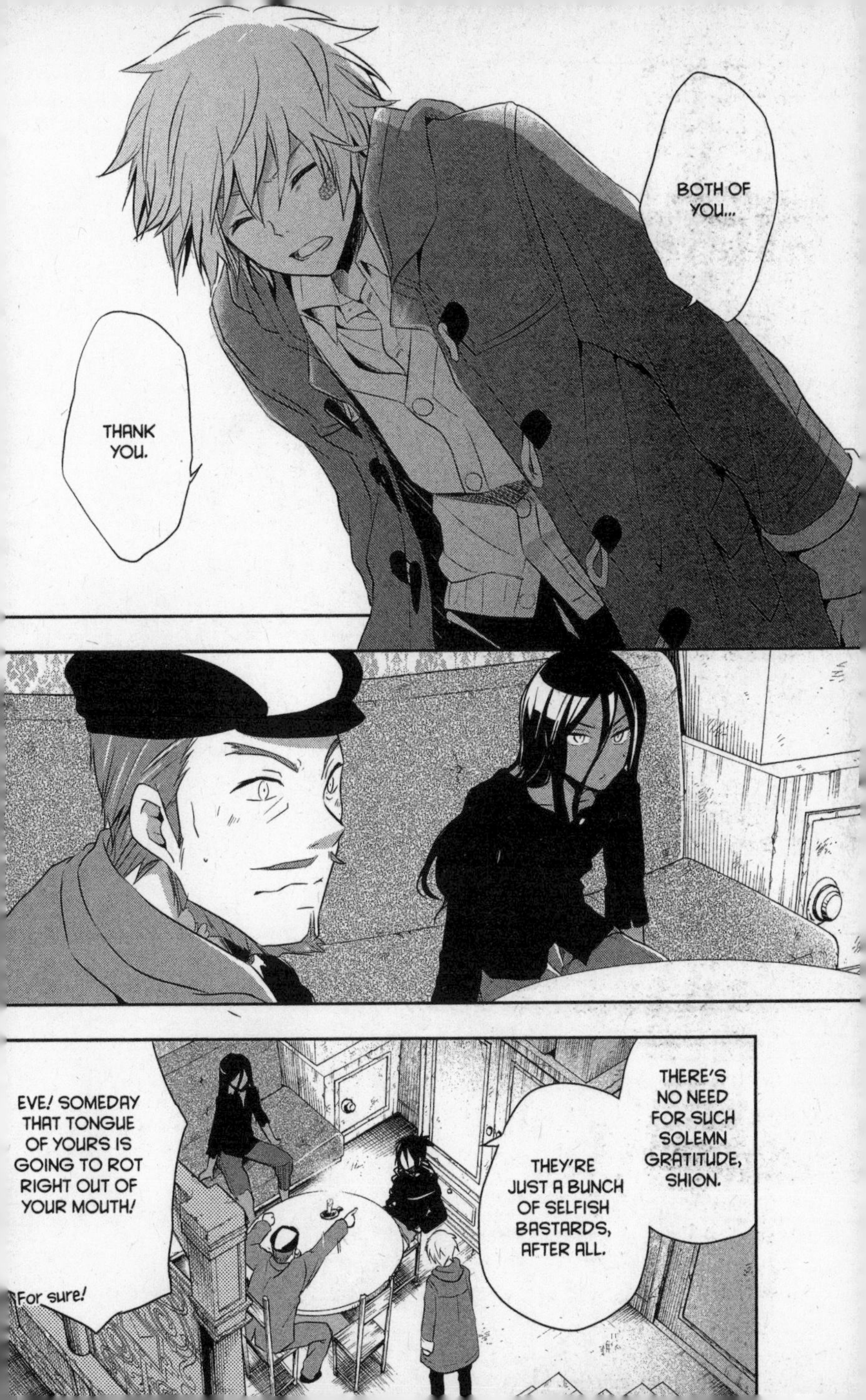
BOTH OF YOU...
THANK YOU.
THERE'S NO NEED FOR SUCH SOLEMN GRATITUDE, SHION.
THEY'RE JUST A BUNCH OF SELFISH BASTARDS, AFTER ALL.
EVE! SOMEDAY THAT TONGUE OF YOURS IS GOING TO ROT RIGHT OUT OF YOUR MOUTH!
For sure!

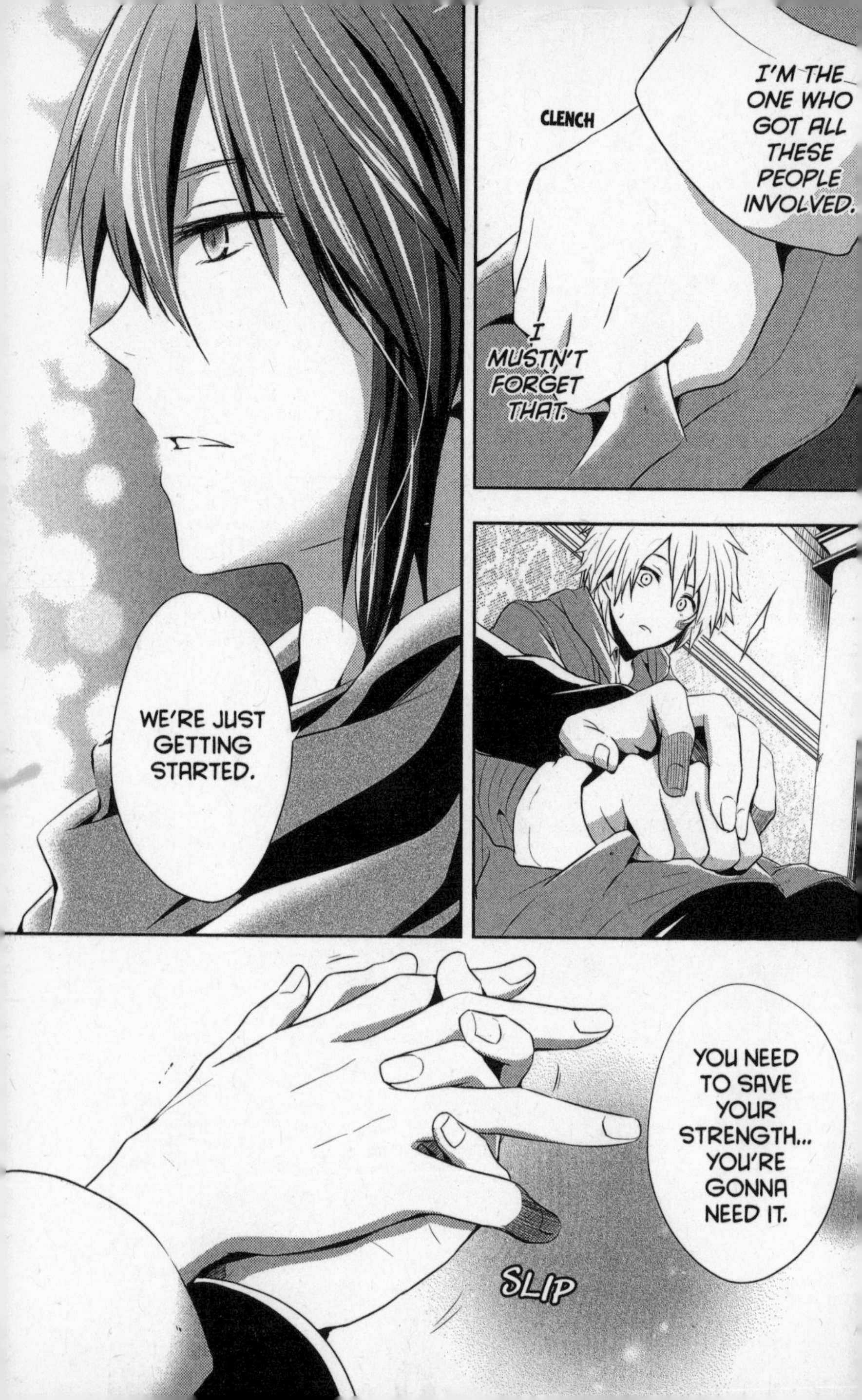
I'M THE ONE WHO GOT ALL THESE PEOPLE INVOLVED.
CLENCH
I MUSTN'T FORGET THAT.
WE'RE JUST GETTING STARTED.
YOU NEED TO SAVE YOUR STRENGTH... YOU'RE GONNA NEED IT.
SLIP

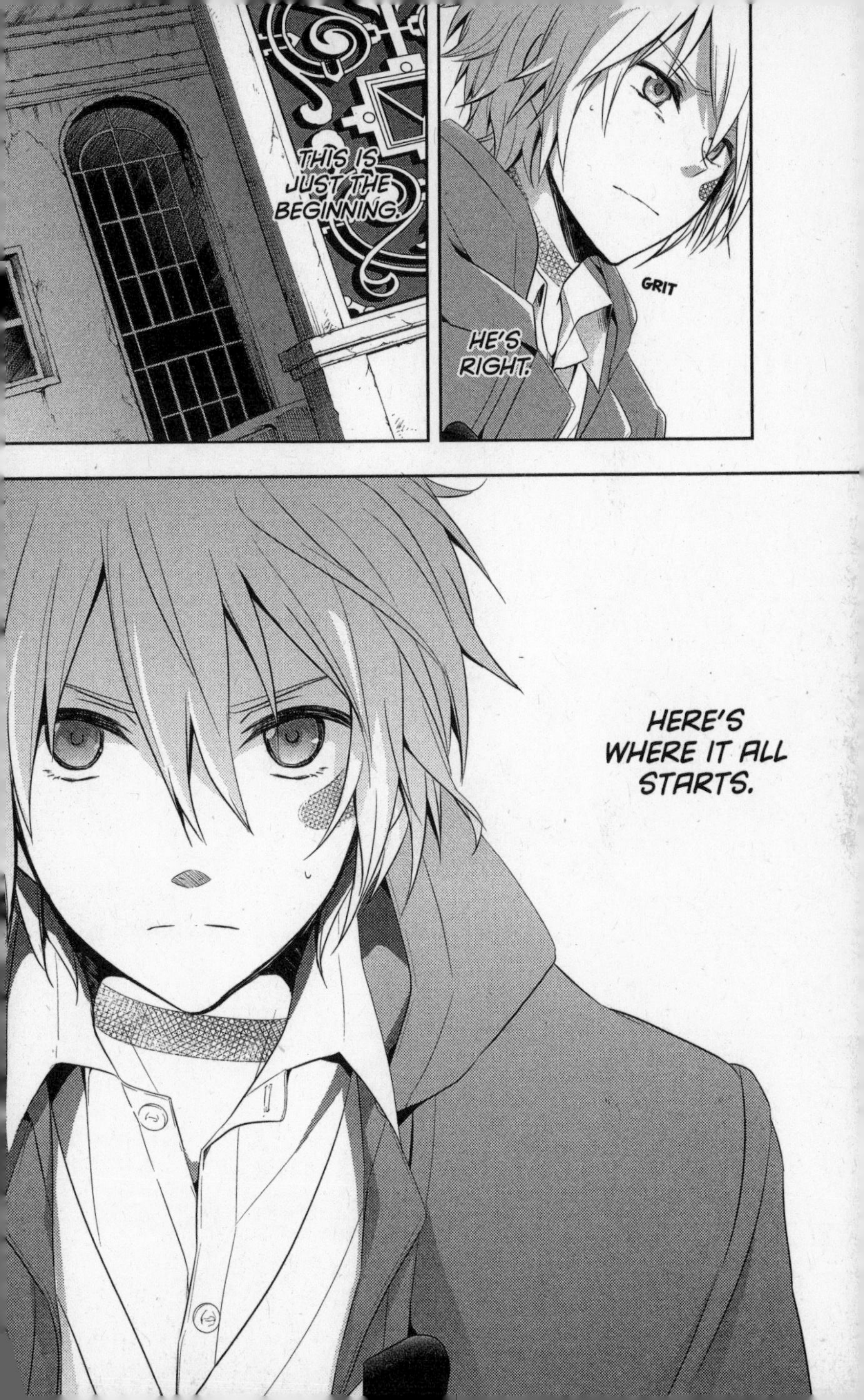
GRIT
HE'S RIGHT.
THIS IS JUST THE BEGINNING.
HERE'S WHERE IT ALL STARTS.

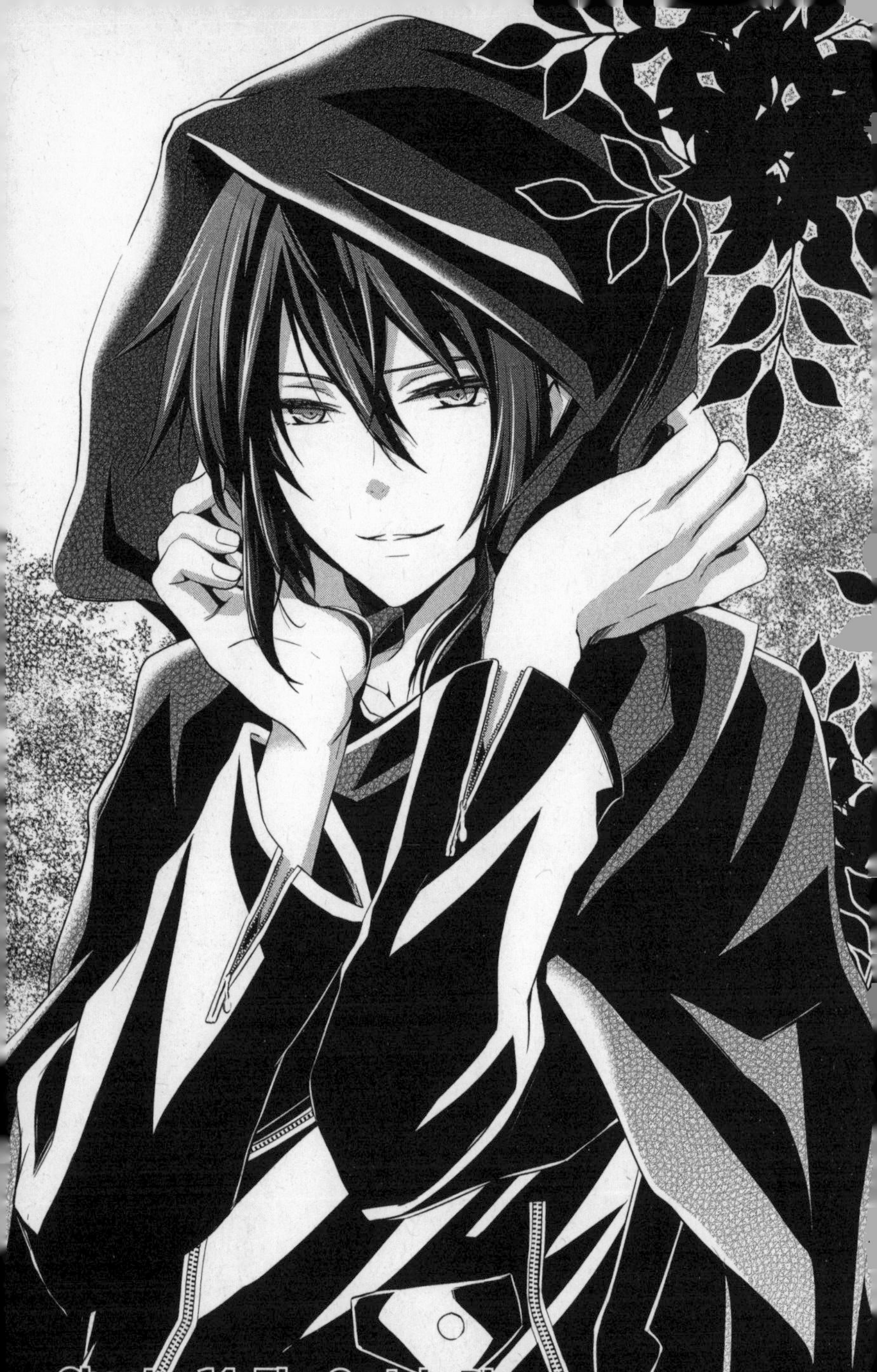

Chapter 14: The Curtain Rises

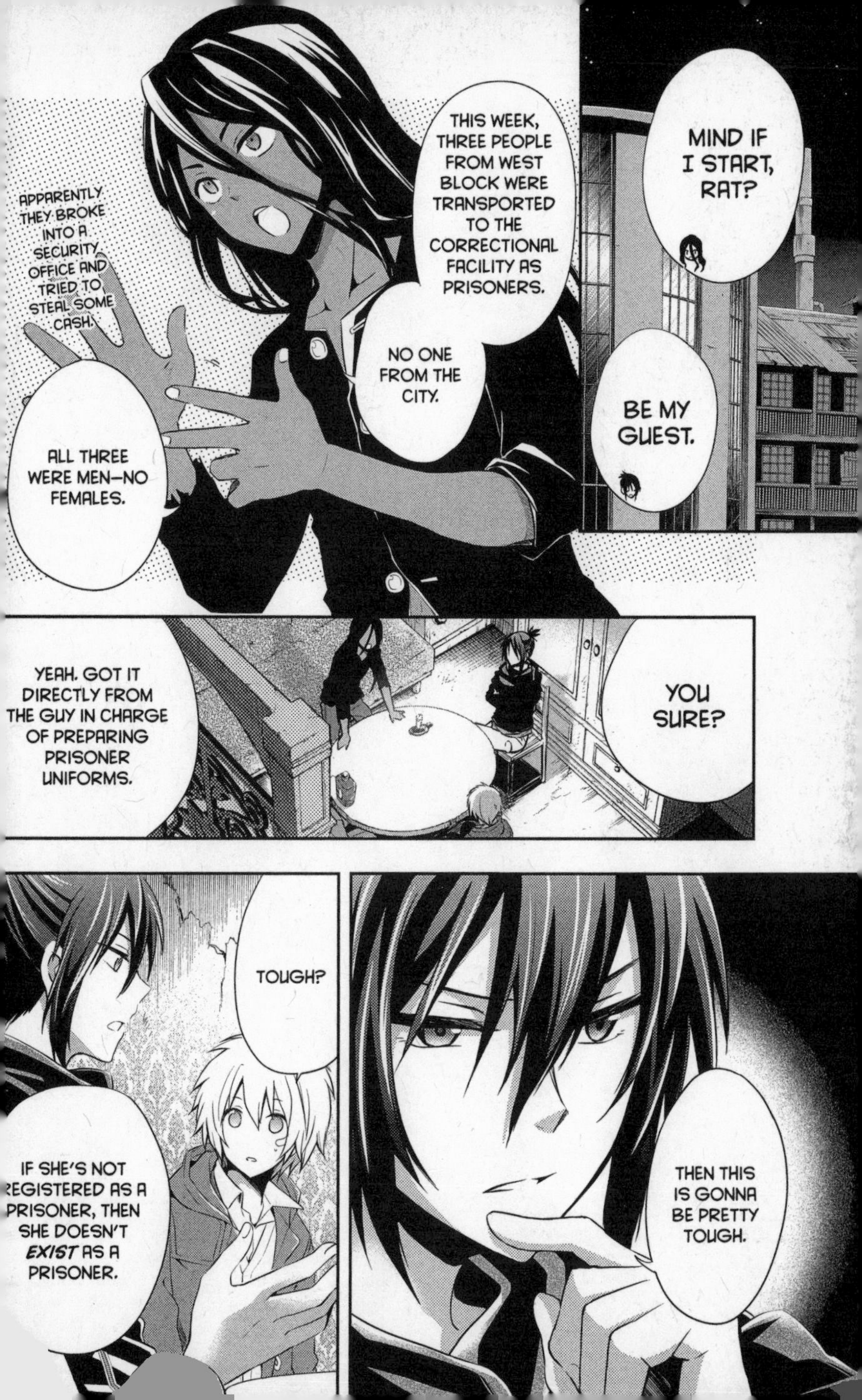
MIND IF I START, RAT?
BE MY GUEST.
THIS WEEK, THREE PEOPLE FROM WEST BLOCK WERE TRANSPORTED TO THE CORRECTIONAL FACILITY AS PRISONERS.
NO ONE FROM THE CITY.
APPARENTLY THEY BROKE INTO A SECURITY OFFICE AND TRIED TO STEAL SOME CASH.
ALL THREE WERE MEN—NO FEMALES.
YOU SURE?
YEAH. GOT IT DIRECTLY FROM THE GUY IN CHARGE OF PREPARING PRISONER UNIFORMS.
THEN THIS IS GONNA BE PRETTY TOUGH.
TOUGH?
IF SHE'S NOT REGISTERED AS A PRISONER, THEN SHE DOESN'T *EXIST* AS A PRISONER.

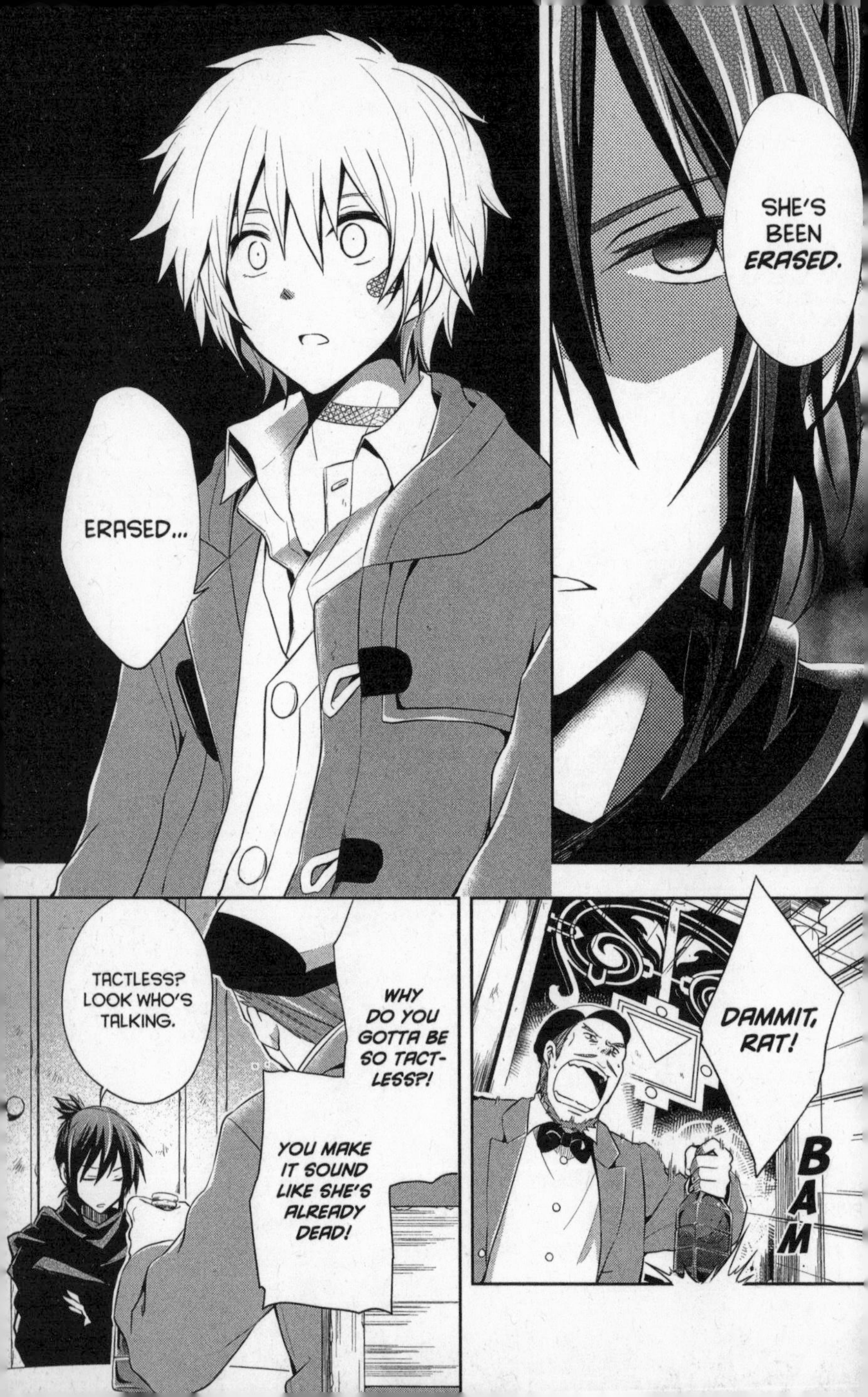
SHE'S BEEN ERASED.
ERASED...
DAMMIT, RAT!
BAM
WHY DO YOU GOTTA BE SO TACT-LESS?!
YOU MAKE IT SOUND LIKE SHE'S ALREADY DEAD!
TACTLESS? LOOK WHO'S TALKING.

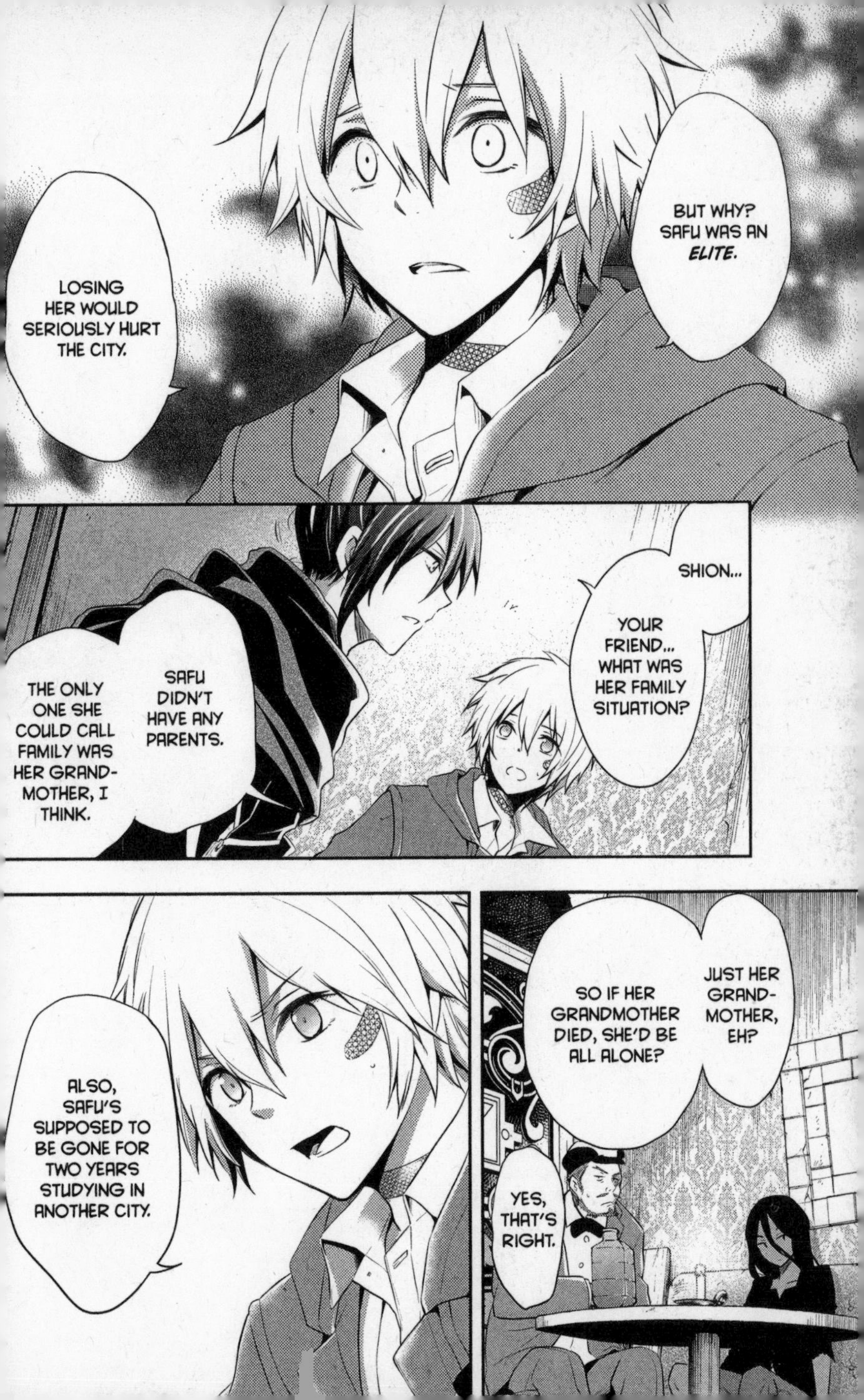
BUT WHY? SAFU WAS AN *ELITE.*
LOSING HER WOULD SERIOUSLY HURT THE CITY.
SHION... YOUR FRIEND... WHAT WAS HER FAMILY SITUATION?
SAFU DIDN'T HAVE ANY PARENTS.
THE ONLY ONE SHE COULD CALL FAMILY WAS HER GRAND-MOTHER, I THINK.
JUST HER GRAND-MOTHER, EH?
SO IF HER GRANDMOTHER DIED, SHE'D BE ALL ALONE?
YES, THAT'S RIGHT.
ALSO, SAFU'S SUPPOSED TO BE GONE FOR TWO YEARS STUDYING IN ANOTHER CITY.

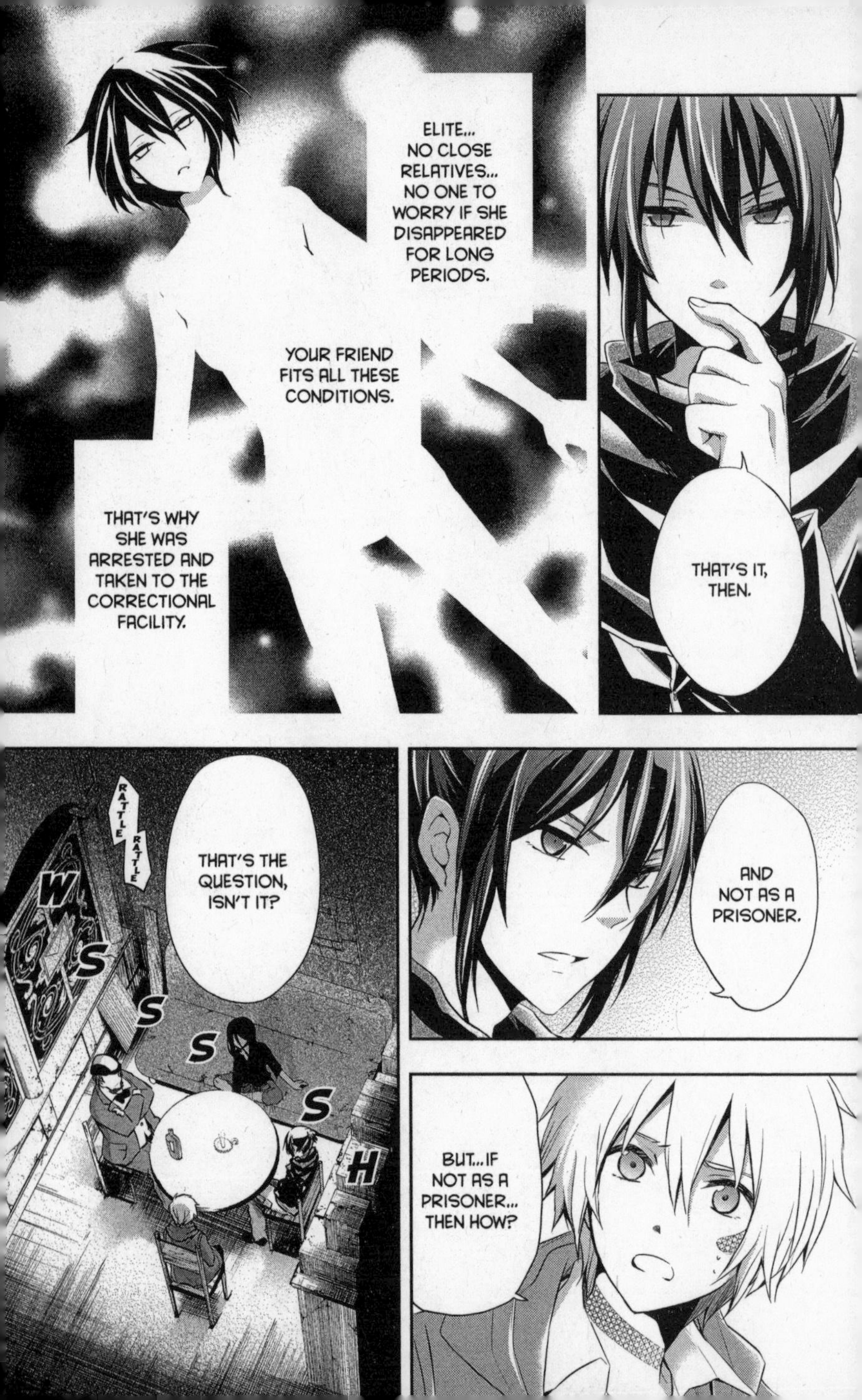

THAT'S IT, THEN.
ELITE... NO CLOSE RELATIVES... NO ONE TO WORRY IF SHE DISAPPEARED FOR LONG PERIODS.
YOUR FRIEND FITS ALL THESE CONDITIONS.
THAT'S WHY SHE WAS ARRESTED AND TAKEN TO THE CORRECTIONAL FACILITY.
AND NOT AS A PRISONER.
BUT... IF NOT AS A PRISONER... THEN HOW?
RATTLE RATTLE
THAT'S THE QUESTION, ISN'T IT?
WSSSSH

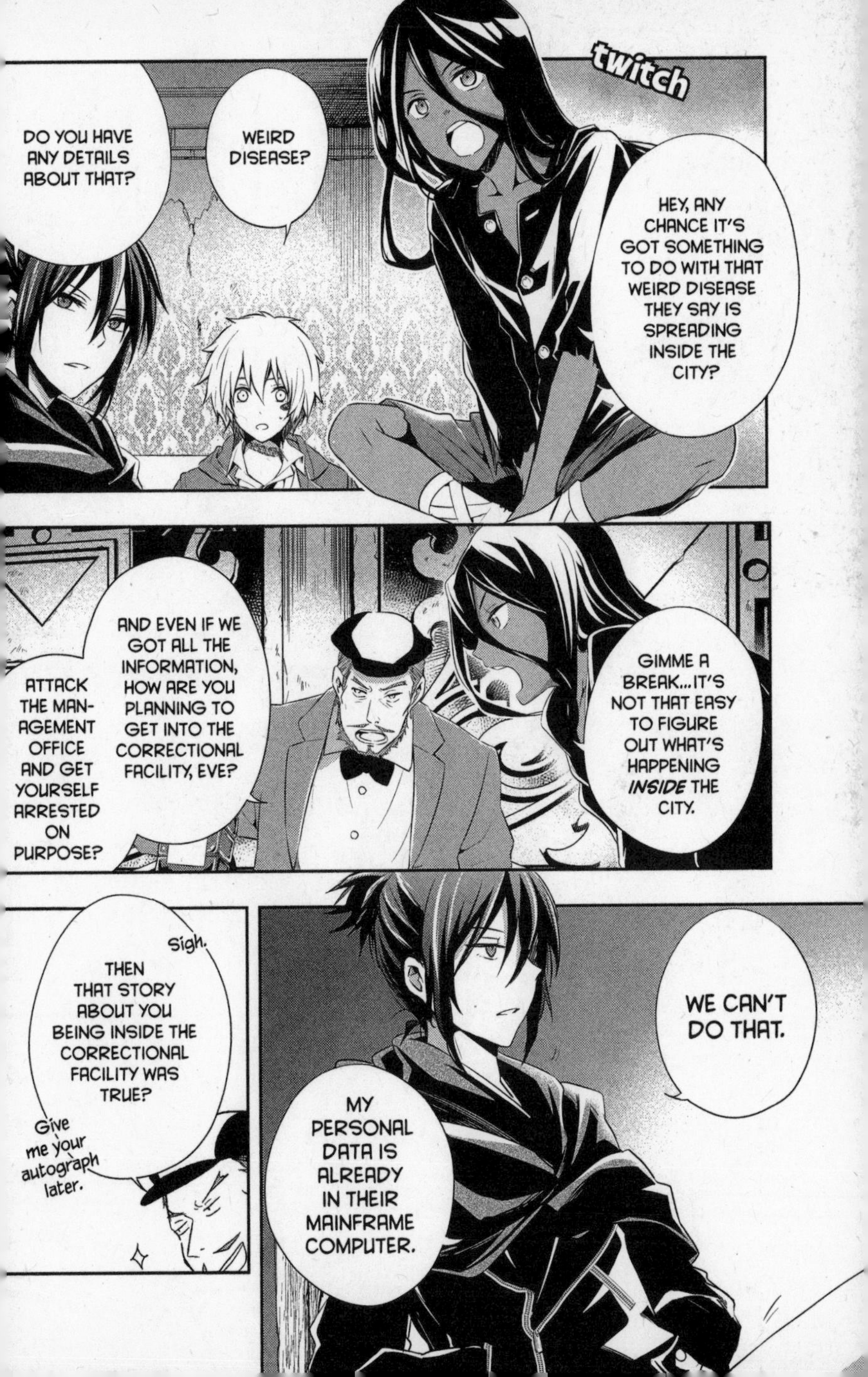
twitch
HEY, ANY CHANCE IT'S GOT SOMETHING TO DO WITH THAT WEIRD DISEASE THEY SAY IS SPREADING INSIDE THE CITY?
WEIRD DISEASE?
DO YOU HAVE ANY DETAILS ABOUT THAT?
GIMME A BREAK...IT'S NOT THAT EASY TO FIGURE OUT WHAT'S HAPPENING *INSIDE* THE CITY.
AND EVEN IF WE GOT ALL THE INFORMATION, HOW ARE YOU PLANNING TO GET INTO THE CORRECTIONAL FACILITY, EVE?
ATTACK THE MAN-AGEMENT OFFICE AND GET YOURSELF ARRESTED ON PURPOSE?
WE CAN'T DO THAT.
MY PERSONAL DATA IS ALREADY IN THEIR MAINFRAME COMPUTER.
Sigh.
THEN THAT STORY ABOUT YOU BEING INSIDE THE CORRECTIONAL FACILITY WAS TRUE?
Give me your autograph later.

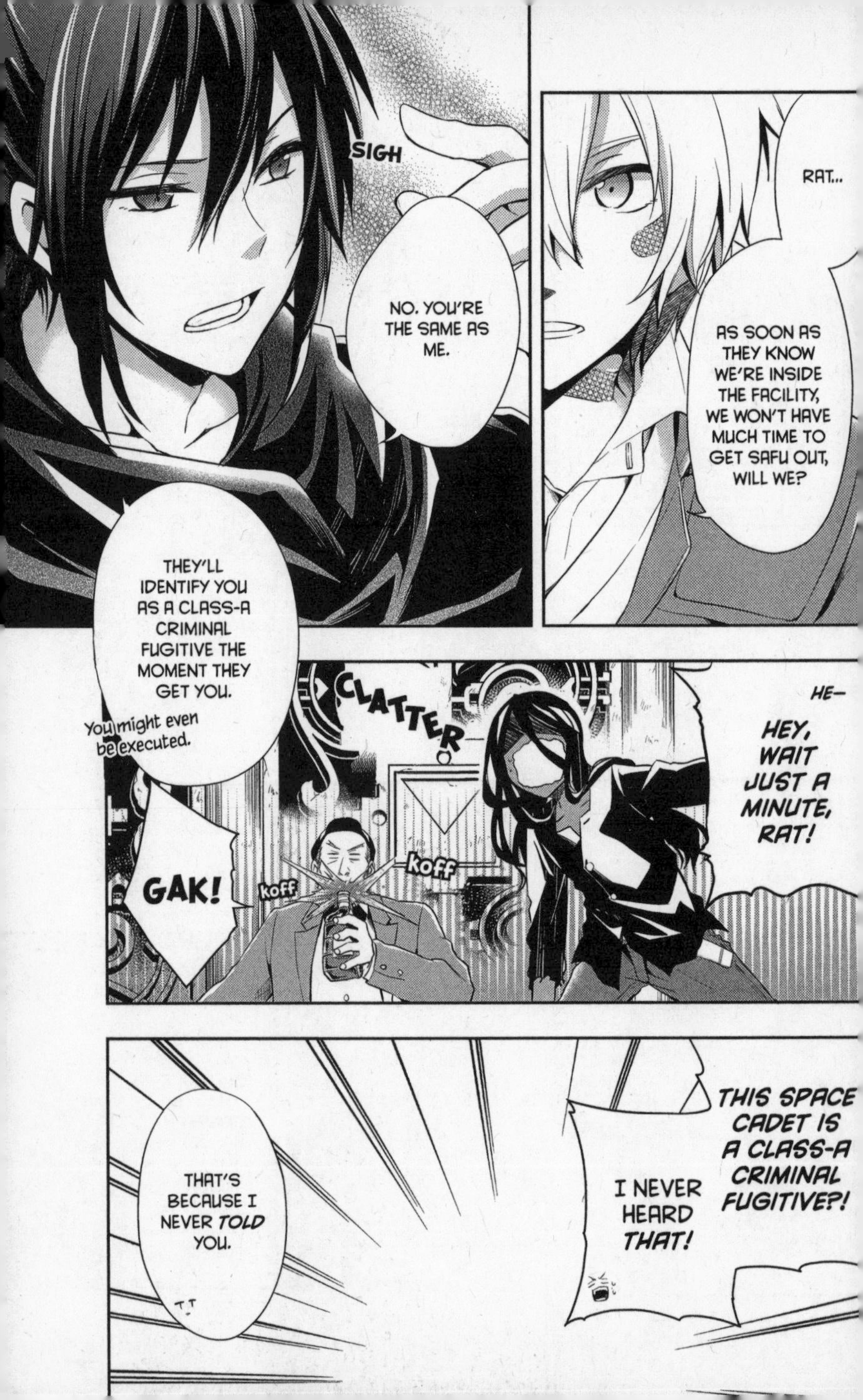
RAT...
AS SOON AS THEY KNOW WE'RE INSIDE THE FACILITY, WE WON'T HAVE MUCH TIME TO GET SAFU OUT, WILL WE?
SIGH
NO. YOU'RE THE SAME AS ME.
THEY'LL IDENTIFY YOU AS A CLASS-A CRIMINAL FUGITIVE THE MOMENT THEY GET YOU.
You might even be executed.
HE—
HEY, WAIT JUST A MINUTE, RAT!
CLATTER
koff
koff
GAK!
THIS SPACE CADET IS A CLASS-A CRIMINAL FUGITIVE?!
I NEVER HEARD THAT!
THAT'S BECAUSE I NEVER TOLD YOU.

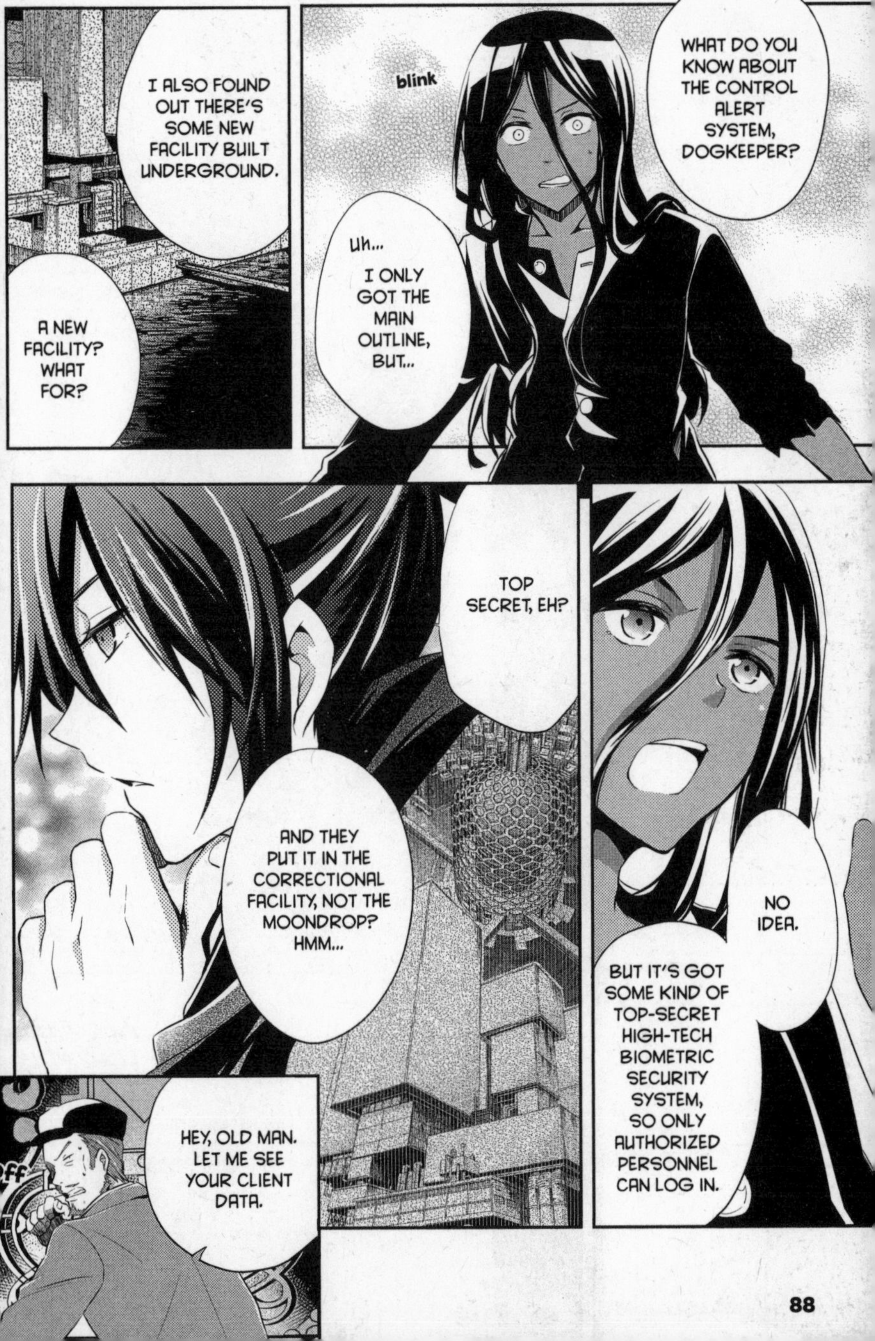
WHAT DO YOU KNOW ABOUT THE CONTROL ALERT SYSTEM, DOGKEEPER?
blink
uh... I ONLY GOT THE MAIN OUTLINE, BUT...
I ALSO FOUND OUT THERE'S SOME NEW FACILITY BUILT UNDERGROUND.
A NEW FACILITY? WHAT FOR?
NO IDEA.
BUT IT'S GOT SOME KIND OF TOP-SECRET HIGH-TECH BIOMETRIC SECURITY SYSTEM, SO ONLY AUTHORIZED PERSONNEL CAN LOG IN.
TOP SECRET, EH?
AND THEY PUT IT IN THE CORRECTIONAL FACILITY, NOT THE MOONDROP? HMM...
HEY, OLD MAN. LET ME SEE YOUR CLIENT DATA.

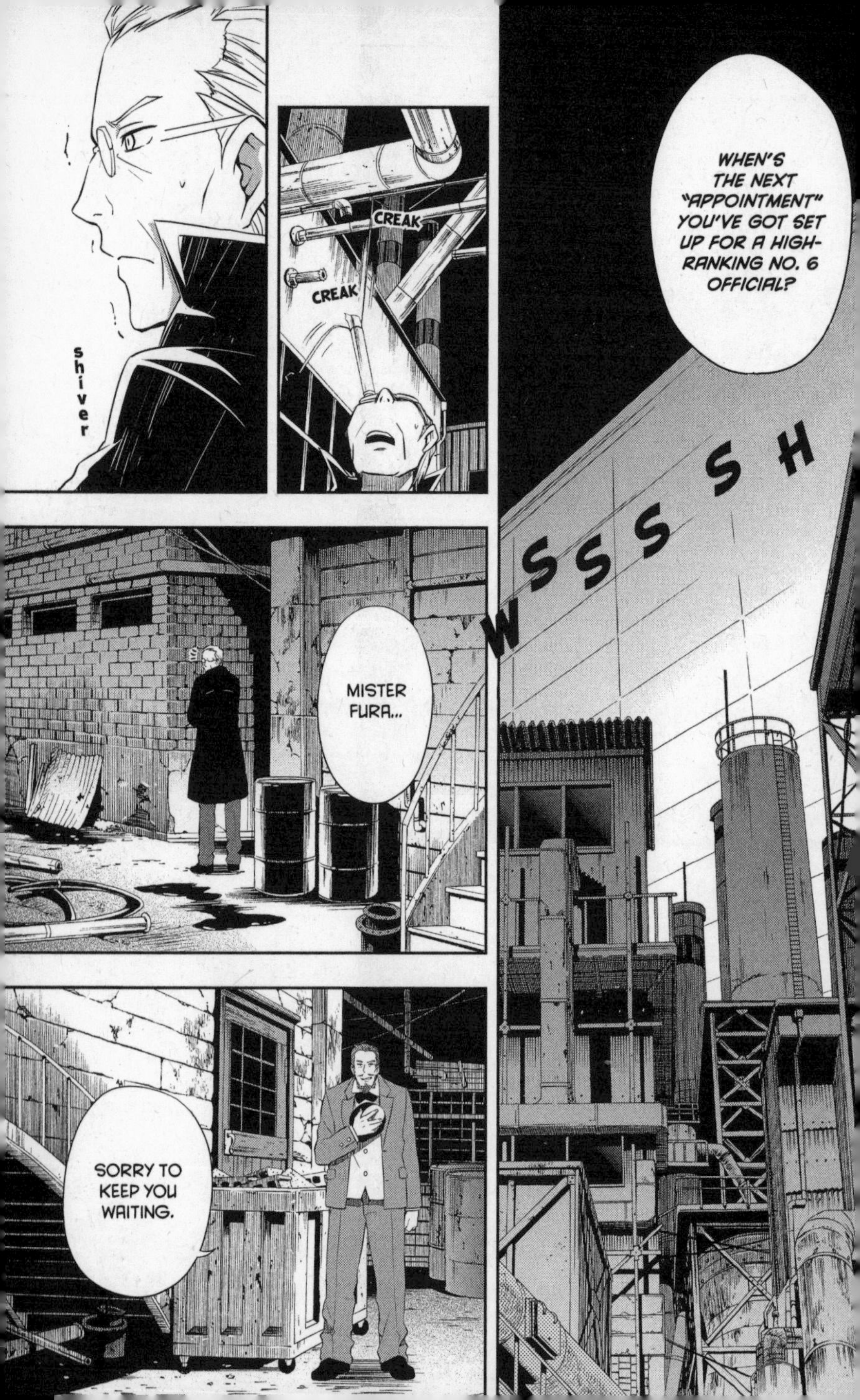
WHEN'S THE NEXT "APPOINTMENT" YOU'VE GOT SET UP FOR A HIGH-RANKING NO. 6 OFFICIAL?
WSSSSH
CREAK
CREAK
shiver
MISTER FURA...
SORRY TO KEEP YOU WAITING.

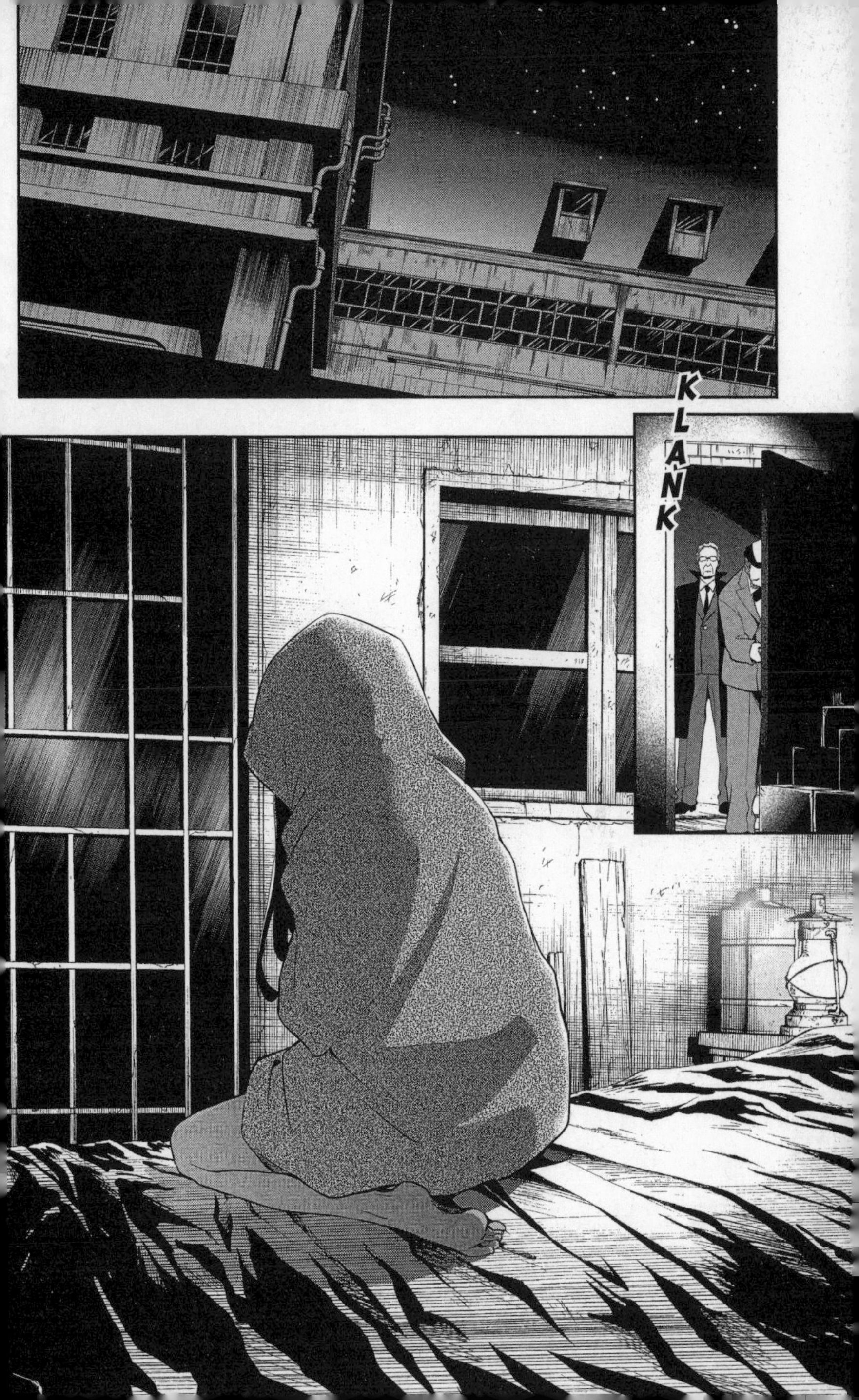
KLANK

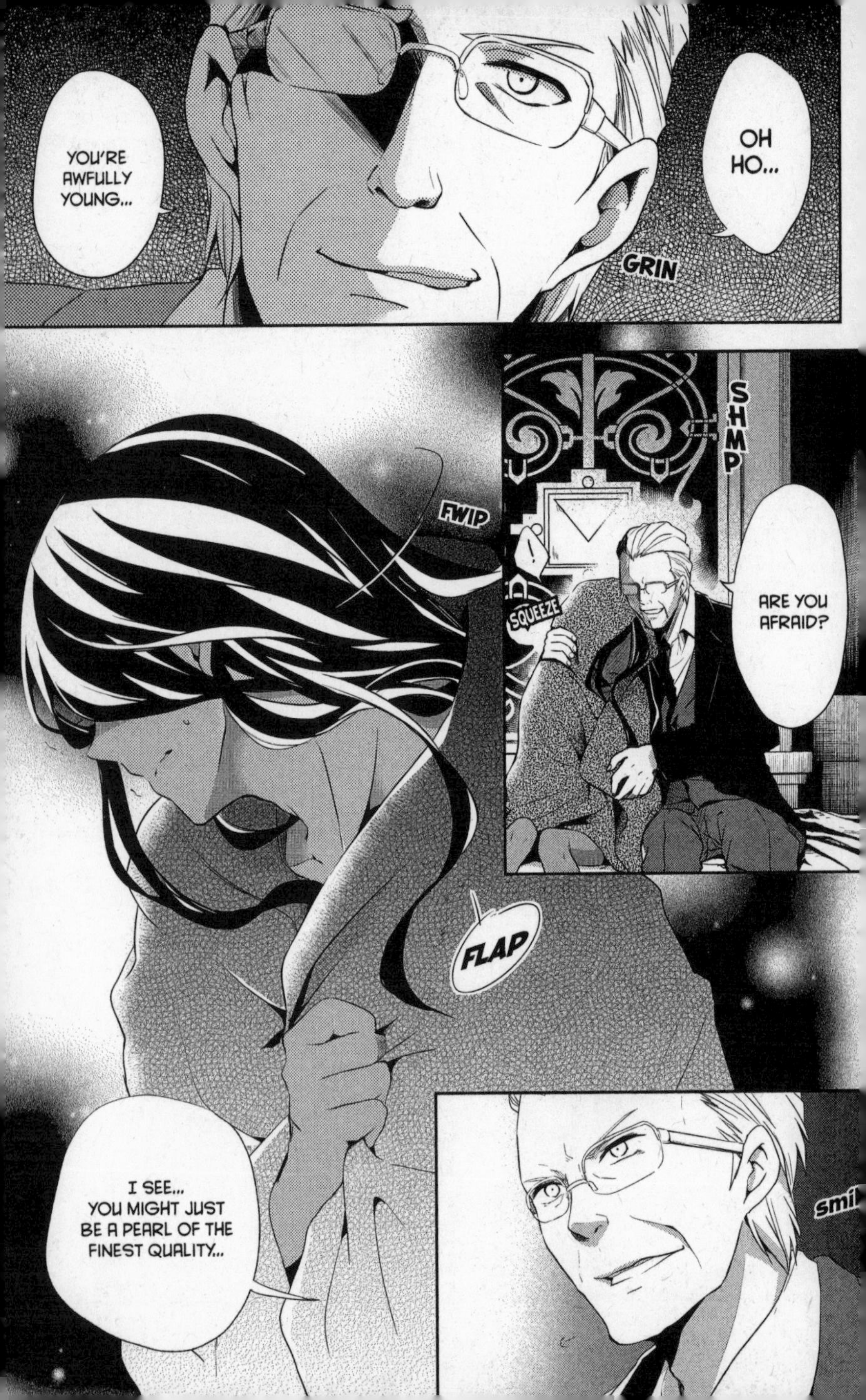
OH HO...
GRIN
YOU'RE AWFULLY YOUNG...
SHMP
ARE YOU AFRAID?
SQUEEZE
FWIP
FLAP
smil
I SEE... YOU MIGHT JUST BE A PEARL OF THE FINEST QUALITY...

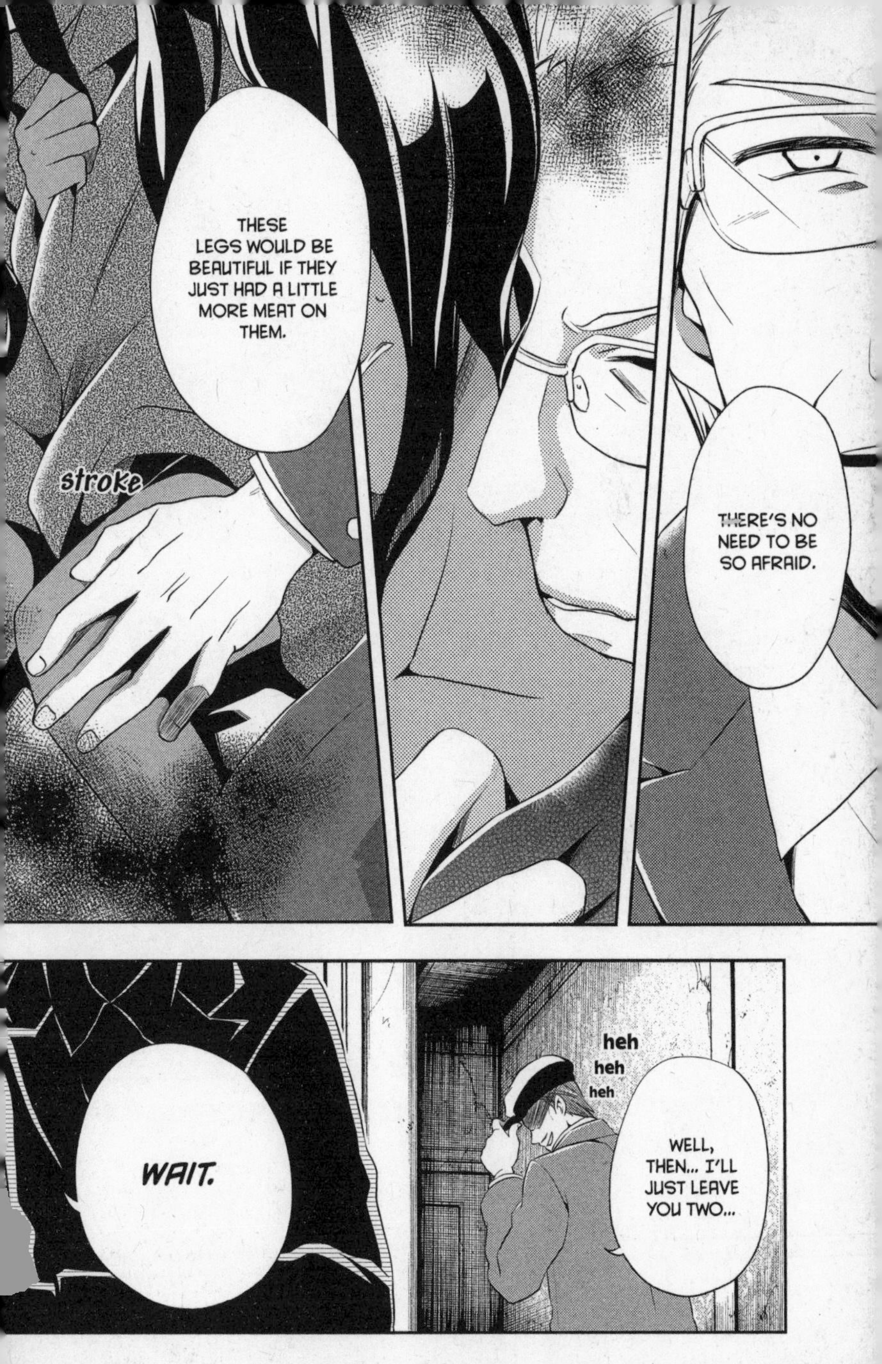
THERE'S NO NEED TO BE SO AFRAID.
THESE LEGS WOULD BE BEAUTIFUL IF THEY JUST HAD A LITTLE MORE MEAT ON THEM.
stroke
heh heh heh
WELL, THEN... I'LL JUST LEAVE YOU TWO...
WAIT.

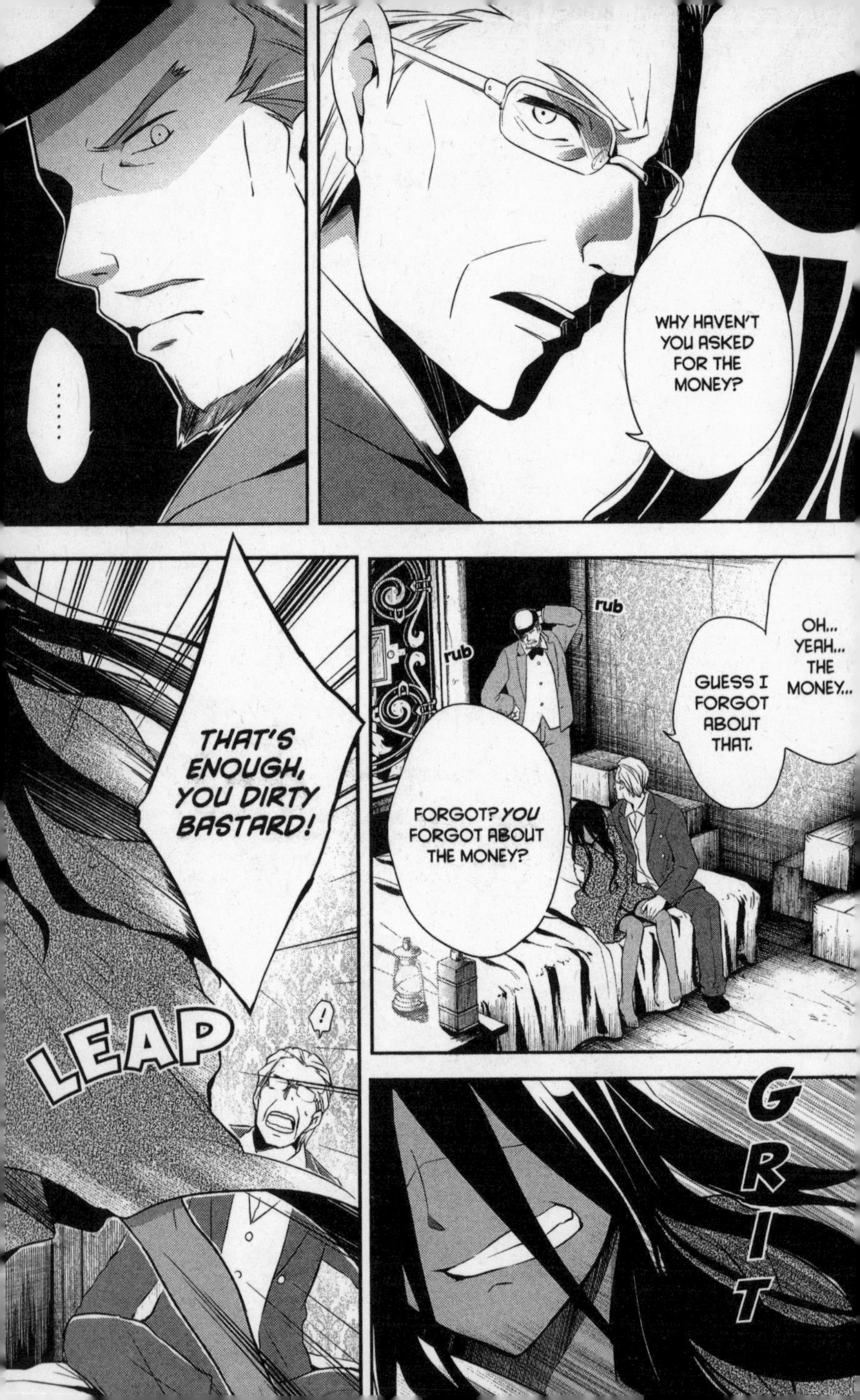
WHY HAVEN'T YOU ASKED FOR THE MONEY?
......
rub
rub
OH... YEAH... THE MONEY...
GUESS I FORGOT ABOUT THAT.
FORGOT? YOU FORGOT ABOUT THE MONEY?
GRIT
THAT'S ENOUGH, YOU DIRTY BASTARD!
!
LEAP

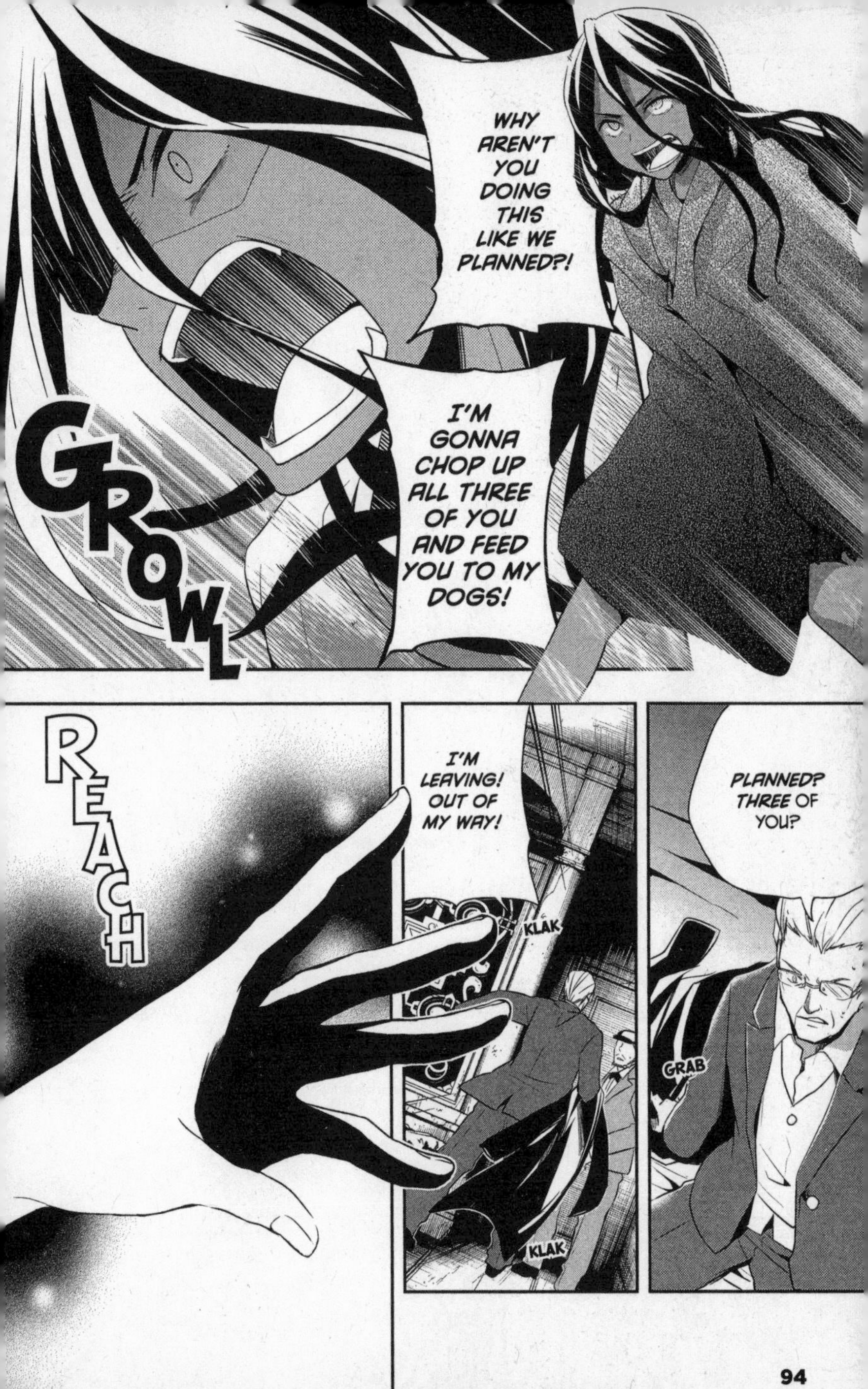
WHY AREN'T YOU DOING THIS LIKE WE PLANNED?!
I'M GONNA CHOP UP ALL THREE OF YOU AND FEED YOU TO MY DOGS!
GROWL
PLANNED? THREE OF YOU?
GRAB
I'M LEAVING! OUT OF MY WAY!
KLAK
KLAK
REACH

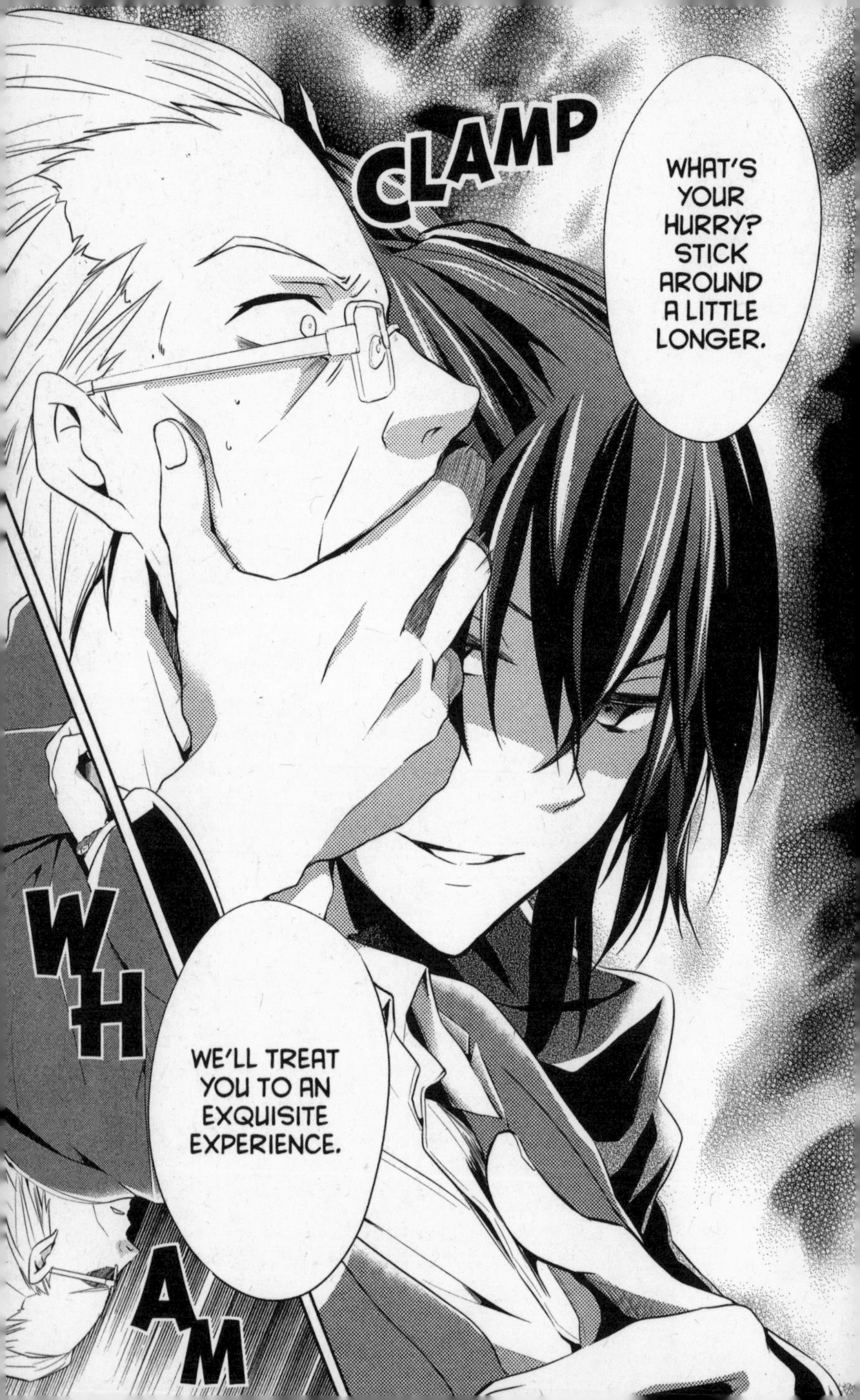
CLAMP
WHAT'S YOUR HURRY? STICK AROUND A LITTLE LONGER.
WHAM
WE'LL TREAT YOU TO AN EXQUISITE EXPERIENCE.

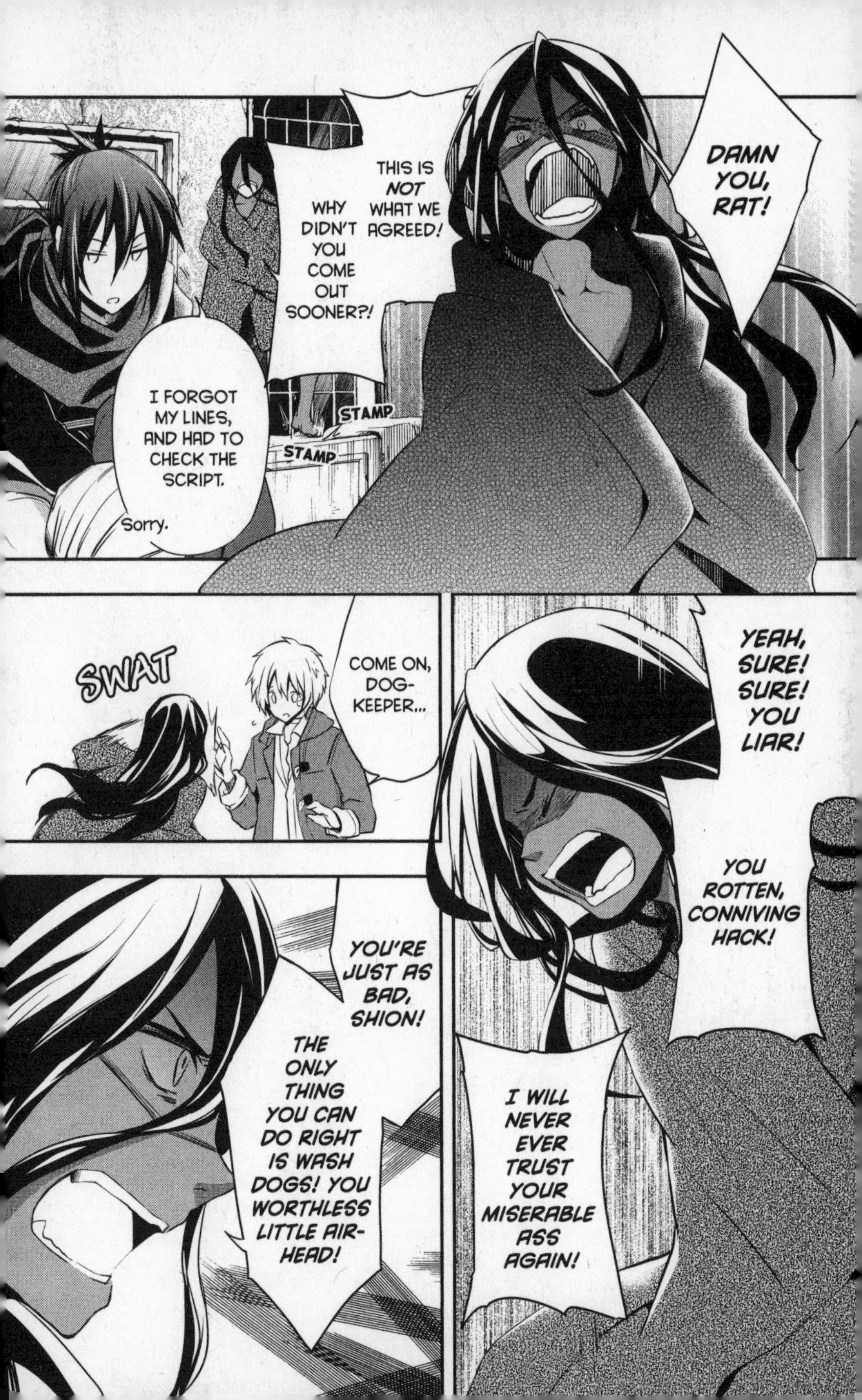
DAMN YOU, RAT!
THIS IS NOT WHAT WE AGREED!
WHY DIDN'T YOU COME OUT SOONER?!
STAMP
STAMP
I FORGOT MY LINES, AND HAD TO CHECK THE SCRIPT.
Sorry.
YEAH, SURE! SURE! YOU LIAR!
YOU ROTTEN, CONNIVING HACK!
I WILL NEVER EVER TRUST YOUR MISERABLE ASS AGAIN!
COME ON, DOG-KEEPER...
SWAT
YOU'RE JUST AS BAD, SHION!
THE ONLY THING YOU CAN DO RIGHT IS WASH DOGS! YOU WORTHLESS LITTLE AIR-HEAD!

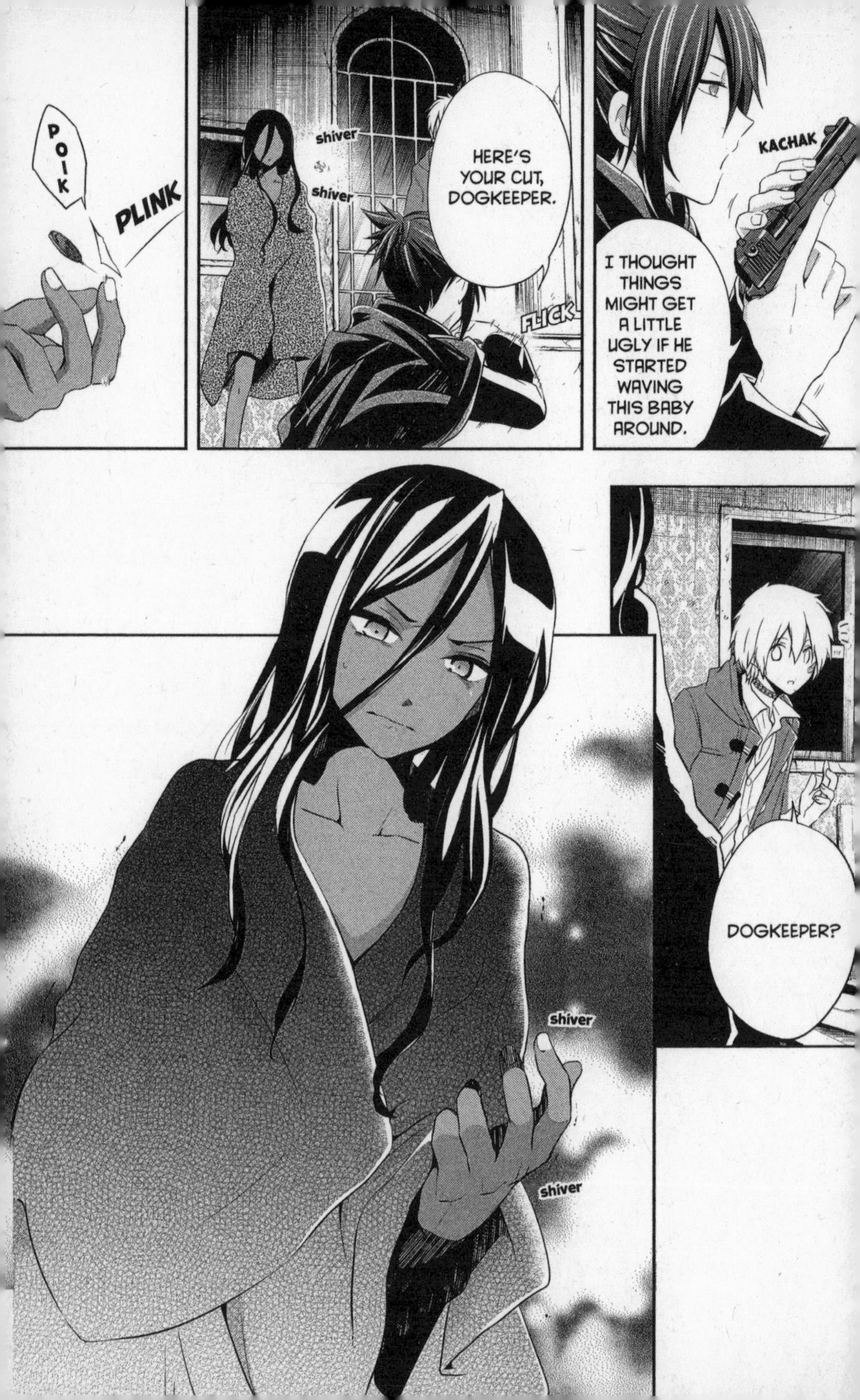
KACHAK
I THOUGHT THINGS MIGHT GET A LITTLE UGLY IF HE STARTED WAVING THIS BABY AROUND.
HERE'S YOUR CUT, DOGKEEPER.
shiver
shiver
FLICK
POIK
PLINK
DOGKEEPER?
shiver
shiver

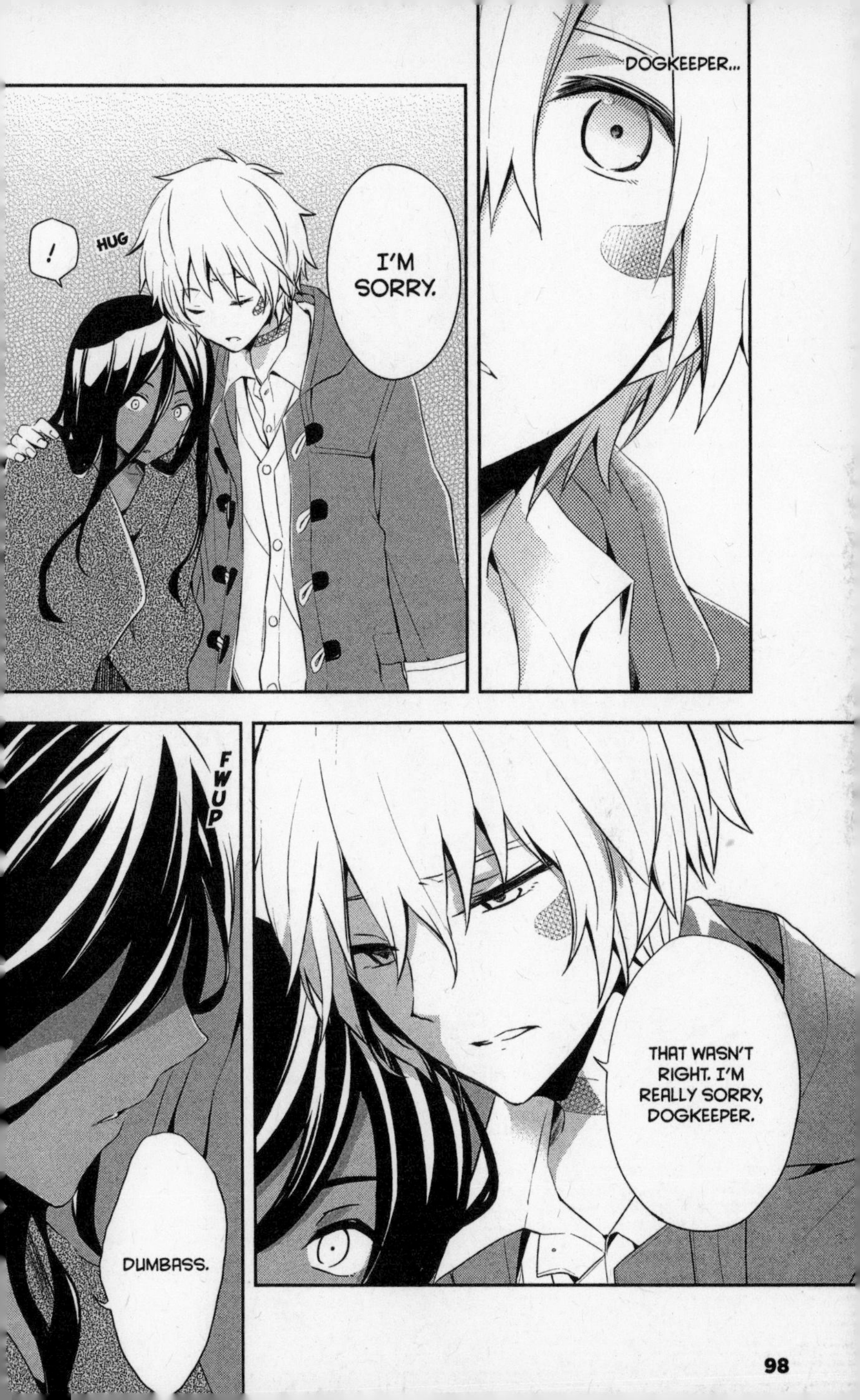
DOGKEEPER...
I'M SORRY.
!
HUG
THAT WASN'T RIGHT. I'M REALLY SORRY, DOGKEEPER.
FWUP
DUMBASS.

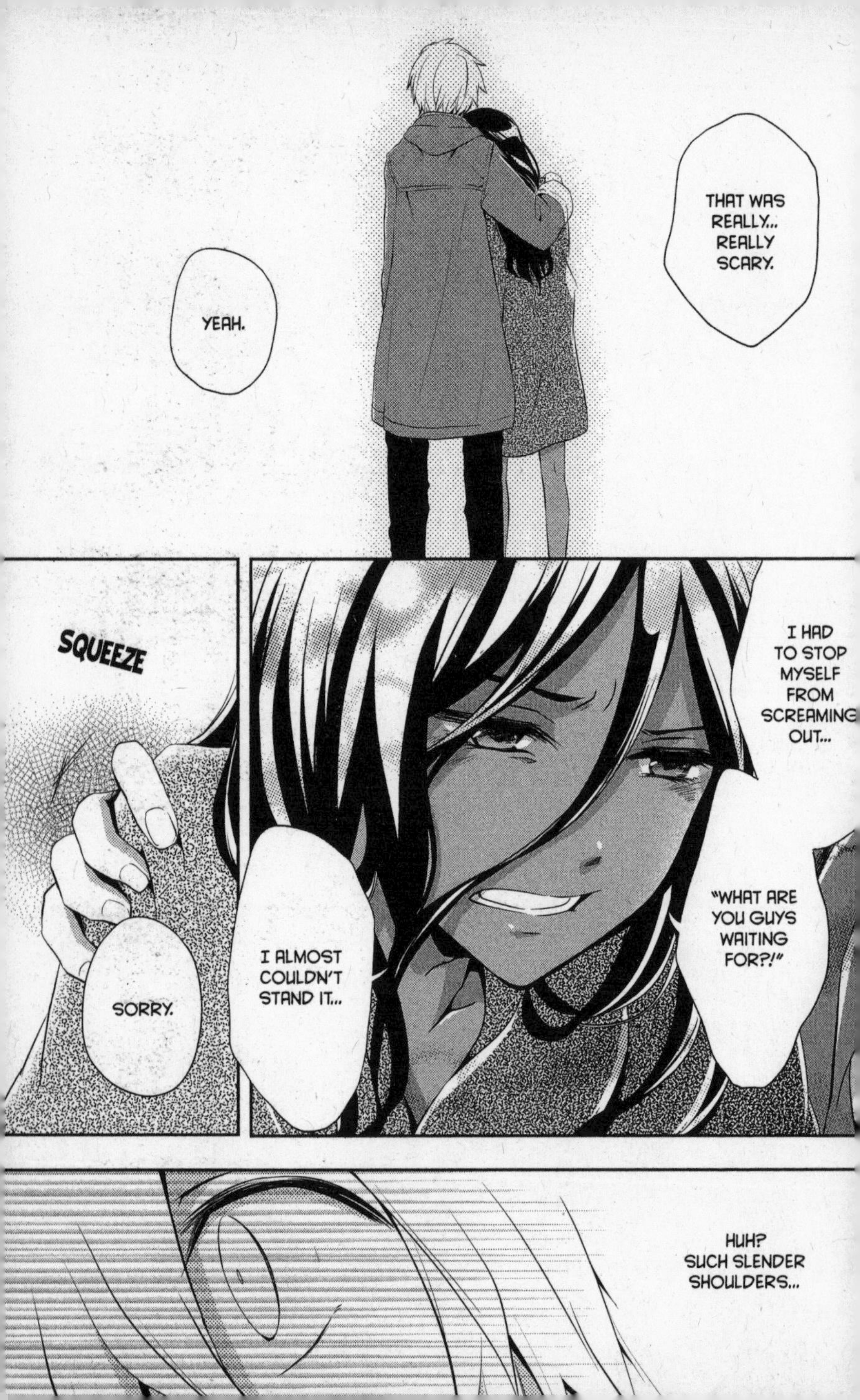
THAT WAS REALLY... REALLY SCARY.
YEAH.
I HAD TO STOP MYSELF FROM SCREAMING OUT...
"WHAT ARE YOU GUYS WAITING FOR?!"
I ALMOST COULDN'T STAND IT...
SQUEEZE
SORRY.
HUH? SUCH SLENDER SHOULDERS...

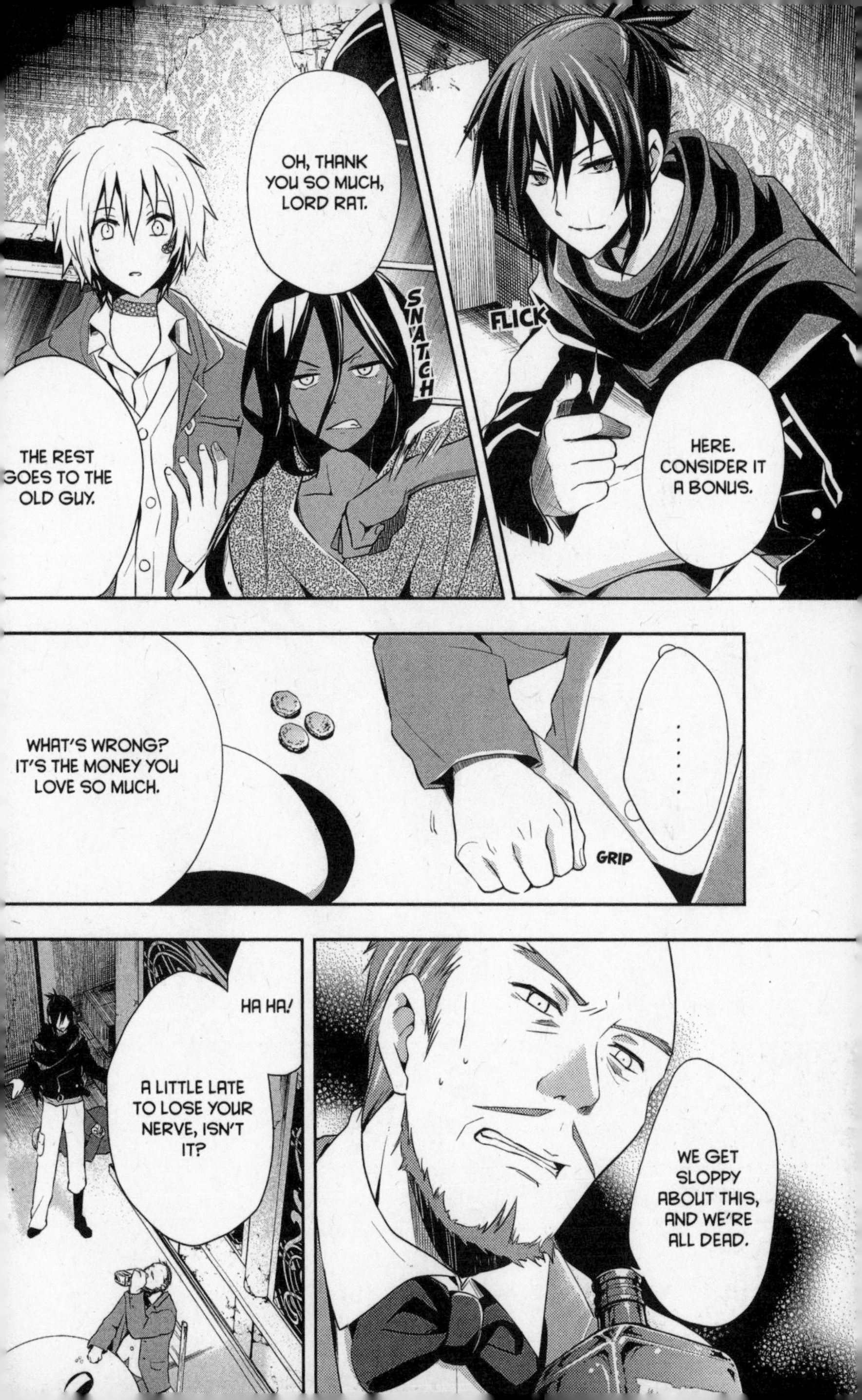
HERE. CONSIDER IT A BONUS.
FLICK
OH, THANK YOU SO MUCH, LORD RAT.
SNATCH
THE REST GOES TO THE OLD GUY.
......
GRIP
WHAT'S WRONG? IT'S THE MONEY YOU LOVE SO MUCH.
WE GET SLOPPY ABOUT THIS, AND WE'RE ALL DEAD.
HA HA!
A LITTLE LATE TO LOSE YOUR NERVE, ISN'T IT?

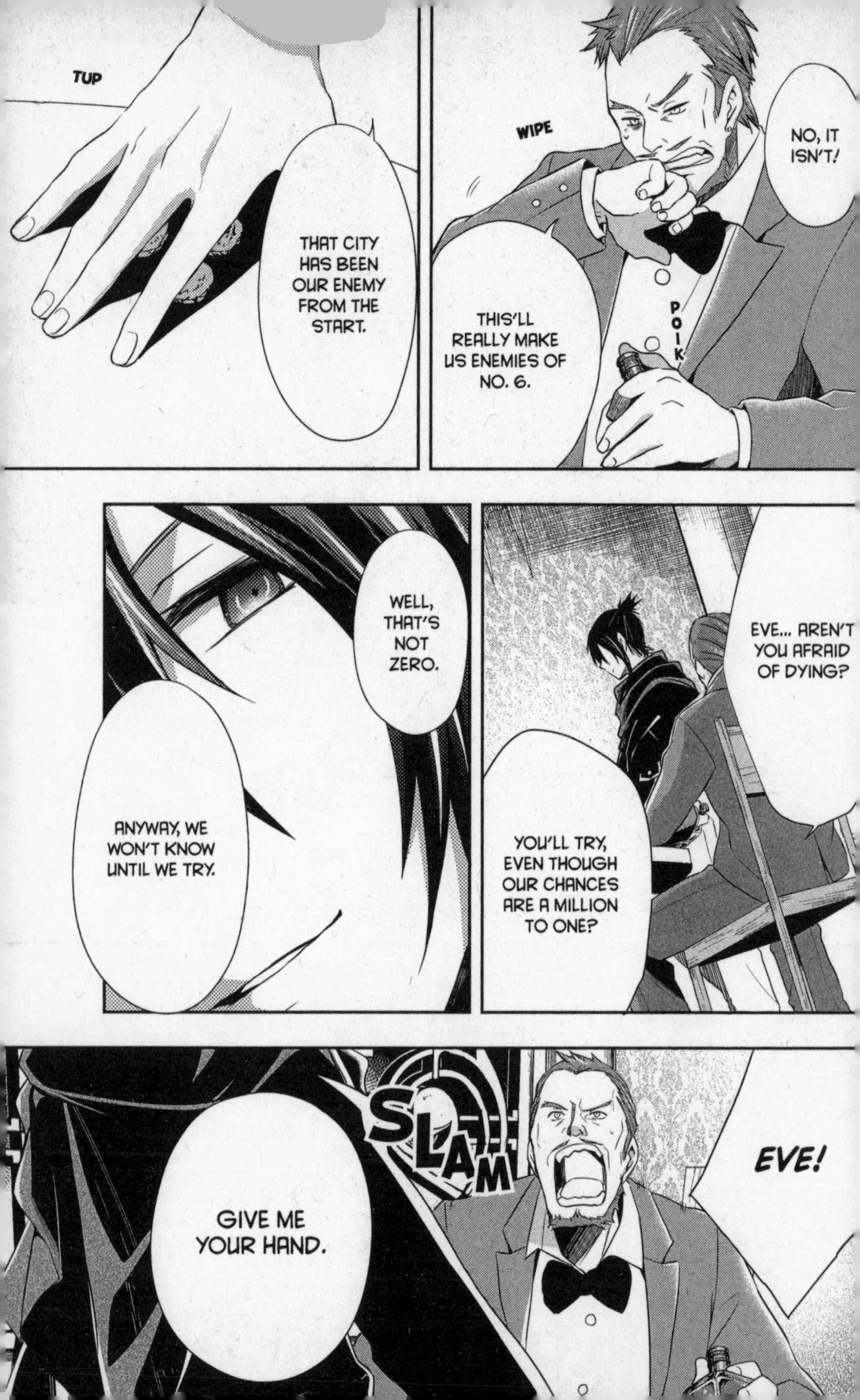
NO, IT ISN'T!
WIPE
POIK
THIS'LL REALLY MAKE US ENEMIES OF NO. 6.
TUP
THAT CITY HAS BEEN OUR ENEMY FROM THE START.
EVE... AREN'T YOU AFRAID OF DYING?
YOU'LL TRY, EVEN THOUGH OUR CHANCES ARE A MILLION TO ONE?
WELL, THAT'S NOT ZERO.
ANYWAY, WE WON'T KNOW UNTIL WE TRY.
EVE!
SLAM
GIVE ME YOUR HAND.

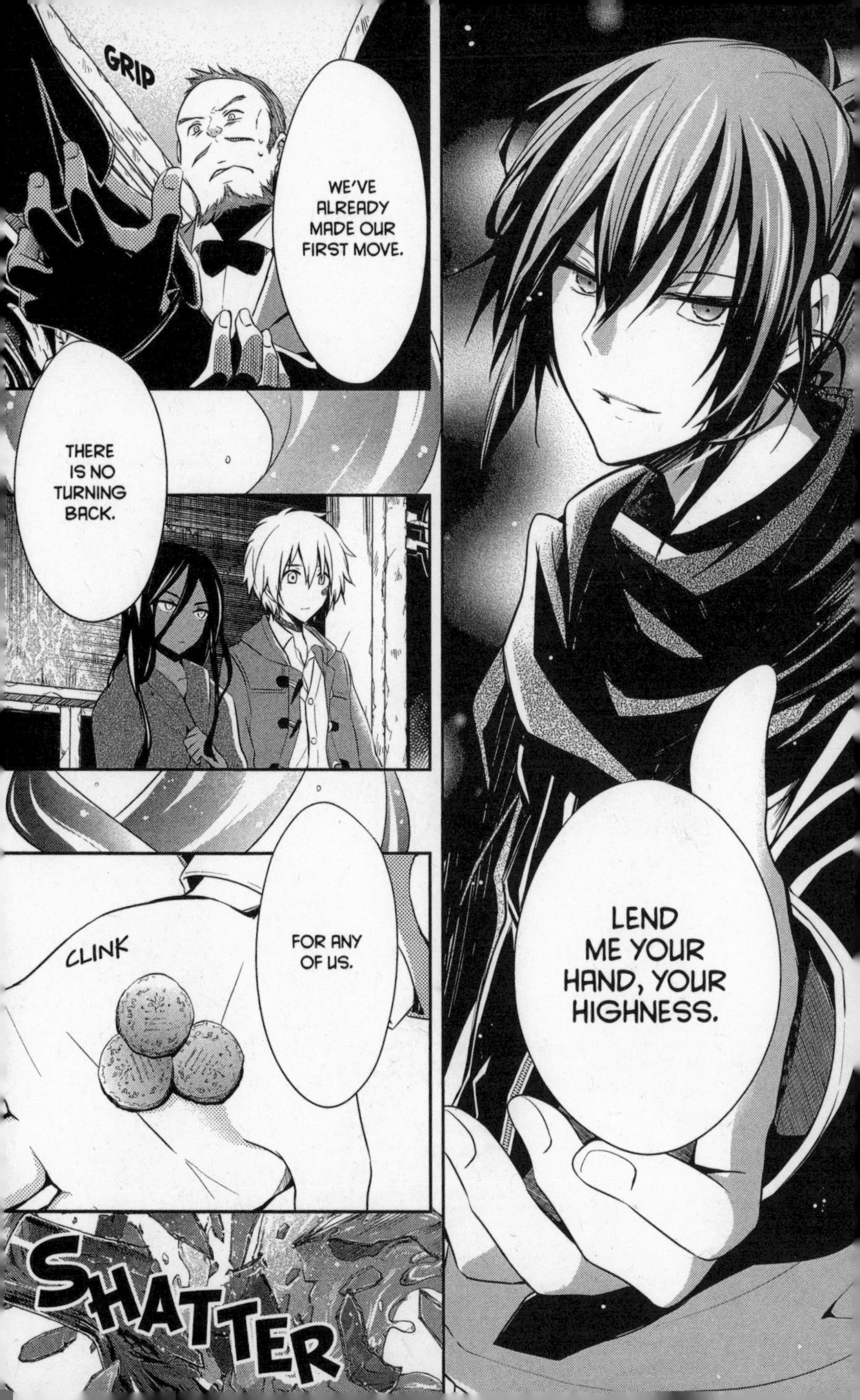
LEND ME YOUR HAND, YOUR HIGHNESS.
WE'VE ALREADY MADE OUR FIRST MOVE.
GRIP
THERE IS NO TURNING BACK.
FOR ANY OF US.
CLINK
SHATTER

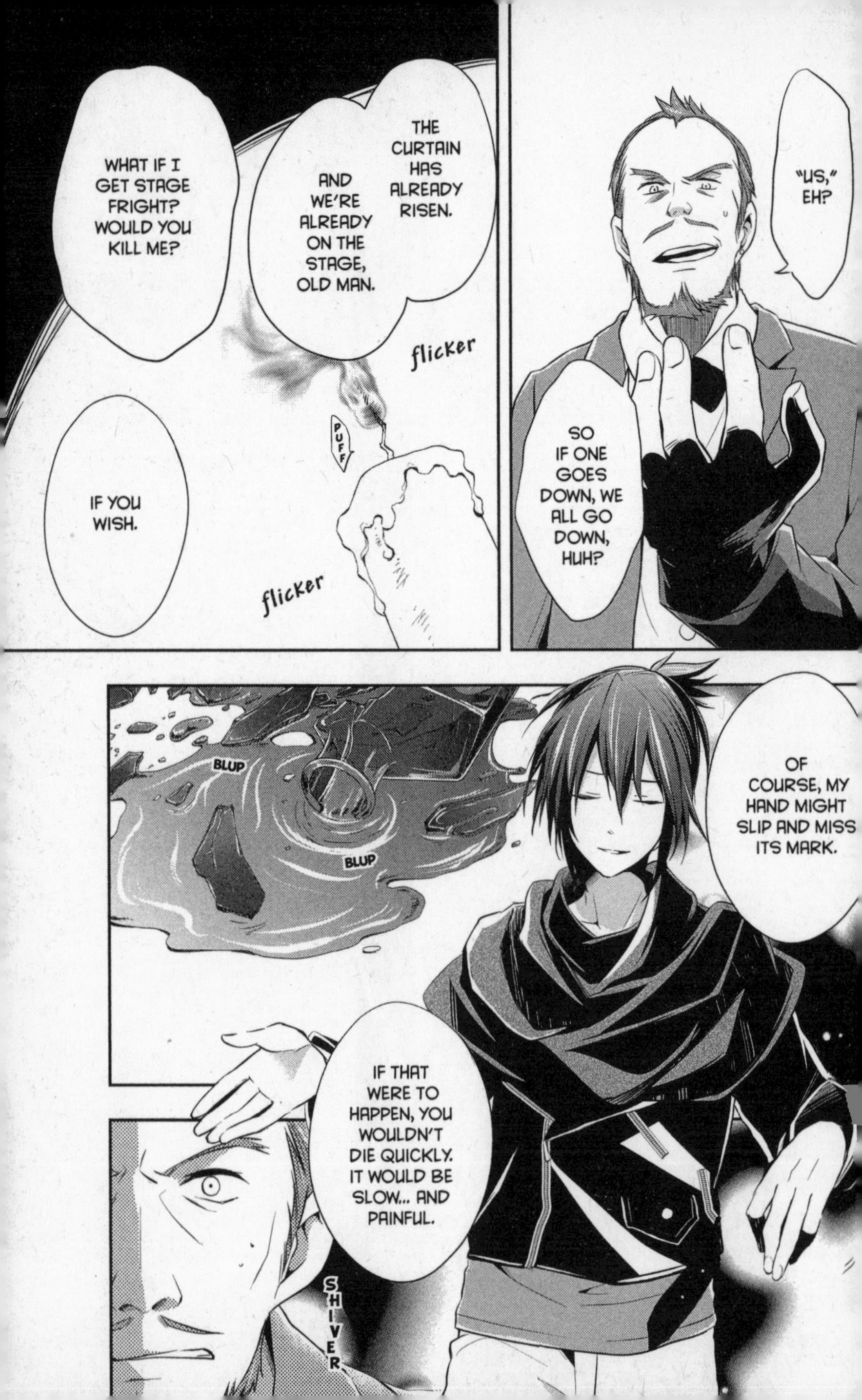
"US," EH?
SO IF ONE GOES DOWN, WE ALL GO DOWN, HUH?
THE CURTAIN HAS ALREADY RISEN.
AND WE'RE ALREADY ON THE STAGE, OLD MAN.
WHAT IF I GET STAGE FRIGHT? WOULD YOU KILL ME?
flicker
PUFF
IF YOU WISH.
flicker
OF COURSE, MY HAND MIGHT SLIP AND MISS ITS MARK.
BLUP
BLUP
IF THAT WERE TO HAPPEN, YOU WOULDN'T DIE QUICKLY. IT WOULD BE SLOW... AND PAINFUL.
SHIVER

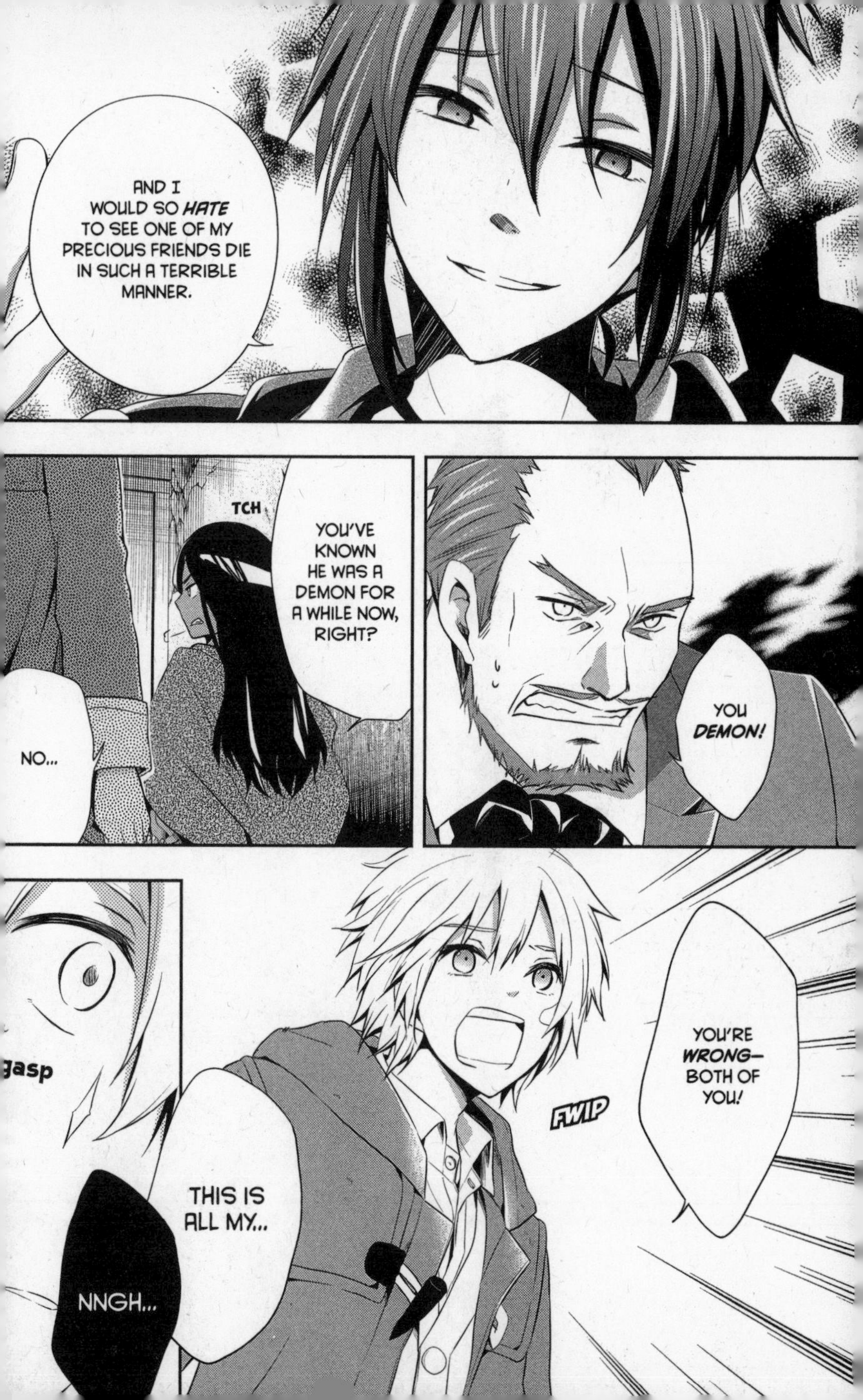
AND I WOULD SO *HATE* TO SEE ONE OF MY PRECIOUS FRIENDS DIE IN SUCH A TERRIBLE MANNER.
YOU *DEMON!*
TCH
YOU'VE KNOWN HE WAS A DEMON FOR A WHILE NOW, RIGHT?
NO...
YOU'RE *WRONG*— BOTH OF YOU!
FWIP
gasp
THIS IS ALL MY...
NNGH...

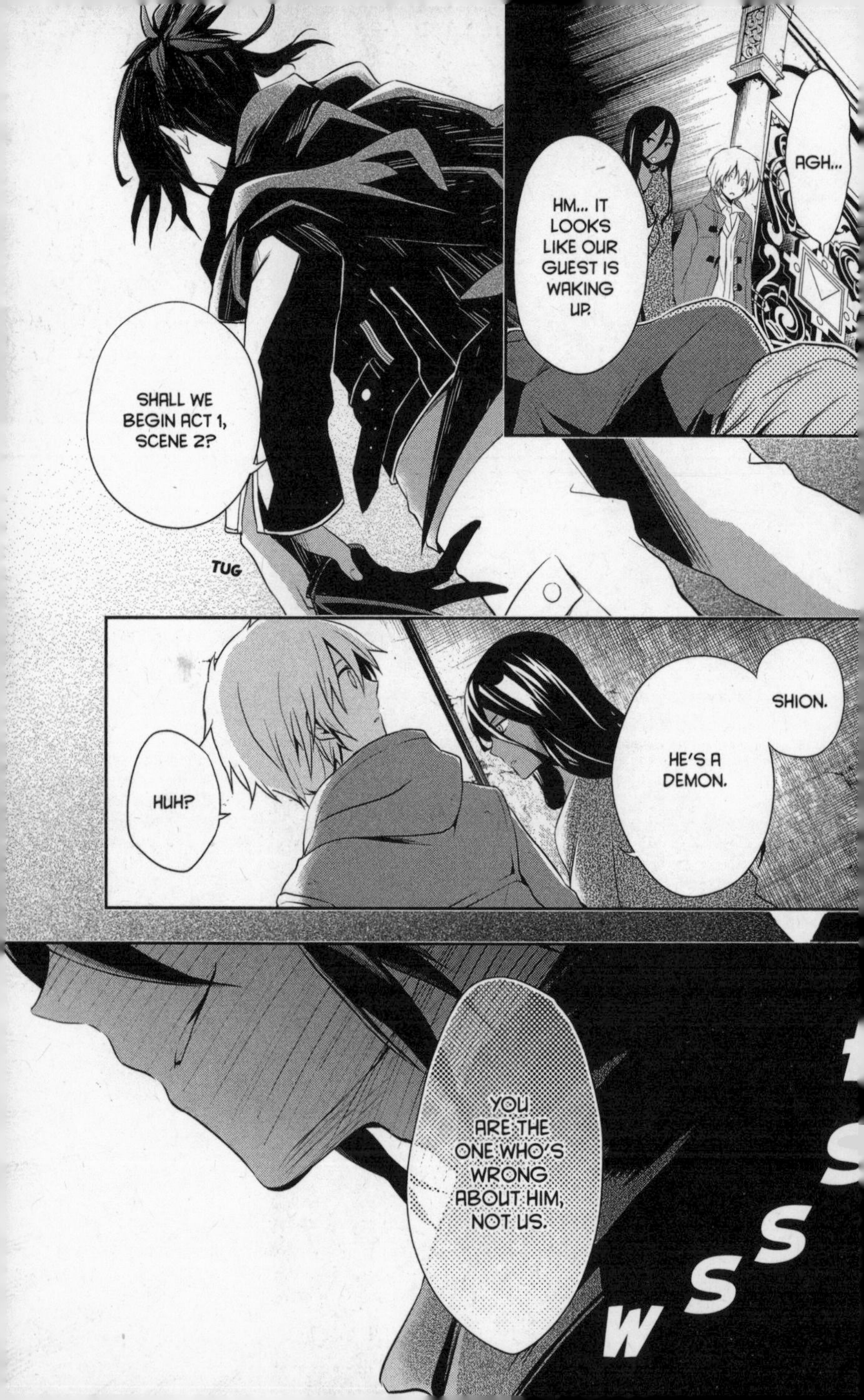
AGH...
HM... IT LOOKS LIKE OUR GUEST IS WAKING UP.
SHALL WE BEGIN ACT 1, SCENE 2?
TUG
SHION.
HE'S A DEMON.
HUH?
YOU ARE THE ONE WHO'S WRONG ABOUT HIM, NOT US.
WSSSS

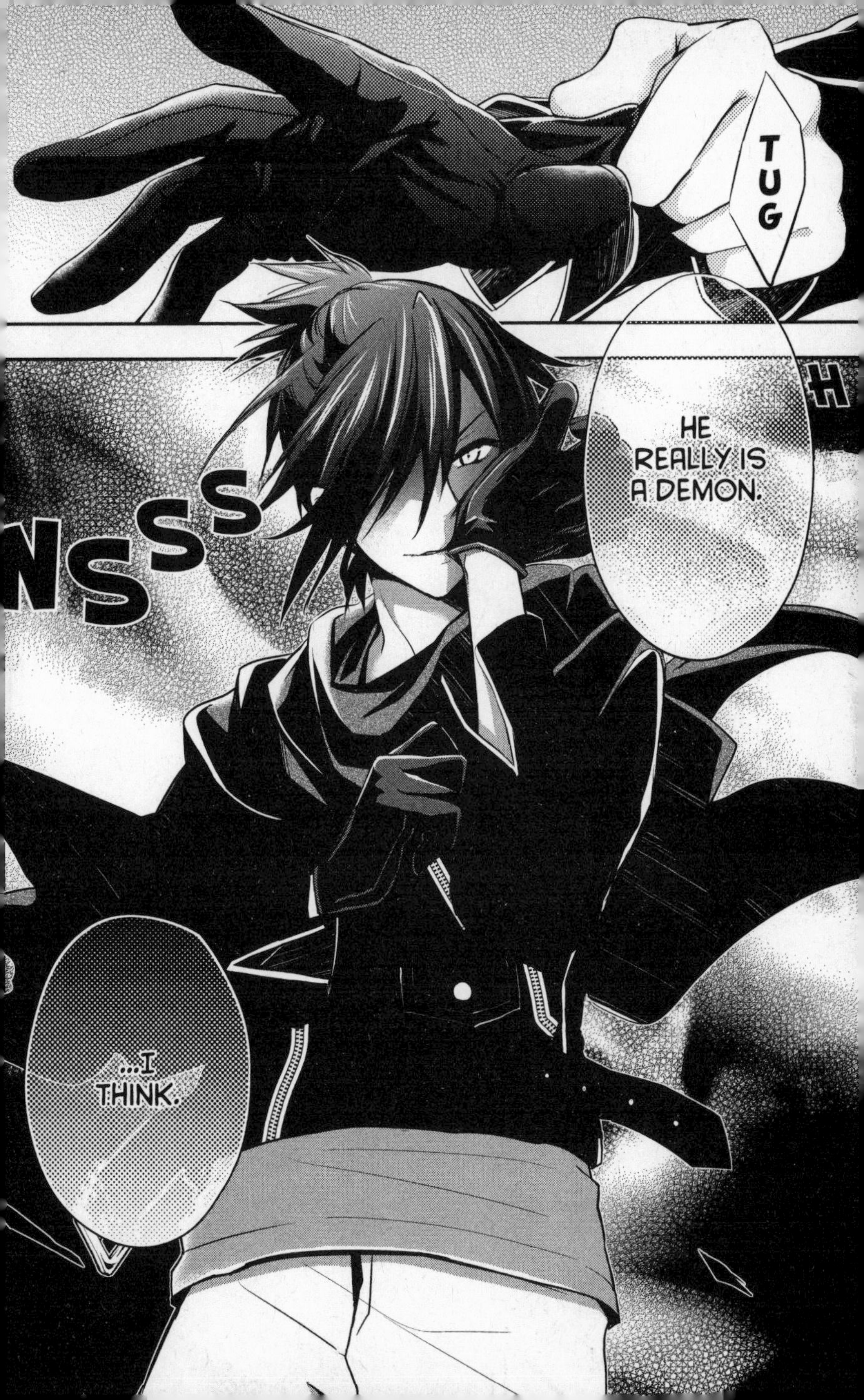
TUG
HE REALLY IS A DEMON.
NSSS
...I THINK.

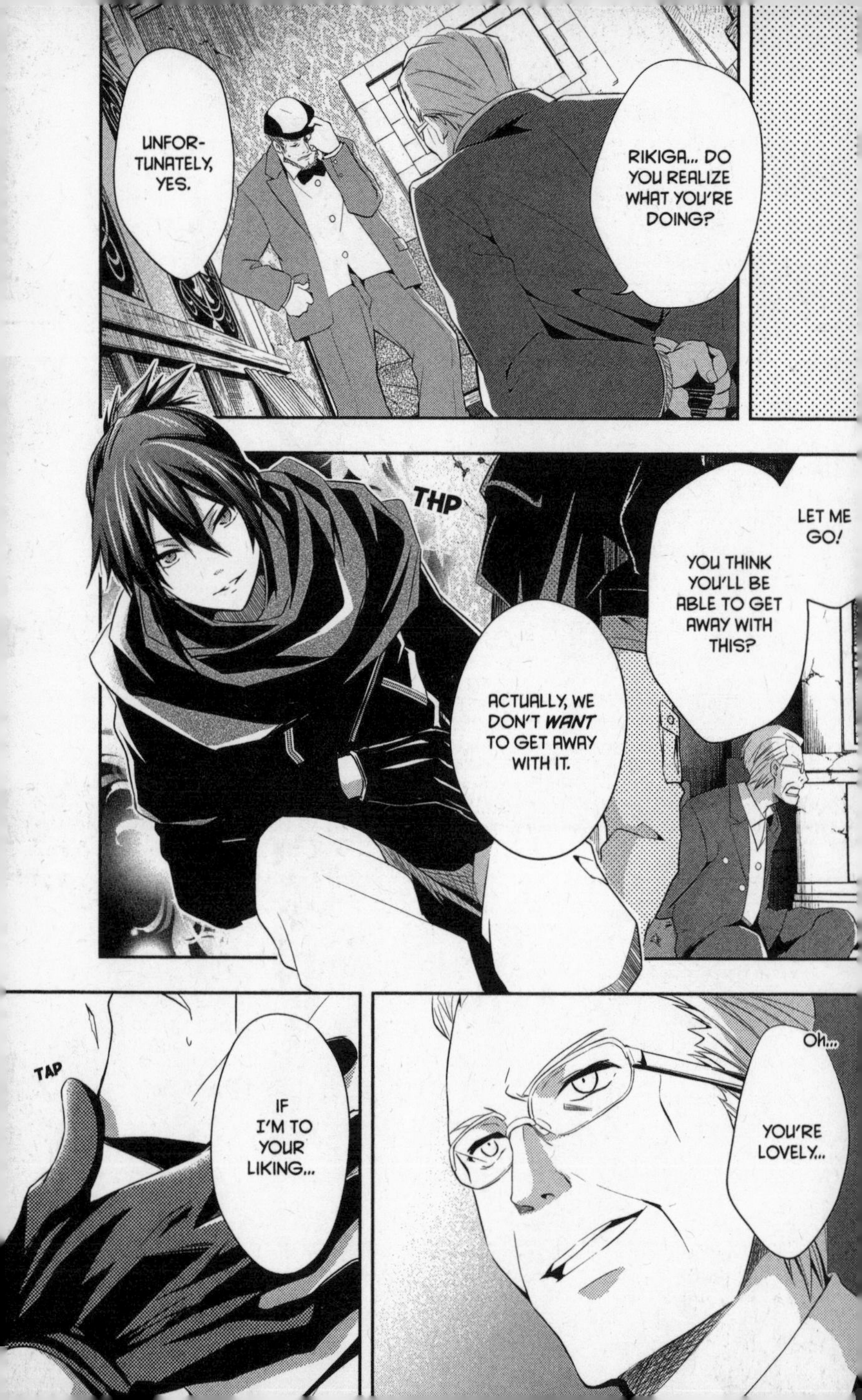
RIKIGA... DO YOU REALIZE WHAT YOU'RE DOING?
UNFOR-TUNATELY, YES.
LET ME GO!
YOU THINK YOU'LL BE ABLE TO GET AWAY WITH THIS?
THP
ACTUALLY, WE DON'T *WANT* TO GET AWAY WITH IT.
Oh...
YOU'RE LOVELY...
IF I'M TO YOUR LIKING...
TAP

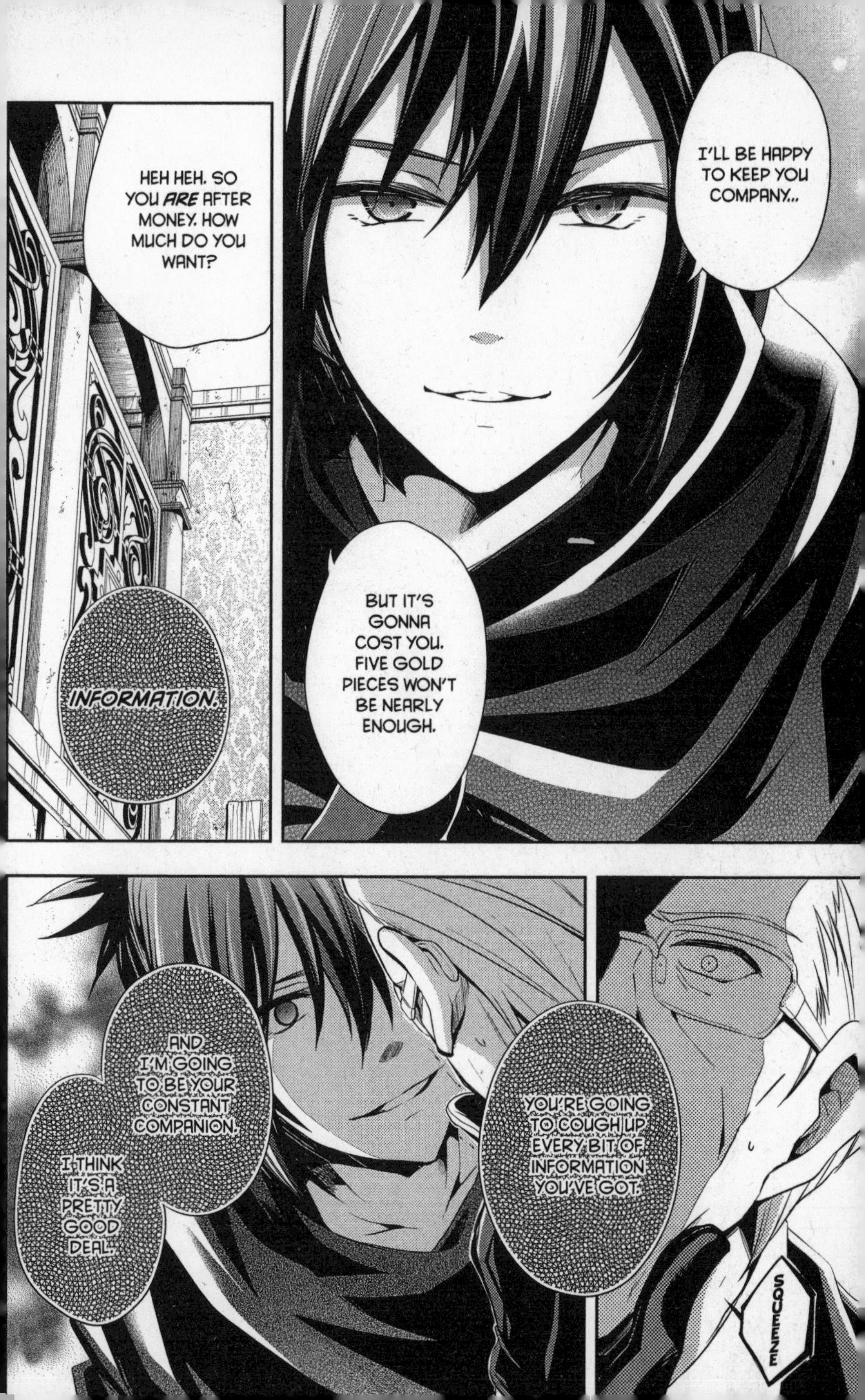
I'LL BE HAPPY TO KEEP YOU COMPANY...
BUT IT'S GONNA COST YOU. FIVE GOLD PIECES WON'T BE NEARLY ENOUGH.
HEH HEH. SO YOU *ARE* AFTER MONEY. HOW MUCH DO YOU WANT?
INFORMATION.
YOU'RE GOING TO COUGH UP EVERY BIT OF INFORMATION YOU'VE GOT.
SQUEEZE
AND I'M GOING TO BE YOUR CONSTANT COMPANION.
I THINK IT'S A PRETTY GOOD DEAL.

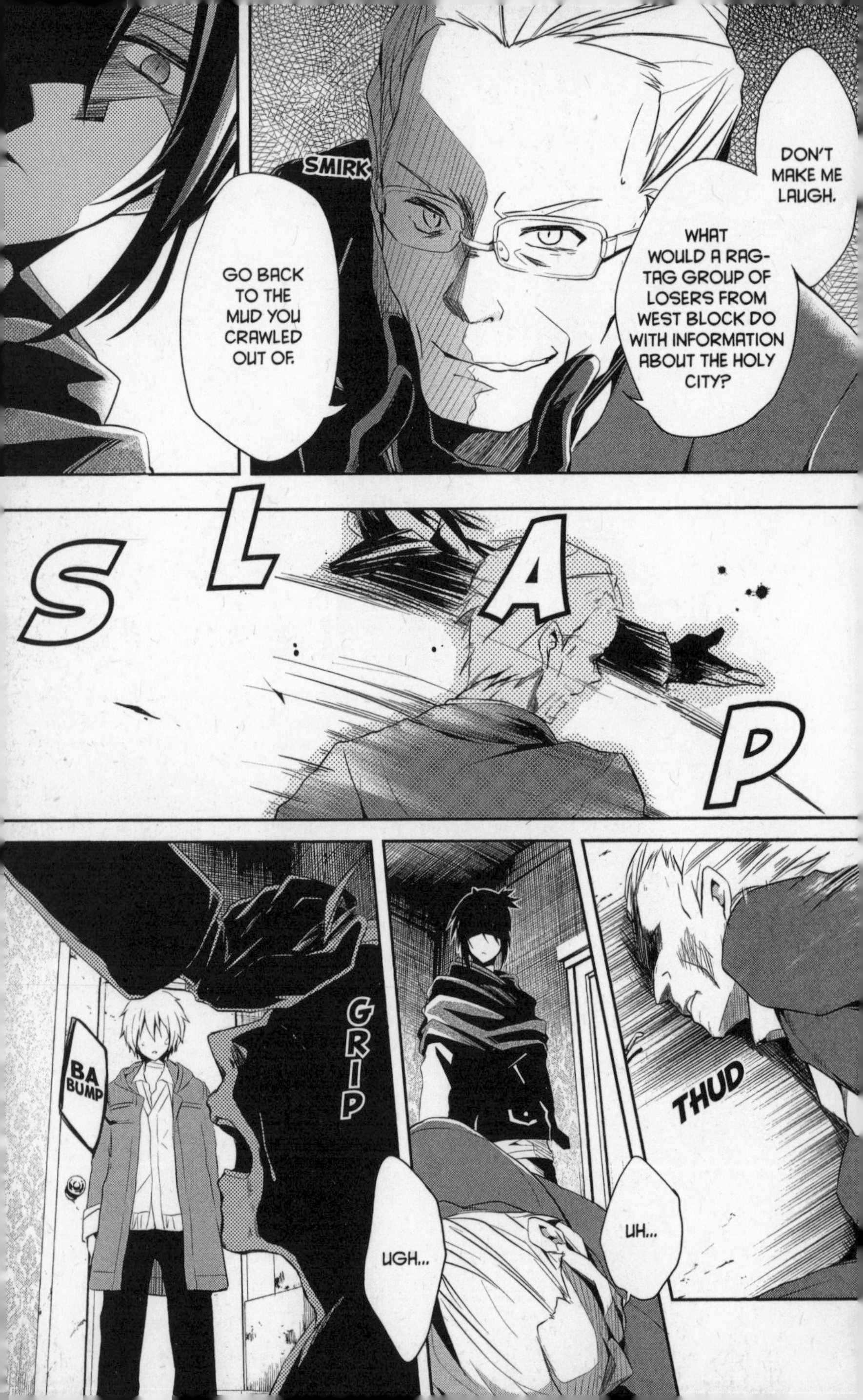
DON'T MAKE ME LAUGH.
WHAT WOULD A RAG-TAG GROUP OF LOSERS FROM WEST BLOCK DO WITH INFORMATION ABOUT THE HOLY CITY?
SMIRK
GO BACK TO THE MUD YOU CRAWLED OUT OF.
SLAP
THUD
UH...
UGH...
GRIP
BA BUMP

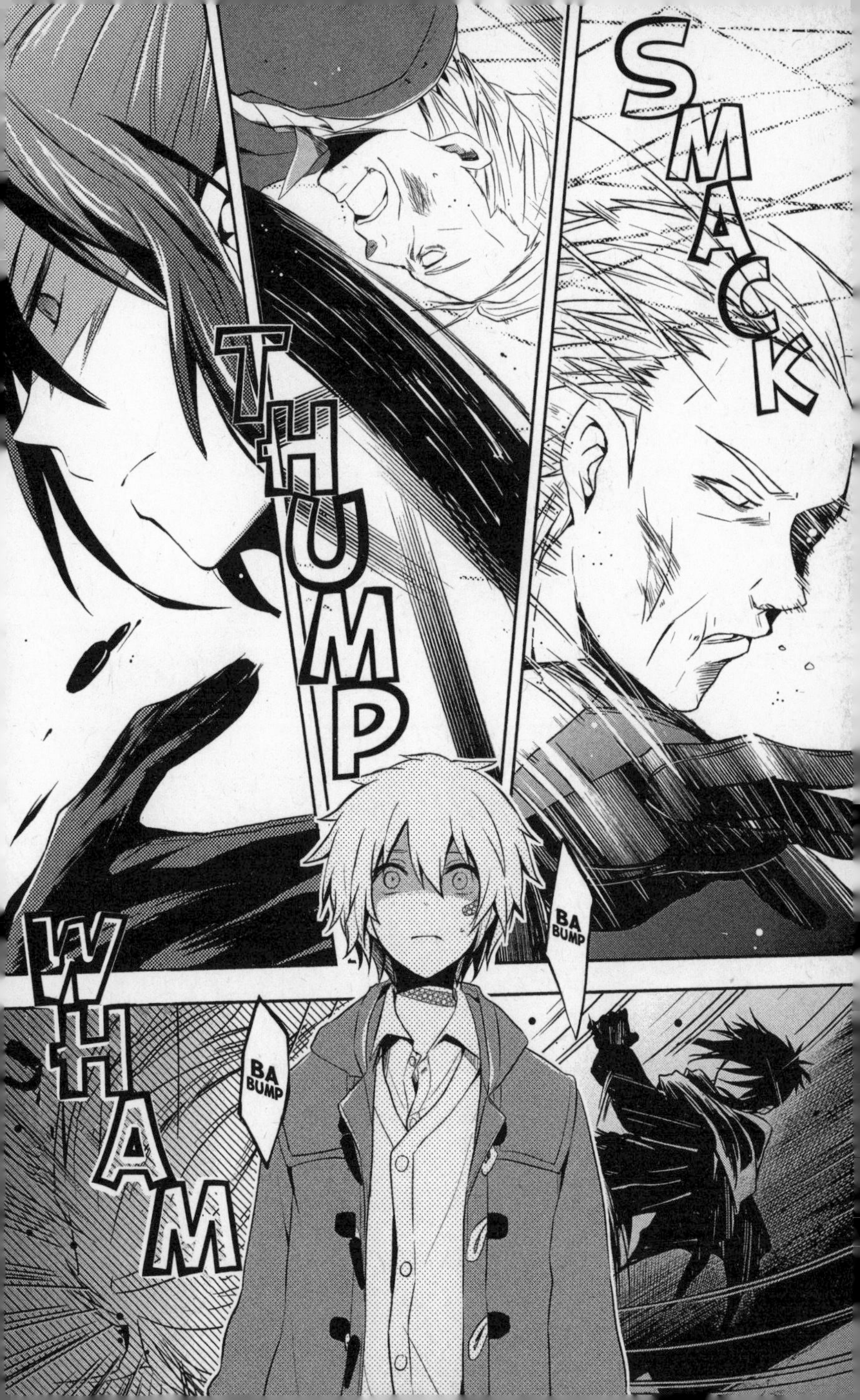
SMACK
THUMP
WHAM
BA BUMP
BA BUMP

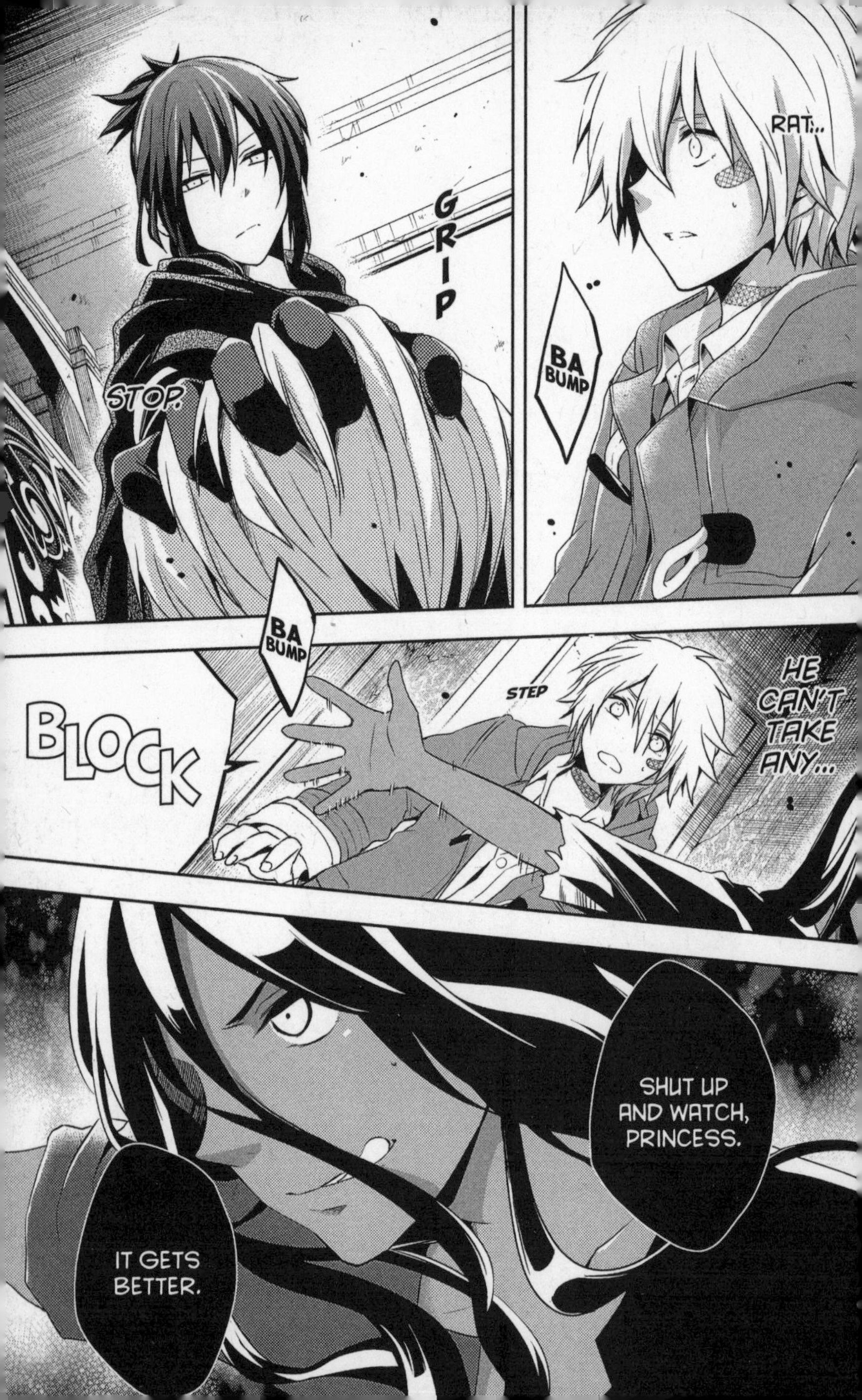
RAT...
BA BUMP
GRIP
STOP.
BA BUMP
HE CAN'T TAKE ANY...
STEP
BLOCK
SHUT UP AND WATCH, PRINCESS.
IT GETS BETTER.

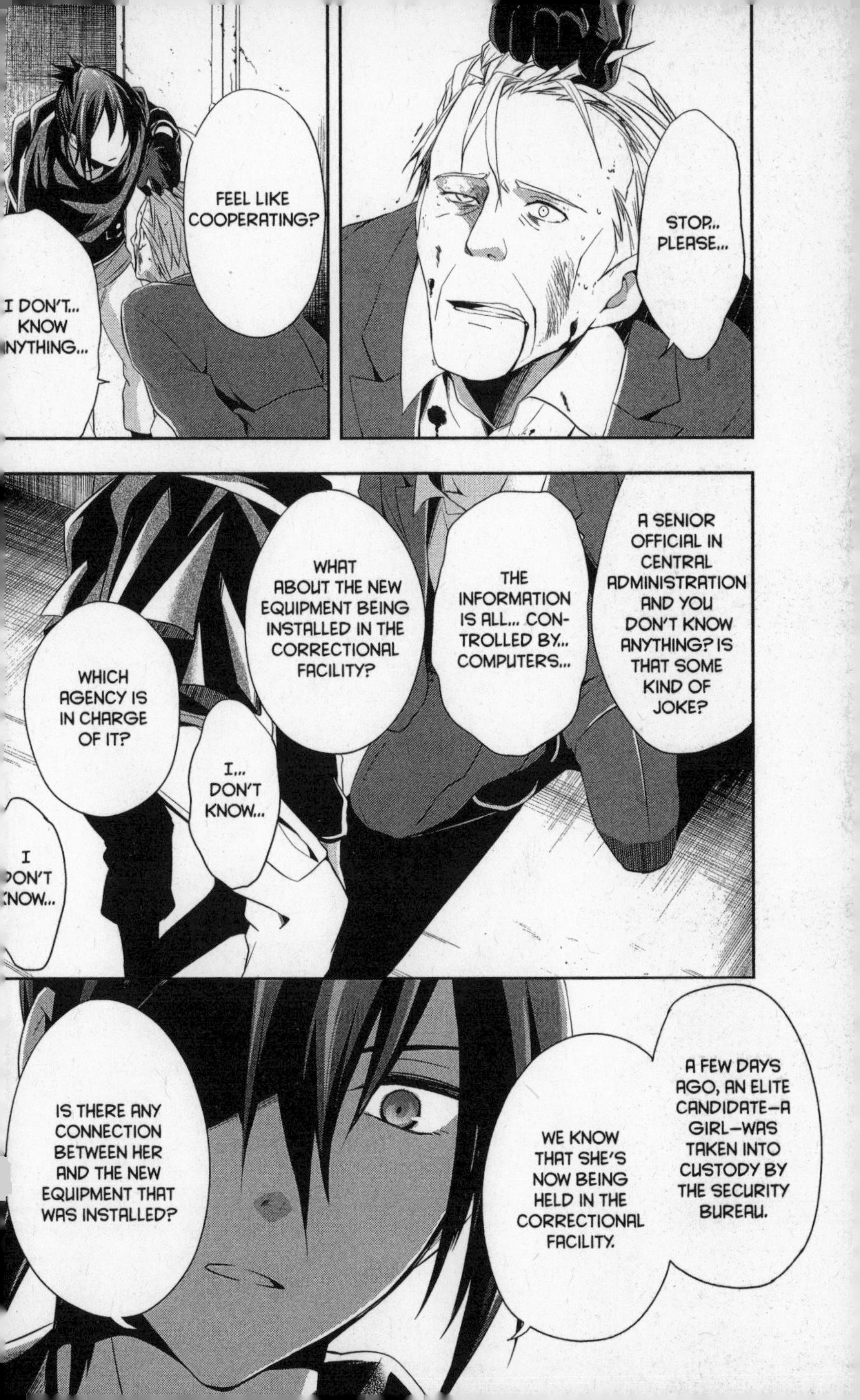
STOP.. PLEASE...
FEEL LIKE COOPERATING?
I DON'T... KNOW ANYTHING...
A SENIOR OFFICIAL IN CENTRAL ADMINISTRATION AND YOU DON'T KNOW ANYTHING? IS THAT SOME KIND OF JOKE?
THE INFORMATION IS ALL... CON-TROLLED BY... COMPUTERS...
WHAT ABOUT THE NEW EQUIPMENT BEING INSTALLED IN THE CORRECTIONAL FACILITY?
WHICH AGENCY IS IN CHARGE OF IT?
I... DON'T KNOW...
I DON'T KNOW...
A FEW DAYS AGO, AN ELITE CANDIDATE—A GIRL—WAS TAKEN INTO CUSTODY BY THE SECURITY BUREAU.
WE KNOW THAT SHE'S NOW BEING HELD IN THE CORRECTIONAL FACILITY.
IS THERE ANY CONNECTION BETWEEN HER AND THE NEW EQUIPMENT THAT WAS INSTALLED?

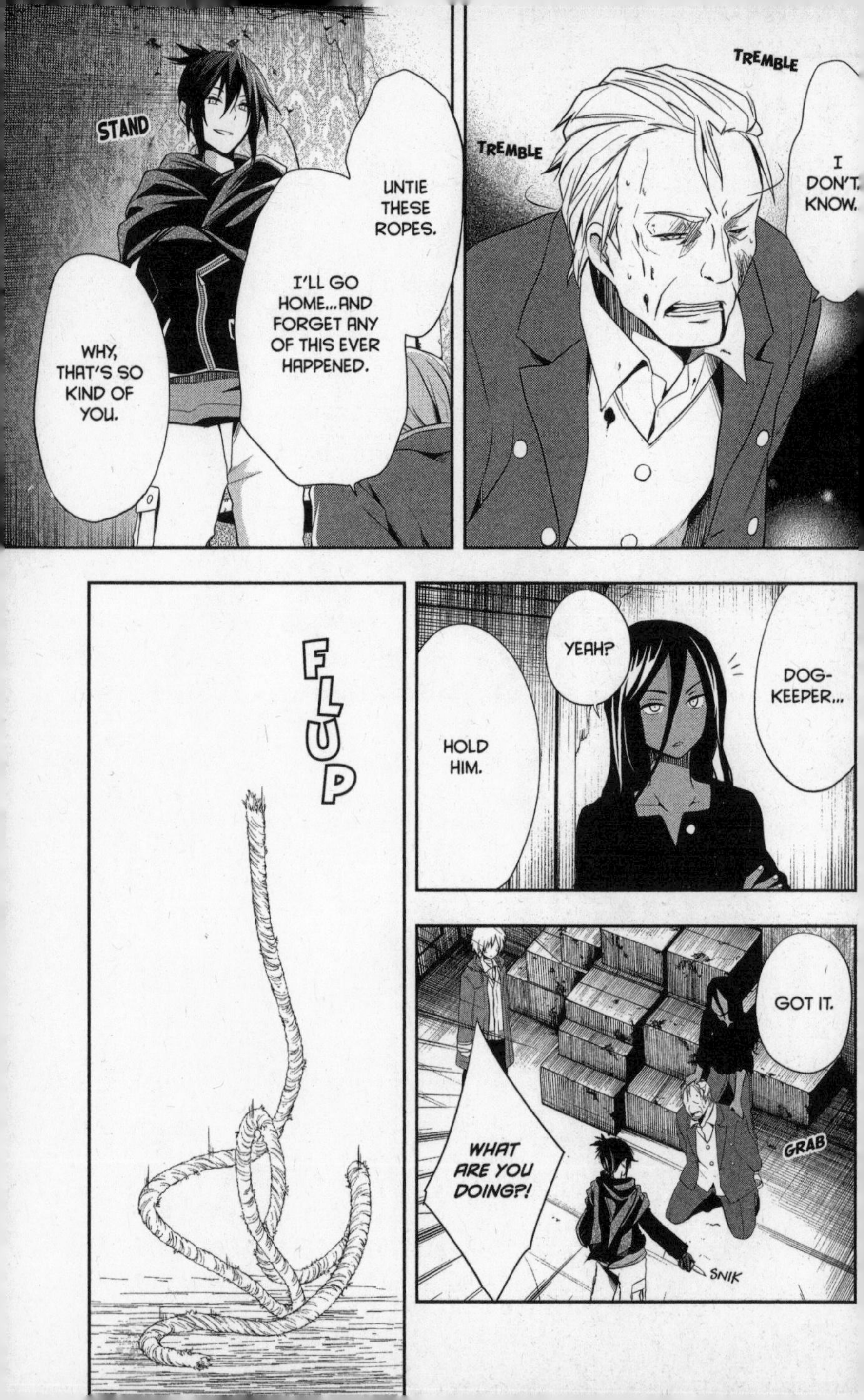
TREMBLE
I DON'T. KNOW.
TREMBLE
UNTIE THESE ROPES.
I'LL GO HOME...AND FORGET ANY OF THIS EVER HAPPENED.
STAND
WHY, THAT'S SO KIND OF YOU.
DOG-KEEPER...
YEAH?
HOLD HIM.
GOT IT.
GRAB
WHAT ARE YOU DOING?!
SNIK
FLUP

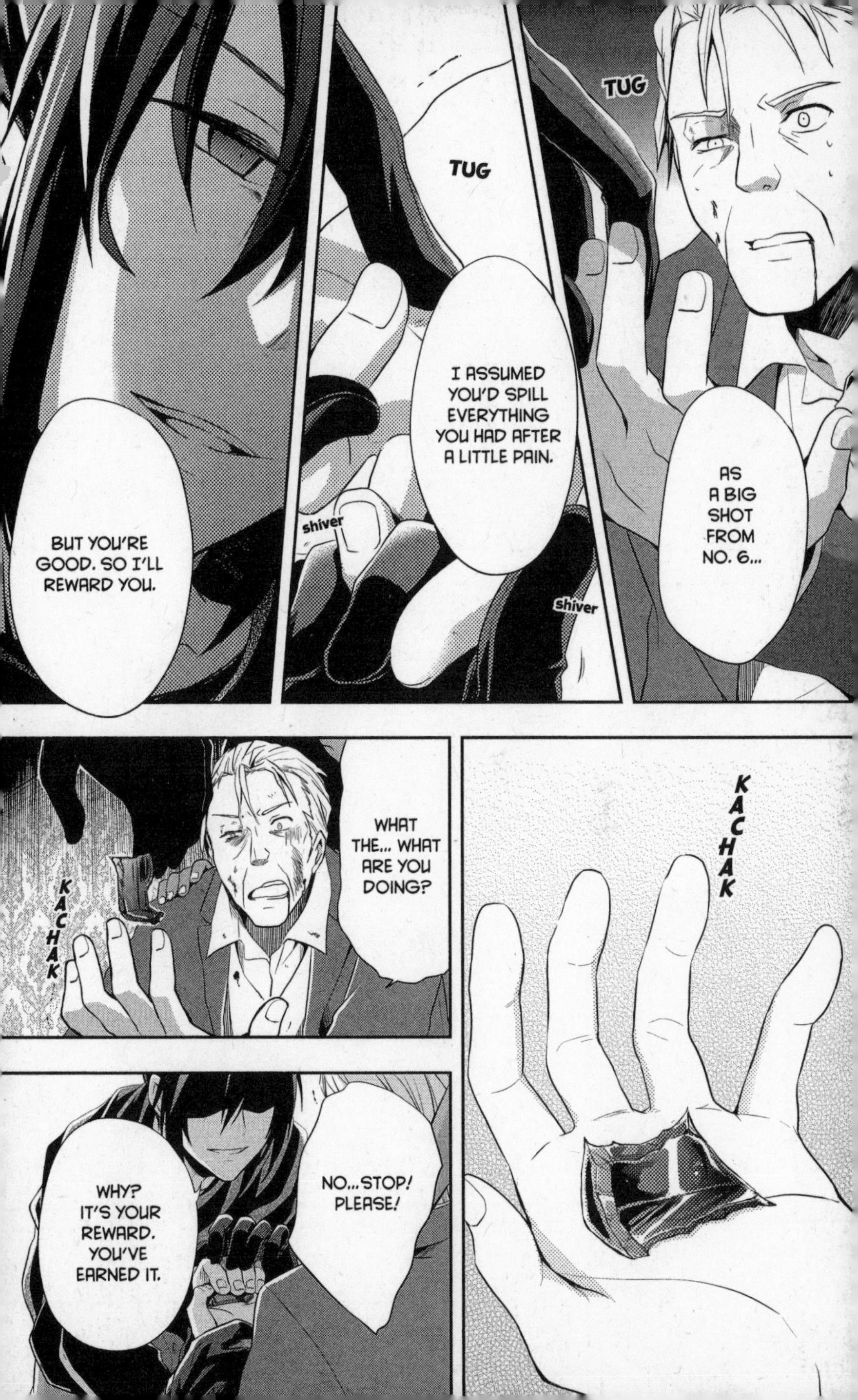
TUG
AS A BIG SHOT FROM NO. 6...
shiver
TUG
I ASSUMED YOU'D SPILL EVERYTHING YOU HAD AFTER A LITTLE PAIN.
shiver
BUT YOU'RE GOOD. SO I'LL REWARD YOU.
KACHAK
WHAT THE... WHAT ARE YOU DOING?
KACHAK
NO...STOP! PLEASE!
WHY? IT'S YOUR REWARD. YOU'VE EARNED IT.

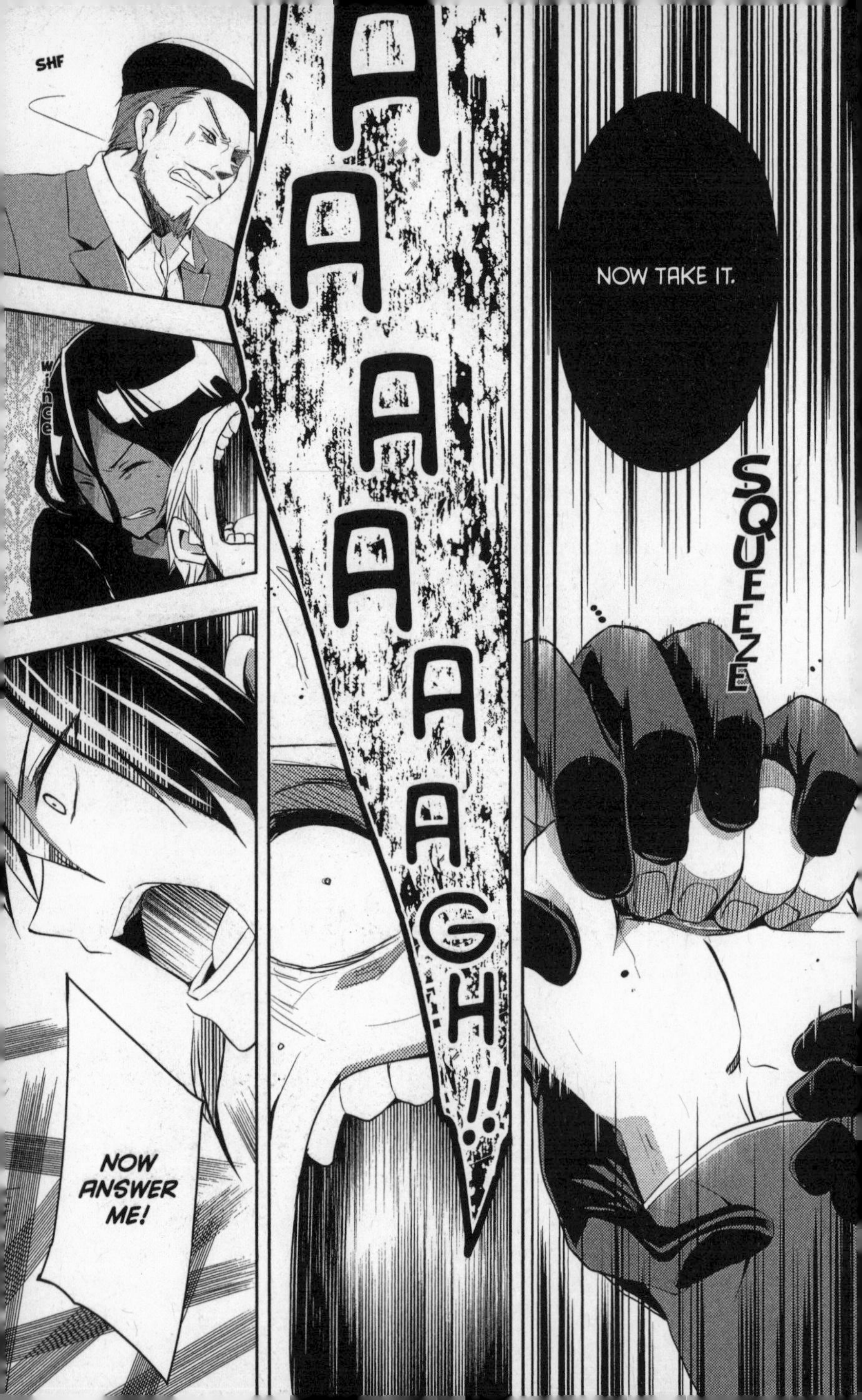
NOW TAKE IT.
SQUEEZE
AAAAAAGH!!
SHF
wince
NOW ANSWER ME!

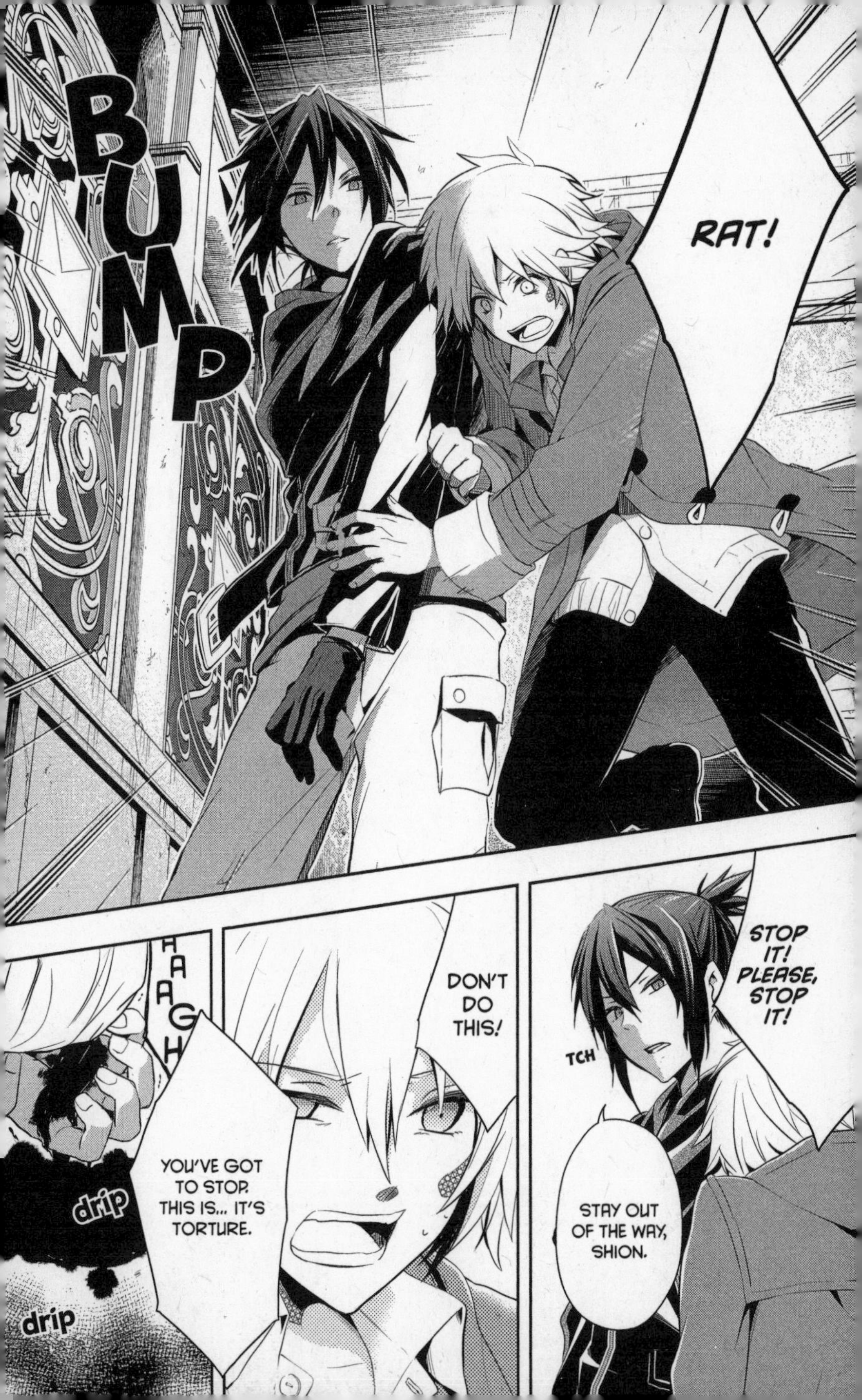
RAT!
BUMP
STOP IT! PLEASE, STOP IT!
TCH
STAY OUT OF THE WAY, SHION.
DON'T DO THIS!
YOU'VE GOT TO STOP. THIS IS... IT'S TORTURE.
HAAGH
drip
drip

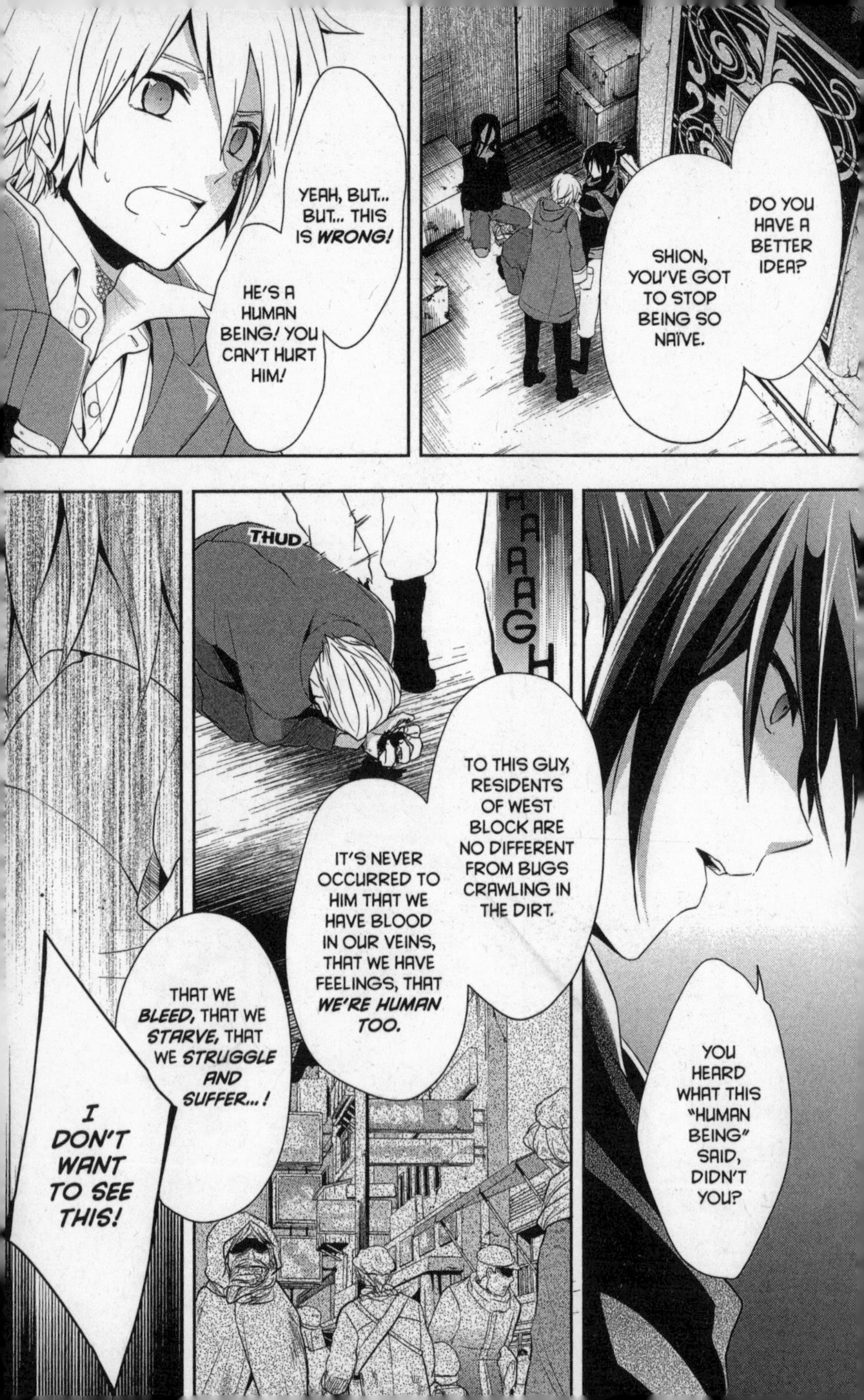
DO YOU HAVE A BETTER IDEA?
SHION, YOU'VE GOT TO STOP BEING SO NAÏVE.
YEAH, BUT... BUT... THIS IS *WRONG!*
HE'S A HUMAN BEING! YOU CAN'T HURT HIM!
YOU HEARD WHAT THIS "HUMAN BEING" SAID, DIDN'T YOU?
AAAAGH
THUD
TO THIS GUY, RESIDENTS OF WEST BLOCK ARE NO DIFFERENT FROM BUGS CRAWLING IN THE DIRT.
IT'S NEVER OCCURRED TO HIM THAT WE HAVE BLOOD IN OUR VEINS, THAT WE HAVE FEELINGS, THAT *WE'RE HUMAN TOO.*
THAT WE *BLEED,* THAT WE *STARVE,* THAT WE *STRUGGLE AND SUFFER...!*
I DON'T WANT TO SEE THIS!

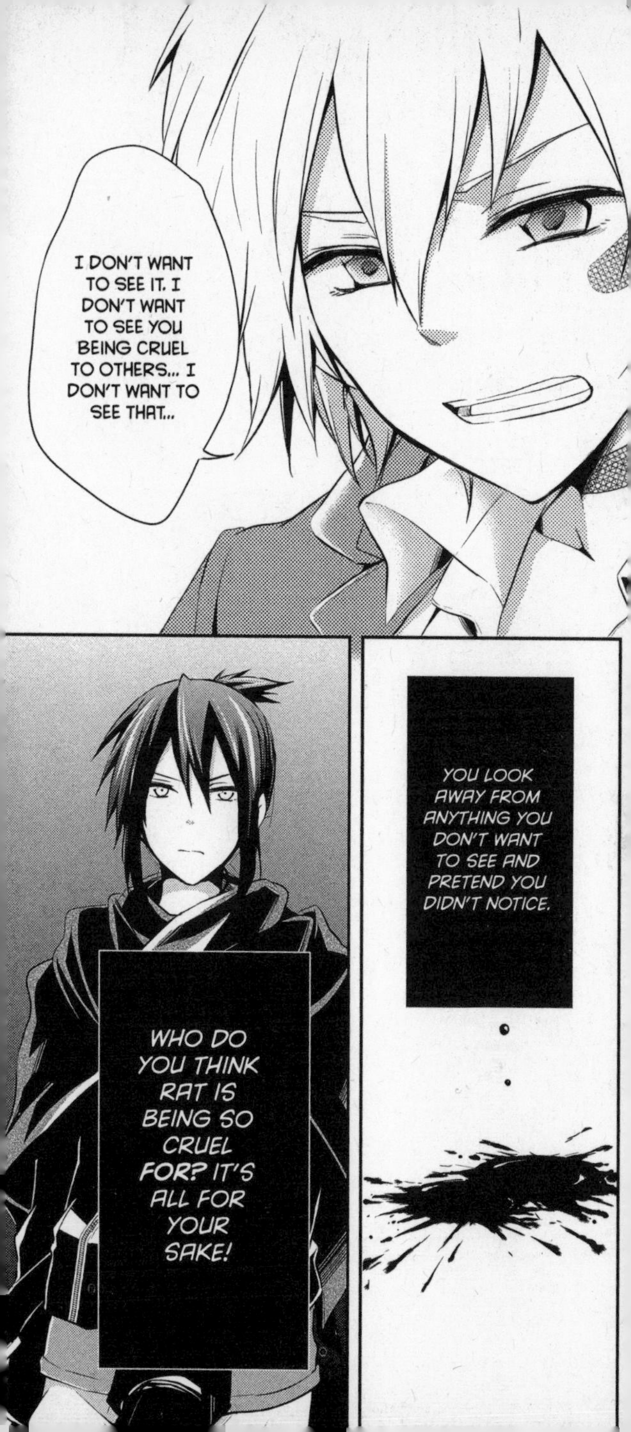
I DON'T WANT TO SEE IT. I DON'T WANT TO SEE YOU BEING CRUEL TO OTHERS... I DON'T WANT TO SEE THAT...
YOU LOOK AWAY FROM ANYTHING YOU DON'T WANT TO SEE AND PRETEND YOU DIDN'T NOTICE.
WHO DO YOU THINK RAT IS BEING SO CRUEL FOR? IT'S ALL FOR YOUR SAKE!

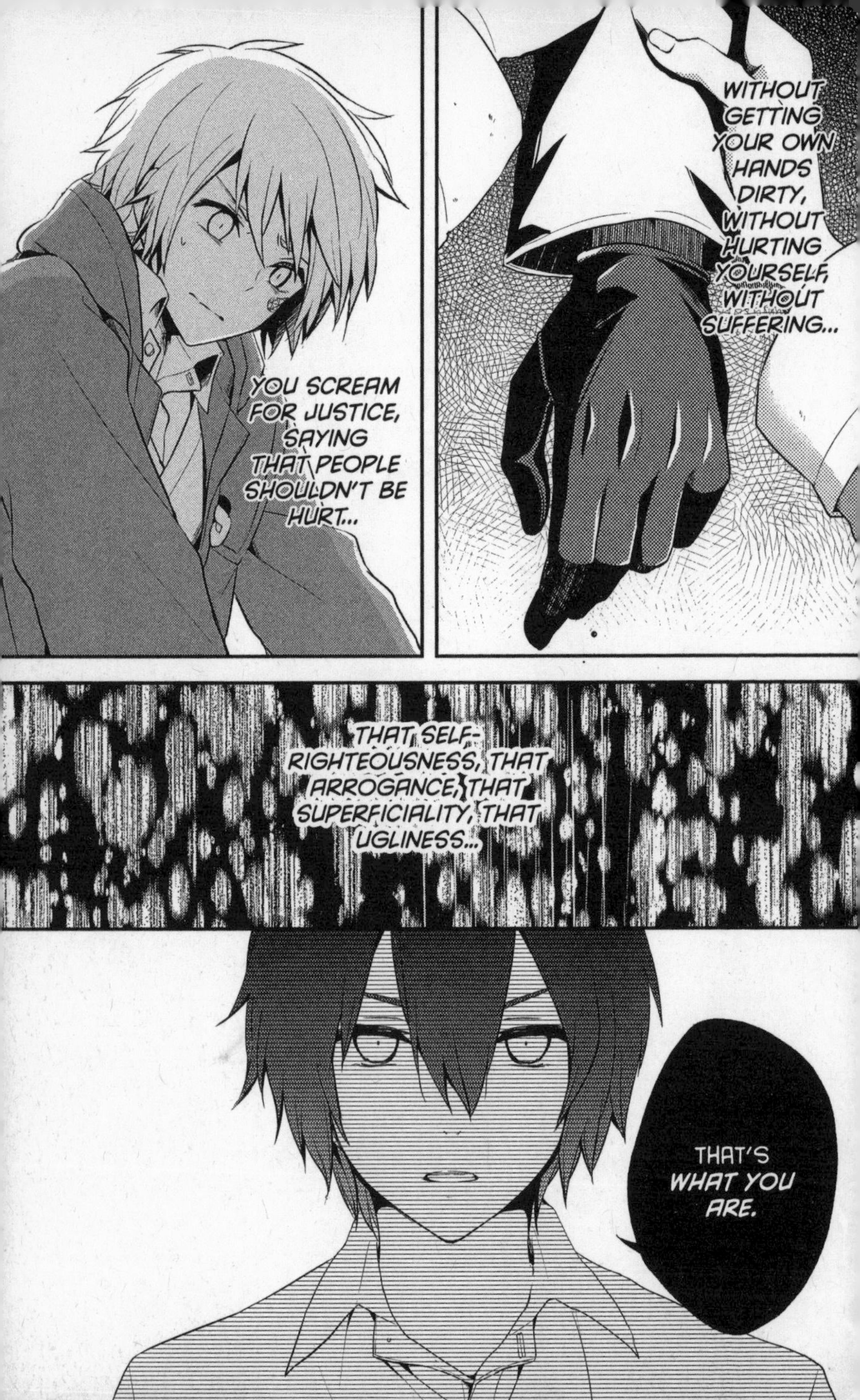

WITHOUT GETTING YOUR OWN HANDS DIRTY, WITHOUT HURTING YOURSELF, WITHOUT SUFFERING...
YOU SCREAM FOR JUSTICE, SAYING THAT PEOPLE SHOULDN'T BE HURT...
THAT SELF-RIGHTEOUSNESS, THAT ARROGANCE, THAT SUPERFICIALITY, THAT UGLINESS...
THAT'S WHAT YOU ARE.

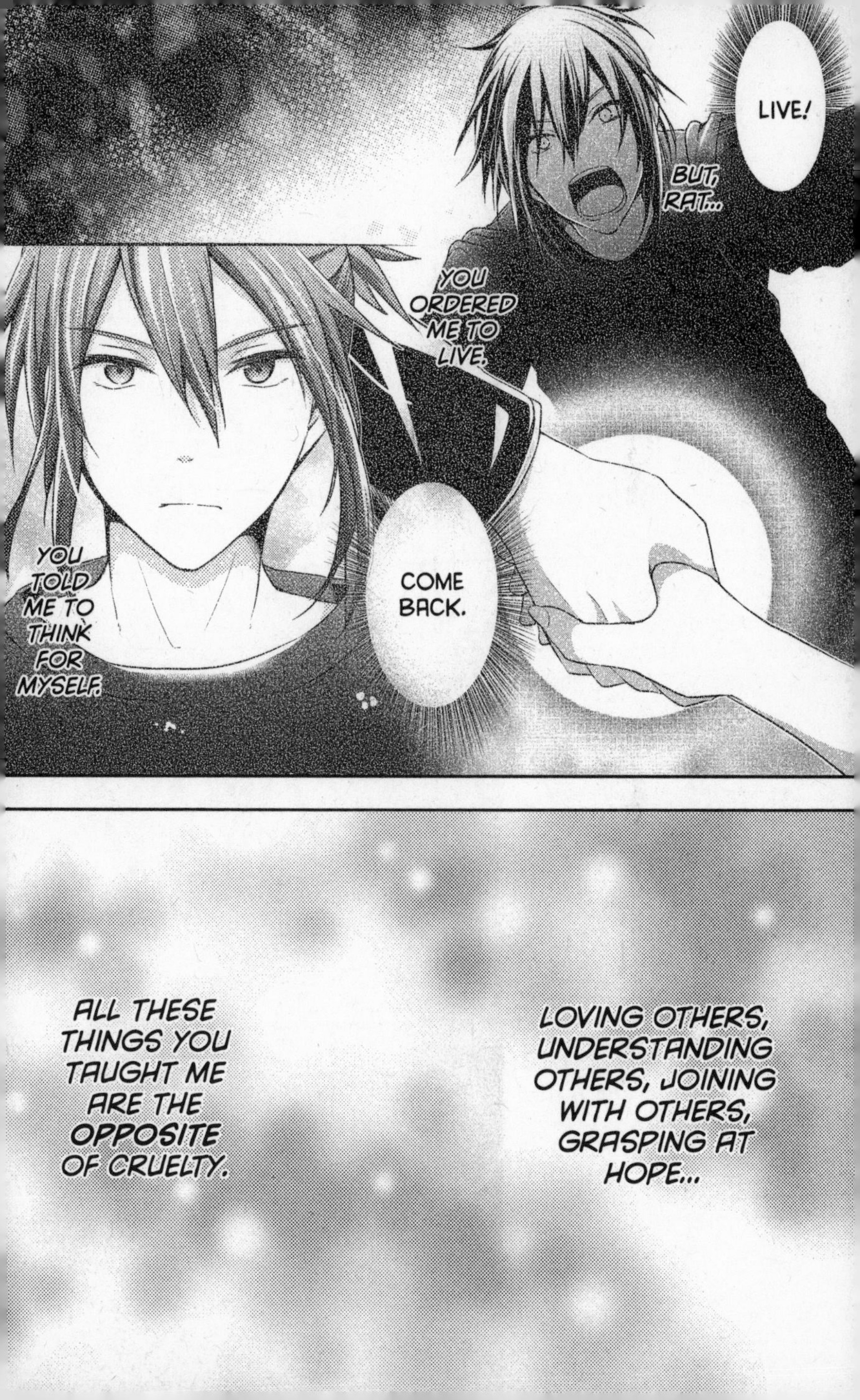
LIVE!
BUT, RAT...
YOU ORDERED ME TO LIVE.
COME BACK.
YOU TOLD ME TO THINK FOR MYSELF.
LOVING OTHERS, UNDERSTANDING OTHERS, JOINING WITH OTHERS, GRASPING AT HOPE...
ALL THESE THINGS YOU TAUGHT ME ARE THE OPPOSITE OF CRUELTY.

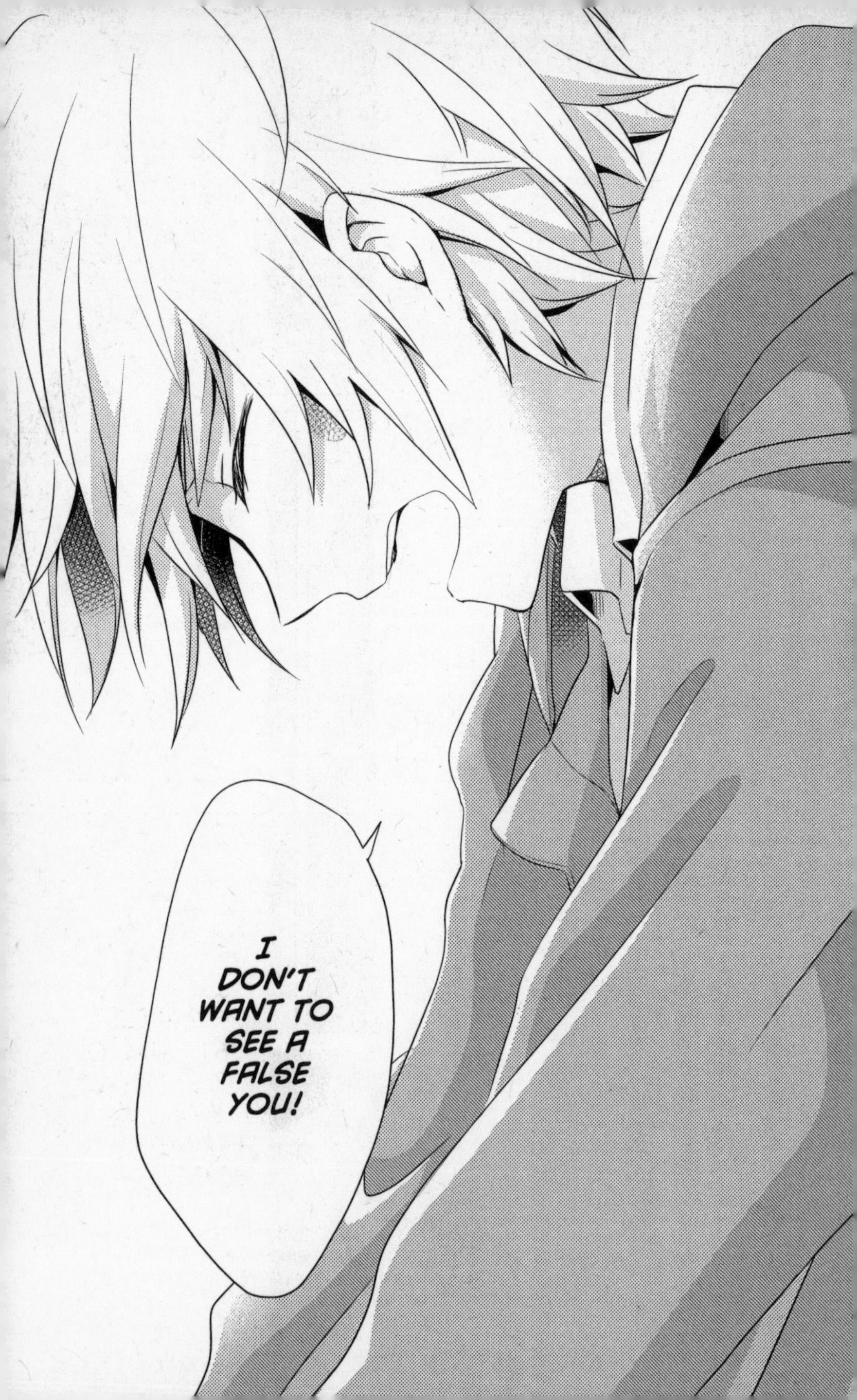
I DON'T WANT TO SEE A FALSE YOU!

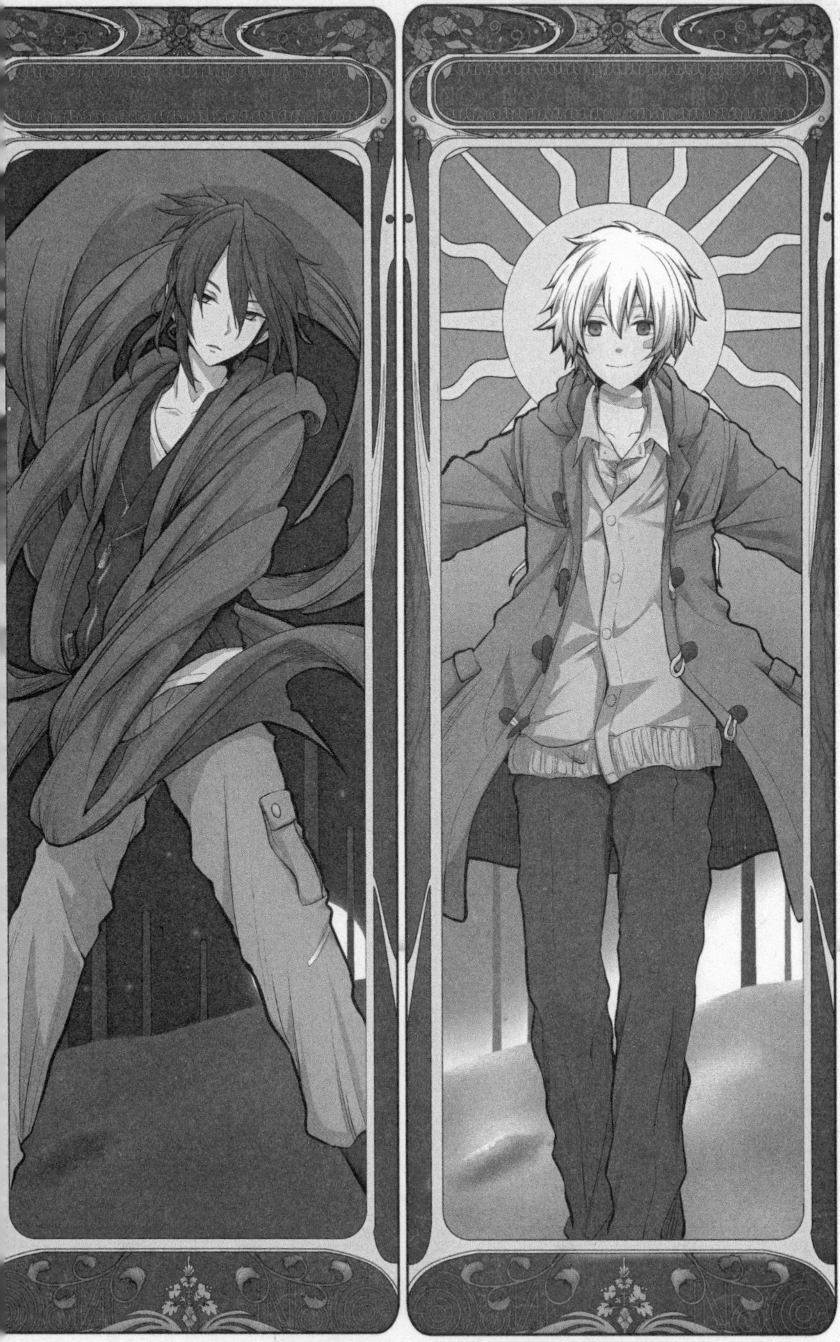

Chapter 15: The Stage Grows Dark

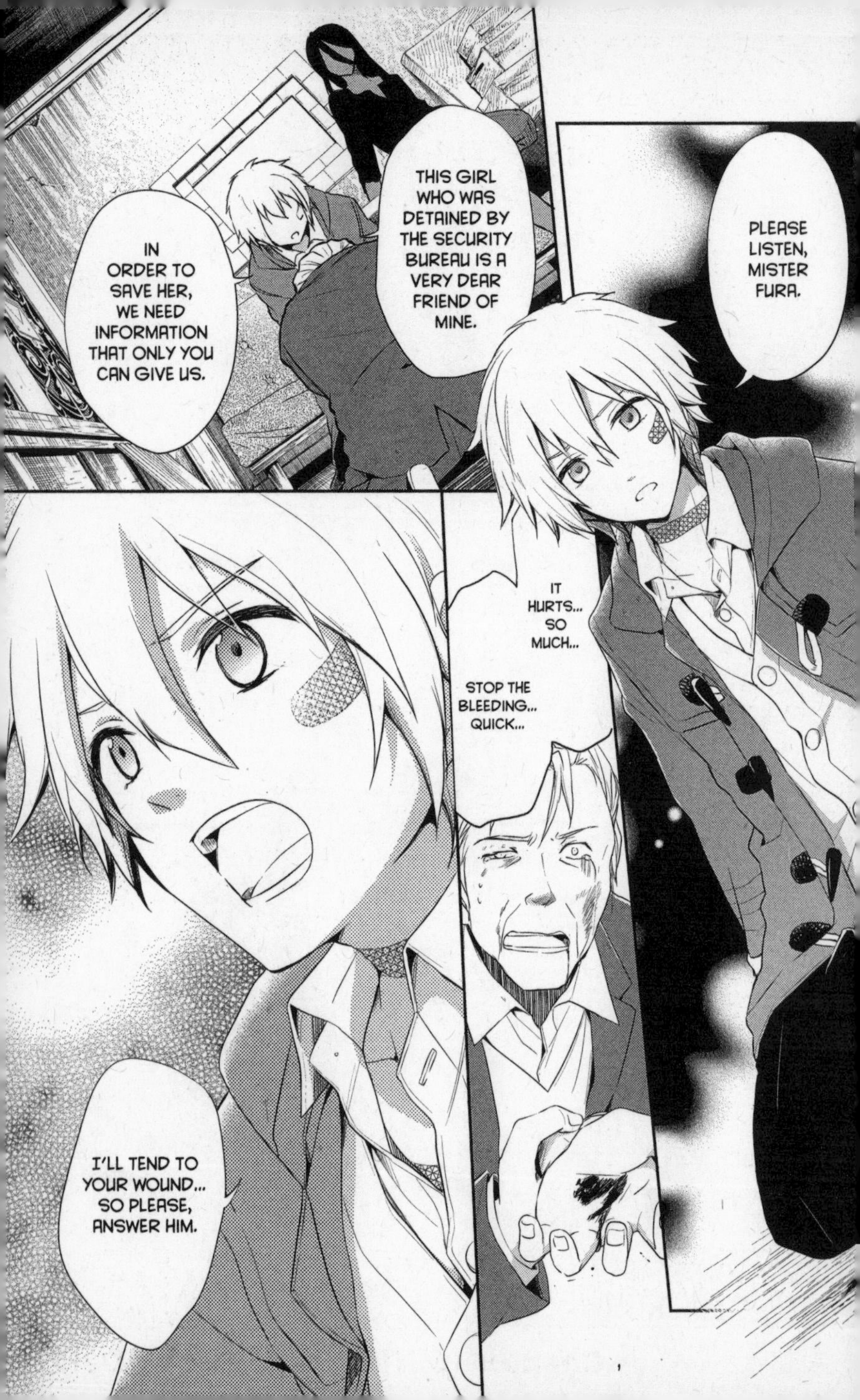
PLEASE LISTEN, MISTER FURA.
THIS GIRL WHO WAS DETAINED BY THE SECURITY BUREAU IS A VERY DEAR FRIEND OF MINE.
IN ORDER TO SAVE HER, WE NEED INFORMATION THAT ONLY YOU CAN GIVE US.
IT HURTS... SO MUCH...
STOP THE BLEEDING... QUICK...
I'LL TEND TO YOUR WOUND... SO PLEASE, ANSWER HIM.

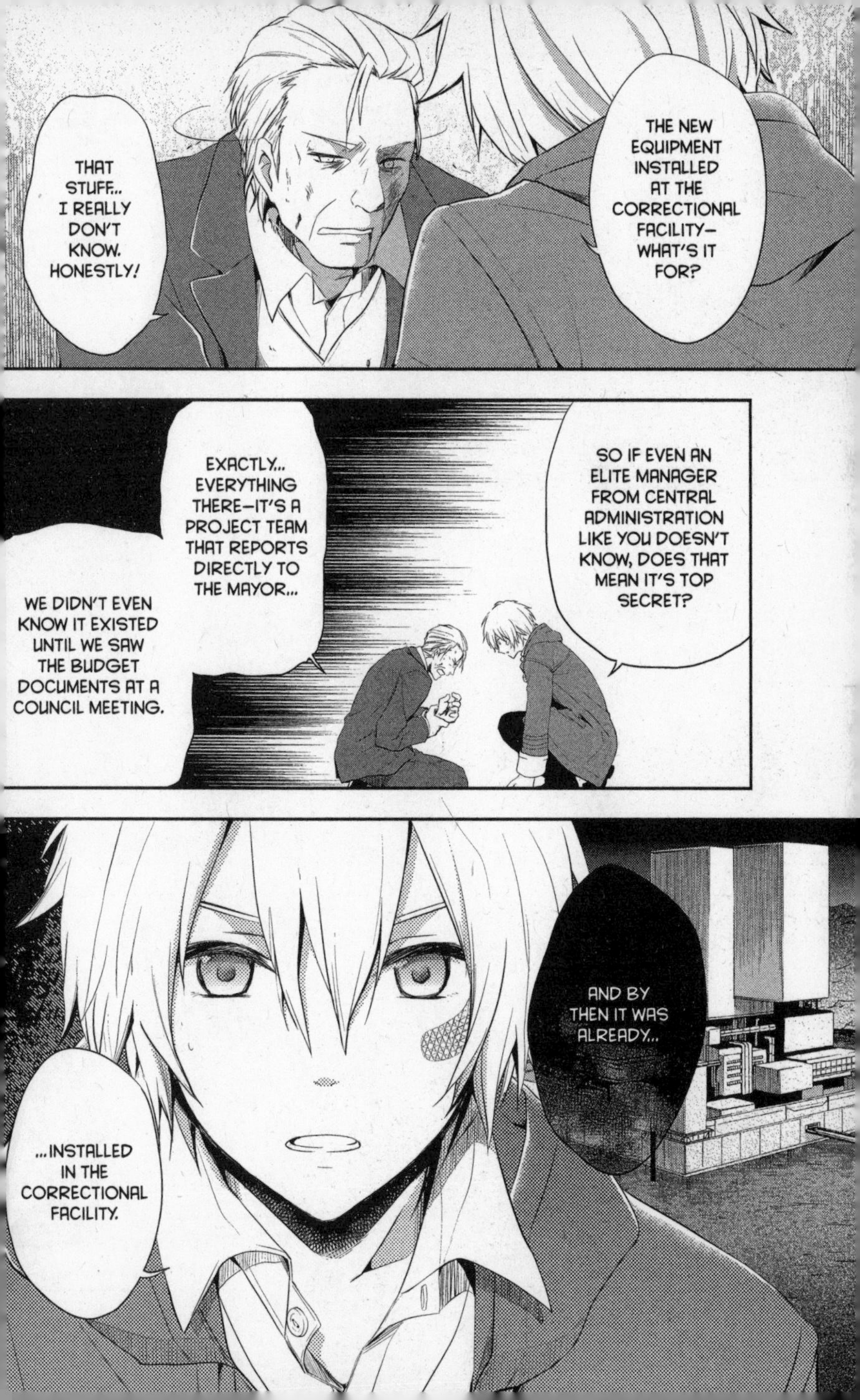
THE NEW EQUIPMENT INSTALLED AT THE CORRECTIONAL FACILITY—WHAT'S IT FOR?
THAT STUFF... I REALLY DON'T KNOW. HONESTLY!
SO IF EVEN AN ELITE MANAGER FROM CENTRAL ADMINISTRATION LIKE YOU DOESN'T KNOW, DOES THAT MEAN IT'S TOP SECRET?
EXACTLY... EVERYTHING THERE—IT'S A PROJECT TEAM THAT REPORTS DIRECTLY TO THE MAYOR...
WE DIDN'T EVEN KNOW IT EXISTED UNTIL WE SAW THE BUDGET DOCUMENTS AT A COUNCIL MEETING.
AND BY THEN IT WAS ALREADY...
...INSTALLED IN THE CORRECTIONAL FACILITY.

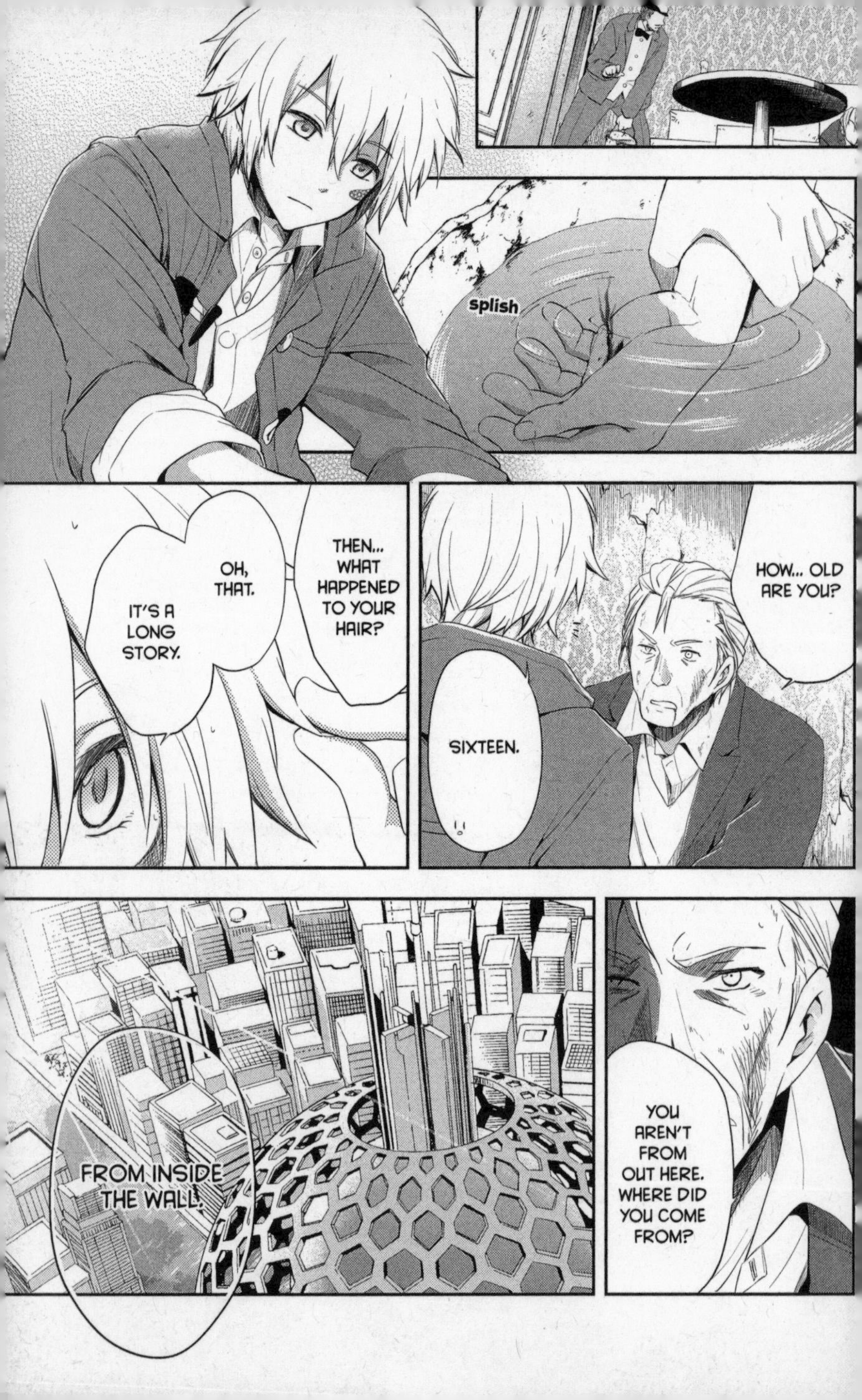
splish
HOW... OLD ARE YOU?
SIXTEEN.
THEN... WHAT HAPPENED TO YOUR HAIR?
OH, THAT.
IT'S A LONG STORY.
YOU AREN'T FROM OUT HERE. WHERE DID YOU COME FROM?
FROM INSIDE THE WALL.

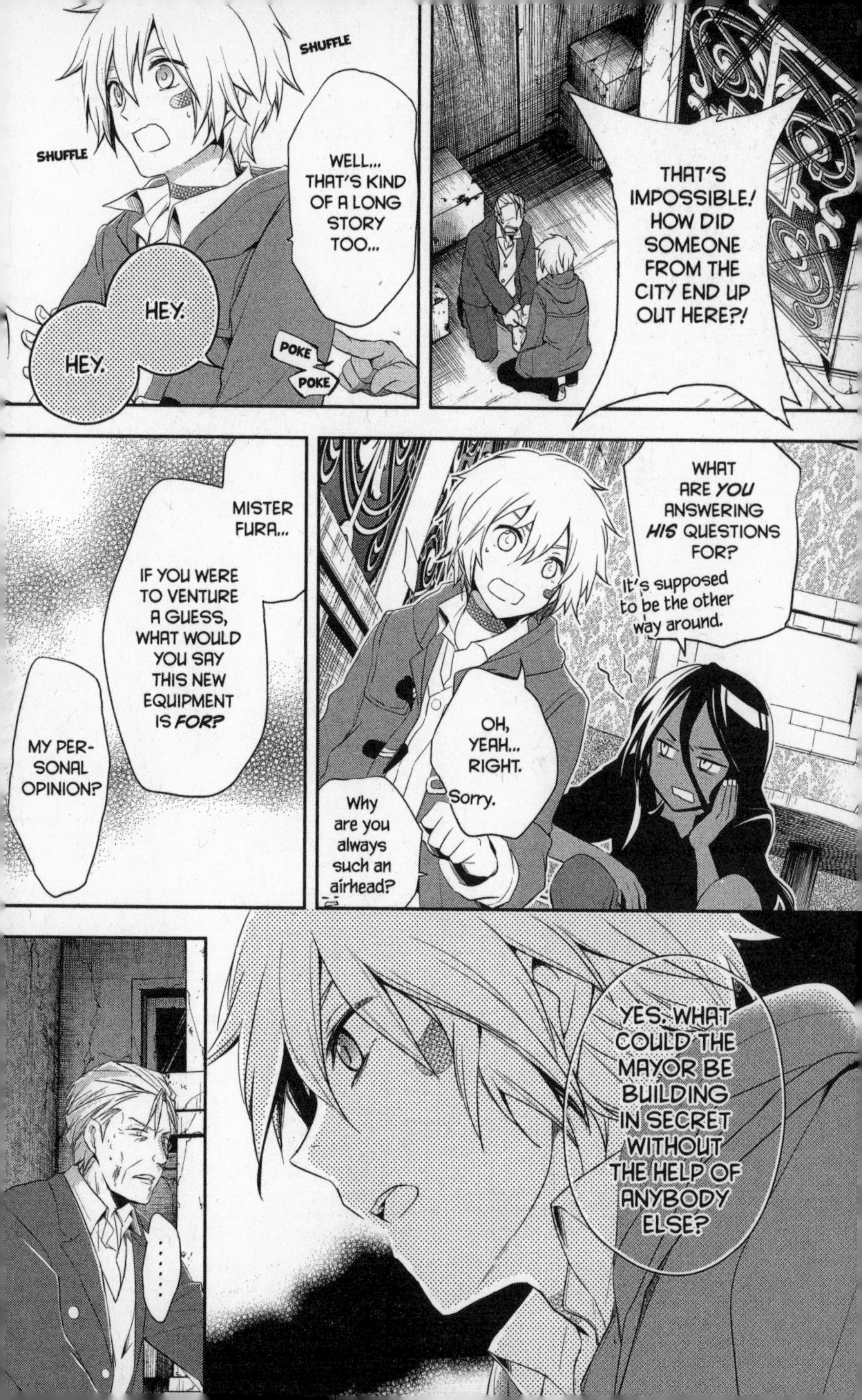
THAT'S IMPOSSIBLE! HOW DID SOMEONE FROM THE CITY END UP OUT HERE?!
SHUFFLE
WELL... THAT'S KIND OF A LONG STORY TOO...
SHUFFLE
HEY.
HEY.
POKE
POKE
WHAT ARE YOU ANSWERING HIS QUESTIONS FOR?
It's supposed to be the other way around.
OH, YEAH... RIGHT.
Sorry.
Why are you always such an airhead?
MISTER FURA...
IF YOU WERE TO VENTURE A GUESS, WHAT WOULD YOU SAY THIS NEW EQUIPMENT IS FOR?
MY PER-SONAL OPINION?
YES. WHAT COULD THE MAYOR BE BUILDING IN SECRET WITHOUT THE HELP OF ANYBODY ELSE?
......

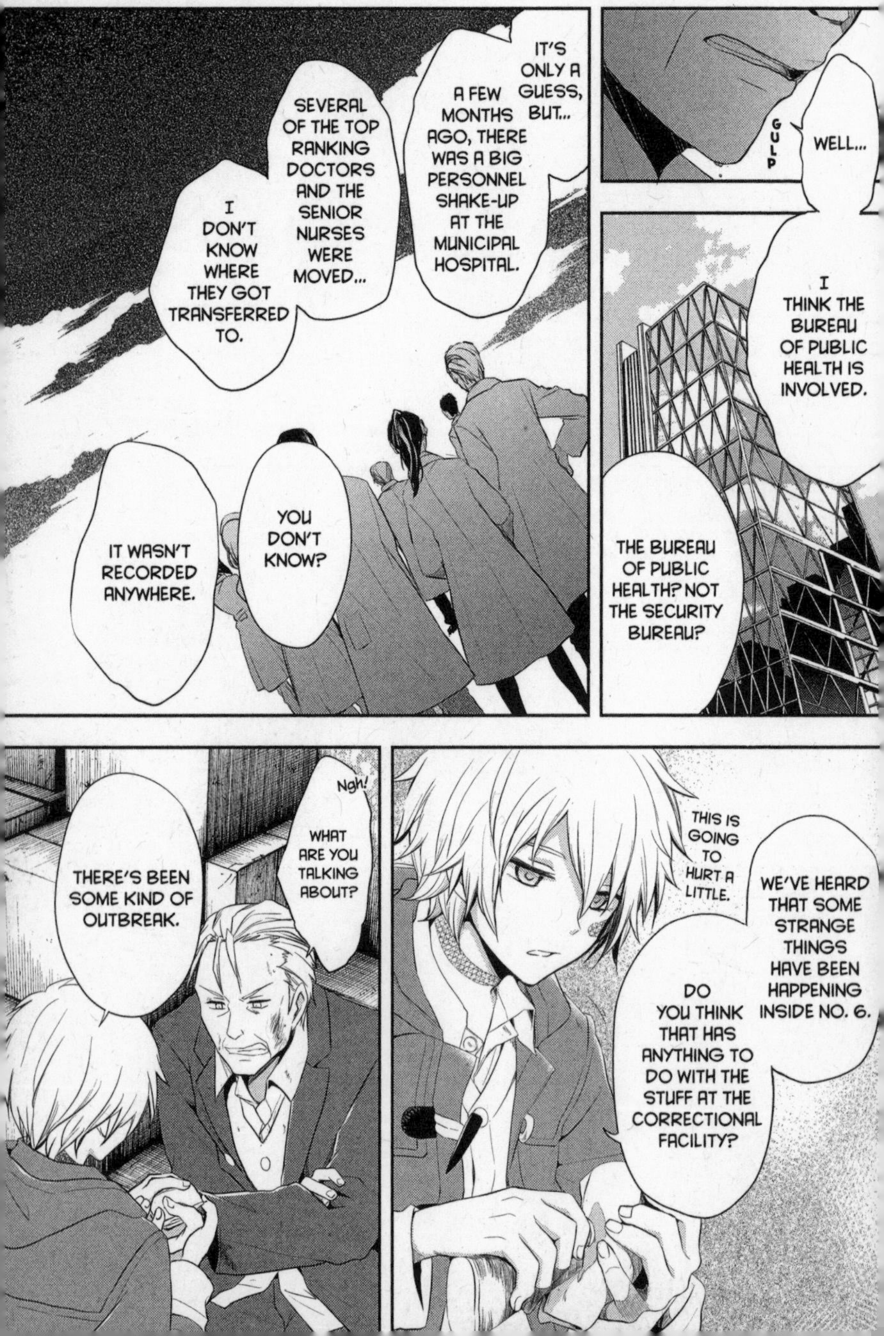
GULP
WELL...
I THINK THE BUREAU OF PUBLIC HEALTH IS INVOLVED.
THE BUREAU OF PUBLIC HEALTH? NOT THE SECURITY BUREAU?
IT'S ONLY A GUESS, BUT...
A FEW MONTHS AGO, THERE WAS A BIG PERSONNEL SHAKE-UP AT THE MUNICIPAL HOSPITAL.
SEVERAL OF THE TOP RANKING DOCTORS AND THE SENIOR NURSES WERE MOVED...
I DON'T KNOW WHERE THEY GOT TRANSFERRED TO.
YOU DON'T KNOW?
IT WASN'T RECORDED ANYWHERE.
WE'VE HEARD THAT SOME STRANGE THINGS HAVE BEEN HAPPENING INSIDE NO. 6.
DO YOU THINK THAT HAS ANYTHING TO DO WITH THE STUFF AT THE CORRECTIONAL FACILITY?
THIS IS GOING TO HURT A LITTLE.
Ngh!
WHAT ARE YOU TALKING ABOUT?
THERE'S BEEN SOME KIND OF OUTBREAK.

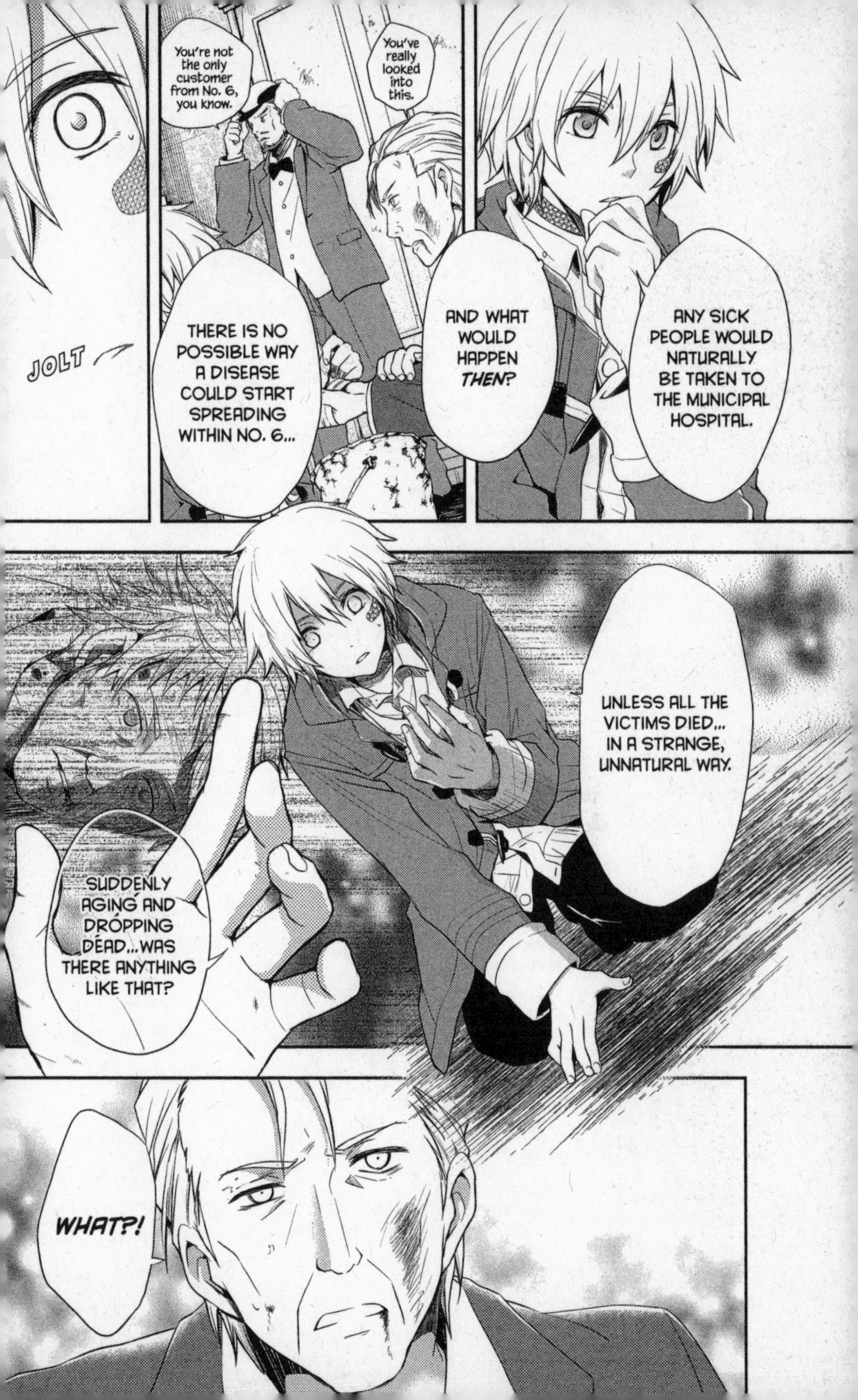
ANY SICK PEOPLE WOULD NATURALLY BE TAKEN TO THE MUNICIPAL HOSPITAL.
You've really looked into this.
You're not the only customer from No. 6, you know.
AND WHAT WOULD HAPPEN *THEN*?
THERE IS NO POSSIBLE WAY A DISEASE COULD START SPREADING WITHIN NO. 6...
JOLT
UNLESS ALL THE VICTIMS DIED... IN A STRANGE, UNNATURAL WAY.
SUDDENLY AGING AND DROPPING DEAD...WAS THERE ANYTHING LIKE THAT?
WHAT?!

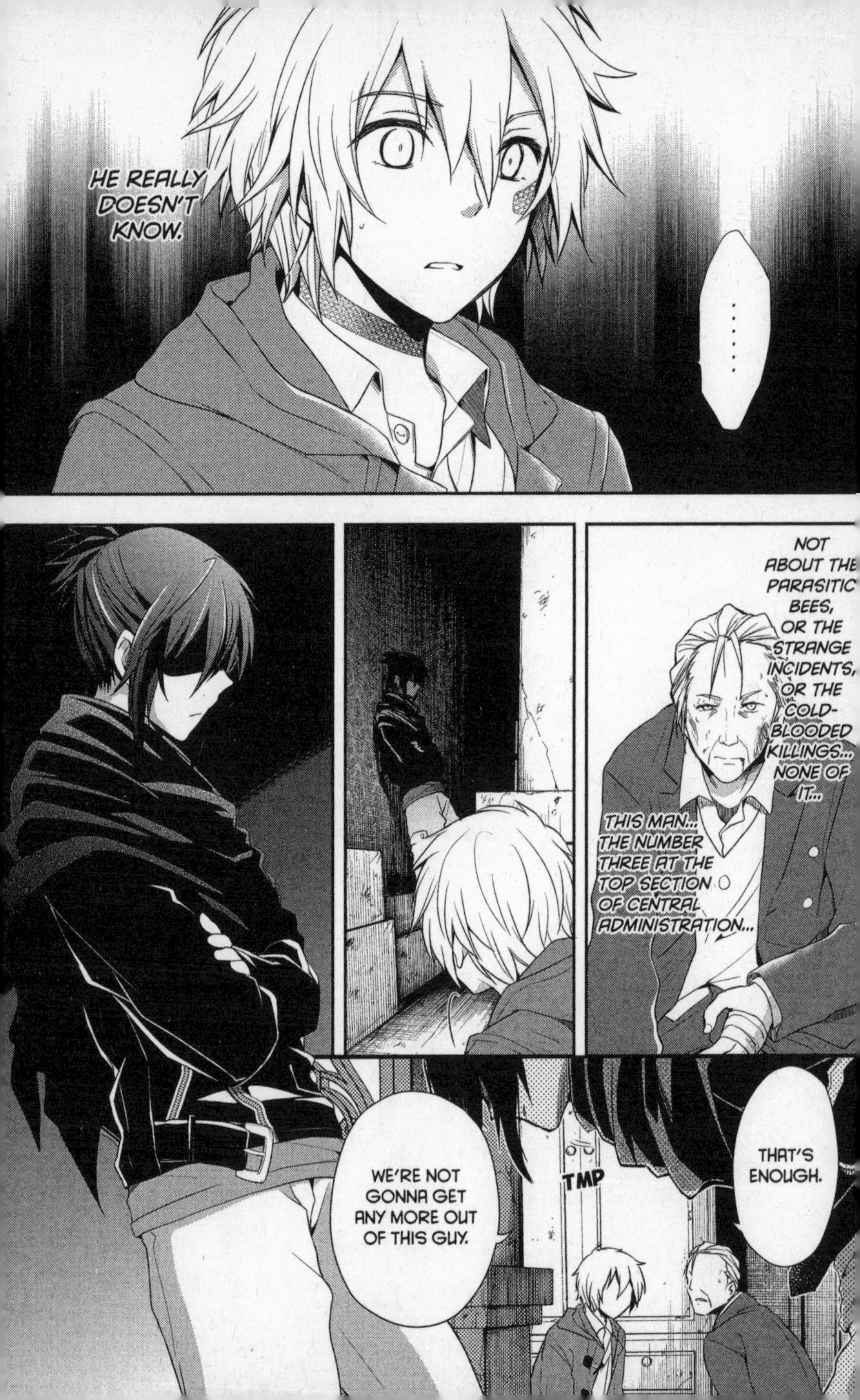
......
HE REALLY DOESN'T KNOW.
NOT ABOUT THE PARASITIC BEES, OR THE STRANGE INCIDENTS, OR THE COLD-BLOODED KILLINGS... NONE OF IT...
THIS MAN... THE NUMBER THREE AT THE TOP SECTION OF CENTRAL ADMINISTRATION...
THAT'S ENOUGH.
TMP
WE'RE NOT GONNA GET ANY MORE OUT OF THIS GUY.

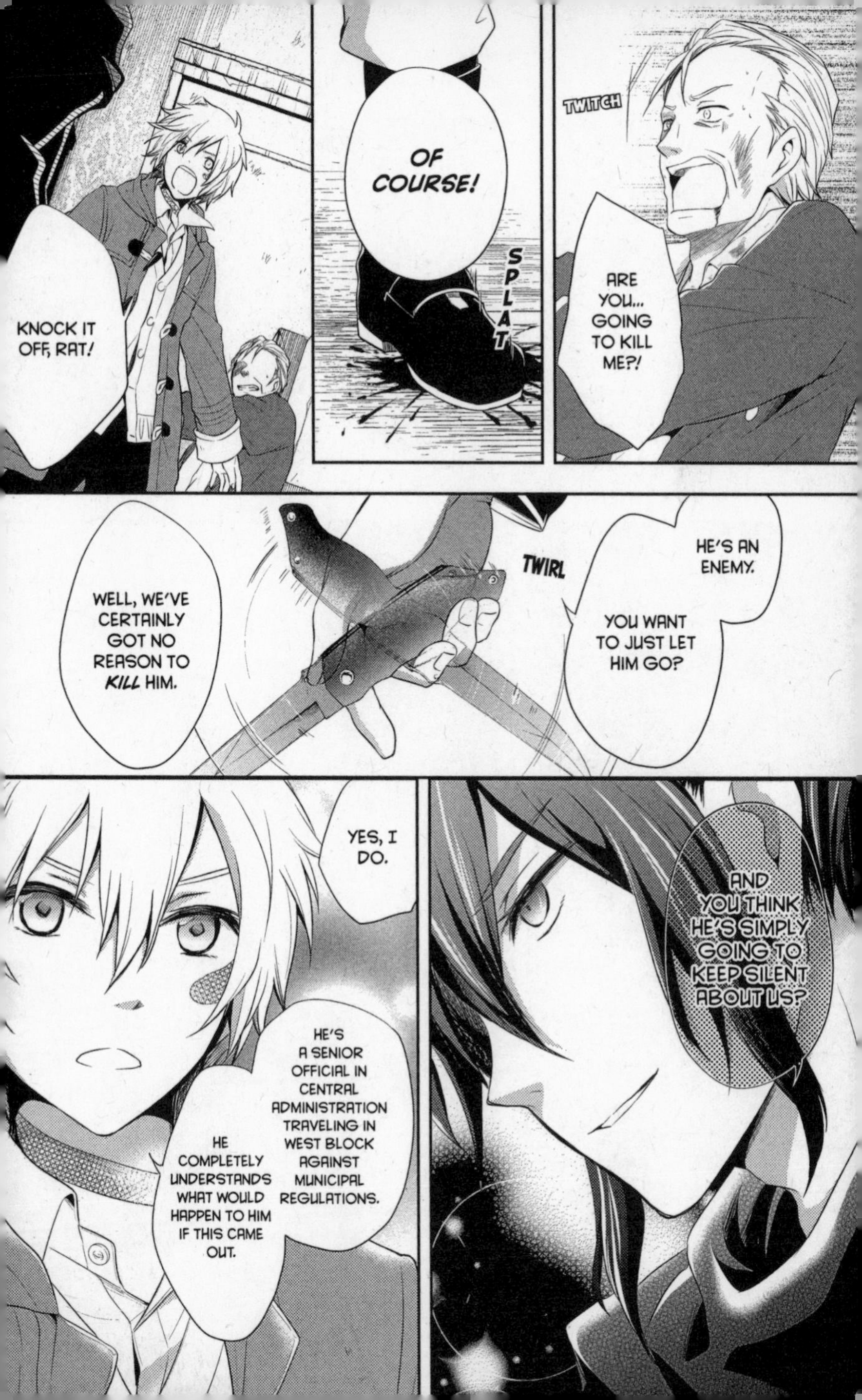
TWITCH
ARE YOU... GOING TO KILL ME?!
OF COURSE!
SPLAT
KNOCK IT OFF, RAT!
HE'S AN ENEMY.
YOU WANT TO JUST LET HIM GO?
TWIRL
WELL, WE'VE CERTAINLY GOT NO REASON TO *KILL* HIM.
AND YOU THINK HE'S SIMPLY GOING TO KEEP SILENT ABOUT US?
YES, I DO.
HE'S A SENIOR OFFICIAL IN CENTRAL ADMINISTRATION TRAVELING IN WEST BLOCK AGAINST MUNICIPAL REGULATIONS.
HE COMPLETELY UNDERSTANDS WHAT WOULD HAPPEN TO HIM IF THIS CAME OUT.

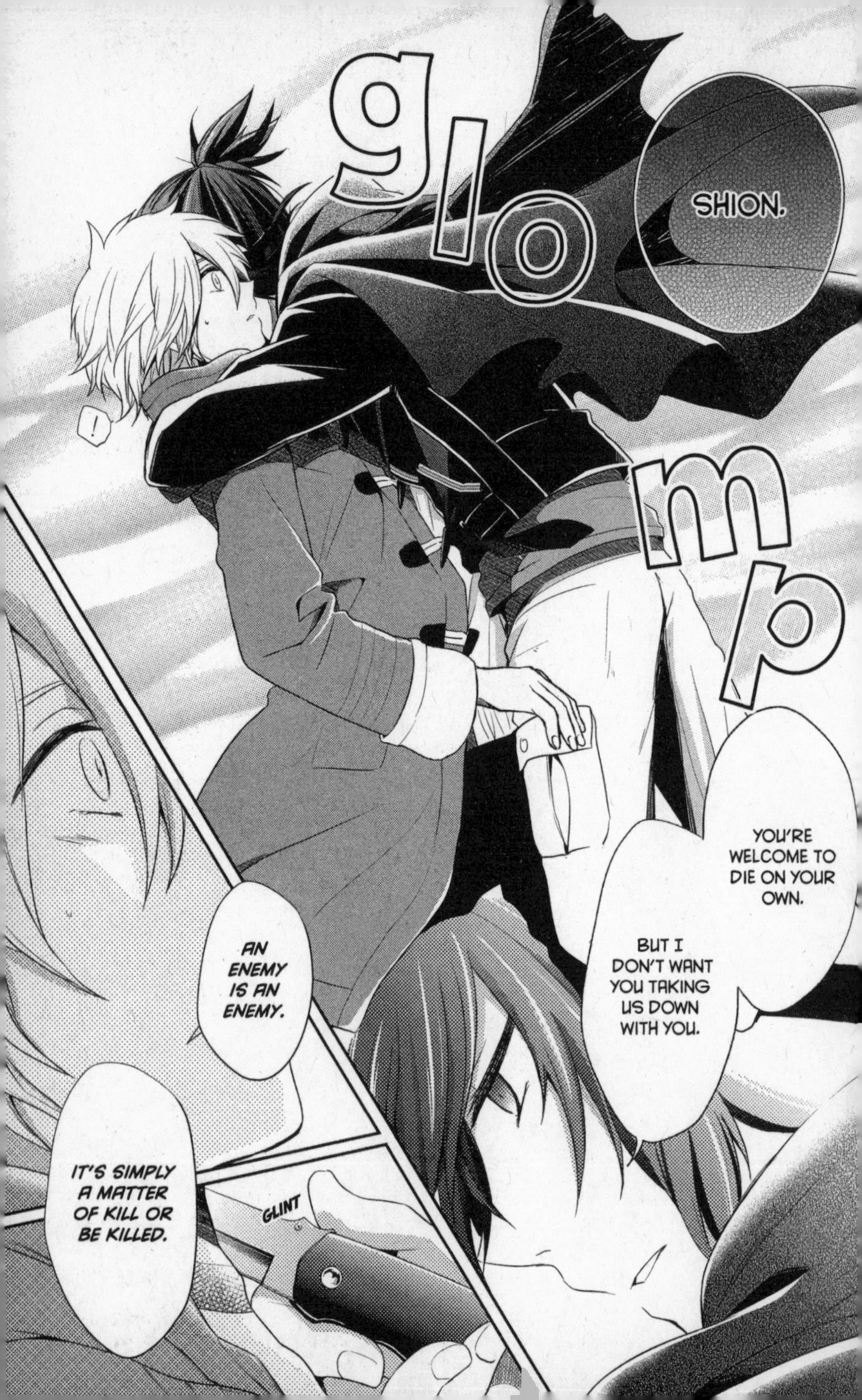
SHION.
glomp
!
YOU'RE WELCOME TO DIE ON YOUR OWN.
BUT I DON'T WANT YOU TAKING US DOWN WITH YOU.
AN ENEMY IS AN ENEMY.
IT'S SIMPLY A MATTER OF KILL OR BE KILLED.
GLINT

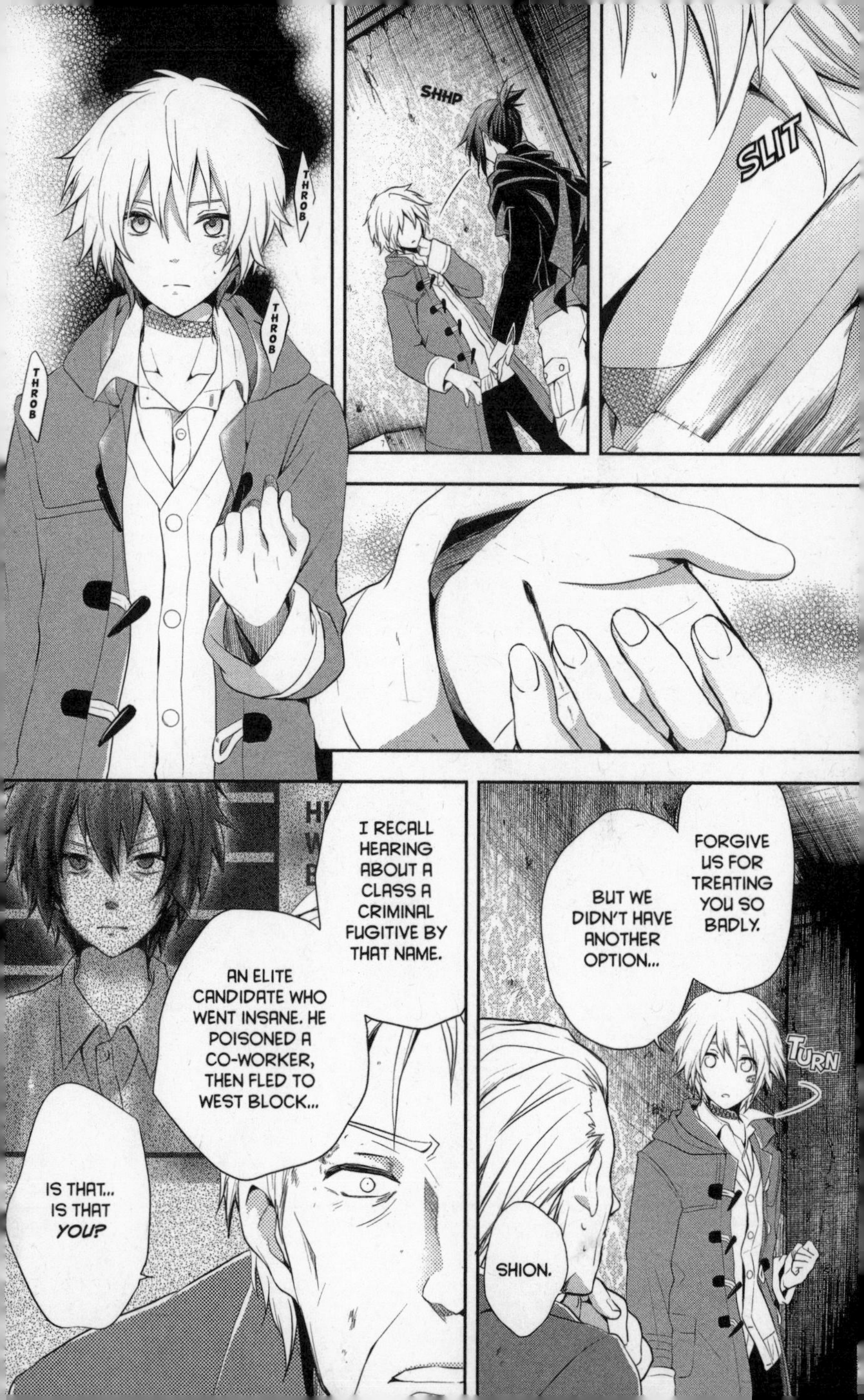
SLIT
SHHP
THROB
THROB
THROB
FORGIVE US FOR TREATING YOU SO BADLY.
BUT WE DIDN'T HAVE ANOTHER OPTION...
TURN
SHION.
I RECALL HEARING ABOUT A CLASS A CRIMINAL FUGITIVE BY THAT NAME.
AN ELITE CANDIDATE WHO WENT INSANE. HE POISONED A CO-WORKER, THEN FLED TO WEST BLOCK...
IS THAT... IS THAT *YOU?*

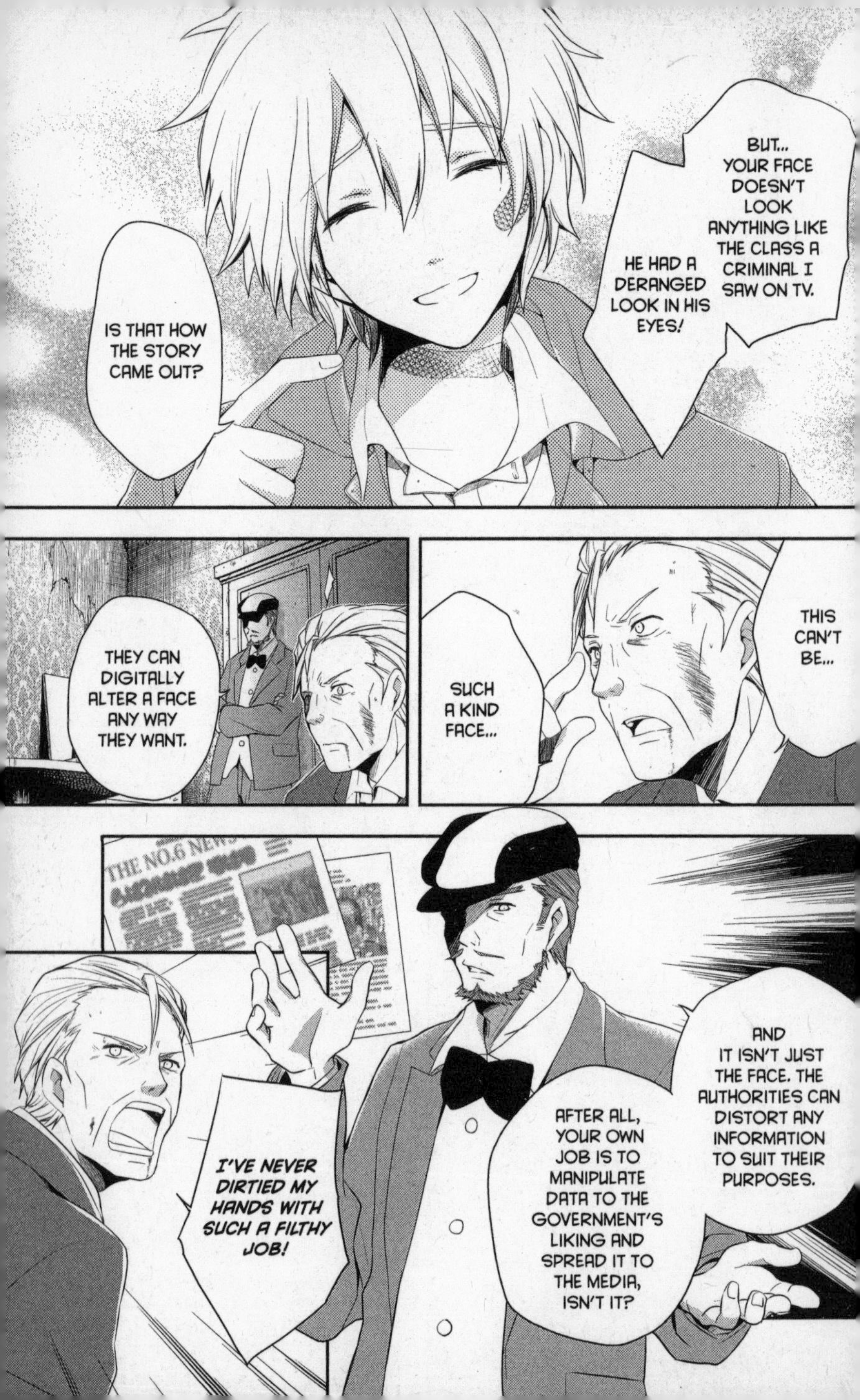

BUT... YOUR FACE DOESN'T LOOK ANYTHING LIKE THE CLASS A CRIMINAL I SAW ON TV.
HE HAD A DERANGED LOOK IN HIS EYES!
IS THAT HOW THE STORY CAME OUT?
THIS CAN'T BE...
SUCH A KIND FACE...
THEY CAN DIGITALLY ALTER A FACE ANY WAY THEY WANT.
AND IT ISN'T JUST THE FACE. THE AUTHORITIES CAN DISTORT ANY INFORMATION TO SUIT THEIR PURPOSES.
AFTER ALL, YOUR OWN JOB IS TO MANIPULATE DATA TO THE GOVERNMENT'S LIKING AND SPREAD IT TO THE MEDIA, ISN'T IT?
THE NO.6 NEWS
I'VE NEVER DIRTIED MY HANDS WITH SUCH A FILTHY JOB!

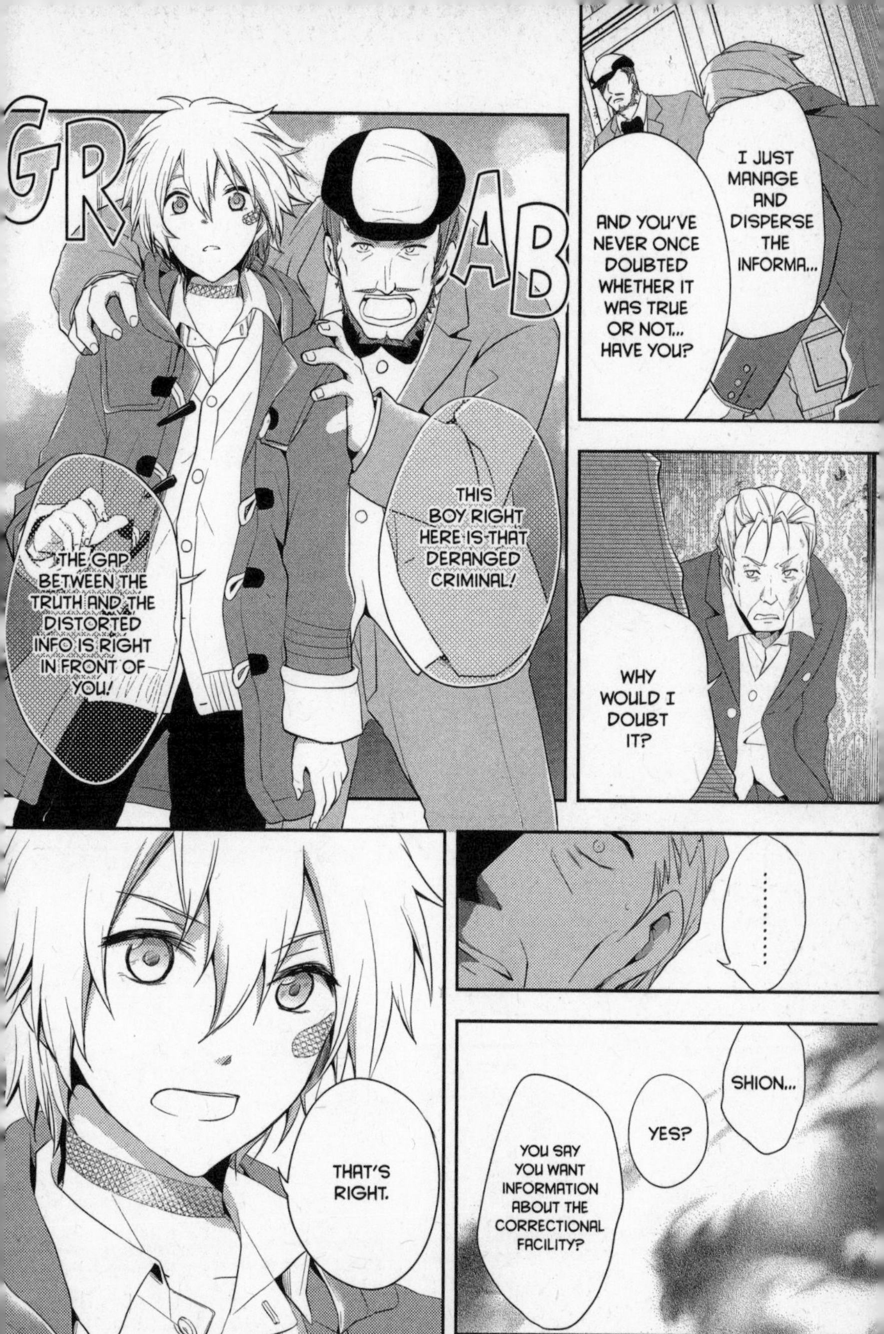
I JUST MANAGE AND DISPERSE THE INFORMA...
AND YOU'VE NEVER ONCE DOUBTED WHETHER IT WAS TRUE OR NOT... HAVE YOU?
WHY WOULD I DOUBT IT?
GRAB
THIS BOY RIGHT HERE IS THAT DERANGED CRIMINAL!
THE GAP BETWEEN THE TRUTH AND THE DISTORTED INFO IS RIGHT IN FRONT OF YOU!
......
SHION...
YES?
YOU SAY YOU WANT INFORMATION ABOUT THE CORRECTIONAL FACILITY?
THAT'S RIGHT.

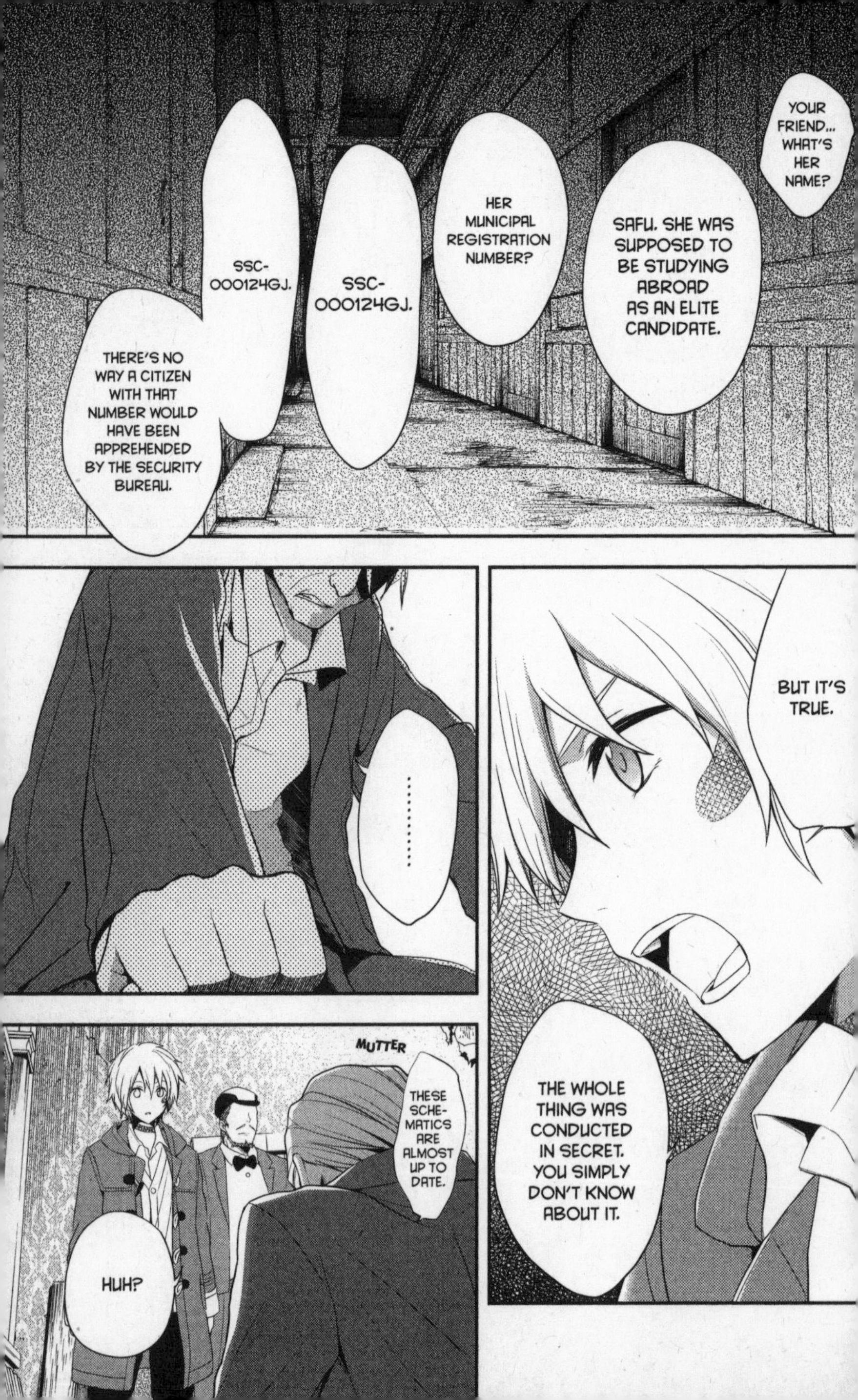

YOUR FRIEND... WHAT'S HER NAME?
SAFU. SHE WAS SUPPOSED TO BE STUDYING ABROAD AS AN ELITE CANDIDATE.
HER MUNICIPAL REGISTRATION NUMBER?
SSC-000124GJ.
SSC-000124GJ.
THERE'S NO WAY A CITIZEN WITH THAT NUMBER WOULD HAVE BEEN APPREHENDED BY THE SECURITY BUREAU.
BUT IT'S TRUE.
THE WHOLE THING WAS CONDUCTED IN SECRET. YOU SIMPLY DON'T KNOW ABOUT IT.
......
MUTTER
THESE SCHE-MATICS ARE ALMOST UP TO DATE.
HUH?

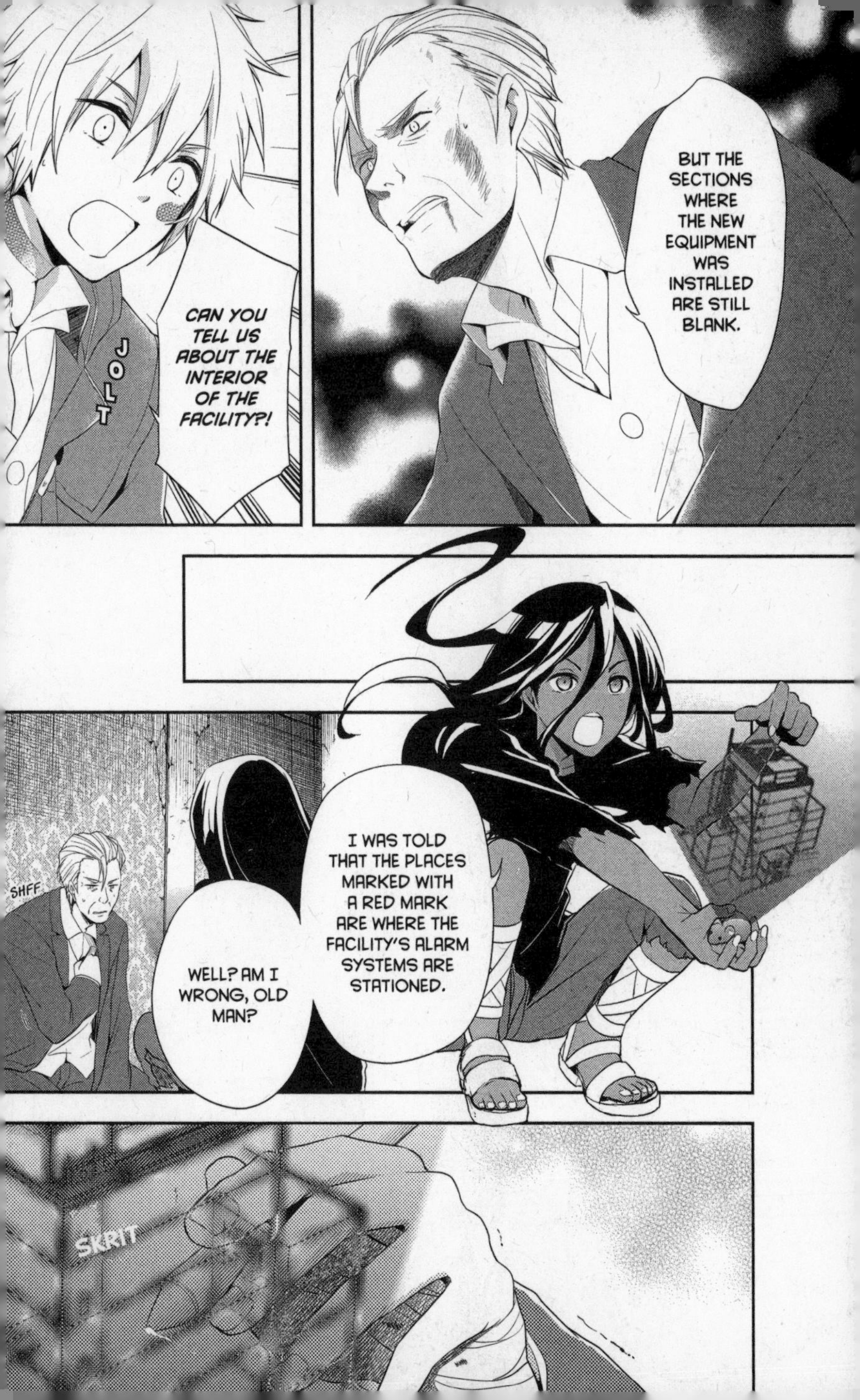
BUT THE SECTIONS WHERE THE NEW EQUIPMENT WAS INSTALLED ARE STILL BLANK.
JOLT
CAN YOU TELL US ABOUT THE INTERIOR OF THE FACILITY?!
I WAS TOLD THAT THE PLACES MARKED WITH A RED MARK ARE WHERE THE FACILITY'S ALARM SYSTEMS ARE STATIONED.
WELL? AM I WRONG, OLD MAN?
SHFF
SKRIT

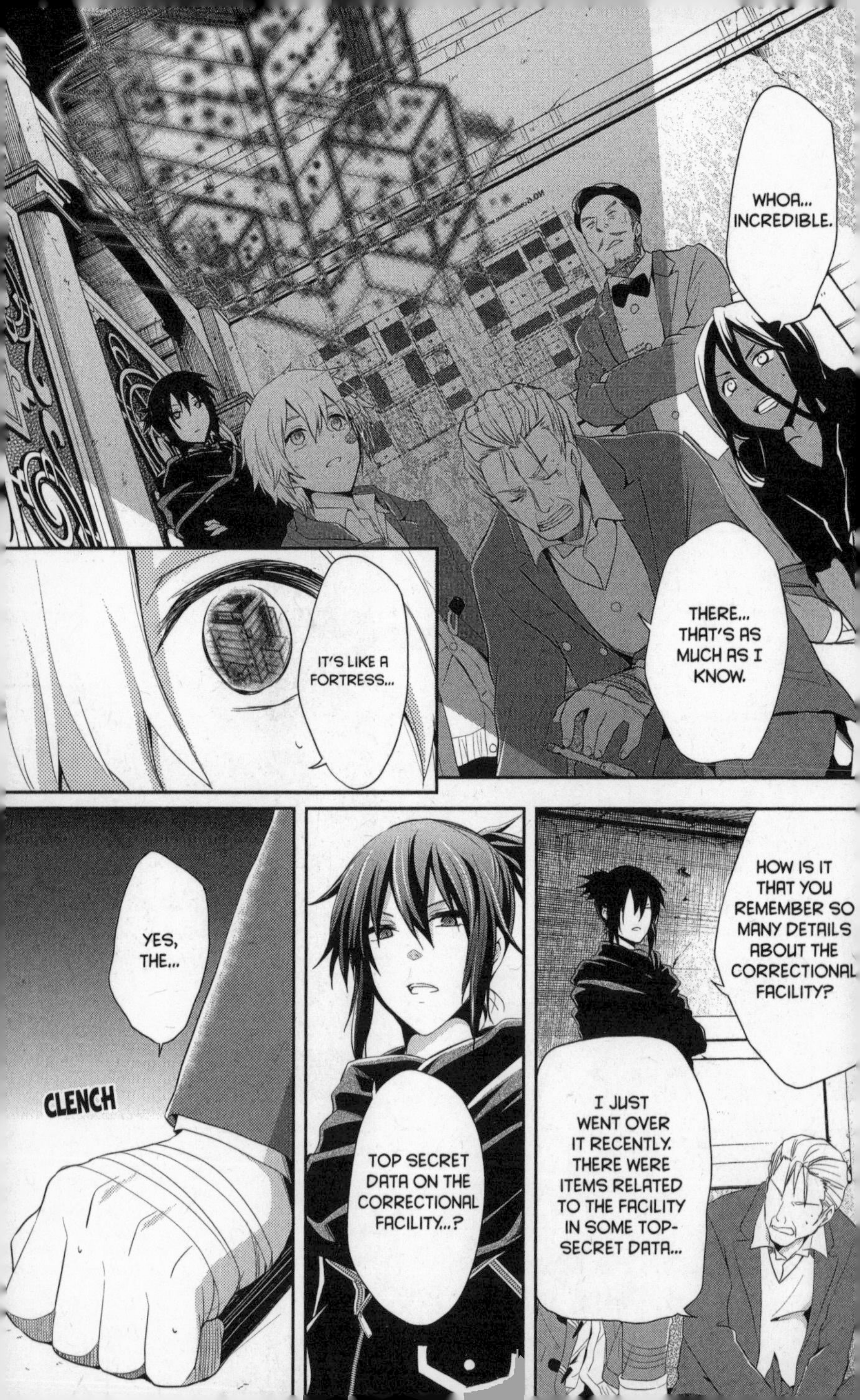
WHOA... INCREDIBLE.
THERE... THAT'S AS MUCH AS I KNOW.
IT'S LIKE A FORTRESS...
HOW IS IT THAT YOU REMEMBER SO MANY DETAILS ABOUT THE CORRECTIONAL FACILITY?
I JUST WENT OVER IT RECENTLY. THERE WERE ITEMS RELATED TO THE FACILITY IN SOME TOP-SECRET DATA...
TOP SECRET DATA ON THE CORRECTIONAL FACILITY...?
YES, THE...
CLENCH

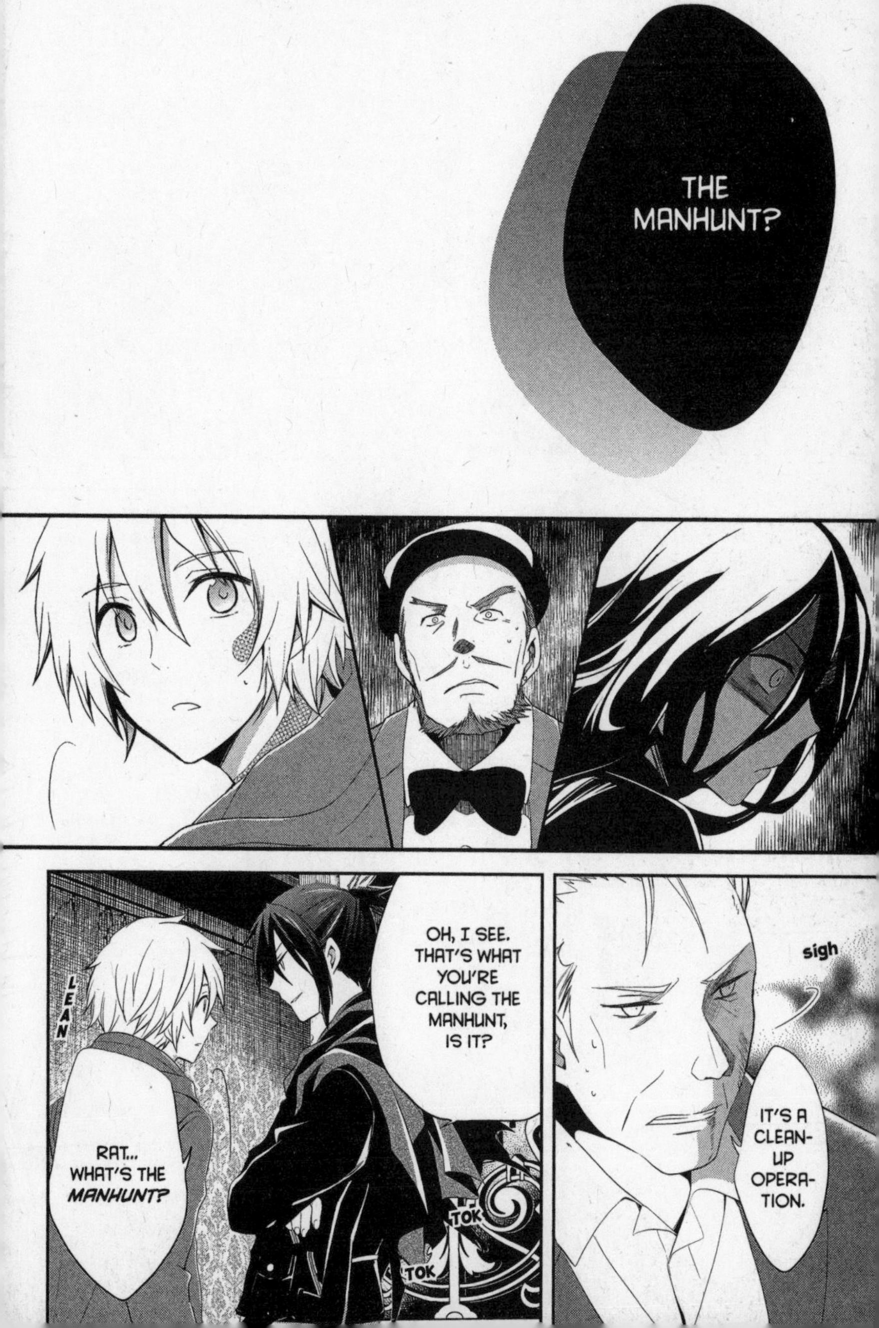
THE MANHUNT?
sigh
IT'S A CLEAN-UP OPERATION.
OH, I SEE. THAT'S WHAT YOU'RE CALLING THE MANHUNT, IS IT?
LEAN
TOK
RAT... WHAT'S THE *MANHUNT?*
TOK

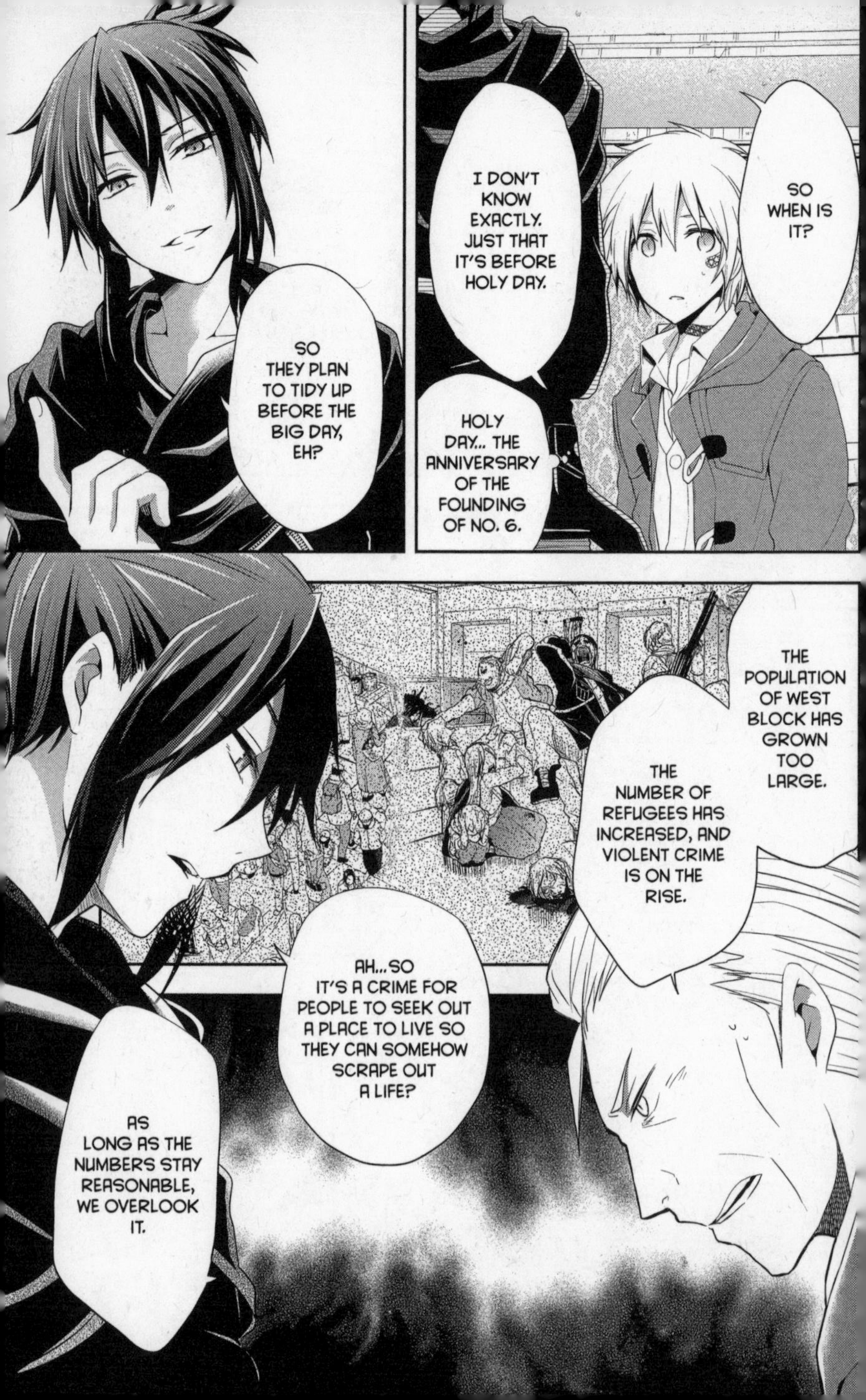
SO WHEN IS IT?
I DON'T KNOW EXACTLY. JUST THAT IT'S BEFORE HOLY DAY.
HOLY DAY... THE ANNIVERSARY OF THE FOUNDING OF NO. 6.
SO THEY PLAN TO TIDY UP BEFORE THE BIG DAY, EH?
THE POPULATION OF WEST BLOCK HAS GROWN TOO LARGE.
THE NUMBER OF REFUGEES HAS INCREASED, AND VIOLENT CRIME IS ON THE RISE.
AH...SO IT'S A CRIME FOR PEOPLE TO SEEK OUT A PLACE TO LIVE SO THEY CAN SOMEHOW SCRAPE OUT A LIFE?
AS LONG AS THE NUMBERS STAY REASONABLE, WE OVERLOOK IT.

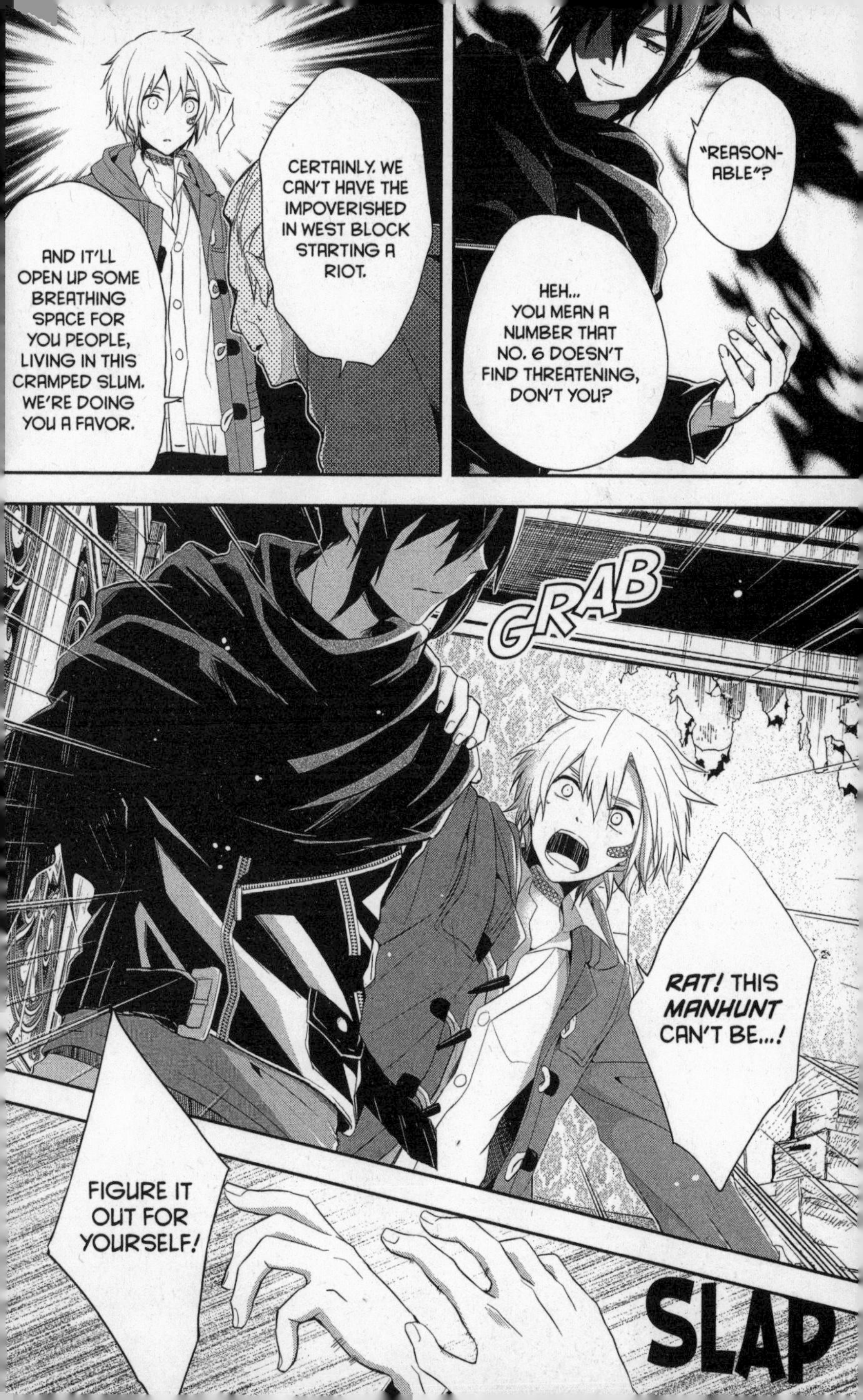
"REASON-ABLE"?
HEH... YOU MEAN A NUMBER THAT NO. 6 DOESN'T FIND THREATENING, DON'T YOU?
CERTAINLY. WE CAN'T HAVE THE IMPOVERISHED IN WEST BLOCK STARTING A RIOT.
AND IT'LL OPEN UP SOME BREATHING SPACE FOR YOU PEOPLE, LIVING IN THIS CRAMPED SLUM. WE'RE DOING YOU A FAVOR.
GRAB
RAT! THIS MANHUNT CAN'T BE...!
FIGURE IT OUT FOR YOURSELF!
SLAP

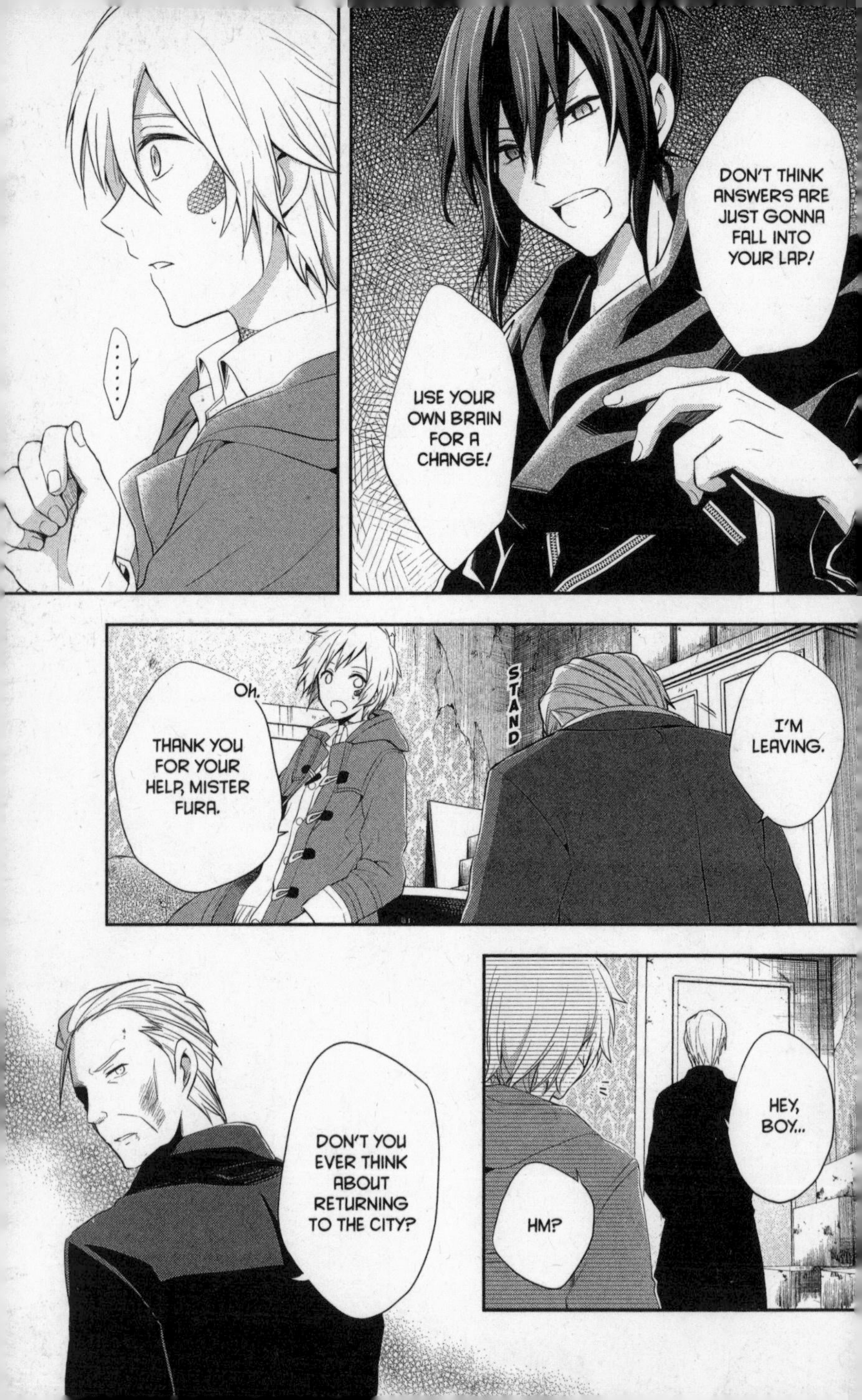
DON'T THINK ANSWERS ARE JUST GONNA FALL INTO YOUR LAP!
USE YOUR OWN BRAIN FOR A CHANGE!
......
I'M LEAVING.
STAND
Oh.
THANK YOU FOR YOUR HELP, MISTER FURA.
HEY, BOY...
HM?
DON'T YOU EVER THINK ABOUT RETURNING TO THE CITY?

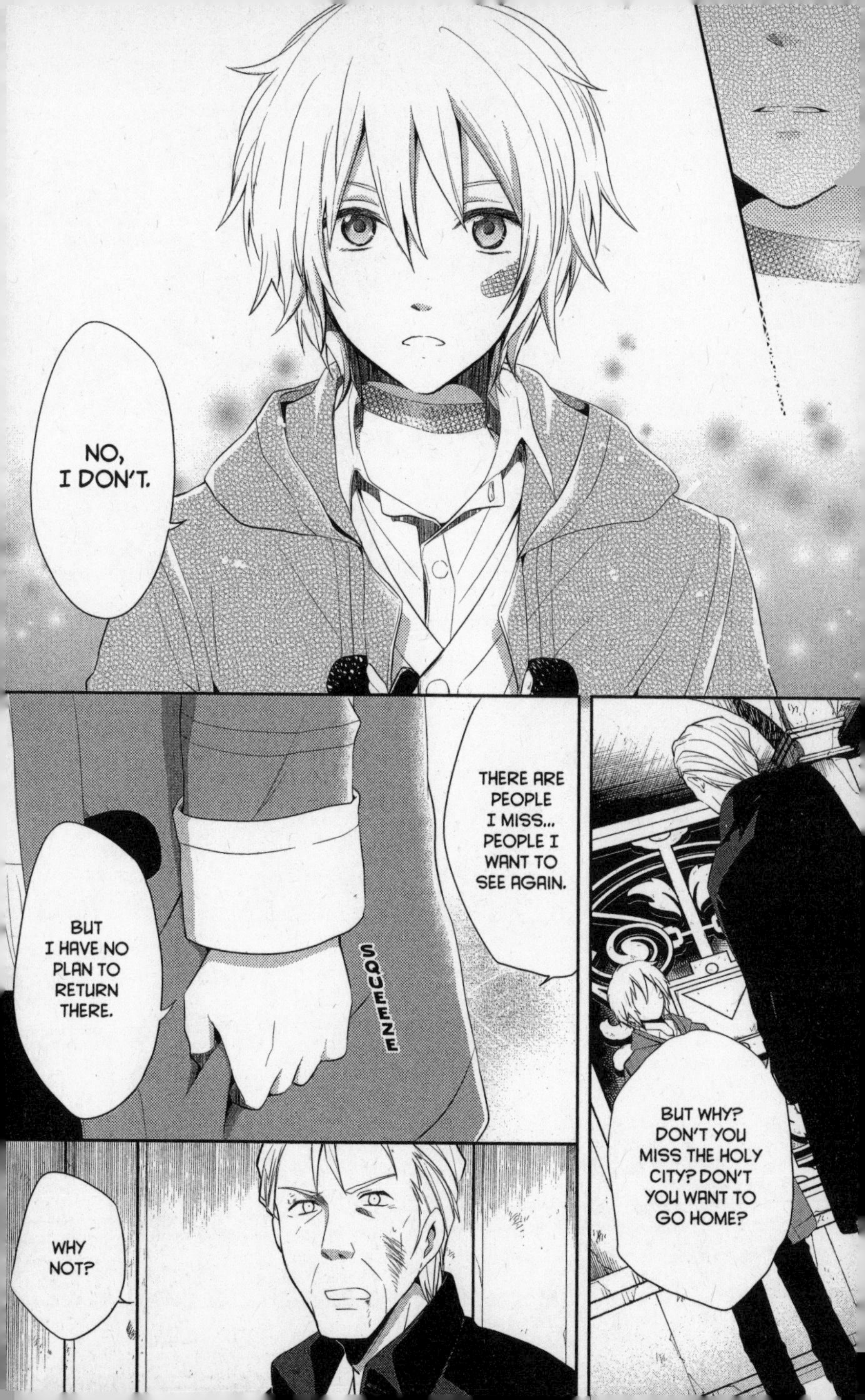
NO, I DON'T.
BUT WHY? DON'T YOU MISS THE HOLY CITY? DON'T YOU WANT TO GO HOME?
THERE ARE PEOPLE I MISS... PEOPLE I WANT TO SEE AGAIN.
SQUEEZE
BUT I HAVE NO PLAN TO RETURN THERE.
WHY NOT?

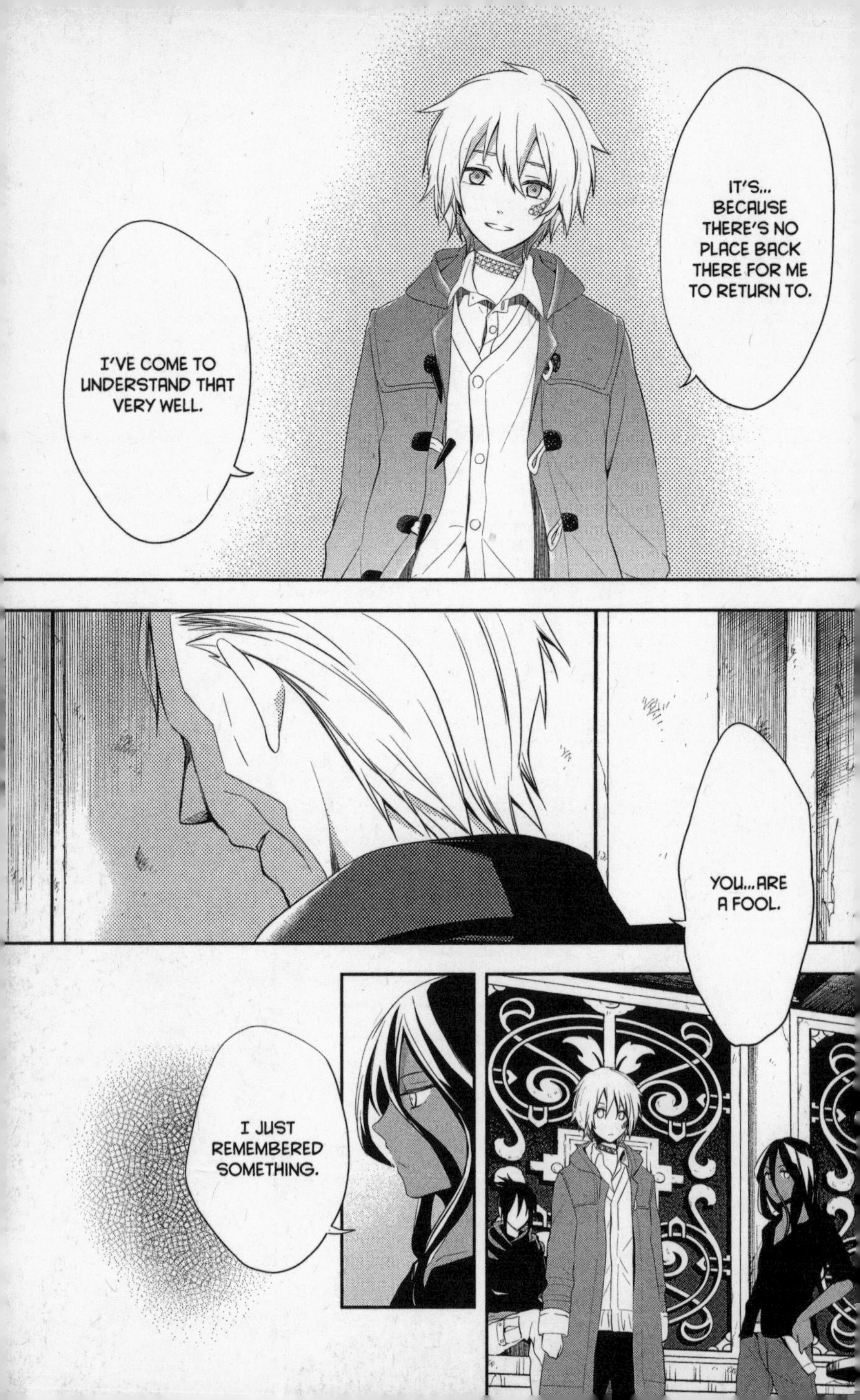
IT'S... BECAUSE THERE'S NO PLACE BACK THERE FOR ME TO RETURN TO.
I'VE COME TO UNDERSTAND THAT VERY WELL.
YOU...ARE A FOOL.
I JUST REMEMBERED SOMETHING.

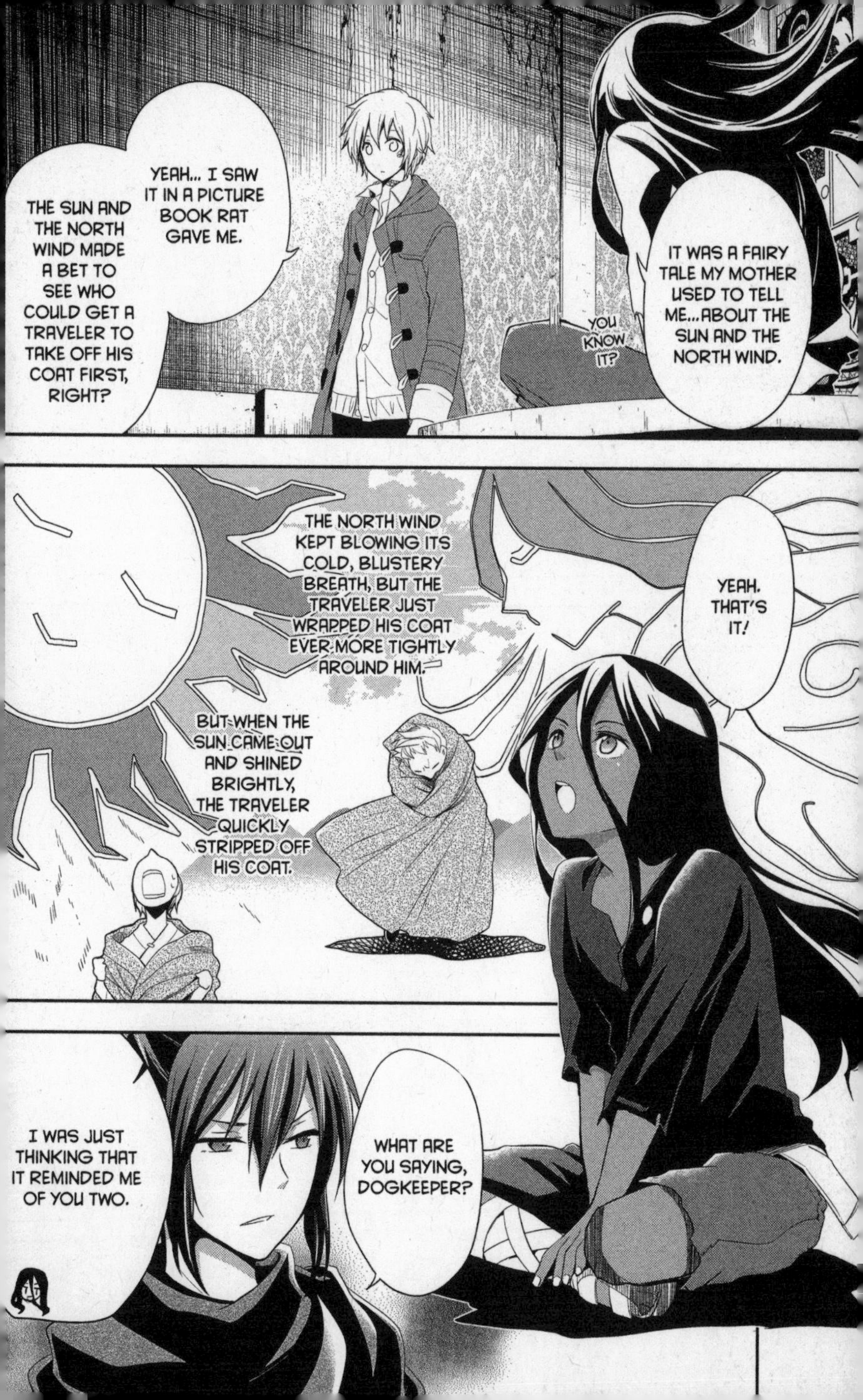
IT WAS A FAIRY TALE MY MOTHER USED TO TELL ME...ABOUT THE SUN AND THE NORTH WIND.
YOU KNOW IT?
YEAH... I SAW IT IN A PICTURE BOOK RAT GAVE ME.
THE SUN AND THE NORTH WIND MADE A BET TO SEE WHO COULD GET A TRAVELER TO TAKE OFF HIS COAT FIRST, RIGHT?
YEAH. THAT'S IT!
THE NORTH WIND KEPT BLOWING ITS COLD, BLUSTERY BREATH, BUT THE TRAVELER JUST WRAPPED HIS COAT EVER MORE TIGHTLY AROUND HIM.
BUT WHEN THE SUN CAME OUT AND SHINED BRIGHTLY, THE TRAVELER QUICKLY STRIPPED OFF HIS COAT.
WHAT ARE YOU SAYING, DOGKEEPER?
I WAS JUST THINKING THAT IT REMINDED ME OF YOU TWO.

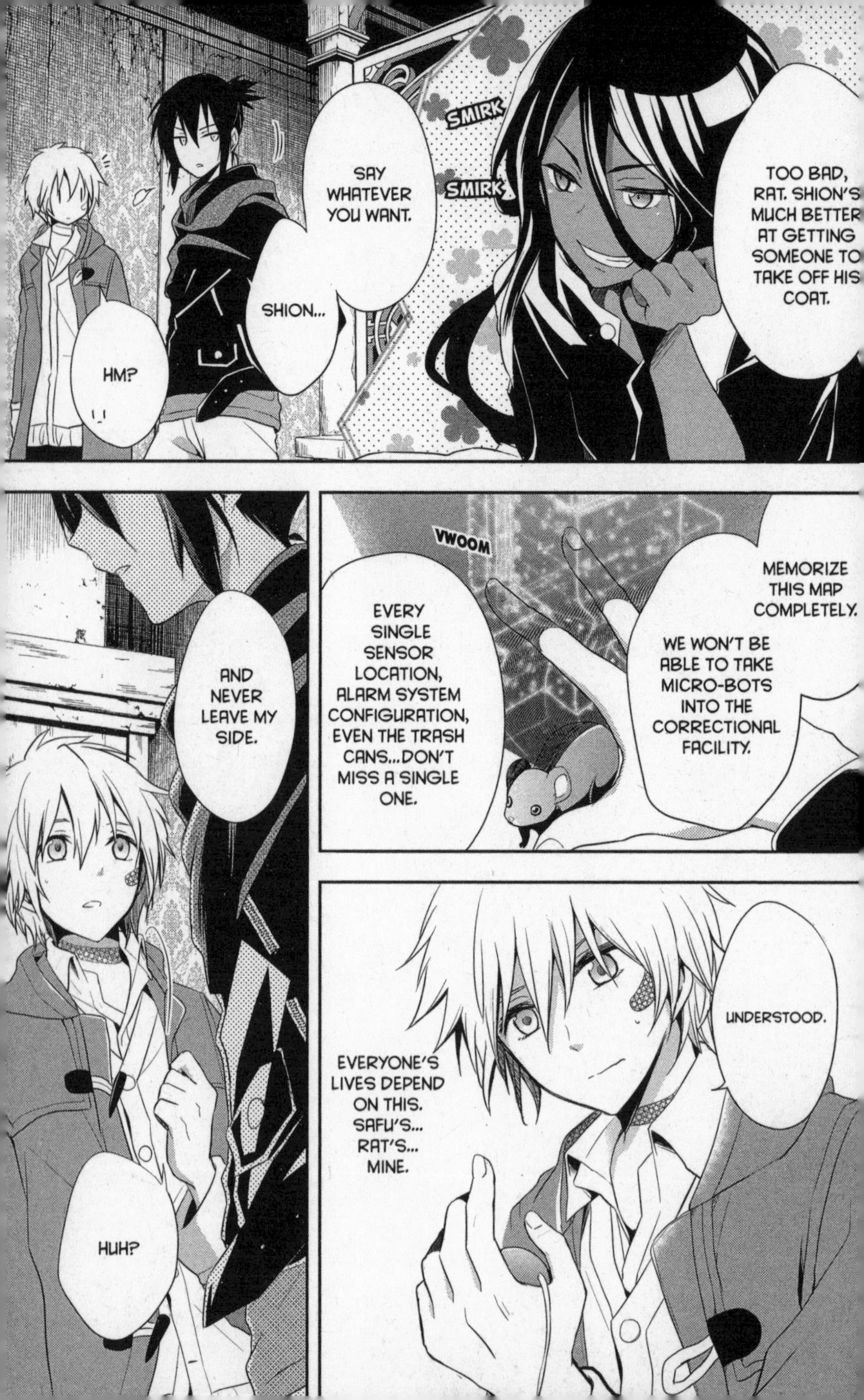
TOO BAD, RAT. SHION'S MUCH BETTER AT GETTING SOMEONE TO TAKE OFF HIS COAT.
SMIRK
SMIRK
SAY WHATEVER YOU WANT.
SHION...
HM?
MEMORIZE THIS MAP COMPLETELY.
WE WON'T BE ABLE TO TAKE MICRO-BOTS INTO THE CORRECTIONAL FACILITY.
VWOOM
EVERY SINGLE SENSOR LOCATION, ALARM SYSTEM CONFIGURATION, EVEN THE TRASH CANS...DON'T MISS A SINGLE ONE.
UNDERSTOOD.
EVERYONE'S LIVES DEPEND ON THIS. SAFU'S... RAT'S... MINE.
AND NEVER LEAVE MY SIDE.
HUH?

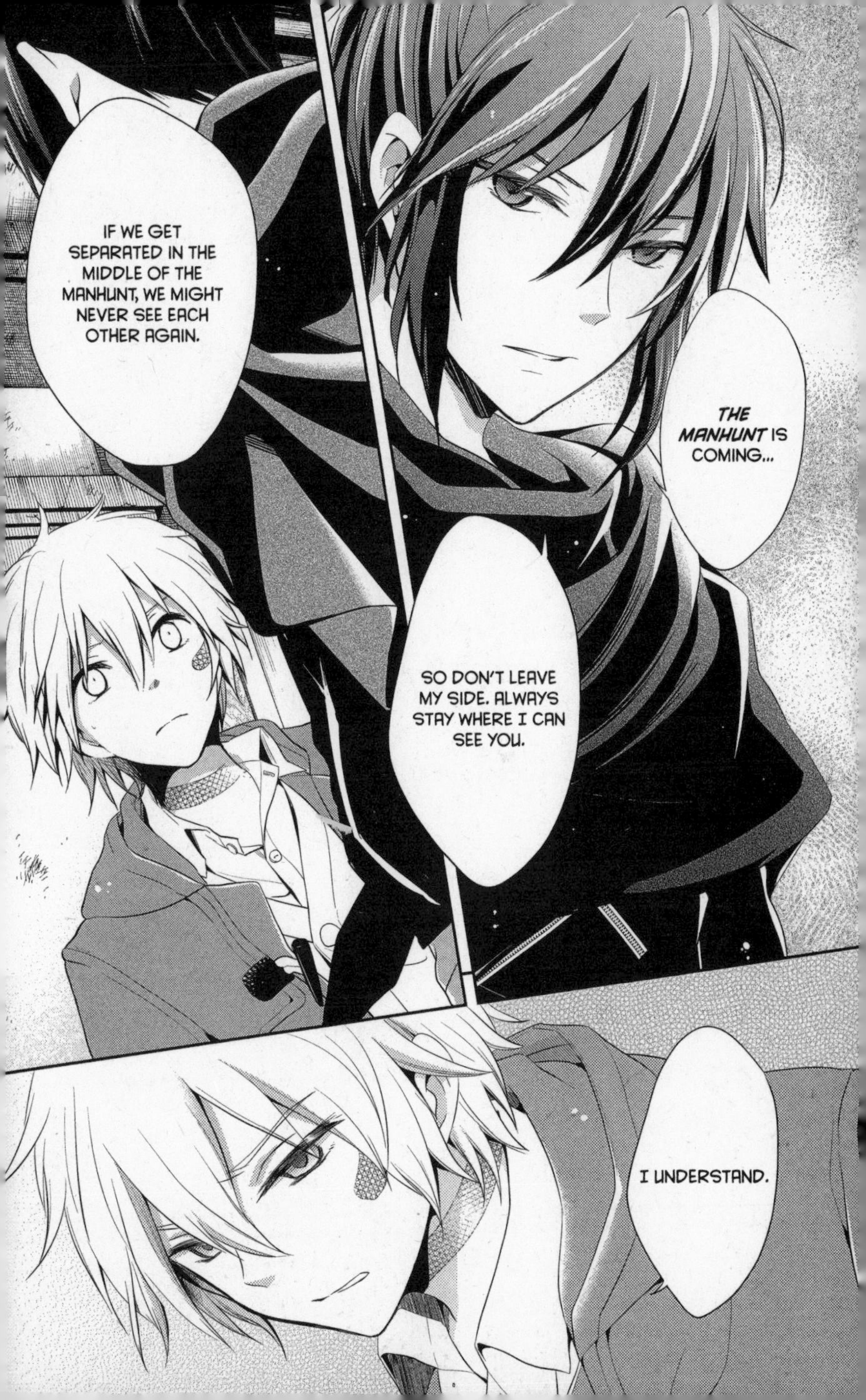
THE *MANHUNT* IS COMING...
IF WE GET SEPARATED IN THE MIDDLE OF THE MANHUNT, WE MIGHT NEVER SEE EACH OTHER AGAIN.
SO DON'T LEAVE MY SIDE. ALWAYS STAY WHERE I CAN SEE YOU.
I UNDERSTAND.

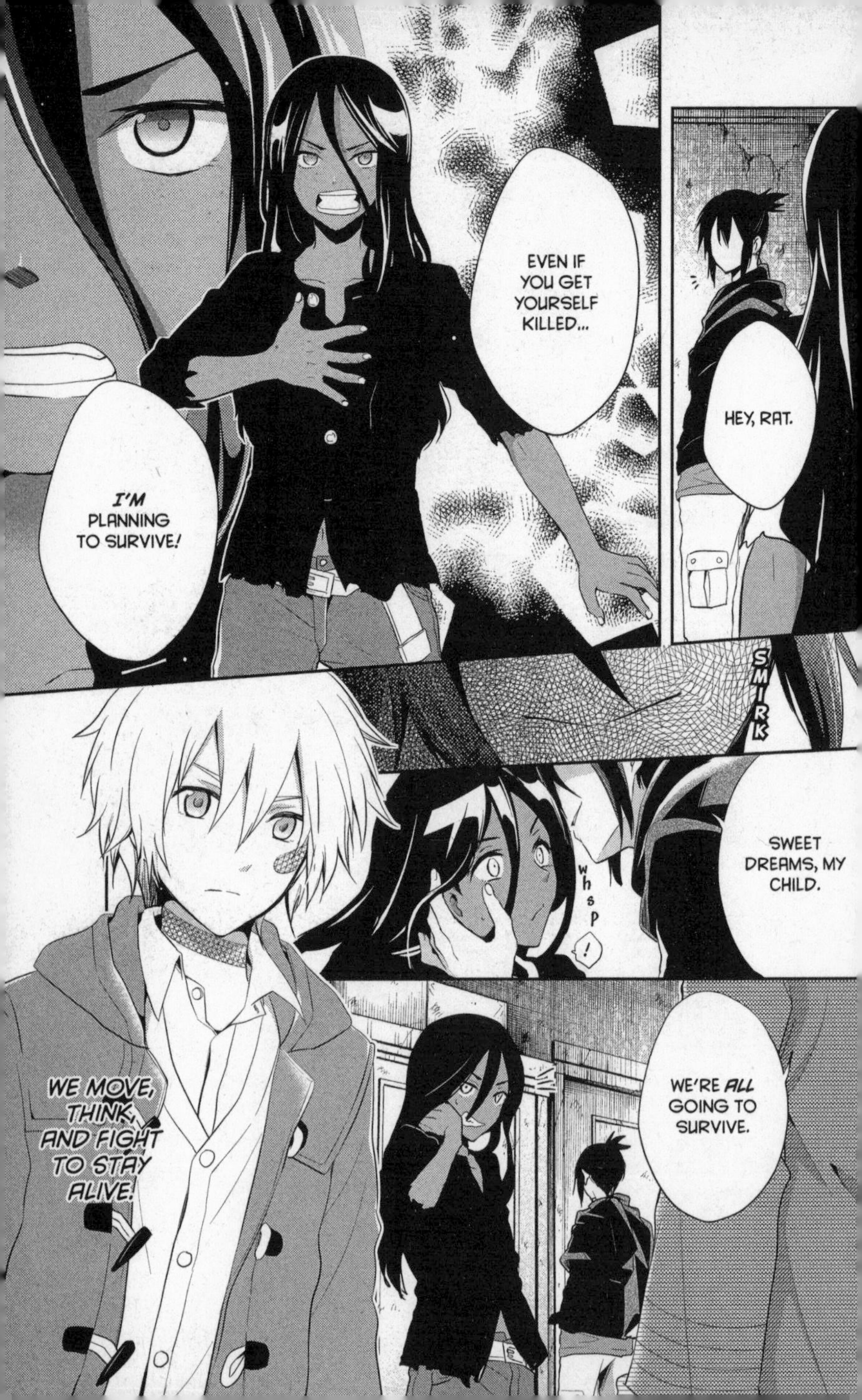
HEY, RAT.
EVEN IF YOU GET YOURSELF KILLED...
I'M PLANNING TO SURVIVE!
SMIRK
SWEET DREAMS, MY CHILD.
whsp
!
WE'RE ALL GOING TO SURVIVE.
WE MOVE, THINK, AND FIGHT TO STAY ALIVE.

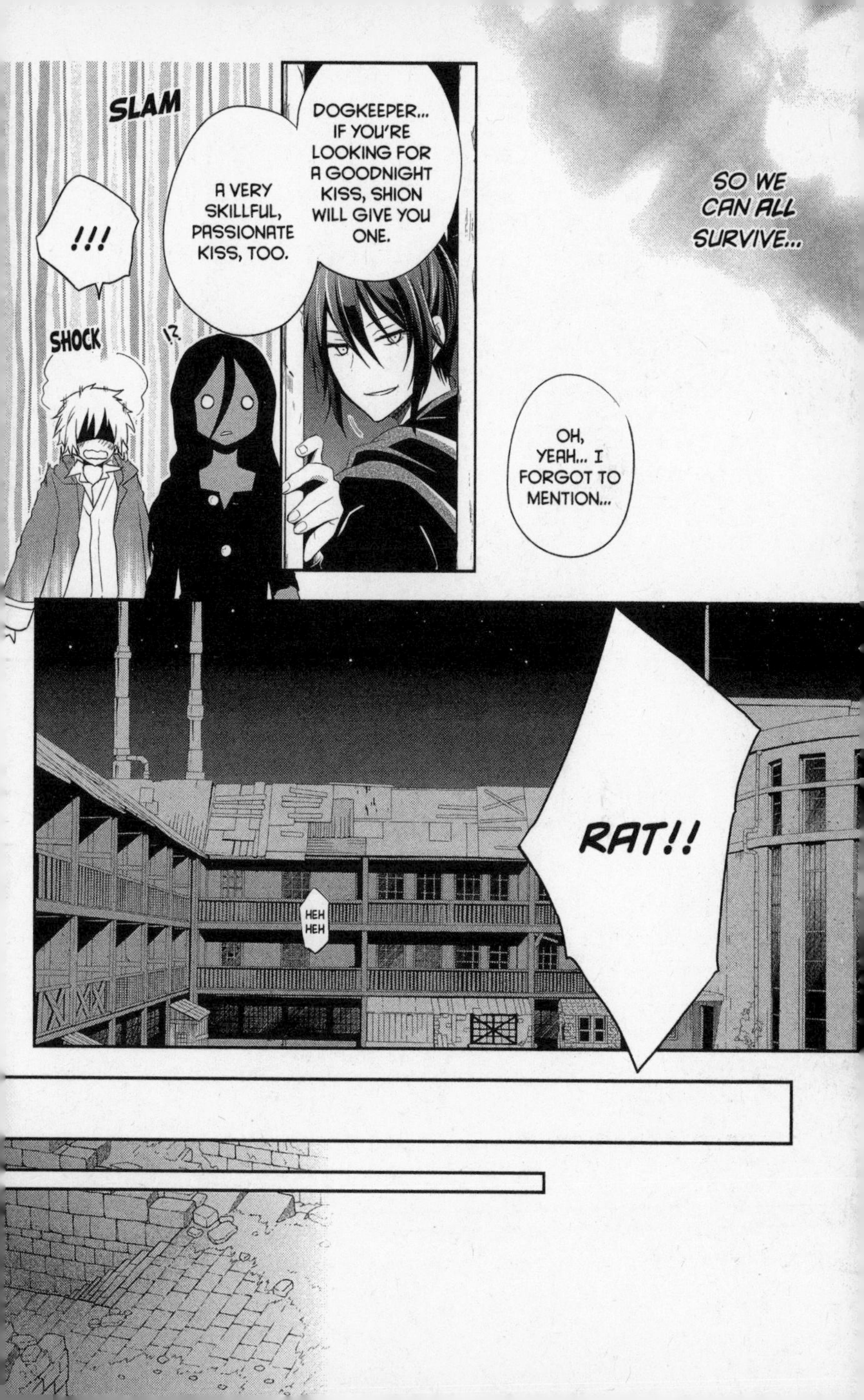
SO WE CAN ALL SURVIVE...
OH, YEAH... I FORGOT TO MENTION...
DOGKEEPER... IF YOU'RE LOOKING FOR A GOODNIGHT KISS, SHION WILL GIVE YOU ONE.
A VERY SKILLFUL, PASSIONATE KISS, TOO.
SLAM
!!!
!?
SHOCK
RAT!!
HEH HEH

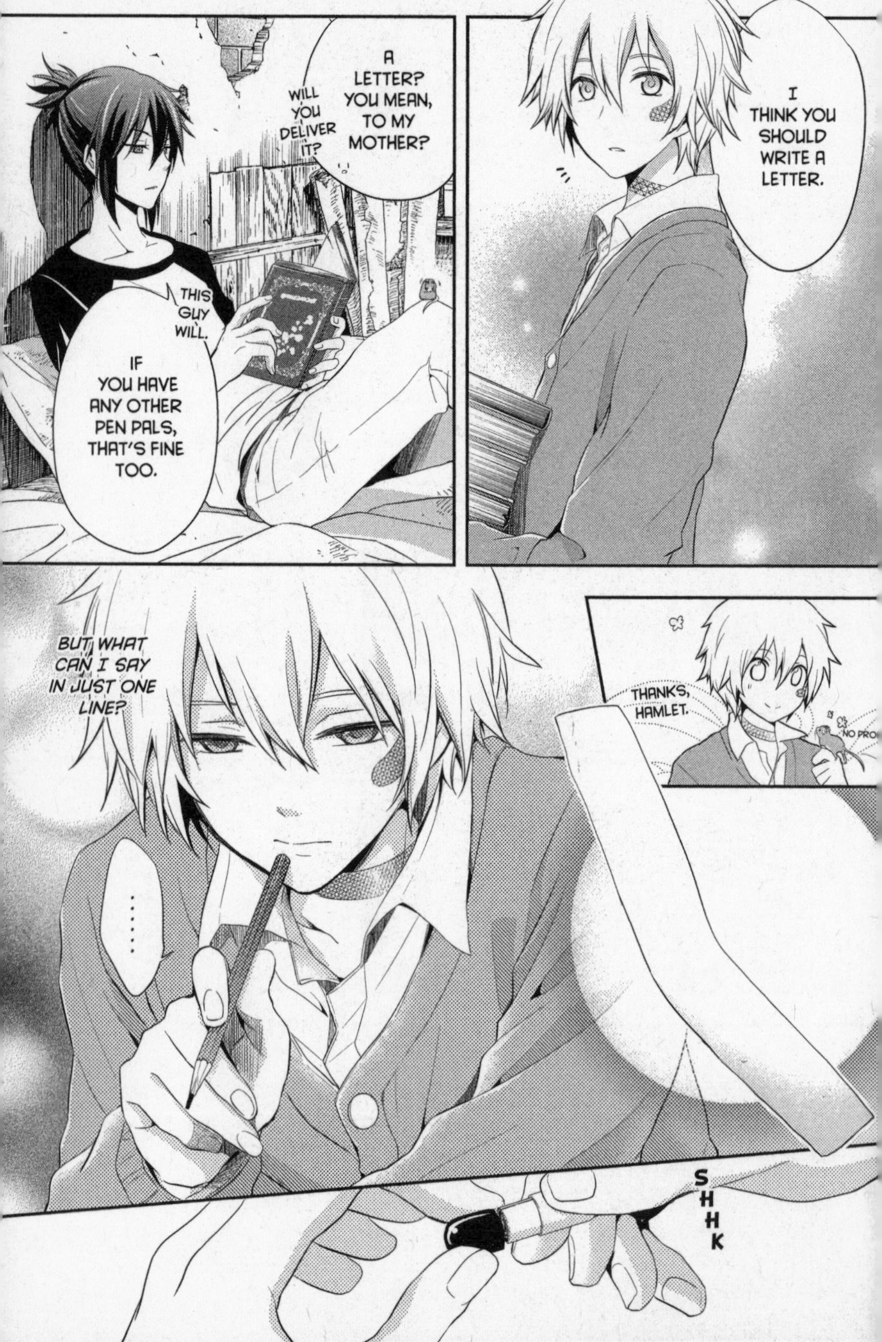
I THINK YOU SHOULD WRITE A LETTER.
A LETTER? YOU MEAN, TO MY MOTHER?
WILL YOU DELIVER IT?
THIS GUY WILL.
IF YOU HAVE ANY OTHER PEN PALS, THAT'S FINE TOO.
THANKS, HAMLET.
NO PRO
BUT WHAT CAN I SAY IN JUST ONE LINE?
......
SHHK

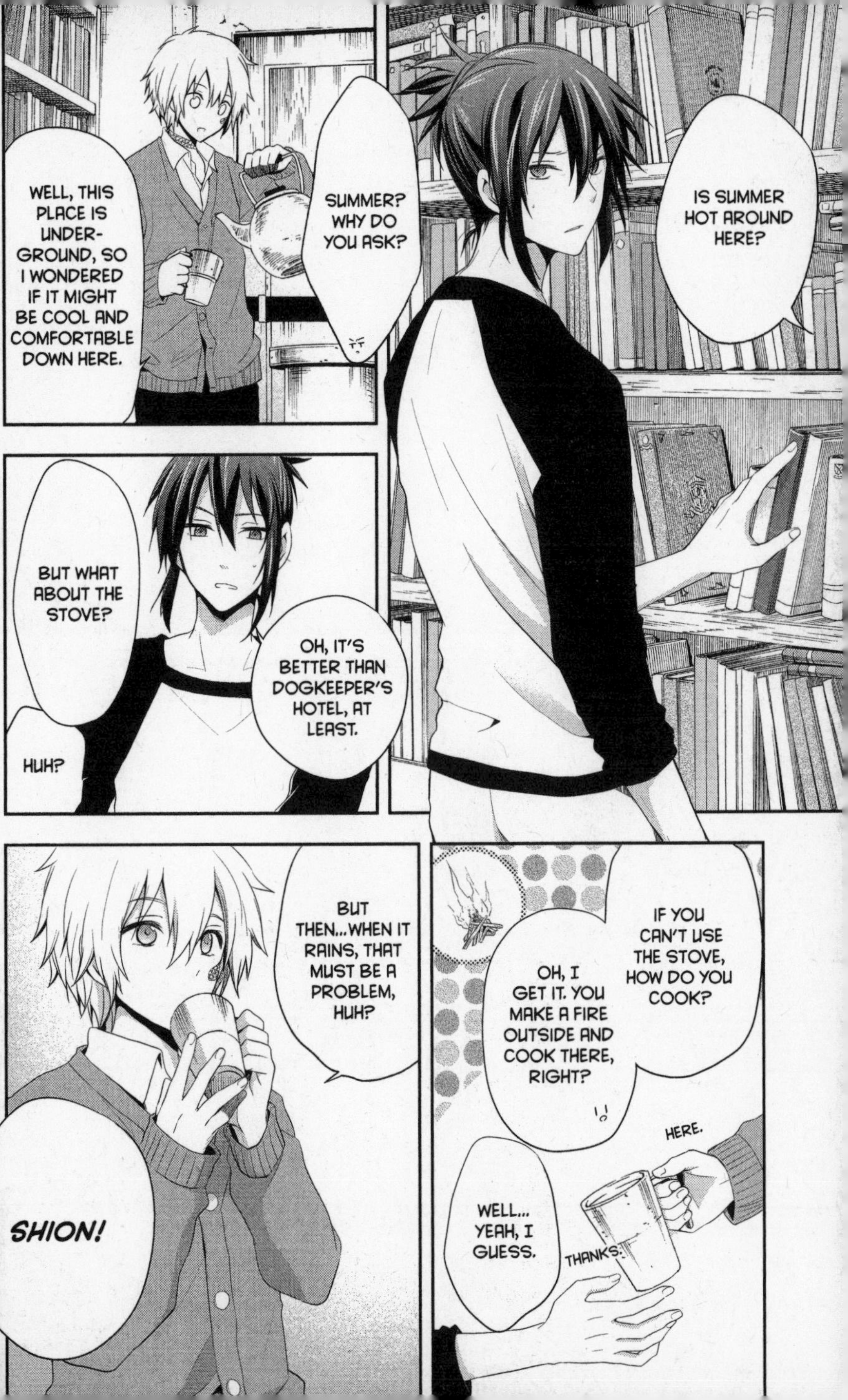
IS SUMMER HOT AROUND HERE?
SUMMER? WHY DO YOU ASK?
WELL, THIS PLACE IS UNDER-GROUND, SO I WONDERED IF IT MIGHT BE COOL AND COMFORTABLE DOWN HERE.
OH, IT'S BETTER THAN DOGKEEPER'S HOTEL, AT LEAST.
BUT WHAT ABOUT THE STOVE?
HUH?
IF YOU CAN'T USE THE STOVE, HOW DO YOU COOK?
OH, I GET IT. YOU MAKE A FIRE OUTSIDE AND COOK THERE, RIGHT?
HERE.
WELL... YEAH, I GUESS.
THANKS.
BUT THEN...WHEN IT RAINS, THAT MUST BE A PROBLEM, HUH?
SHION!

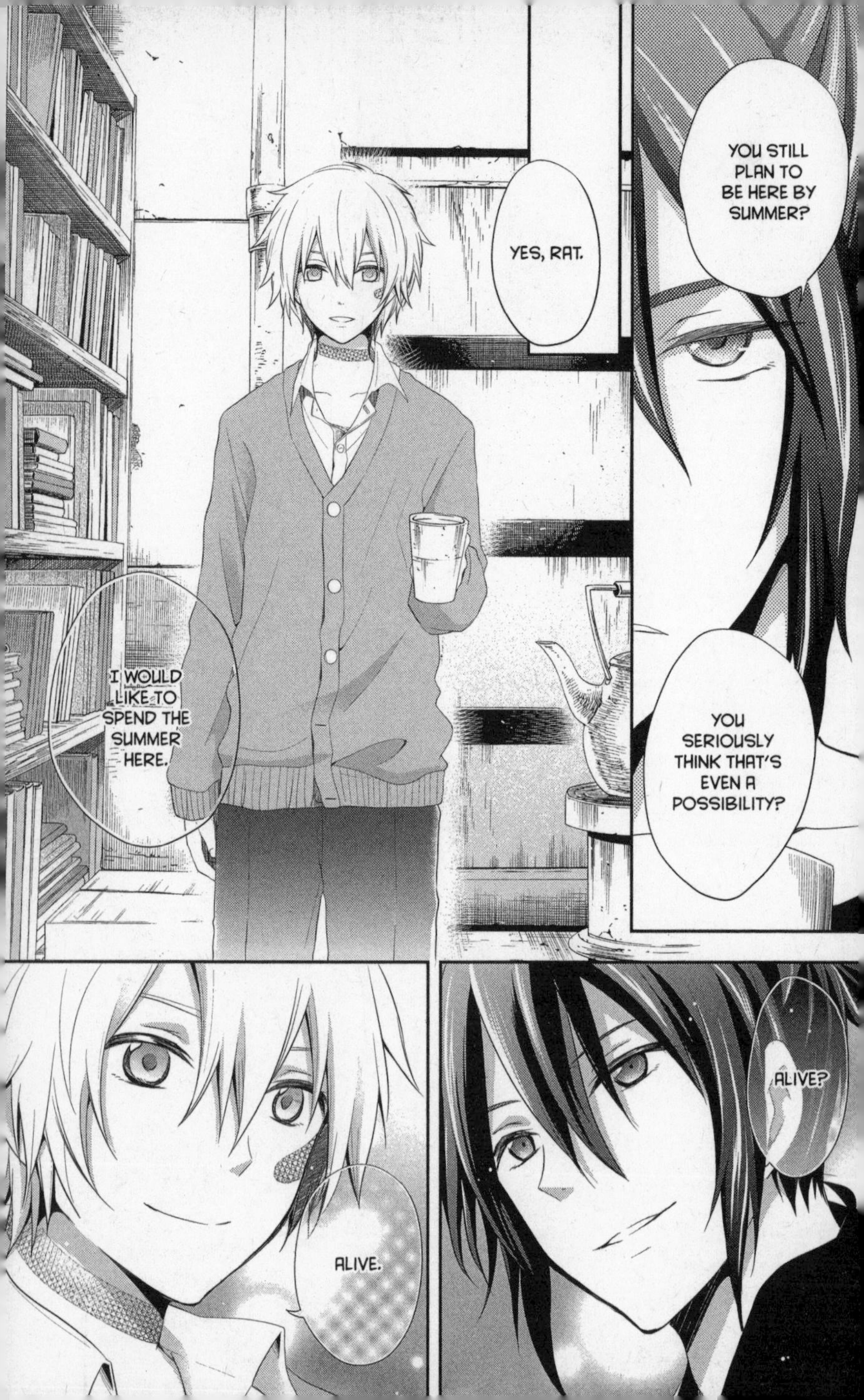
YOU STILL PLAN TO BE HERE BY SUMMER?
YOU SERIOUSLY THINK THAT'S EVEN A POSSIBILITY?
YES, RAT.
I WOULD LIKE TO SPEND THE SUMMER HERE.
ALIVE?
ALIVE.

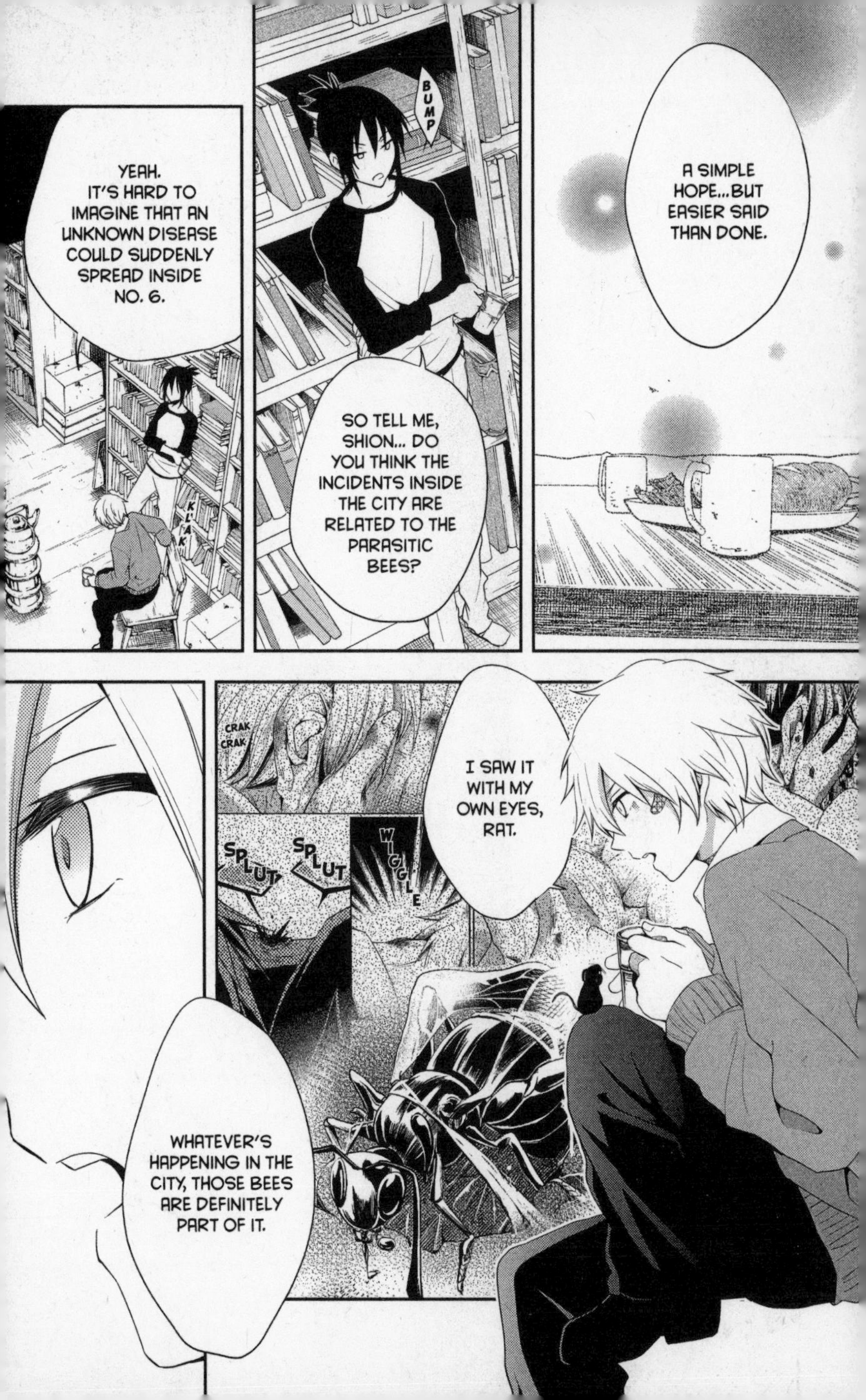
A SIMPLE HOPE...BUT EASIER SAID THAN DONE.
BUMP
SO TELL ME, SHION... DO YOU THINK THE INCIDENTS INSIDE THE CITY ARE RELATED TO THE PARASITIC BEES?
YEAH. IT'S HARD TO IMAGINE THAT AN UNKNOWN DISEASE COULD SUDDENLY SPREAD INSIDE NO. 6.
KLAK
I SAW IT WITH MY OWN EYES, RAT.
CRAK CRAK
WIGGLE
SPLUT
SPLUT
WHATEVER'S HAPPENING IN THE CITY, THOSE BEES ARE DEFINITELY PART OF IT.

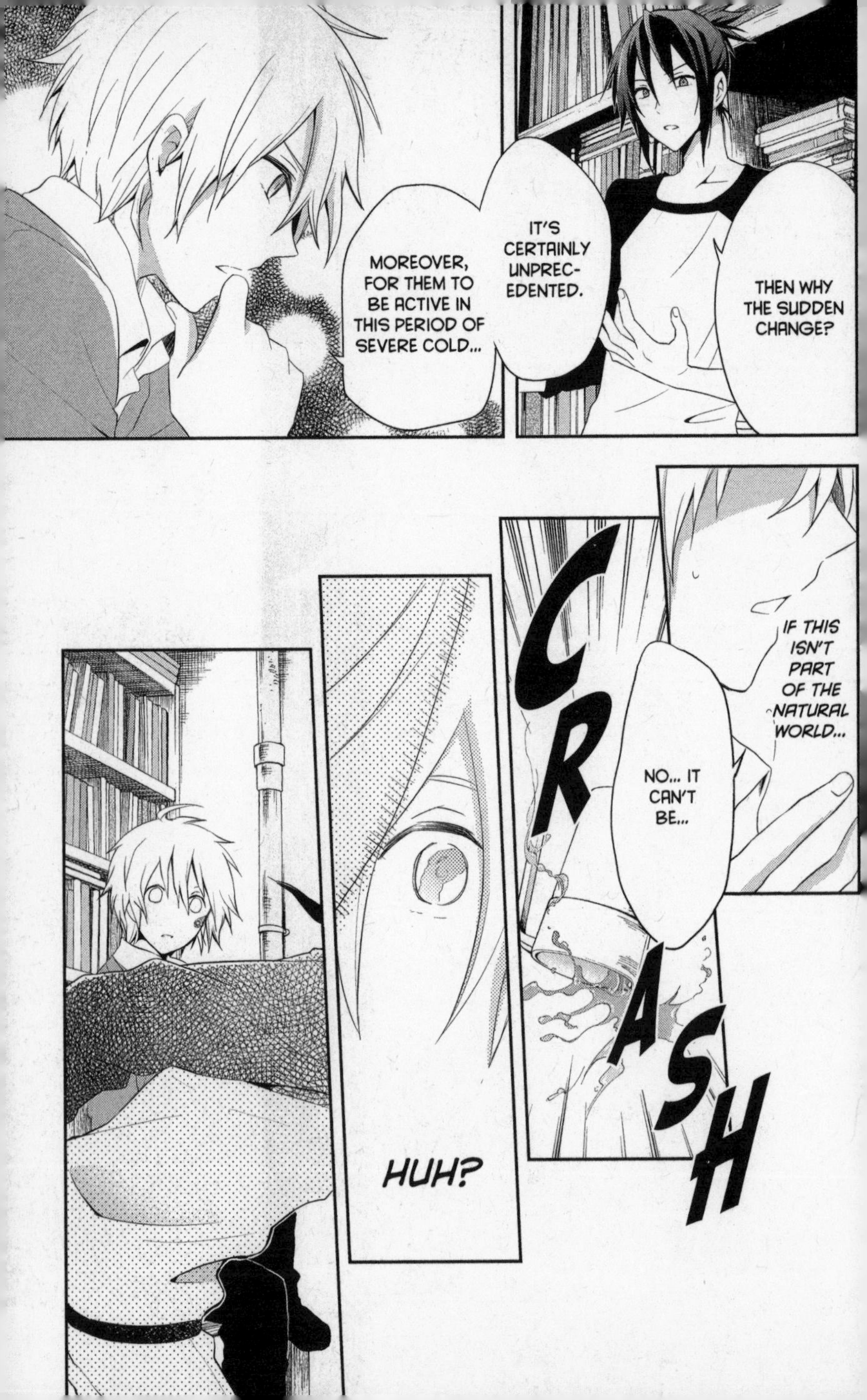
THEN WHY THE SUDDEN CHANGE?
IT'S CERTAINLY UNPREC-EDENTED.
MOREOVER, FOR THEM TO BE ACTIVE IN THIS PERIOD OF SEVERE COLD...
IF THIS ISN'T PART OF THE NATURAL WORLD...
NO... IT CAN'T BE...
CRASH
HUH?

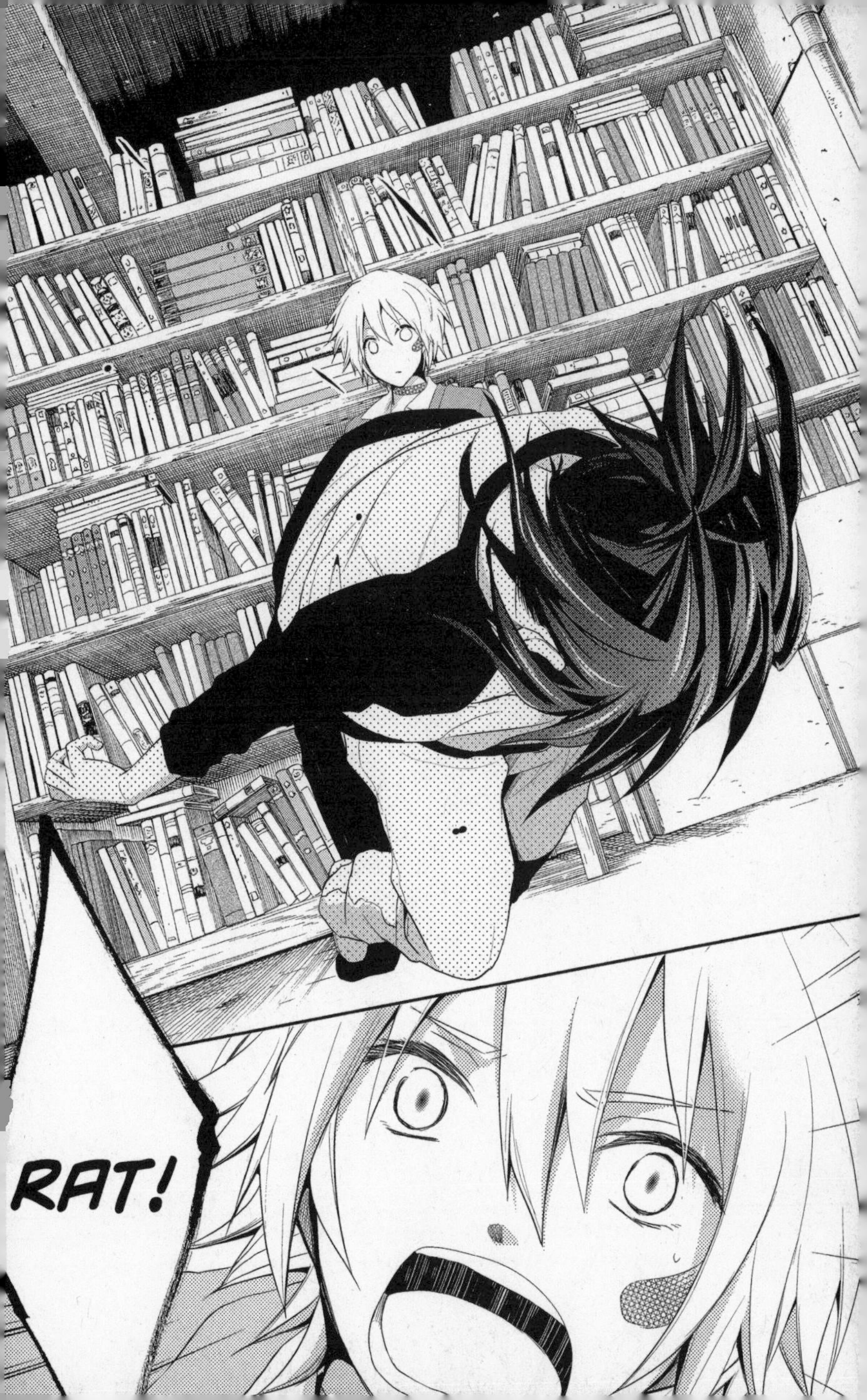
RAT!

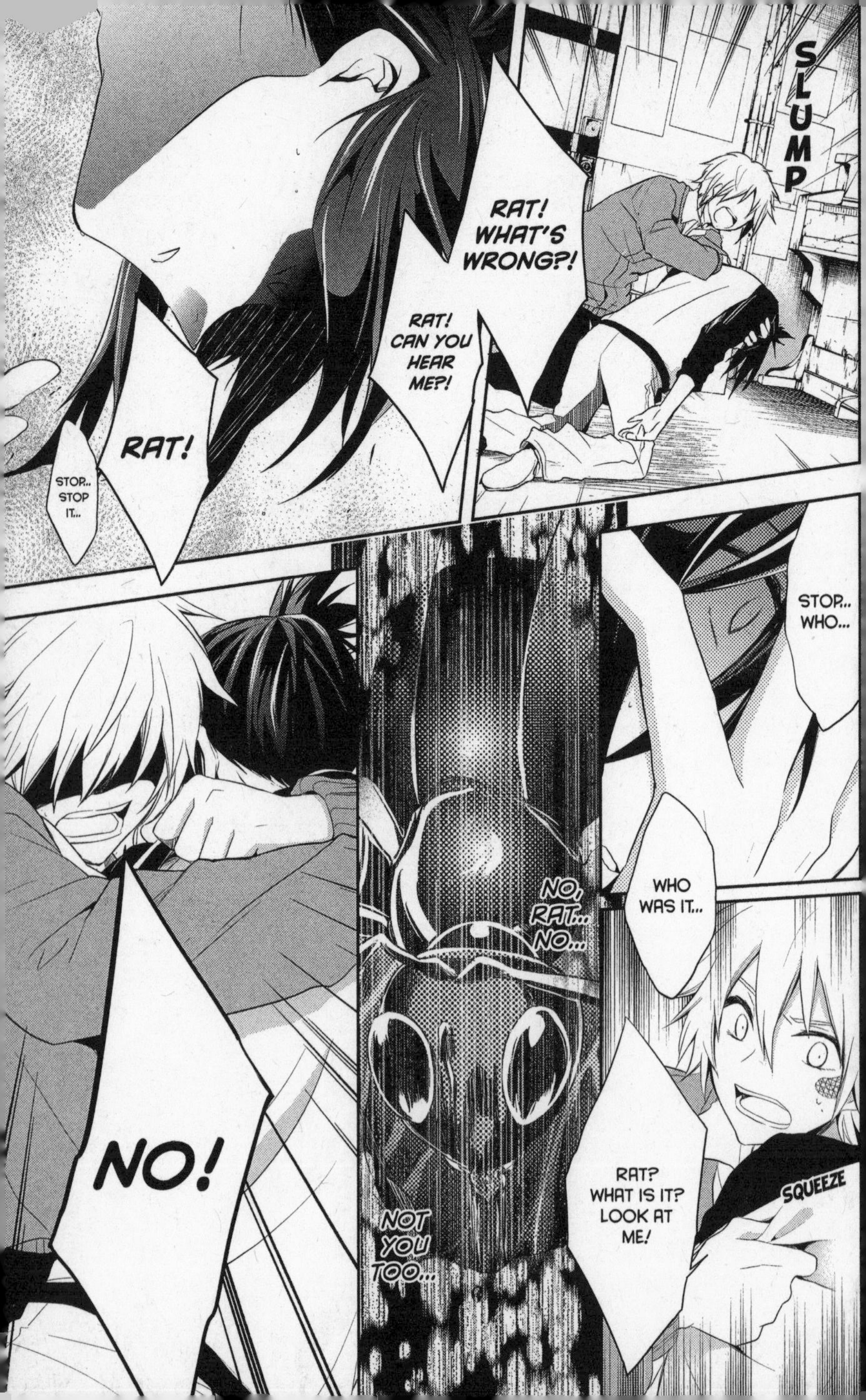
SLUMP
RAT! WHAT'S WRONG?!
RAT! CAN YOU HEAR ME?!
RAT!
STOP.. STOP IT...
STOP... WHO...
WHO WAS IT...
RAT? WHAT IS IT? LOOK AT ME!
SQUEEZE
NO, RAT... NO...
NOT YOU TOO...
NO!

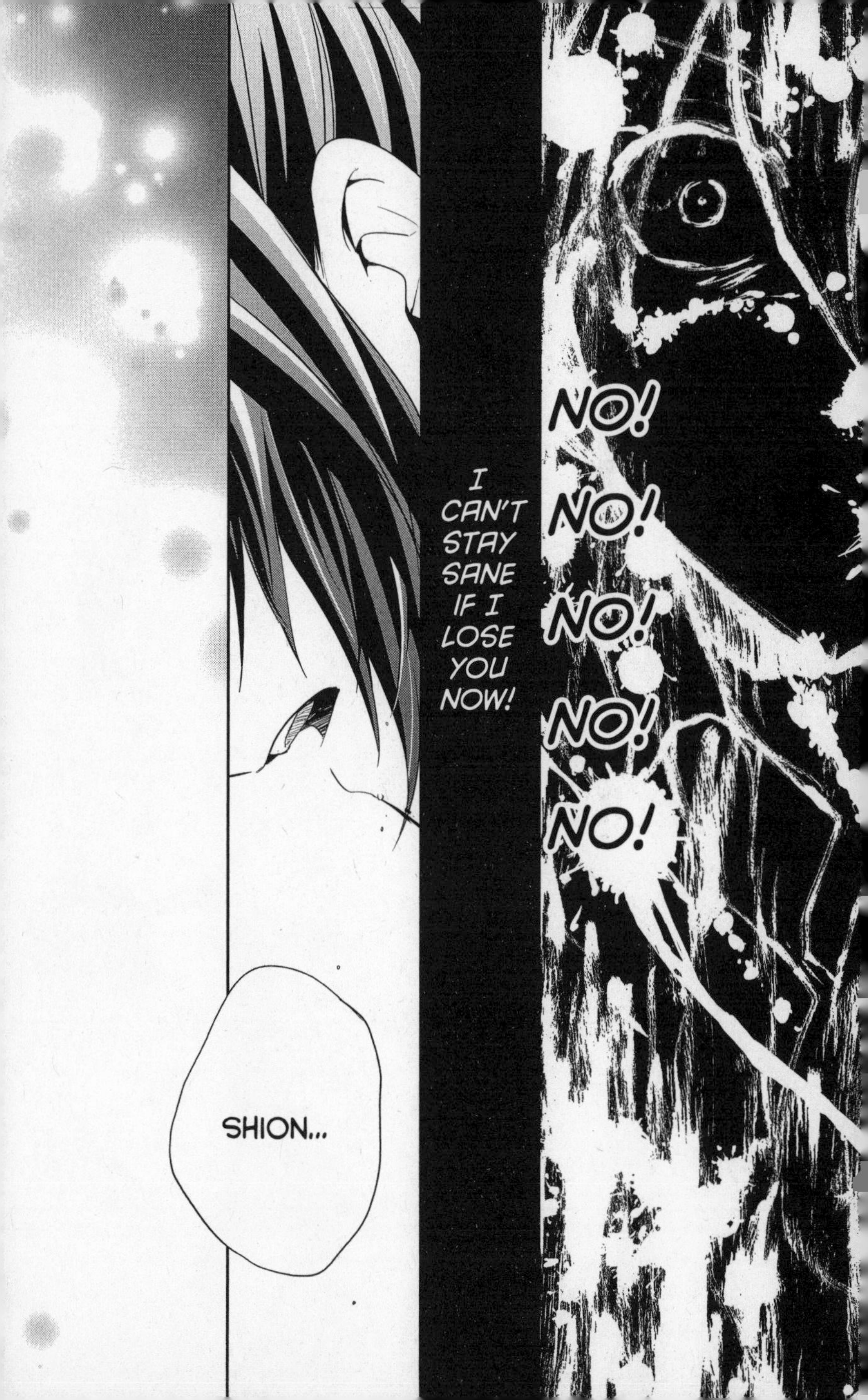
NO!
NO!
NO!
NO!
NO!
I CAN'T STAY SANE IF I LOSE YOU NOW!
SHION...

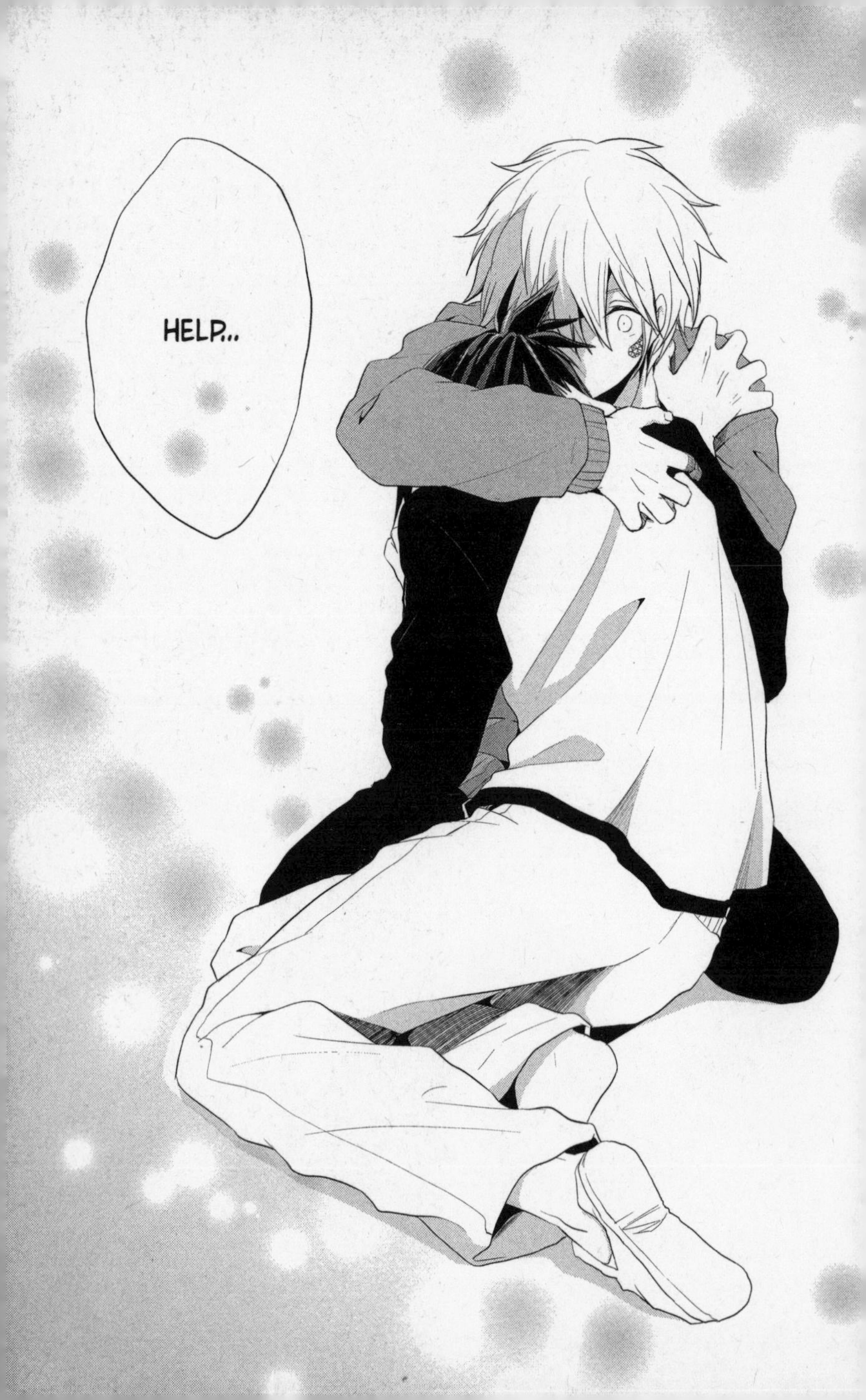
HELP...

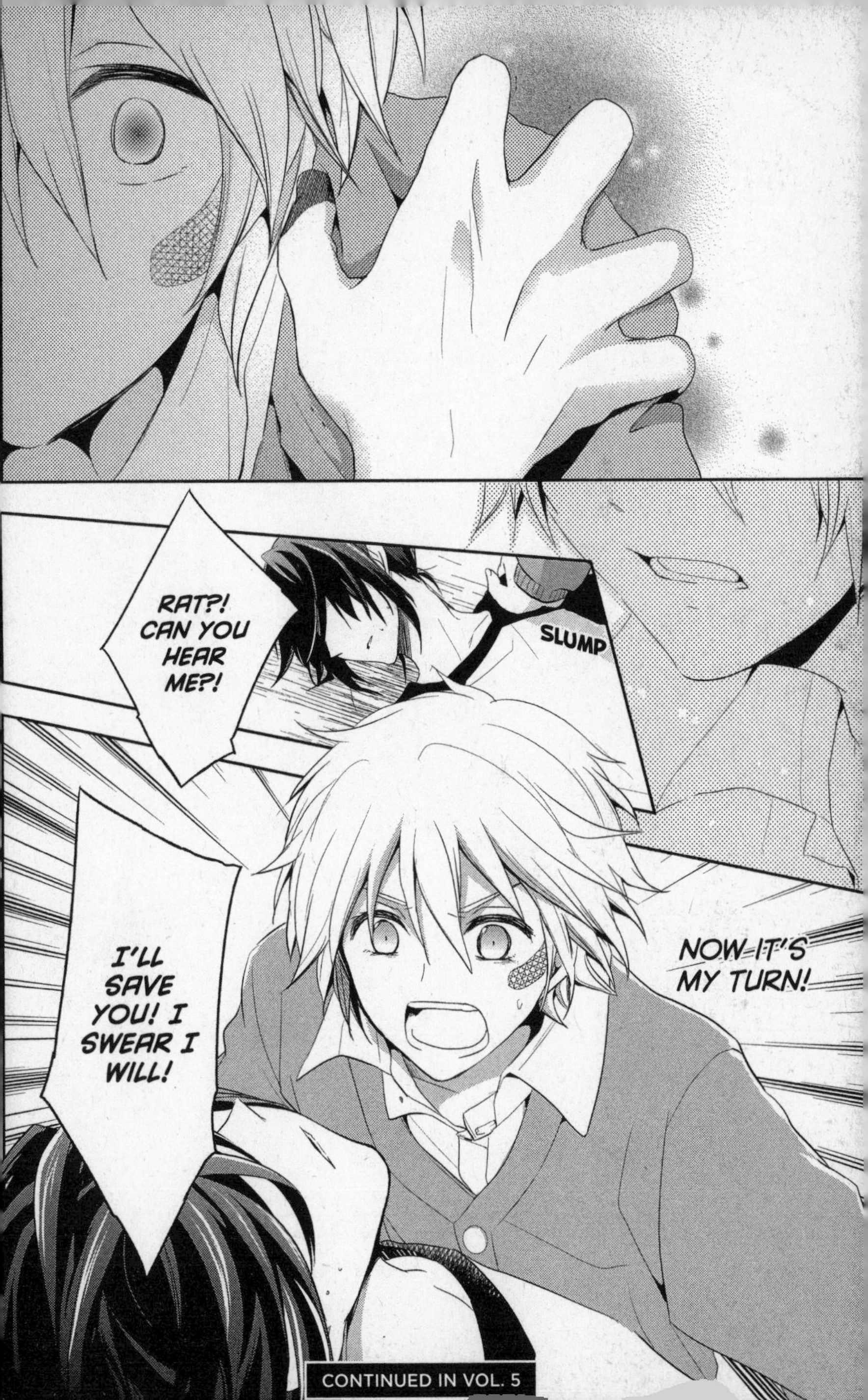
SLUMP
RAT?! CAN YOU HEAR ME?!
NOW IT'S MY TURN!
I'LL SAVE YOU! I SWEAR I WILL!
CONTINUED IN VOL. 5

NO.6

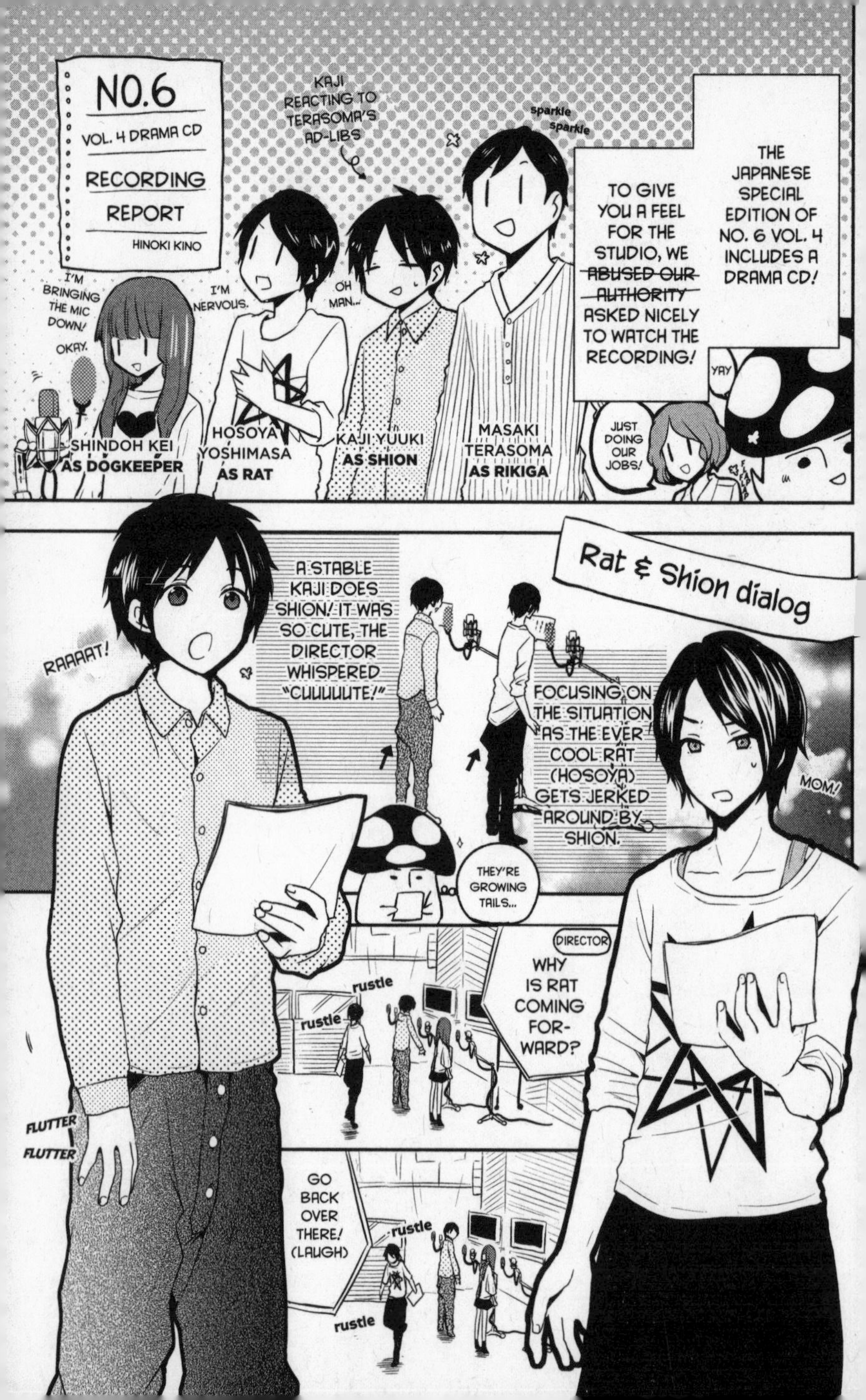
THE JAPANESE SPECIAL EDITION OF NO. 6 VOL. 4 INCLUDES A DRAMA CD!
TO GIVE YOU A FEEL FOR THE STUDIO, WE ~~ABUSED OUR AUTHORITY~~ ASKED NICELY TO WATCH THE RECORDING!
YAY
JUST DOING OUR JOBS!
sparkle sparkle
MASAKI TERASOMA AS RIKIGA
KAJI REACTING TO TERASOMA'S AD-LIBS
OH MAN...
KAJI YUUKI AS SHION
NO.6
VOL. 4 DRAMA CD
RECORDING REPORT
HINOKI KINO
I'M NERVOUS.
HOSOYA YOSHIMASA AS RAT
I'M BRINGING THE MIC DOWN!
OKAY.
SHINDOH KEI AS DOGKEEPER
Rat & Shion dialog
MOM!
FOCUSING ON THE SITUATION AS THE EVER COOL RAT (HOSOYA) GETS JERKED AROUND BY SHION.
A STABLE KAJI DOES SHION! IT WAS SO CUTE, THE DIRECTOR WHISPERED "CUUUUUTE!"
THEY'RE GROWING TAILS...
DIRECTOR
WHY IS RAT COMING FOR-WARD?
rustle
rustle
GO BACK OVER THERE! (LAUGH)
rustle
rustle
RAAAAT!
FLUTTER
FLUTTER

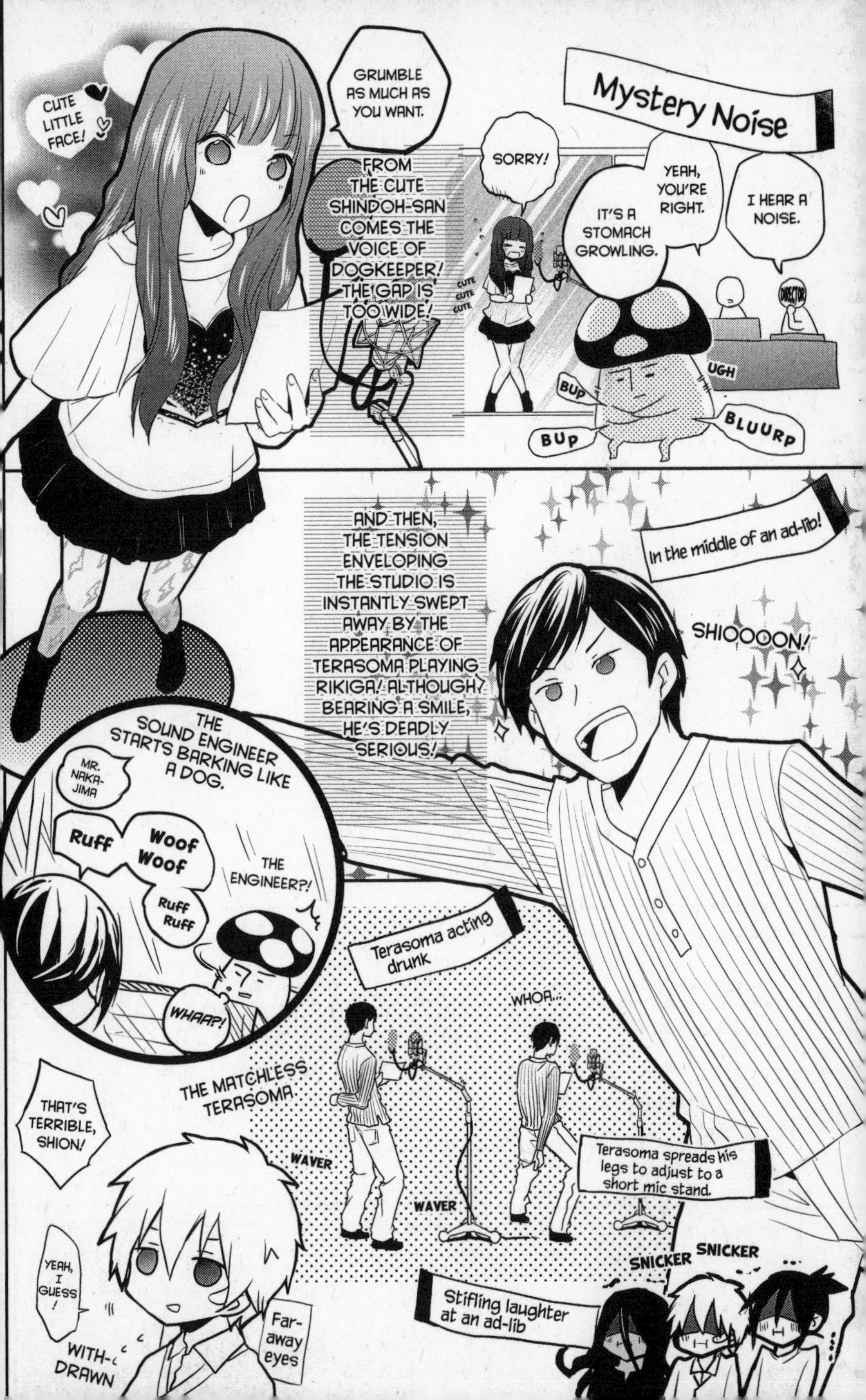
Mystery Noise
I HEAR A NOISE.
YEAH, YOU'RE RIGHT.
IT'S A STOMACH GROWLING.
SORRY!
CUTE CUTE CUTE
DIRECTOR
UGH
BUP
BLUURP
BUP
GRUMBLE AS MUCH AS YOU WANT.
FROM THE CUTE SHINDOH-SAN COMES THE VOICE OF DOGKEEPER! THE GAP IS TOO WIDE!
CUTE LITTLE FACE!
In the middle of an ad-lib!
SHIOOOON!
AND THEN, THE TENSION ENVELOPING THE STUDIO IS INSTANTLY SWEPT AWAY BY THE APPEARANCE OF TERASOMA PLAYING RIKIGA! ALTHOUGH BEARING A SMILE, HE'S DEADLY SERIOUS!
THE SOUND ENGINEER STARTS BARKING LIKE A DOG.
MR. NAKAJIMA
Woof Woof
Ruff
THE ENGINEER?!
Ruff Ruff
WHAA?!
Terasoma acting drunk
WHOA...
Terasoma spreads his legs to adjust to a short mic stand.
WAVER
WAVER
THE MATCHLESS TERASOMA
Stifling laughter at an ad-lib
SNICKER
SNICKER
THAT'S TERRIBLE, SHION!
YEAH, I GUESS!
Far-away eyes
WITH-DRAWN

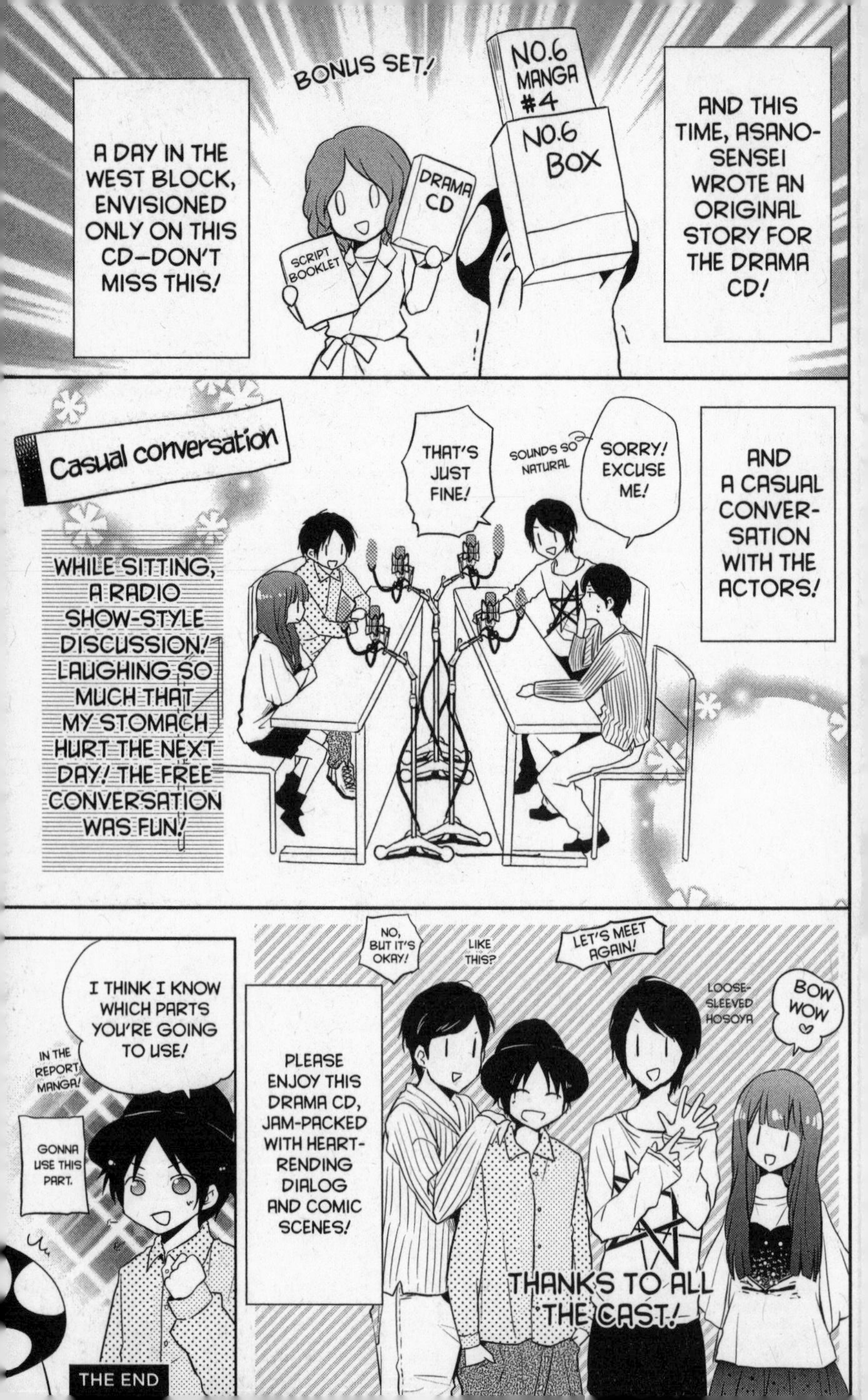
AND THIS TIME, ASANO-SENSEI WROTE AN ORIGINAL STORY FOR THE DRAMA CD!
NO.6 MANGA #4
NO.6 BOX
BONUS SET!
DRAMA CD
SCRIPT BOOKLET
A DAY IN THE WEST BLOCK, ENVISIONED ONLY ON THIS CD—DON'T MISS THIS!
AND A CASUAL CONVERSATION WITH THE ACTORS!
SORRY! EXCUSE ME!
SOUNDS SO NATURAL
THAT'S JUST FINE!
Casual conversation
WHILE SITTING, A RADIO SHOW-STYLE DISCUSSION! LAUGHING SO MUCH THAT MY STOMACH HURT THE NEXT DAY! THE FREE CONVERSATION WAS FUN!
BOW WOW
LOOSE-SLEEVED HOSOYA
LET'S MEET AGAIN!
LIKE THIS?
NO, BUT IT'S OKAY!
PLEASE ENJOY THIS DRAMA CD, JAM-PACKED WITH HEART-RENDING DIALOG AND COMIC SCENES!
THANKS TO ALL THE CAST!
I THINK I KNOW WHICH PARTS YOU'RE GOING TO USE!
IN THE REPORT MANGA!
GONNA USE THIS PART.
THE END

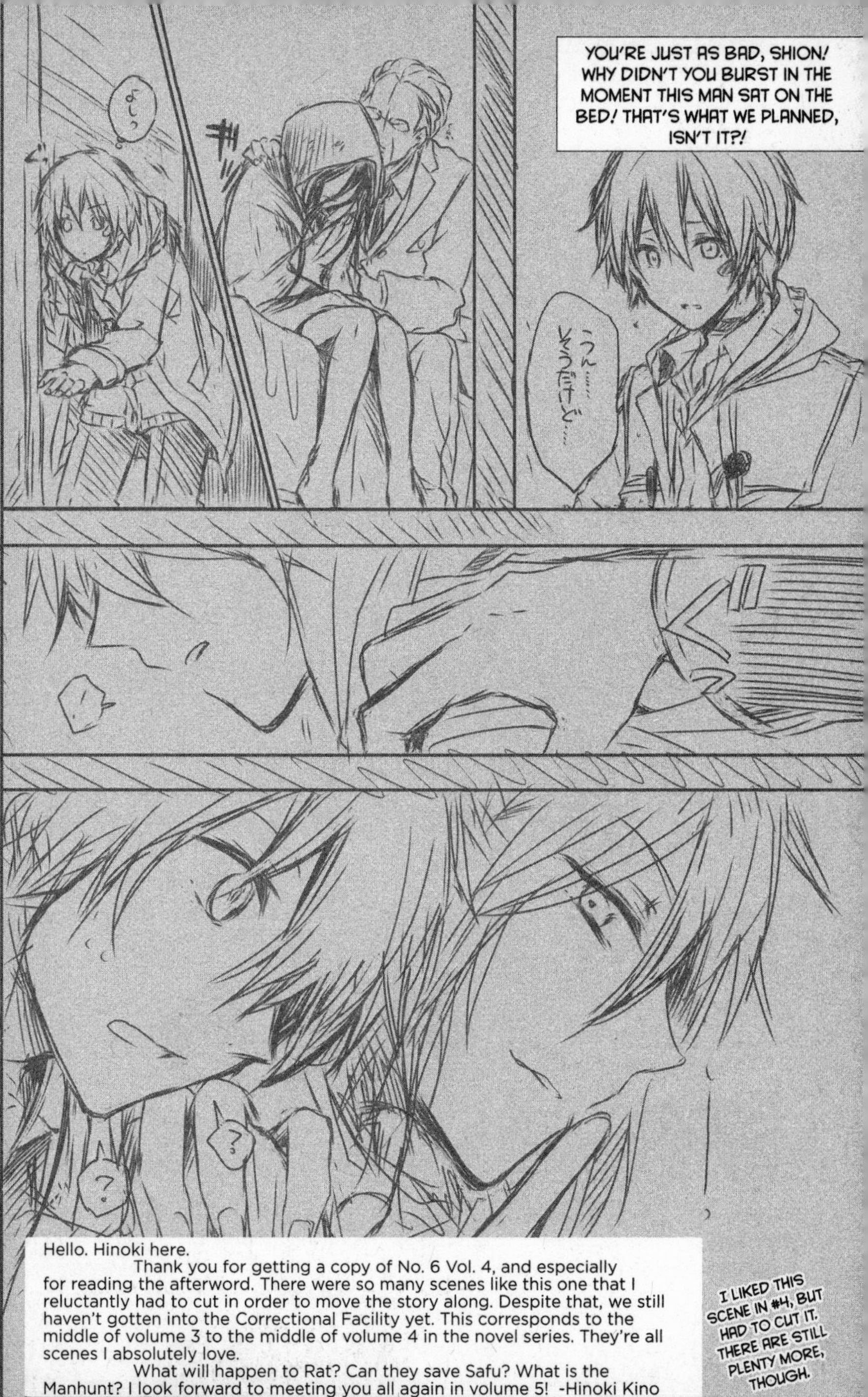
YOU'RE JUST AS BAD, SHION! WHY DIDN'T YOU BURST IN THE MOMENT THIS MAN SAT ON THE BED! THAT'S WHAT WE PLANNED, ISN'T IT?!
うん……そうだけど…
よしっ
I LIKED THIS SCENE IN #4, BUT HAD TO CUT IT. THERE ARE STILL PLENTY MORE, THOUGH.

Hello. Hinoki here.

Thank you for getting a copy of No. 6 Vol. 4, and especially for reading the afterword. There were so many scenes like this one that I reluctantly had to cut in order to move the story along. Despite that, we still haven't gotten into the Correctional Facility yet. This corresponds to the middle of volume 3 to the middle of volume 4 in the novel series. They're all scenes I absolutely love.

What will happen to Rat? Can they save Safu? What is the Manhunt? I look forward to meeting you all again in volume 5! -Hinoki Kino

SPECIAL THANKS!

Atsuko Asano-sensei

Everyone in the Kodansha
Aria Editorial Department

Everyone on the No. 6 Team
Editor K
toi8
Everyone on the anime staff
Everyone at NARTi;S
Ginkyo

* Production Cooperation
Honma
Megi
Netanon
Noguchi Sayuri (Ch. 13)
Kurosoh Yui (Ch. 14)

* Finishing
Tsunocchi

* 3D
Rinkan Kei

* Color Backgrounds
Mr. dominori (Big Brother)
My family (Dad, Mom,
brother, sister, Grandma,
dog)

And everyone else who
helped out

Also, all you readers!

Thank you all so very much!

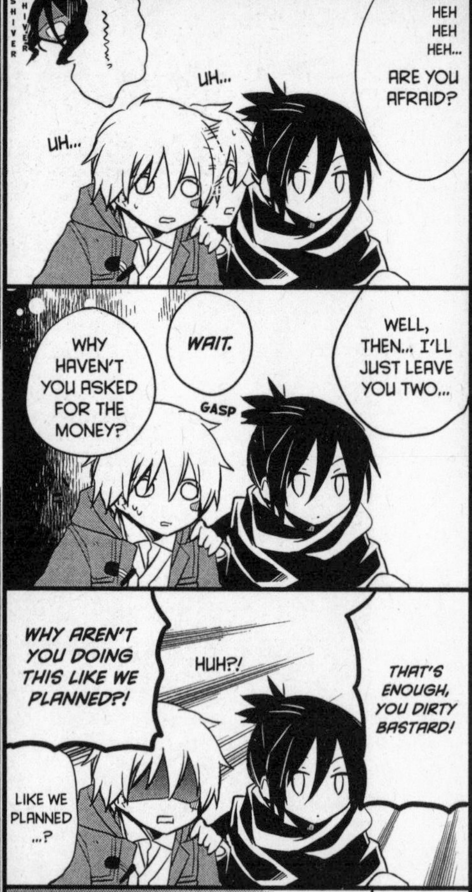

HEH HEH HEH... ARE YOU AFRAID?
UH...
UH...
SHIVER SHIVER
WELL, THEN... I'LL JUST LEAVE YOU TWO...
WAIT.
GASP
WHY HAVEN'T YOU ASKED FOR THE MONEY?
THAT'S ENOUGH, YOU DIRTY BASTARD!
HUH?!
WHY AREN'T YOU DOING THIS LIKE WE PLANNED?!
LIKE WE PLANNED ...?
I'M LEAVING! OUT OF MY WAY!
CRASH
DASH
HUH?!
LEFT BEHIND.

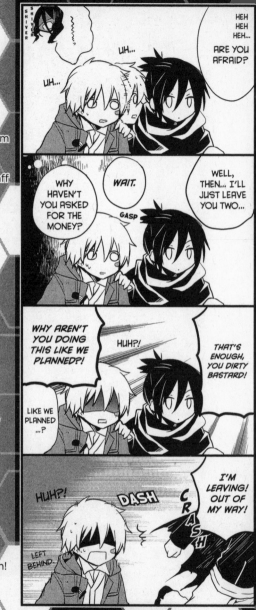

No. 6
Volume 5
Preview

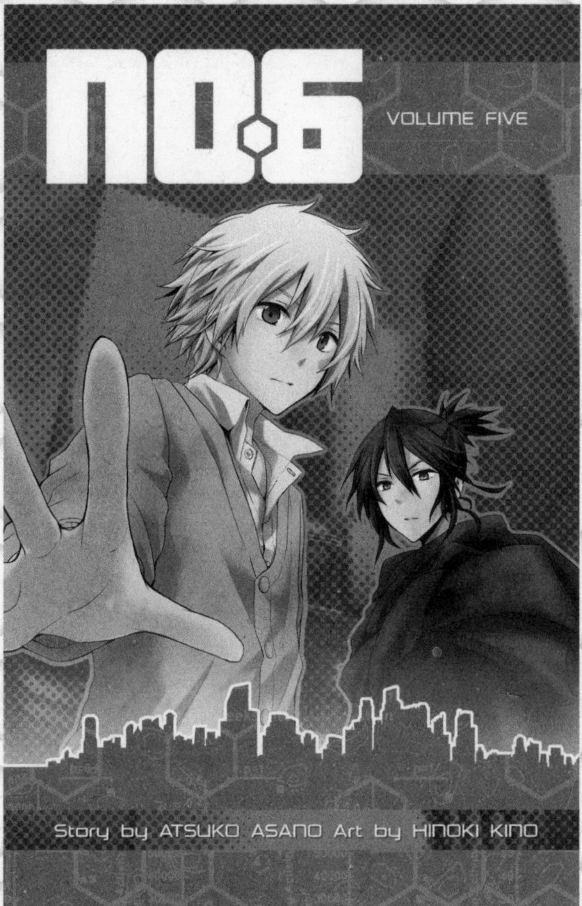
NO.6
VOLUME FIVE
Story by ATSUKO ASANO Art by HINOKI KINO

Coming February 2014

Chapter 16: Stage of Disaster

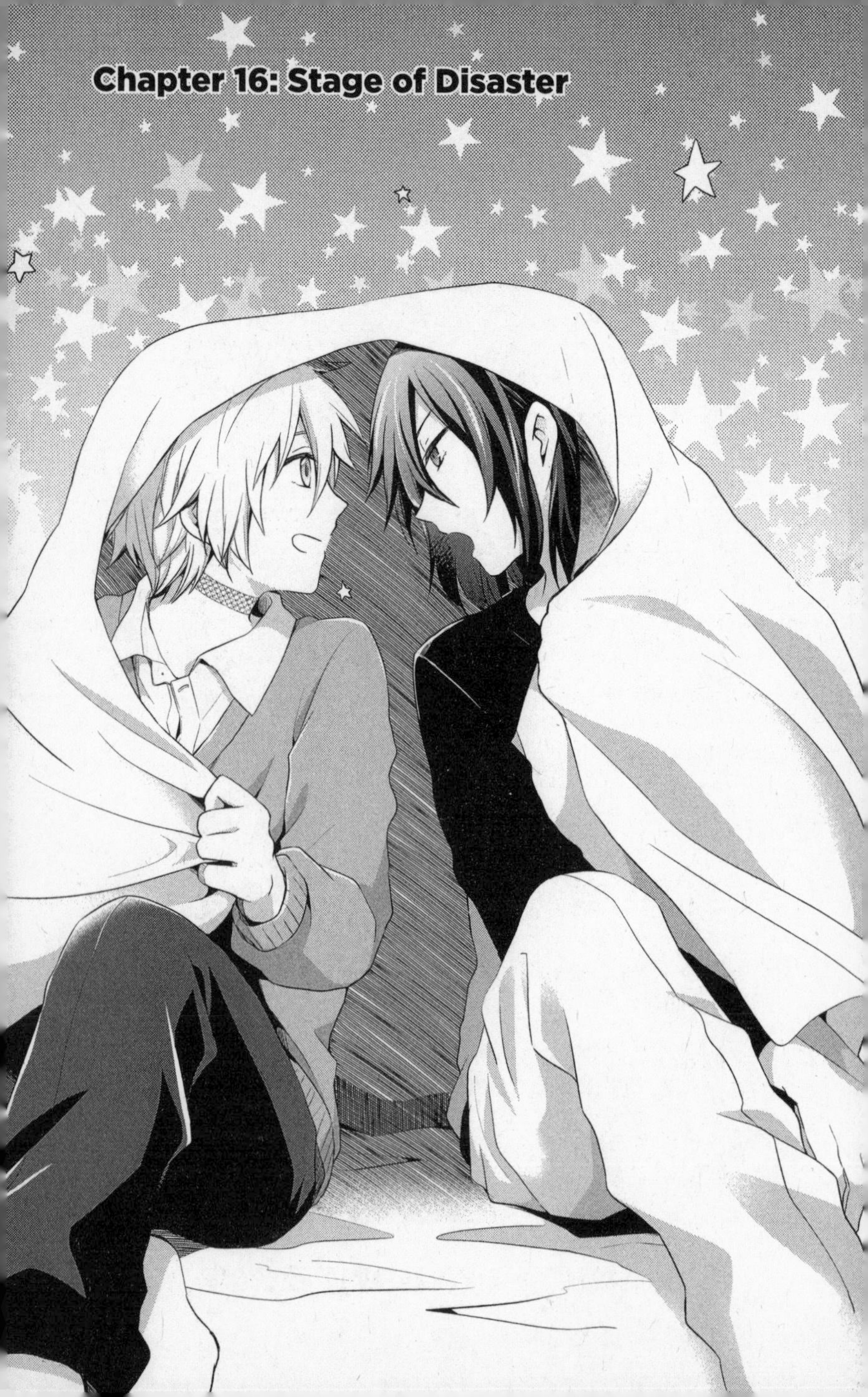

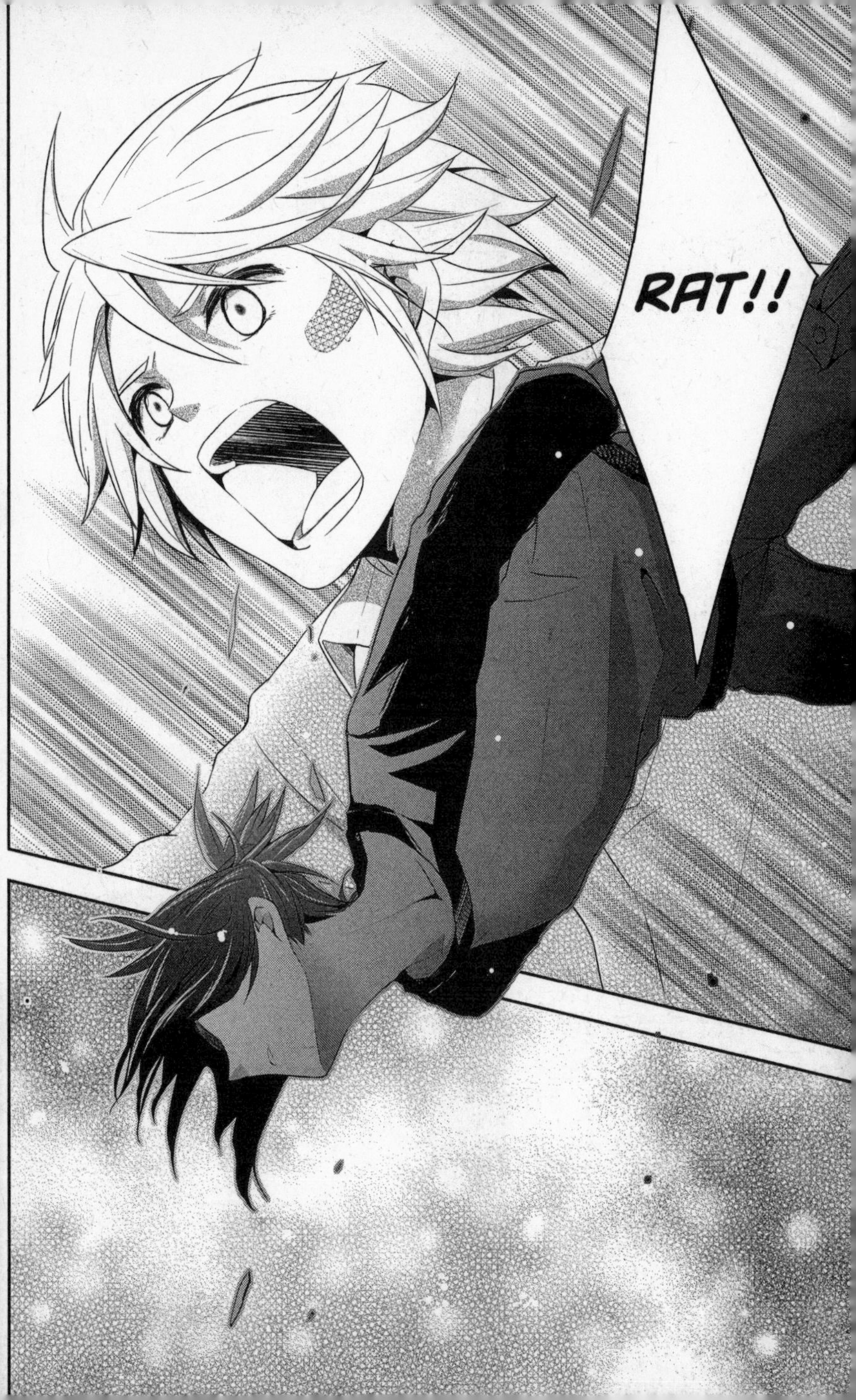
RAT!!

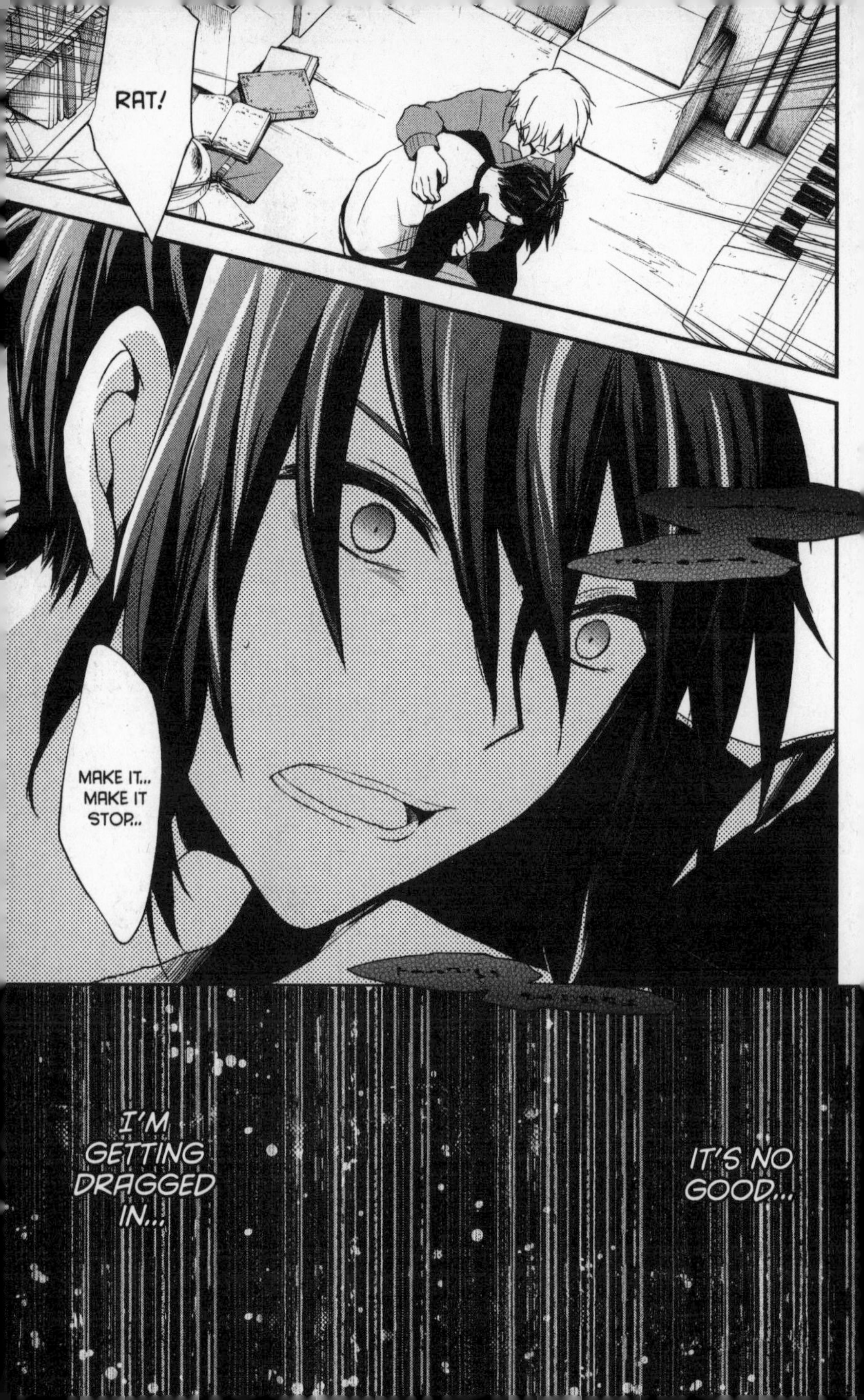
RAT!
MAKE IT... MAKE IT STOP...
IT'S NO GOOD...
I'M GETTING DRAGGED IN...

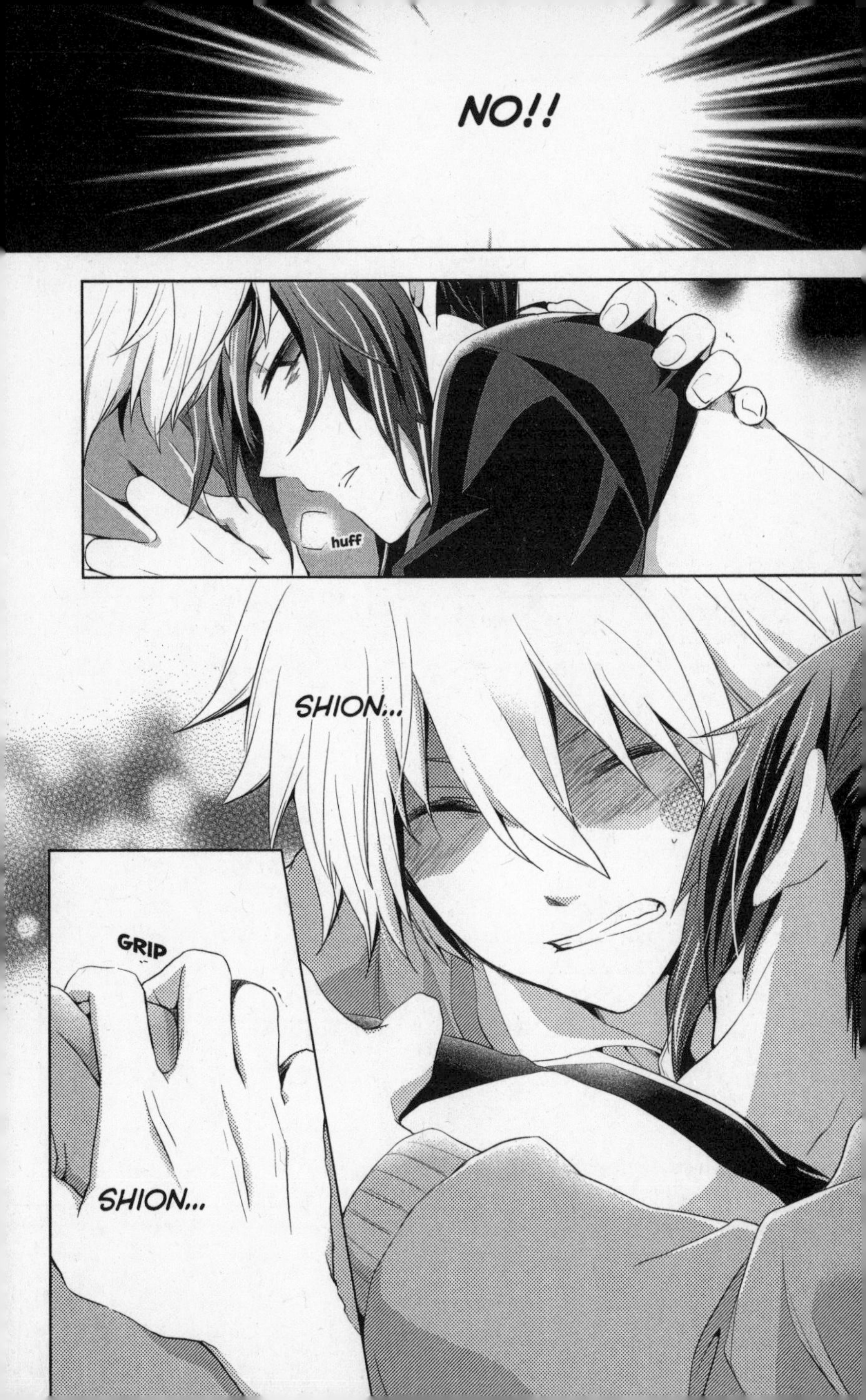
NO!!
huff
SHION...
GRIP
SHION...

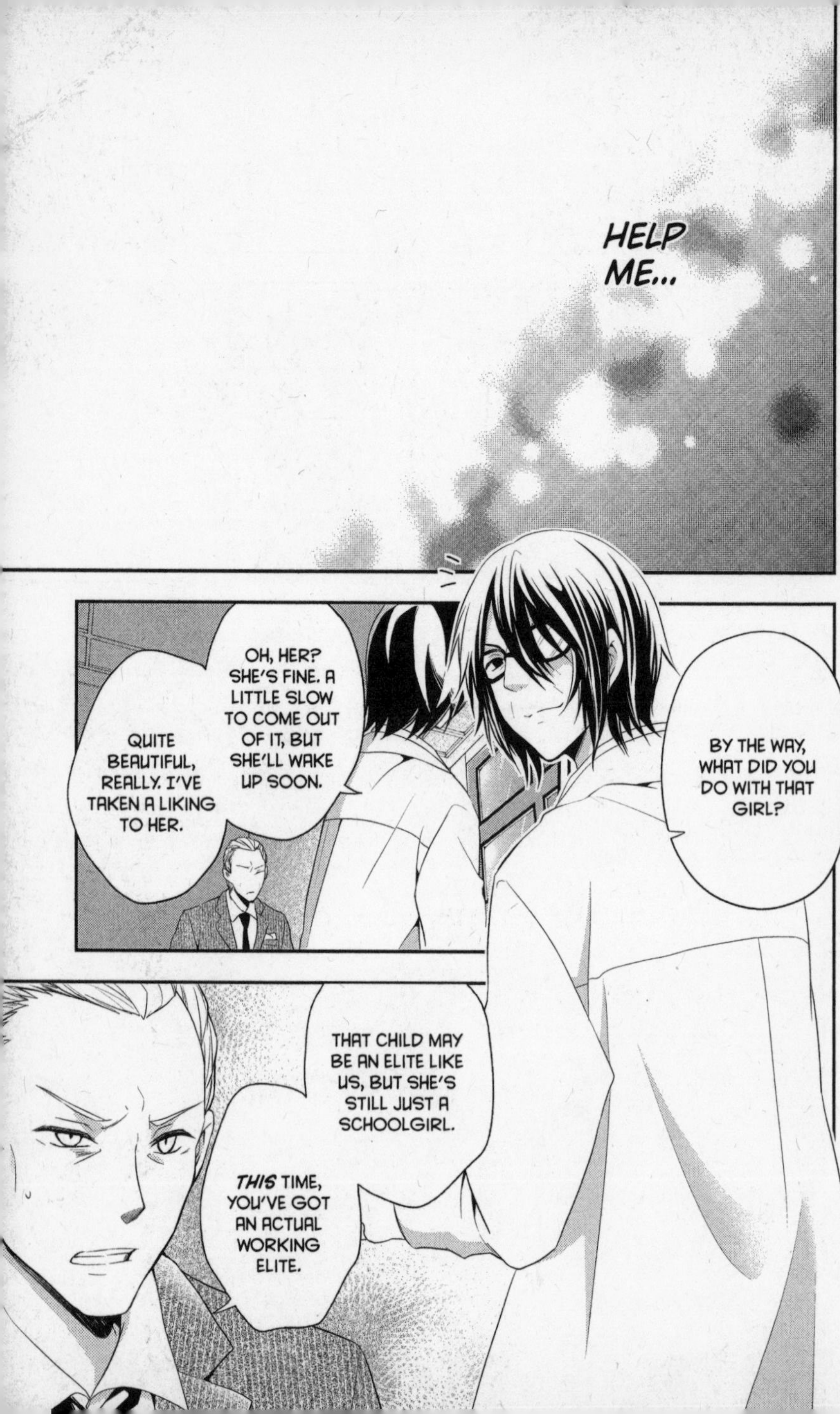
HELP ME...
BY THE WAY, WHAT DID YOU DO WITH THAT GIRL?
OH, HER? SHE'S FINE. A LITTLE SLOW TO COME OUT OF IT, BUT SHE'LL WAKE UP SOON.
QUITE BEAUTIFUL, REALLY. I'VE TAKEN A LIKING TO HER.
THAT CHILD MAY BE AN ELITE LIKE US, BUT SHE'S STILL JUST A SCHOOLGIRL.
THIS TIME, YOU'VE GOT AN ACTUAL WORKING ELITE.

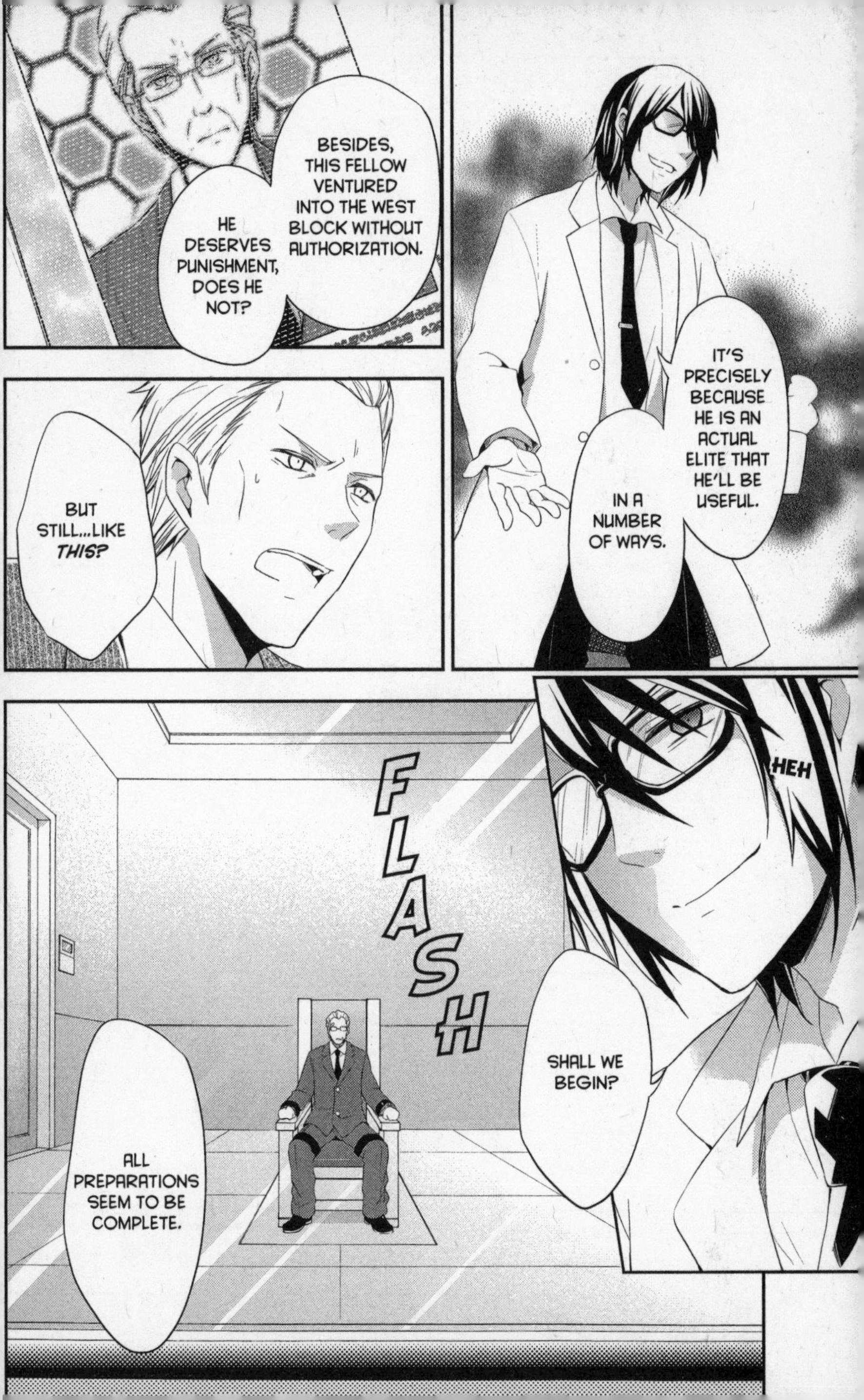
IT'S PRECISELY BECAUSE HE IS AN ACTUAL ELITE THAT HE'LL BE USEFUL.
IN A NUMBER OF WAYS.
BESIDES, THIS FELLOW VENTURED INTO THE WEST BLOCK WITHOUT AUTHORIZATION.
HE DESERVES PUNISHMENT, DOES HE NOT?
BUT STILL...LIKE *THIS?*
HEH
SHALL WE BEGIN?
FLASH
ALL PREPARATIONS SEEM TO BE COMPLETE.

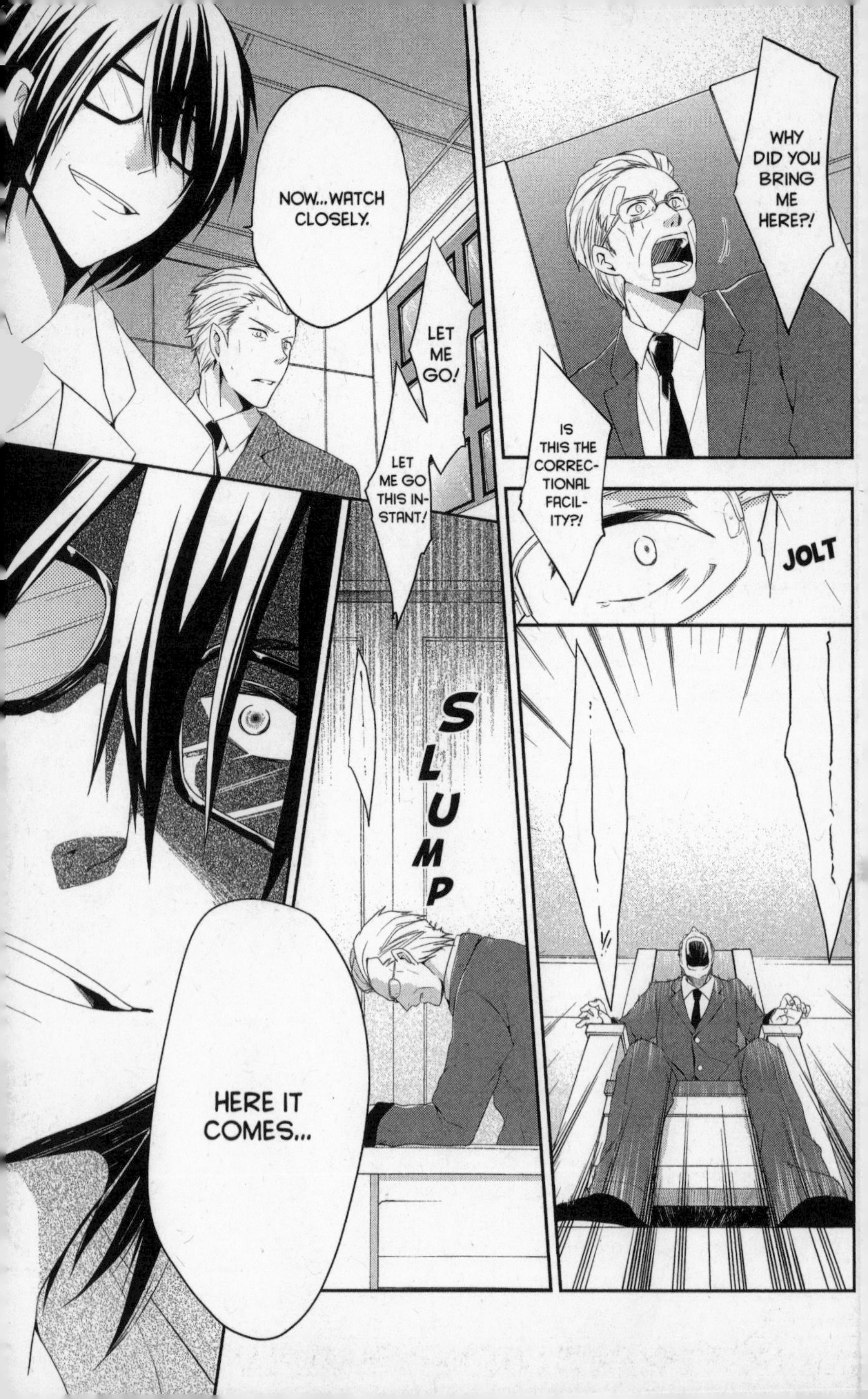
WHY DID YOU BRING ME HERE?!
IS THIS THE CORRECTIONAL FACILITY?!
LET ME GO!
LET ME GO THIS INSTANT!
NOW...WATCH CLOSELY.
JOLT
SLUMP
HERE IT COMES...

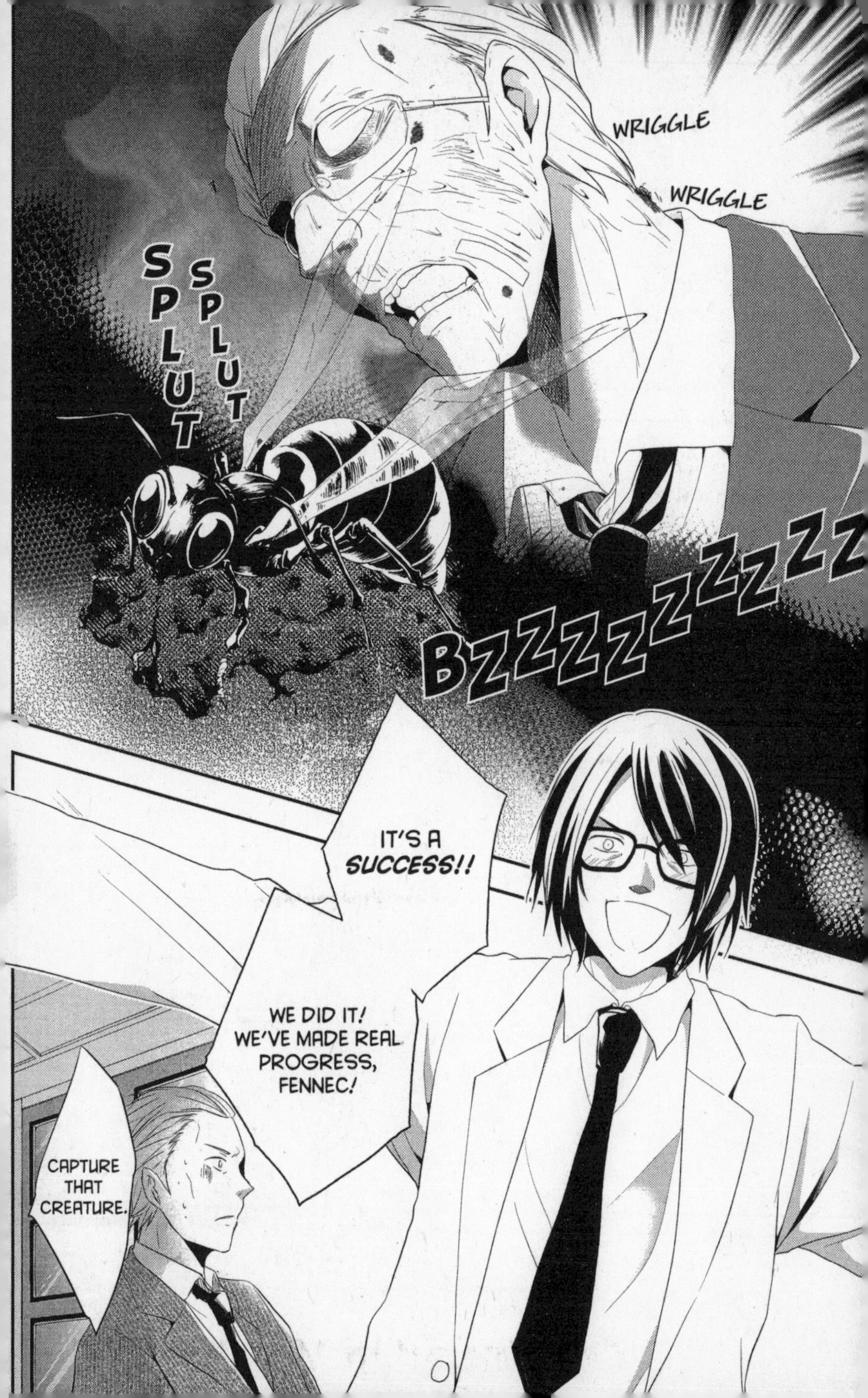
WRIGGLE
WRIGGLE
SPLUT
SPLUT
BZZZZZZZZZZ
IT'S A SUCCESS!!
WE DID IT! WE'VE MADE REAL PROGRESS, FENNEC!
CAPTURE THAT CREATURE.

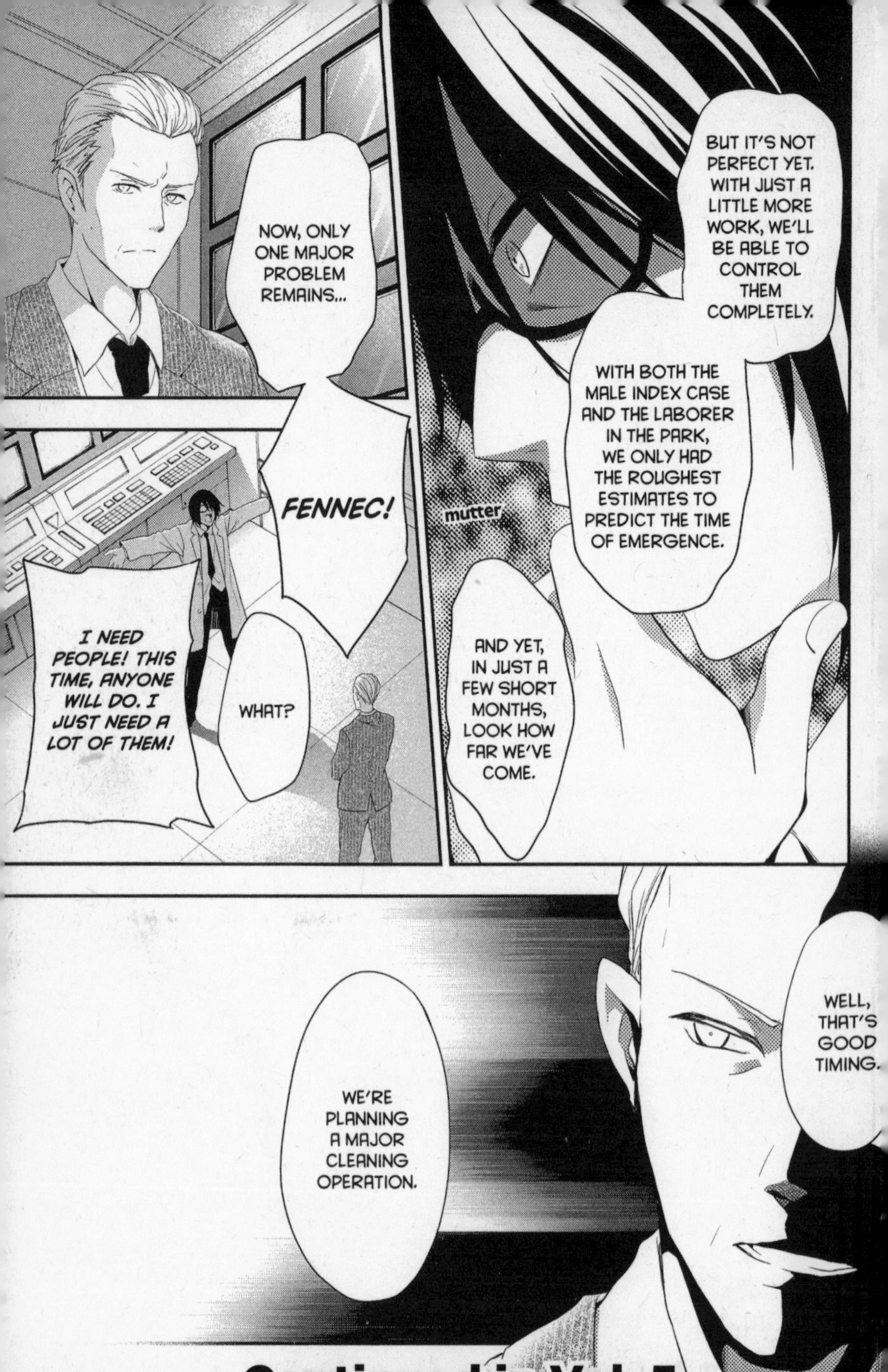
BUT IT'S NOT PERFECT YET. WITH JUST A LITTLE MORE WORK, WE'LL BE ABLE TO CONTROL THEM COMPLETELY.
WITH BOTH THE MALE INDEX CASE AND THE LABORER IN THE PARK, WE ONLY HAD THE ROUGHEST ESTIMATES TO PREDICT THE TIME OF EMERGENCE.
mutter
AND YET, IN JUST A FEW SHORT MONTHS, LOOK HOW FAR WE'VE COME.
NOW, ONLY ONE MAJOR PROBLEM REMAINS...
FENNEC!
WHAT?
I NEED PEOPLE! THIS TIME, ANYONE WILL DO. I JUST NEED A LOT OF THEM!
WELL, THAT'S GOOD TIMING.
WE'RE PLANNING A MAJOR CLEANING OPERATION.

Continued in Vol. 5

No. 6 volume 4 is a work of fiction. Names, characters, places, and incidents are the products of the author's imagination or are used fictitiously. Any resemblance to actual events, locales, or persons, living or dead, is entirely coincidental.

A Kodansha Comics Trade Paperback Original.

Published in the United States by Kodansha Comics, an imprint of Kodansha USA Publishing, LLC, New York.

Publication rights for this English edition arranged through Kodansha Ltd., Tokyo.

First published in Japan in 2012 by Kodansha Ltd., Tokyo
ISBN 978-1-61262-358-0

Printed in the United States of America.

www.kodanshacomics.com

9 8 7 6 5 4 3 2 1

Translation: Jonathan Tarbox and Kazuko Shimizu
Lettering: Christy Sawyer
Editing: Ben Applegate